THE
ASCENSION
MYSTERIES

ALSO BY DAVID WILCOCK

The Source Field Investigations
The Synchronicity Key

THE
ASCENSION
MYSTERIES

Revealing the Cosmic Battle

Between Good and Evil

DAVID WILCOCK

P

PROFILE BOOKS

First published in Great Britain in 2017 by Souvenir Press,
an imprint of Profile Books Ltd
3 Holford Yard
Bevin Way
London
WC1X 9HD
www.profilebooks.com

ISBN 978 0 28564 362 8
eISBN 978 0 28564 363 5

Printed and bound in Great Britain by Clays Ltd, Elcograf S.p.A.

FSC
www.fsc.org
MIX
Paper from
responsible sources
FSC® C018072

This book is dedicated to those brave souls who have laid their lives on the line, or even paid the ultimate price, to fight for a better world for all of us.

Contents

List of Figures

THE
ASCENSION
MYSTERIES

CHAPTER ONE

Introduction

Imagine a life of supernatural, godlike powers. Instantaneous telepathy, where you read others' minds so effectively that words are obsolete. Levitation, where you soar into the air with nothing more than the power of your thoughts. Telekinesis, where you levitate objects, even of colossal size, and command them to move with your mind. Materialization, where you can create anything you want as easily as you once opened your mouth to speak. Time travel, where you jump into the past and fast-forward into the future with stunning clarity. The "veil" between living and dying, which caused you to forget that you had a greater identity beyond each mortal life, has now dropped. In every moment you are fully aware that you are a soul having a human experience. Your level of intelligence is now vastly greater than anything you had access to in the past.

Is this a dream? A case of ridiculous wishful thinking that has no grounding in reality? Or is it possible that the world's great spiritual teachers were telling you the truth? Are you walking around in a state of amnesia, oblivious to who and what you really are? Could the choices you make and the thoughts you think be far more important than you might ever realize? Is there a cosmic battle between good and evil playing out in the seemingly mundane struggles of your everyday life? Is this hidden battle also raging behind the headlines of many of the world's

most noteworthy events? Is ascension—a graduation into a higher level
of existence—your ultimate goal for being human? And are there negative forces in the universe that feed on your fear, anger, guilt, and shame
and will stop at nothing to prevent you from achieving this quantum
leap in your evolution? Are we witnessing a tremendous competition over
who gets to control our planet? Would these negative forces literally die
without our selfishness, jealousy, materialism, greed, and loneliness providing them with an energy supply? Have these forces been fighting a
battle that has gone on for hundreds of thousands of years—in their own
conscious memory?

You are about to enter a world where all these questions have answers.
We are threatened with doom and destruction from a seemingly impossible array of villainous forces. Not only do we have an "elite" who appear
to thrive on creating wars, financial catastrophes, plagues, and chaos,
nature itself appears to have betrayed us. Our planet is dying. The water
is disappearing. The animals are being hunted into extinction. Every year
the temperatures are getting hotter. Earthquakes, volcanoes, tsunamis,
hurricanes, and superstorms threaten our lives and planet.

People tend to think the ancient spiritual tales are only "mythology,"
whereas we live in the "real world," which is far more lonely and threatening. Humans often use denial and addictive behaviors to push the
unpleasant and seemingly inevitable truth of mass destruction out of our
minds. Then, when the truth comes blasting out of its feeble packaging,
it triggers a hidden sense of hopelessness once more, and we crash-land
into another deep, dark depression of profound loneliness. Now we believe in God—when things are at their worst—and in our private hell we
cry out, "Why? Why? Why?"

You may have been fortunate enough to come into contact with what
many visionaries have called "ageless wisdom." You may have had a near-
death experience, where you caught a glimpse of the greater reality beyond the veil of living and dying. You may have had a dream so beautiful
and breathtaking that you woke up in tears, longing for the promise of
a new tomorrow. You may have had a peak emotional event, either of
extreme terror or utter ecstasy, and broken through to that resplendent

calm that is the bounty enjoyed by all the great masters—where time slows to a crawl and you see your life from an "overview" perspective. Something may have happened to you that was so utterly bizarre, so undeniably supernatural, that your entire being seemed to tingle and vibrate in amazement. For those few precious moments, you touched the essence of something truly profound. You experienced a reality where there is no fear, no pain, no loss or loneliness—only love, joy, happiness, and boundless, brilliant white light.

This expansive, awe-inspiring sense of eternity often seems fleeting. You get a brief glimpse of the magic, but all too soon the mundane realities of everyday life surround you once more. The candle flame of infinite potential is snuffed by the cold, hard wind of reality—as most now see it. Thankfully, it doesn't have to be that way. One of the great mysteries of our time is that positive spiritual beings do exist, and if you follow certain guidelines, you can make direct contact with them. I get letters almost every day from people experiencing bizarre and mystical phenomena. I worked very hard to achieve contact with spiritual beings, and the results have been extremely profound and meaningful.

I am going to tell you the story of my experiences in this book—how one person moved through incredible hardship to discover dazzling hidden truths about ascension and our future. The Gnostic spiritual tradition teaches us that information is alive, and exposing ourselves to information about the true nature of the cosmos can trigger a metamorphosis within us that ultimately promotes ascension. My previous books have presented this information from a scientific perspective, but in the first half of this book I will reveal how this metaphysical truth manifests in your life on a personal level.

The Mysteries of History

Science teaches us that you evolved from a spectacularly boring life in caves, in which your distant forefathers were illiterate hunter-gatherers who were forced to survive against the elements. Your ancient ancestors eventually became intelligent enough to invent the wheel, plant crops, domesticate animals, develop systems of trade, build sturdy shelters, and gather together in towns and cities. Civilizations arose gradually, and we developed written language, mathematics, ceramics, metallurgy, astronomy, governments, laws, and religion.

We also worshipped gods. Virtually every culture on Earth reported some form of direct contact with advanced beings of significantly higher intelligence. Civilization, so we are told, did not arise randomly. We were taught how to speak, how to read, how to write, how to grow crops, build shelters, study the stars, and understand the universal language of science by sophisticated beings. Again and again, our own written records soberly tell the tale of advanced, human-looking people handing us these keys to knowledge. In many cases these people walked with us for hundreds if not thousands of years, governing the affairs of our world with the presumably divine right of kings. Some of these "gods" taught us to be more loving and forgiving of others, and helped originate our major religions—which may hold deep mysteries that few of us truly understand at this time. Other "gods" were nowhere near as kind or benevolent. They warred with one another, were petty and conniving, lied and deceived, and in many cases were overthrown and destroyed when their angry and betrayed subjects finally rose up against them.

Is it possible that these "gods" of antiquity were, in fact, extraterrestrial beings? This is a question that I have been publicly tackling for twenty years in a variety of forms, including my website, DivineCosmos .com; my books, *The Source Field Investigations* and *The Synchronicity Key*; and well over eighty different episodes of *Ancient Aliens*, the number one show on the History Channel, entering its tenth season at the time of this writing. Yet many are still acting like the priests who refused to look through Galileo's telescope. The worldview most people now take for granted is nothing more than a belief system, much like any other religion. We defend our current scientific models like Bible-thumping zealots, claiming there is only one truth, and the magi of science have all the answers.

The "Story" Has Changed

Traditionally, skeptics have defended their belief systems by invoking science as the ultimate authority. This should be a confusing time for them, because those same authorities are continually changing the story. Everything we were taught to believe was quietly transformed on October 22, 2013, in a paper that was published in the *Proceedings of the National Academy of Sciences*, without any major media publicity. A team of three scientists, led by Dr. Erik Petigura, used NASA's Kepler telescope to study 42,000 nearby stars that are similar to our own Sun. They were looking for moments when the brightness of each star plunged in a measurable way. These dimmings are caused when a planet crosses in front of the star. Petigura's team found a total of 603 planets. Ten of them were Earth-sized and orbited in the "habitable zone"—where oceans can form because the planet is neither too hot nor too cold. Petigura's team already had the data to tell them these ten planets likely had liquid water. When you combine two hydrogen atoms with one oxygen atom, you get water. NASA has already proven that stars give off countless tons of hydrogen and oxygen gas. When these gases reach a planet with the right temperature, they combine into water—and form atmospheres, rainfall, and oceans.

Petigura's study concluded that an astonishing 22 percent of all Sun-like stars in the universe have watery, Earth-like planets orbiting around them—in the zone where life has the proper conditions to appear. The closest star with an Earth-like planet around it is only twelve light years away, making it easy to reach in one human lifetime if our technology advances to a point where we can travel at light speed. However, the real magic occurs when we take this 22 percent figure and extend it out into the known universe. The results are absolutely astonishing, and were summarized in an article entitled "The Fermi Paradox" on the website WaitButWhy.com.[1]

There are an estimated 100 to 400 billion stars in the Milky Way galaxy alone. We now know that for every star in the Milky Way, there is an entire galaxy in the universe. A galaxy is nothing but a huge grouping of stars. Once we are armed with these numbers, we can prove that for every grain of sand on Earth, there are ten thousand stars in the universe. That number alone seems impossible to comprehend, since we have thoughtlessly walked over countless grains of sand all our lives. Our story gets even more outrageous once we estimate that 5 percent of those stars will be Sun-like, as NASA's data has suggested. That means there are 500 quintillion, or 500 billion billion Sun-like stars in the universe.

Each of these Sun-like stars will have a "habitable zone," where a planet could develop oceans of liquid water. If 5 percent of all the stars in the universe are like our Sun, and Petigura's team discovered that one-fifth of these stars will have Earth-like planets orbiting around them, then that means 1 percent of all the stars in the universe could be home to another planet we could live on. There would be 100 billion billion Earth-like planets in the cosmos. This means that for every single grain of sand on Earth, there are a hundred Earth-like planets in the universe. Based on these numbers, there are about a billion Earths in our own galaxy alone. If we then assume that only 1 percent of those watery worlds have developed some form of life, then every grain of sand on Earth represents an inhabited, Earth-like planet in the universe.

Let's assume that a mere 1 percent of those inhabited planets have life that has evolved into an intelligent civilization, like what we now see on Earth. That would mean there are 10 quadrillion, or 10 million billion intelligent civilizations in our universe. When we apply this same logic to the Milky Way, we have 100,000 intelligent civilizations seeded among the billion Earth-like planets out there waiting for us. This is a radical re-envisioning of everything we think we know, coming directly from official sources working with NASA data. And with these numbers, the idea that we are alone in the universe becomes utterly ridiculous—akin to an extreme fundamentalist religious belief that is easily dismissed.

"The Fermi Paradox" also asks us to consider the age of the universe, currently estimated to be about 13 billion years. Earth was formed only 4.54 billion years ago. It is entirely conceivable that an Earth-like planet could have emerged 8 billion years ago around an older, Sun-like star. Now let's imagine that this planet evolved to our current level of intelligence and technology in the same length of time that it took to flourish here on

Earth—4.54 billion years. That would mean that this planet had 3.46 billion years to evolve beyond the level we have reached today. The degree of technology, intelligence, and sophistication that could develop during that time may be beyond our ability to even comprehend.

On March 5, 2015, NASA announced that nearly half of Mars was once covered with an ocean, like those on Earth, that was up to a mile deep.[2] Then, on September 28, 2015, NASA revealed that Mars still has liquid water on its surface today, in limited quantities.[3] Finally, on November 5, 2015, NASA announced that Mars once had an atmosphere like Earth's that was wiped out, perhaps by some form of solar event.[4] Pluto has an oddly Earth-like atmosphere. According to a BBC article from March 12, 2015, which quoted NASA, Jupiter's moon Ganymede was found to have a subsurface ocean as well as a variety of other satellites: "These include the dwarf planets Pluto and Ceres; other Jupiter moons—Europa and Callisto; Saturn's moons Enceladus, Titan, and Mimas; and possibly Neptune's moon, Triton. 'The Solar System is now looking like a pretty soggy place,' joked Jim Green, the US space agency's director of planetary science."[5]

These official discoveries are changing everything we were taught to believe. There are multiple places within our own solar system that are suitable for life—in one form or another. Mars appears to have been Earth-like enough that an intelligent civilization could have thrived on it in our own past. These utterly life-changing findings are being released here and there in the media, one at a time. They get a day or two of minor headlines, which are easily overlooked in today's world of information saturation, and are then forgotten. By simply putting the pieces together, we can build a radically different worldview than what most people now believe to be the absolute truth.

The Cosmic Seed

Another scientific revolution occurred just a month before the *Proceedings of the National Academy of Sciences* study, in September 2013. It was too late to include the data in *The Synchronicity Key*, but I certainly wish I could have. I can still see every detail of the plane I was sitting in when I read "A Jewel at the Heart of Quantum Physics" in *Quanta* magazine.[6] Even though we were still climbing in altitude, I wanted to unbuckle my seat belt and run up and down the aisle, shouting with joy and amazement. So many years of scientific research and journalism had paid off—in a way I honestly had never expected would happen. Hundreds of puzzle pieces snapped together in my mind, and for the first time I was able to see the grand solution that unified them all into a single, complete whole.

Most of us believe that the universe originated in a "Big Bang." In this model, we are taught that "in the beginning, there was nothing." Then, this "nothing" became "something." In fact, "nothing" supposedly created all the matter in the universe in a single, sudden explosion—i.e., a "Big Bang." It is obviously very problematic to tell us that "nothing exploded," and in that one moment the entire universe was created. We still come back to the core problem, which is that science is telling us that we get something out of nothing. If we can accept this idea, then why would matter only be created once, at the very beginning of the universe? Why wouldn't there be an ongoing transformation of some form of invisible energy, or "nothing," into the matter that we see today?

The Big Bang model was given scientific support by the black hole theories of Stephen Hawking. However, the Big Bang is still an unproven assumption. Hardly anyone is aware that Hawking's own senior professor, Sir Roger Penrose, was working on a very different theory about the origin and nature of the universe. Hawking and Penrose have publicly debated about their two models for many years now, but Penrose's concepts have been completely ignored by the media. Penrose was studying the movements of energy we see at the quantum level and looking for a hidden pattern that unified them. He found compelling evidence that everything we see in the universe—all space and all time—was being formed from a single point, moment by moment. This would mean that there is no space, no matter, no energy, and no time as we know it—only "distortions" of this one single point. The beginning, middle, and ending of the universe all exist simultaneously.

The story gets even weirder when we see that Penrose believed this "point" was actually an odd-looking three-dimensional geometric shape, made predominantly out of triangles, as you can see here.

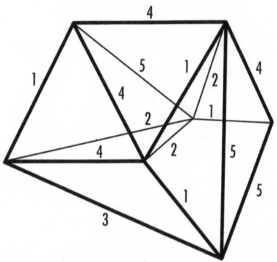

Sir Roger Penrose's Model of a Universal Geometric Seed

Penrose was working on the math to prove that this is how the universe works, and he had made compelling progress, but he hit a brick wall. His theory sat around as an intriguing but unproven scientific mystery until Nima Arkani-Hmed and Jaroslav Trnka, two scientists at the California Institute of Technology (Caltech), reopened the investigation. Through a staggering feat of mathematical genius, they were able to prove that Penrose's basic idea was correct—he just didn't have the right shape. By finally getting the math right, these scientists effectively proved that the universe as we know it does not exist. It behaves like a hologram: it appears to be solid and three-dimensional but nothing is really there. This also means if we zoom into the quantum level deeply enough, we will ultimately find a single "particle" that is making the entire universe—including all space and all time. This "particle" looks like a group of four triangular pyramids, or tetrahedrons, that have all been stuck together:

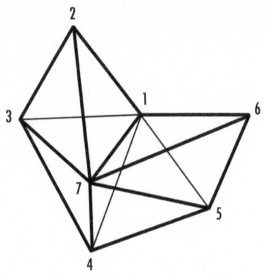

The "Amplituhedron"—Geometric Seed of the Universe

Although we see 100 to 400 billion galaxies in the universe, and potentially 100 billion billion Earth-like planets—a hundred watery worlds for every grain of sand on Earth—we now have proof that they are all emanating from this single geometric shape. The universe becomes like a vast tree with countless branches that all grew out of a single seed that is almost impossibly small. And, as confusing as this may seem, the seed is all that really exists. The tree is only an illusion. There is no beginning and no ending. The seed and the tree coexist at the same time.

Sacred Geometry

The question then becomes, *What is the universe?* How do we explain all the seemingly solid matter that we see out there? In my first book, *The Source Field Investigations,* I presented extensive evidence that atoms and molecules are not made of particles, but energy that is appearing in geometric patterns.[7] Science tells us the nucleus of the atom is made of protons and neutrons. One of the founding fathers of the atomic bomb, Dr. Robert

Moon, discovered in 1987 that many of the greatest mysteries of the atom could be solved if we see each proton as the corner of a simple geometric shape—like the cube. This elegantly solves the problem of wave-particle duality, the idea that subatomic particles can act like waves and vice versa. Dr. Moon concluded that there are no particles in the atom—only waves of energy that form certain geometric shapes. The simplest example of this is with oxygen. There are eight protons in an oxygen molecule. Dr. Moon identifies these eight protons as the eight corners of a cube. That means if we could see the nucleus of an oxygen atom, we would be looking at a cube. The cube isn't solid—it is only a wave.

As we then go into heavier elements, the cube remains inside the nucleus, and its corners still count as protons, but new geometric shapes start forming over it. This begins with the octahedron, then the icosahedron, then the dodecahedron. This nest of shapes cranks out some of the most stable and abundant elements on Earth—oxygen (cube), silicon (octahedron), iron (icosahedron), and palladium (dodecahedron)—and solves an impressive number of quantum physics problems.

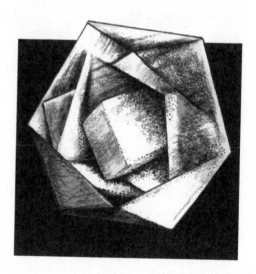

Dr. Robert Moon's Geometric
Model of the Atom

Although I love to explore these technical details, *The Source Field Investigations* has already been written. This book is not intended to present another scientific discourse on consciousness, biology, and physics, though we will revisit some of those concepts. The most important point we need to know now is that geometry is the visible form of vibration. This was very elegantly proven by Dr. Hans Jenny, who generated beautiful geometric patterns—including the cube—in a drop of water. Dr. Jenny started with sand that was floating in a drop of water. This created what looked like a muddy, whitish liquid. Then he vibrated the drop of water with pure tones of sound, like what we hear when we play the white keys on the piano. Miraculously, the sand particles arranged into beautiful geometric wave patterns—as if they were under the influence of some mysterious, unseen force.

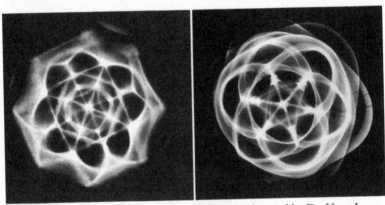

Geometric Patterns in a Vibrating Drop of Water Observed by Dr. Hans Jenny

The same drop of water, with the same sand, will create totally different geometric patterns—including the cube—depending upon what sound you play into it. As you can see, a three-dimensional Star of David–type pattern of triangles appears in the water at certain sound frequencies. This pattern has astonishing similarities to the triangular shape our Caltech scientists discovered as being the seed of the universe.

Most of us still believe matter is made of particles that are hard, solid, and tangible. If we retool our scientific models to see that atoms are geometric energy patterns, then that means all matter could be formed by something akin to a sound wave—that has reverberated throughout the entire universe. This is exactly what the ancient spiritual traditions tell us. Hindus and Buddhists believe the universe was formed from a primordial sound they call the *aum*. They will spend hours chanting this sound, and believe it gets them closer to the Creator. The book of Genesis says, "In the beginning, there was the word." Native Americans beat a drum in honor of the heartbeat of the Mother—i.e., the universe.

Let's assume for a moment that our Caltech scientists are correct, and the entire universe is emanating from a single seed. We know that we are living and conscious beings. We are surrounded by a wealth of biological life. We appear to be separate from everything else around us, but we are connected by the hidden energy in the quantum realm that flows through and creates all matter. All life on Earth is ultimately the fruit of this universal seed, if this new model is correct. Therefore, the seed must have all the ingredients needed to make biological life and consciousness. The seed itself must be alive and intelligent. Everything we need to make intelligent civilizations like the ones we now see on Earth would be contained within the seed. That means the ingredients to make intelligent life are cosmic in nature, and sentient life may very well have flowered throughout the universe. This also means that life could have an energetic component that would not require any physical biological material to exist. The energy itself is alive, forming what I call the "Source Field"—and all matter in the universe is part of a living cosmos.

If you have already read *The Source Field Investigations* and *The Synchronicity Key*, then you have seen extensive scientific proof to support these assertions. The cosmos is not a void of darkness peppered with unthinking blobs of gas burning away with nuclear fusion. The universe is alive, aware, and intelligent. It is designed to make biological life. The codes that make DNA, proteins, and cells are directly written into the laws of quantum physics. My favorite proof of this came from the Nobel Prize–winning biologist Dr. Luc Montagnier.[8] He was able to transform ordinary water molecules, in a sealed container, into DNA. All he needed was another nearby sealed tube of water with DNA in it and some static electricity. The hydrogen and oxygen in the plain water somehow transmuted into complex amino acids that assembled themselves into DNA. Montagnier's experiments are very sound, and he repeated them many times. As you might expect, hardly any media outlets covered this story, even after his research was formally presented at the United Nations in

2014.[9] If this really works—and again, remember he won a Nobel Prize—then why would our own human DNA be any different? The code that makes human life could be written into the universe itself. There may be people living on a majority of those 100 billion billion Earth-like planets out there.

"The Law of One," a body of spiritual work we will explore later in this book, tells us that roughly 40 percent of all intelligent life throughout the universe may be human or at least hominid in appearance—meaning having a head, eyes, nose, mouth, and ears, walking upright on two legs, and with two arms with some form of hands for toolmaking. We are also told that there are more than 67 million inhabited worlds in our galaxy alone—or about 67 percent of all Earth-like planets in Petigura's estimate.

If the universe is making all of us out of a single seed, then what are we doing here? What is the greater purpose for our lives on Earth? Why does our planet seem so incredibly damaged—surfing right on the brink of total catastrophe? Why are so many people suffering through such intense pain and loneliness? Why do we seem hopelessly confused, with no definitive proof that we are not alone in the universe? If other intelligent civilizations do exist, they have been humming along just fine—whether we realize they are out there or not. Why don't they just show up, tell us who they are, and reveal the true nature of the universe? Perhaps we simply haven't matured enough, as a planet, to be given the secret.

Destroying the UFO Cover-up

Another central mystery we will explore in this book is the shadowy world of government secrecy. The Snowden documents were released in June 2013, right after I had finished writing *The Synchronicity Key*, which predicted that information like this would be revealed.[10] Suddenly, whistle-blowers who had been ridiculed for years as "conspiracy theorists" became brave harbingers of a terrifying truth. An overwhelming amount of information was released in the first six months alone, and the disclosures have been ongoing ever since. We now know that we are under constant surveillance in almost every form imaginable. Nothing is private. If we take nude photos of ourselves, someone like Snowden working at the NSA has the software to look at them whenever he wants. We can be watched through the cameras on our smartphones and laptops. Every conversation can be transcribed into text with a system like Apple's Siri, and those transcripts can then be organized in vast databases to look for keywords. And this "all-seeing eye" was in place for many years, cloaked in total secrecy. Snowden proved that astonishingly elaborate secrets are being hidden from us—secrets that would profoundly change everything we think we know about our lives on Earth.

In this book I will combine the testimony of multiple whistle-blowers who have information that makes Snowden's revelations seem like kindergarten class. We have overwhelming evidence that UFOs and extraterrestrials do exist—not just in our own time, but throughout our recorded history. For most people, "Are we alone?" is still an intriguing question with no absolute proof. However, I have met multiple whistle-blowers who have had face-to-face, in-person contact with a variety of humanlike ETs—and no longer have the luxury of doubting that UFOs are real.

Some of these people have already gone public, and I will give you all the links you need to follow up and hear more of what they said for yourself. Others have only spoken to me personally, and the stories they have to share are absolutely astonishing. The insiders present us with the tempting idea that a wide variety of intelligent civilizations are already here now—and the truth has been carefully hidden from us. Millions of people have avidly followed the work I have put out in YouTube videos and television shows, on my website and elsewhere, and the vast majority of you have said you want to hear what these insiders have revealed. It is quite a story, and in order to properly tell it, I need to summarize twenty-two years' worth of "leaks" from a variety of fascinating characters. Some of these people need to have their identities hidden for their own safety, and in the second half of this book I will focus on what they told me—and how it all fits together into a grand mosaic.

Ask yourself this: Isn't it strange that we had the technology to land on the Moon as early as 1969, and then we never went back? Isn't it strange that the space shuttle program was completely discontinued, as if there was nothing out there worth seeing? Did you know that the US government revealed they had a secret space plane, the X-37B, that was orbiting the Earth for nearly two years before landing? What were they doing up there? Is it possible that there have been ongoing missions to the Moon and even Mars, and we already have bases there? I have spoken with multiple insiders who claim to have lived and worked in bases on the Moon, Mars, and elsewhere in our solar system—and beyond. Many of these insiders say they have had contact with extraterrestrials. The most surprising thing they say is that these extraterrestrials are predominantly human-looking, or at the very least hominid in appearance.

Henry Deacon claims to have met about forty-three different human-looking extraterrestrials. Pete Peterson claims to have seen about thirteen varieties. Both of these men came forward in Project Camelot videos I was featured in. Sergeant Clifford Stone went public at the Disclosure Project event in May 2001 and said he was personally aware of fifty-seven varieties operating in Earth's own airspace. I was there at this groundbreaking event, where Dr. Steven Greer brought together thirty-nine different high-level whistle-blowers to share what they knew at the National Press Club in Washington, DC—in front of the world's media. Each insider offered to testify before Congress, swearing to tell the truth under oath, and subjecting themselves to rigorous cross-examination. Nothing ever happened. None of them were subpoenaed. Yet I had a chance to talk to the majority of them while I was there. The stories are extremely fascinating and still largely unknown to most people. Other insiders who appeared to me later in our story had much more information than anyone at the Disclosure Project.

I understand how ridiculous this must sound, particularly if this is all new to you. I encourage you to have an open mind and not immediately decide that this is all nonsense. One of the most fascinating features of this investigation has been that different insiders have continually said the same things over these past twenty-two years. I deliberately withheld the majority of what they were telling me so I could weed out the real people from the frauds, charlatans, and fakers. There are countless examples of people making up stories on the Internet and looking to cash in on the quick fame that can occur when an interesting new story "goes viral" in the UFO community. My policy has never been to accuse anyone of making up stories. I try not to say anything about the suspected fakes one way or the other. I discovered a long time ago that this unleashes hordes of angry followers who will then do whatever it takes to try to destroy you and your reputation online. There are dozens of examples of people who pretend to be insiders, and then come out with "new information" a week or two after I release a little more of what I was told. Then all the emails come in from people who are excited about what they just heard, and they do not realize that I had already leaked that exact same information a week or two before.

One major clue that an insider is the real deal is when I hear twenty or thirty different things in a single conversation that others have already shared with me, which have never been revealed online. This is what we would expect to occur when there is a common body of truth that each of these people has come into contact with. Some skeptics argue that the government can't even find a piece of paper in a file cabinet, never mind keep a secret, but this is not true. The Manhattan Project proved that the government can keep very big secrets from us. More than 130,000 employees worked to develop the nuclear bomb in the Manhattan Project over the course of a decade, including Dr. Robert Moon, who discovered the geometric nature of the atom. Many of them had no idea what they were doing. The facilities were kept secret, as was the technology. Not one employee ever leaked their secrets. It was only once the bomb was actually detonated that they found out what they had been working on for all those years.

In a similar sense, one of my insiders claims to have had a job at a military base where all he did was autopsy various extraterrestrial corpses and look for identifiable organ systems. For the first nine months, he was handed little "salmon filets" of biological tissue and told to dissect and analyze them. In his second nine-month term, he started getting body parts like arms and legs that were humanlike but different. Then in his third nine-month term, he got intact or semi-intact corpses. He was never told they were extraterrestrial. He was never allowed to ask a single question about where they were from or what he was doing. He claims to have personally autopsied approximately two thousand different varieties of humanlike ETs. They ranged from less than a foot tall to over forty-five feet in height. A high-ranking friend of his eventually sneaked him into a hangar that was on the same base and showed him a very bizarre diamond-shaped craft. He was apprehended, beaten, threatened with death if he told anyone what he had just seen, and fired. He then was captured, threatened, and beaten again just for riding his bike in the mountains near where he used to work. These experiences caused him to have severe PTSD—post-traumatic stress disorder—that he still suffers with today. He has never wanted to come forward and has not profited from this in any way. He knew many of the same secrets other proven insiders had shared with me privately.

There is a single mega-story that emerges from this collective body of insider information, and in this book we will give a summary overview of it—both on the personal level as well as the cosmic. To begin with, we find out that there are good ETs and bad ETs, and they have been warring with one another in our solar system for hundreds of thousands of years. Both types of ETs are making direct contact with certain people on Earth who are receptive to the messages they have to share. The negative ETs are apt to contact those who already have great money and power, and will give them tools to further enhance their control. The positive ETs are far more apt to contact private individuals who are judged by the quality and virtue of their character—their forgiveness, acceptance, patience, and love. Their method of contact is thoroughly outlined in this book, through my own direct personal example. They deliberately approach you through the imagination first. You are not sure whether what you are seeing and hearing is real or just a dream. Your life becomes filled with ever increasingly bizarre coincidences. You suspect something but are not sure, and flip-flop between understanding and great confusion. All this is done to prevent fear, and to give you a gentle, peaceful introduction into this greater reality.

Both types of ETs have walked the Earth's surface themselves at various times in our past. And the choices we all make as a people, both individually and collectively, will determine the outcome of this battle for each of us. Both the positive and negative ETs are bound by a Prime

Directive, just like the one we hear about in *Star Trek*, stating they cannot openly reveal themselves to us or interfere in our development until a sufficient majority of us welcome them to do so. Scientific explorers from our own time follow a similar policy when dealing with indigenous tribes. If they show up and introduce themselves, a phenomenon called "enculturation" occurs. The indigenous tribes quickly give up their own language, culture, and customs, and adopt the food, language, technology, information, and beliefs of their visitors.

Many insiders have said that a gradual plan to reveal the truth has been under way for many years—at least since the 1950s. Some have referred to this as the Processed Release of Information, or PRI. We are publicly told that UFOs do not exist, while countless films and television programs talk about it as if the truth is obvious—and even make jokes about how ridiculous it is for anyone to doubt it. More and more, the greatest skeptics end up looking like religious zealots.

The greatest secret these insiders have shared with me is that a massive energetic shift is happening on Earth. We are apparently moving into a dense cloud of highly charged energetic particles in our galaxy. This zone of higher energy is having an effect on our consciousness as well as our DNA. For many years I had read spiritual sources saying that this was happening. Versions of this story appear in the Bible, the Koran, the Hindu scriptures, the Buddhist scriptures, and many other ancient texts. Collectively, there are thirty-five different ancient spiritual traditions that predict a time of great strife and pain on Earth that then leads to a Golden Age, much greater than anything we are seeing now. Over the years I have done the hard work to put together a scientific case that could prove this is really happening.

In the past I have tackled this investigation by integrating a wealth of scientific data together. I have also extensively explored the mysteries of ancient civilizations, where "gods" walked among us and were said to have built massive stone structures we can still visit today. Many of these structures were created with stones that are so heavy we still do not have any crane on Earth that is large enough to lift them. An ancient temple in Baalbek, Lebanon, has three huge rectangular stone slabs in it that weigh more than a thousand tons each, and are supported by a structure

keeping them feet above the ground. In 2015, an even larger carved rectangular stone was found nearby, weighing an astonishing 1,650 tons with
a length of sixty-five feet. This stone was discovered beneath another
loose stone that was almost as heavy, indicating that the upper stone
would have to have been lifted away in order to sculpt the lower one.
Mainstream archeologists have tried to explain all this away as the
work of primitive savages rolling them along on greased-up logs, pulling
them with makeshift ropes in huge teams. In *The Source Field Investigations*, I reviewed some of the evidence that reveals this idea is thoroughly
impossible, even ridiculous. Why do these gigantic stone structures appear in so many different cultures, worldwide, that are completely isolated from one another? Why would apparently primitive people want to
tackle engineering projects that are still almost impossible to achieve—
even with today's technology? If it were so easy for primitive people to fit
hundred-ton or even thousand-ton blocks of stone together into huge,
beautiful monuments, then why don't we see any primitive cultures
building structures like this today?

Asking these questions, and being willing to search for the answers,
is all a part of growing up, in the spiritual sense. We need to have the
strength to risk being laughed at and ridiculed by our friends and family.
Our history reveals countless examples in which we thought we knew
everything, only to have major discoveries completely change our worldview. We did not understand that there were creatures too tiny for the
eye to see that could cause infections, and thus doctors did not wash
their hands when performing surgeries. We thought that various health
conditions were caused by "bad blood," and that "bleeding" a person
could make them better. We thought the Earth was flat, and was the
center of our solar system, with the Sun orbiting around it just like the
other planets. We thought objects fell by magic, and did not understand
gravity, until Newton. Even in the twentieth century, prominent scientists were saying heavier-than-air flight was impossible, and were de-
bunking the Wright Brothers' invention of the airplane for four full years
after it was first successfully flown at Kitty Hawk.

It appears that the single most important thing the positive ETs want
you to hear is the spiritual message given to us in the great world

religions. The world seems to be impossibly broken, and every day we face problems that seem to have no solution. But no matter how dire, depressing, and hopeless someone's life may be, everyone is capable of undergoing massive transformation. Many of my readers and viewers look up to me as an authority figure, and do not realize how profoundly I have suffered to reach this point. Now you will know. If you were to zoom in on my life as a teenager, you would see someone who appeared to be on a road to nowhere. I was significantly overweight, had long hair that I never bothered to comb, wore black rock-and-roll T-shirts, and did not want to talk to anyone. I was extremely shy, terrified of rejection, and let my friends and classmates walk all over me. Bullies could basically do whatever they wanted with no fear of reprisal. The people at my twenty-year high school reunion were utterly astonished when they saw me and realized how much I had turned my life around.

I originally did not want to include personal information in this book at all. Everything changed when I took one of the only real vacations I have ever had in my adult life, and got away to the mountains of Banff, in Alberta, Canada, for a whole month. I went back and actually read the four main texts of the New Testament—the books of Matthew, Mark, Luke, and John. I had felt so alienated from Christianity as a whole that I had never read those books before. Once I actually saw the words, I realized that there were dozens of references to ascension—both on a personal and global level—that I had missed.

I was very reluctantly forced to admit that all the key elements of my investigations were right there in the Bible. We have a global villain that is far more evil than most people ever allow themselves to see. It has penetrated almost all aspects of our society, including the government, the military, the financial system, the mainstream media, and corporations. Insiders have revealed this entity is secretly being supported, if not controlled by, extraterrestrial humans who are very, very evil. These beings have a hatred of us that is so pure as to be the perfect embodiment of evil. On the opposite end of the spectrum, we have Jesus, who gave the same teachings I have been hearing and sharing all these years about loving and forgiving others—and who said love was the key to saving the world. There are multiple references in the Bible to some sort of celestial "moment of truth," when we undergo a spontaneous, mass evolution. This seems to involve an incredible release of blindingly bright light from the Sun that utterly transforms us into a new level of human evolution.

Once I found this new evidence in the Bible, I went back to the original references I had found to this same type of event in the Hindu and Zoroastrian scriptures. The Hindus referred to this solar flash as the Samavartaka fire, and the Zoroastrians referred to it as an event they called Fraso-kereti. Both of these stories were briefly mentioned in *The Source Field Investigations.* The very end of *The Synchronicity Key* presents several quotes from the Koran that predict the same type of event. Now I went back into a variety of spiritual and philosophical scriptures and looked for as many details as I could find. Certain keywords opened up worlds of forgotten data I had never before encountered. I started finding scholarly papers that may have had only twenty-seven views online, but were discussing this same solar event in academic terms. I discovered many other references to such an event in a wide variety of cultures—references that were very specific. As a result, I now feel as if I have finally solved the grand puzzle of the Ascension Mysteries that I have been navigating all these years. There is overwhelming evidence that we are heading into a massive event that will utterly and completely transform life on Earth as we know it. If this is really going to happen, and is an unavoidable natural phenomenon, then the best thing we can possibly do is to prepare ourselves for it. It appears that the more we prepare for ascension on the personal level, the sooner we will "authorize" it to occur on the collective level.

Repetition Compulsion

The vast majority of spiritual sources I have found on this subject agree that the most important way to prepare yourself for ascension is to "do the work" of being more loving and forgiving toward yourself and others in your daily life. This practice is not as easy as it sounds, as we can become physically addicted to drama, stress, and unhealthy situations. Dr. Sigmund

Freud, the father of psychotherapy, named this "repetition compulsion." In 1989, Dr. Bessel A. van der Kolk gave an excellent summary of this phenomenon in *The Compulsion to Repeat the Trauma*. This study has so many reference numbers at the end of its sentences that I removed them here to make it easier to read:

> Many traumatized people expose themselves, seemingly compulsively, to situations reminiscent of the original trauma. These behavioral re-enactments are rarely consciously understood to be related to earlier life experiences. This "repetition compulsion" has received surprisingly little systematic exploration during the 70 years since its discovery, though it is regularly described in the clinical literature. . . . Re-enactment of victimization is a major cause of violence. Criminals have often been physically or sexually abused as children. . . . Self-destructive acts are common in abused children. . . . In one study of adults who had recently been in accidents, 57 per cent showed behavioral re-enactments, and 51 per cent had recurrent intrusive images. . . . At least four studies of family violence have found a direct relationship between the severity of childhood physical abuse and later marital violence. Interestingly, nonhuman primates subjected to early abuse and deprivation also are more likely to engage in violent relationships with their peers as adults. . . .
>
> Some traumatized people remain preoccupied with the trauma at the expense of other life experiences and continue to re-create it in some form for themselves or for others. War veterans may enlist as mercenaries, victims of incest may become prostitutes, and victims of childhood physical abuse seemingly provoke subsequent abuse in foster families or become self-mutilators. Still others identify with the aggressor and do to others what was done to them. Clinically, these people are observed to have a vague sense of apprehension, emptiness, boredom, and anxiety when not involved in activities reminiscent of the trauma. . . . Many observers of

traumatic bonding have speculated that victims become addicted to their victimizers. Erschak asks why the batterer does not stop when injury and pain are apparent and why does the victim not leave? He answers that "they are addicted to each other and to abuse. The system, the interaction, the relation takes hold; the individuals are as powerless as junkies."[11]

Dr. van der Kolk goes on to reveal that this addiction is actually biochemical in nature. The body has natural "opioid systems" that release the same basic chemicals as heroin or morphine. When we engage in repetition compulsion of our traumas, we are actually getting high from it. This is dangerously addictive, creating a full-body pain-relief sensation called "stress-induced analgesia":

> Starr, Solomon, Erschak and others may be right in postulating that people can become physiologically addicted to each other. . . . High levels of stress, including social stress, also activate opioid systems. Animals exposed to inescapable shock develop stress-induced analgesia (SIA) when re-exposed to stress shortly afterward. . . . We found that seven of eight Vietnam veterans with PTSD showed a 30 percent reduction in perception of pain when viewing a movie depicting combat in Vietnam. . . . This amount of analgesia produced by watching 15 minutes of a combat movie was equivalent to that which follows the injection of 8 mg. of morphine. . . . Depending on which stimuli have come to condition an opioid response, self-destructive behavior may include chronic involvement with abusive partners, sexual masochism, self-starvation, and violence against self or others. . . . This pattern is reminiscent of spouse abuse described by Walker: "tension gradually builds, an explosive battering (self-mutilating) incident occurs, and a 'calm, loving respite' follows."[12]

The great villains in our planetary script constantly fill the headlines with fear and trauma. Terrifying media, presenting horrors such as the threat of mass destruction, triggers a morphine response that gets us high—which I have termed "fear porn." Some people are then influenced to abuse others, whereas others get high from feeling victimized. I feel the best way to understand this phenomenon and deactivate the system is to study the personal testimony of someone who has identified the addiction and recovered from it. Breaking this habit, I believe, is the core of the ascension process, and it is the main reason why I am sharing so much of myself with you in this book. It took a great deal of time, meditation, and concentration to remember all the most significant details from my childhood. The timing of my memories was often calibrated by things like movies, albums, and television shows, for which I could use the Internet to find out exactly when they happened. Significant events in the world and in my own family also provided clues. It was quite interesting to discover that one memory would immediately cause two or three more to appear. I was able to rebuild an incredible number of things I had forgotten, and once I remembered them, the memories became crystal clear. This has been quite a journey of healing, and I found out that Tibetan monks do a very similar "life review" while they spend years meditating alone in caves.

The villains are doing everything they can to make you ignore your spirituality, fall into jealousy, materialism, and fear, and prevent you from being ready for this epic change. The only way to break the trauma addiction is to learn to love and protect yourself, and then to be able to forgive those who have harmed you. The positive forces cannot just appear in the sky and tell you what is going to happen in our future. They need to present you with information that you can choose to either accept or reject with your own free will. One of the most fascinating things I have gotten out of writing this is seeing how life can appear to be right on the edge, damaged beyond all possibility of repair, and yet the higher beings working with us are completely at peace in this zone. They know every twist and turn of the path, from the brightest to the darkest, and can help us out of the most impossible-seeming paradoxes. I was told that by sharing my own story of awakening, you may be able to see how a life that seems impossibly painful, broken, and wasted can be turned around into something that can create genuine value and uplifting inspiration for others. Ultimately, you don't have to be perfect. If you can learn to love yourself and love other people, your life will transform as if by magic. If you remain addicted to fear, new traumas will keep reappearing, and the highs will never last very long. You may indulge in all sorts of addictive behaviors, including stress eating, compulsive spending, and chemical dependency, to cope with daily life. If you demonstrate love, patience, humility, acceptance, forgiveness, and the courage to face the truth, ascension is in your grasp. You may just leap into an entirely new level of human evolution—and gain all the abilities of masters like Jesus.

CHAPTER TWO

A Battle Against Darkness

I t was a cold, dark night in the fall of 1978 when I discovered I was levitating over my bed. The ceiling was much closer than it was supposed to be. Everything around me seemed to be pulsating with an unseen energy. I pushed my arms down and nothing was there to stop them. I then lifted my left shoulder, dropped my right shoulder, twisted my torso, and was able to turn over in the air. To my incredible surprise, I could now see my own five-year-old body sleeping peacefully in bed. My chest was rising and falling, so I clearly was not dead. My first thought was, "If that's me down there, then who the heck am I?" Fascination quickly took over, as my floating body was fully clothed—wearing the same pair of yellow pajamas with the red cuffs that I was wearing in bed. How in the world could a simple pair of pajamas, made out of cheap "plastic" polyester material, have suddenly doubled? The experience lasted several minutes, and everything around me stayed stable and vividly realistic the entire time.

When I finally emerged from this incredible event, I was so dazzled I could barely fall back asleep. I immediately knew I had discovered a new frontier that most people were completely unaware of. I no longer had to wonder about whether there was life after death. Even if my physical body died, I would still have this energetic body—my soul—afterward. Life was not simply about flesh and blood. There is something much greater about who and what we are than we normally realize. I was so profoundly transformed by this event that I saved the pajamas and still have them in my closet right now. What ended up surprising me the most was that this appeared to be a natural event, something anybody could potentially do, but hardly anyone had experienced it—or even believed it was possible. That was a big clue that something was really wrong with the world as it is today. I realized that I could potentially travel long distances, observe things that were happening somewhere else, and gain valuable information. It also occurred to me that there must be some part of me that is doing this all the time. Either I did not remember these experiences consciously, or I thought they were only dreams. Little did I know at the time that this was also the first glimpse of a stunning new reality that could provide humanity with real hope—to defeat a global villain far beyond most people's wildest imagination. Our collective fear of "the monster under the bed" might make us high as each new threat occurs, but until we soberly face the truth on a collective level, we can never hope to break the addiction and heal our world.

The British Invasion

Both of my parents shared a nation's grief when a very well-liked American president, John Fitzgerald Kennedy, was murdered in broad daylight, receiving gunshot wounds to the head. The Warren Commission explained away what clearly appeared to be multiple bullets from different locations as the work of a single bullet that zigzagged around. Like most Americans, my parents knew the story didn't add up. It was all too convenient to blame everything on one gunman, Lee Harvey Oswald, who was shot to death before he could ever stand trial. At the time, no one wanted to consider that elements of the US government itself may have been responsible for Kennedy's murder. Everyone chose to stay asleep and keep their heads down as they felt the morphine response from the terror this caused. There were no mass protests or calls for a new investigation that created any tangible results. Kennedy's vice president, Lyndon Baines Johnson, was sworn in as president—and ramped up a "police action" that soon became known as the Vietnam War. The first deployment of 3,500 Marines was in March 1965, and it was increased to 200,000 troops that December.

Less than three months after the Kennedy assassination in November 1963, the new "British Invasion" came to America in the form of the Beatles. As I said in *The Synchronicity Key,* the ear splitting screaming and crying of female Beatle fans seemed to be a mass cathartic purging of the trauma of JFK's assassination—and of the government and media participating in an obviously botched cover-up. John, Paul, George, and Ringo suddenly became new heroes, filling the epic void that Kennedy had left behind and creating a musical legacy and celebrity that has still never been duplicated or outmatched. In a sense, the Beatles created a new high that allowed people to forget the traumas of their immediate past—and never look back. The band was so besieged by screaming, crying fans that they quit touring after their fourth album and spent most of their time in the studio. The classic albums *Rubber Soul* and *Revolver* were followed by *Sgt. Pepper's Lonely Hearts Club Band* in early 1967, which strongly influenced what was called the "Summer of Love."

The Beatles used their fame to fight back against the death-dealing powers of the day by releasing "All You Need Is Love" as a single on June 25, 1967. It was performed live during a show called *Our World,* which was the first to fully utilize new satellite-based broadcast technology.[13] This would prove to be the most popular moment in television history, watched by more than 400 million people in twenty-five countries. The Beatles changed the song they were scheduled to perform at the last minute and brilliantly touched off a youth revolution in the process. Unlike during World Wars I and II, Britain did not have a draft, and they sent only about two thousand soldiers into Vietnam—but the Beatles were obviously greatly concerned about what was happening to their American brothers and sisters. My parents were two people among millions of young adults who were profoundly affected by all the changes taking place at this time. It became clear that silence equaled death, and they needed to stand up to the forces in power in order to secure their own future.

Their Britannic Majesties Request

The only other British band that was competing on the same level as the Beatles in the transformative period of the late 1960s was the Rolling Stones. On December 8 of the magical year 1967, in the aftermath of the Summer of Love, the Rolling Stones released a bizarre album called *Their Satanic Majesties Request*. The title was a play on the text that appears in every British passport, beginning with *"Her Britannic Majesty requests and requires."* Mick Jagger, the lead singer of the band, was pictured wearing a dunce cap, suggesting he was the fool, or court jester—the character who often reveals secret political information in Shakespearean plays. It thus appeared that the "court jester" was introducing the British empire as "Their Satanic Majesties." The cover art and musical style were obviously intended to copy the Beatles' classic record from that same year, but the Stones were doing a lot of drugs at the time and *Satanic Majesties* did not have the timeless quality of *Sgt. Pepper*.

Oddly, the drummer of the band was pictured in a costume that looked exactly like that of Henry VIII, the legendary British king. Henry had six wives, two of whom he assassinated, and he was famous for breaking away from the Roman Catholic Church. Henry created radical changes to the British constitution, instituting the Divine Right of Kings, and also declared the British sovereign to have full supremacy over the Church of England—effectively putting himself and his successors in a godlike role over Christianity. Henry also executed many of his dissenters without a formal trial through the use of "bills of attainder," which lobbed charges of treason and heresy that could not be questioned. It was very puzzling to see the Beatles' main competitor come out with an album that very openly mentioned and endorsed Satanism, and that suggested it was woven directly into the British empire, just six months after the Beatles had triggered a revolution by saying "All You Need Is Love."

Satanic Majesties also had intriguing suggestions that it was written to honor an extraterrestrial civilization that had fallen to Earth. A ringed planet, perhaps Saturn, appears behind the band in the cover photo. Due to copyright laws, we cannot feature all the lyrics here, but it is worth a look.

The song "2000 Man" has a chorus that says: "Oh Daddy, proud of your planet, oh Mummy, proud of your sun. . . . Did you come down crashing?" After hearing the insider testimony I received in 2014, which I will review in the second half of this book, I realized these lyrics could be describing a civilization from another planet and sun coming down and crash-landing on Earth—led by an extraterrestrial being we now call Lucifer, who arrived here along with his supporters, the "fallen angels" in the Bible.

How could anyone on Earth support a being like Lucifer? It doesn't even seem possible. Up until recently, you would open yourself up to ridicule and ostracism from your friends and family if you even dared to believe such an idea. It took a great deal of time, energy, research, insider testimony, and personal risk for me to discover that there is a vast, secretive cult on Earth that considers Lucifer to be the good guy. Some people call this group the "New World Order," the Bilderbergers, the Trilateral Commission, or the Illuminati, but here we will call them the Cabal.

This Cabal believes the Christian god is the embodiment of evil—suppressing knowledge, freedom, sexuality, and scientific progress. Even more outrageously, this group has amassed incredible power—including a shocking degree of control over the media, the financial system, Western governments, and the military-industrial complex. It can be deeply upsetting, if not almost impossible to face—but hiding from the truth and hoping it will "just go away" is much more dangerous than educating yourself about it. Once you finally come into contact with enough evidence that you are convinced, you end up going through a "dark night of the soul"—a deep grieving process during which you realize you have been lied to all your life, and a terrifying global villain is leering at you from all sides. This is an essential step in the awakening process, as ultimately you realize you have been living in a world of illusion—and much of what you were taught to believe has been deliberately manipulated by those in power.

A variety of insiders have risked their lives to reveal these hidden truths. Today's youth are being forced to confront this on a much greater level than any previous generation. Unlike the brief signs of trouble that were seen in albums like *Satanic Majesties,* millennials are now being inundated with a seemingly nonstop bombardment of Luciferian symbolism in movies, music videos, Super Bowl halftime shows, music awards ceremonies, video games, and television shows. Pop music icons such as Lady Gaga, Katy Perry, Rihanna, Nicki Minaj, and Miley Cyrus have music videos and live performances that are astonishingly full of "Illuminati" symbolism, such as the All-Seeing Eye. This Cabal now appears to be on a very aggressive advertising campaign, hoping to make their religion seem hip and trendy.[14] Nonetheless, this does not necessarily mean that the stars themselves support the message, and insiders say these stars are often severely abused. The singer Kesha openly accused her former producer of raping her. She gained widespread sympathy from other pop stars, including Adele, Taylor Swift, and Lady Gaga, after having her case dismissed in the spring of 2016.[15] At least eighteen different celebrities voiced their support for Kesha.[16]

Many insiders told me this secretive group is building up to a formal announcement of their presence that they have called "The Great Revealing." Luckily, a tremendous number of YouTube videos now exists that expose the agenda—and many of them have millions of views. This has become the next great youth revolution—far greater in numbers and potential impact than the original Woodstock. Many overlooked and forgotten clues from the past are now being unearthed and reexamined as part of a massive, generations-wide investigation into these mysteries.

It is important to note that these elites do not think they are doing anything bad. They believe they are liberating us from weakness and ignorance. Anyone who dies along the way toward their pursuit of a "New World Order" is considered to be an acceptable loss as we move toward what they consider to be "enlightenment." One of their most highly guarded secrets is that they believe they are the direct bloodline descendants of ancient extraterrestrial human visitors to Earth who were more advanced than the rest of us and became pharaohs, kings, and gods. This "magical blood" is used as an excuse for them to feel superior to everyone else, thus giving them the right—and the need—to rule the Earth. The best intel we now have from high-level insiders suggests they were an extraterrestrial refugee group who crash-landed here 55,000 years ago. They were badly defeated in a war and did not have the technology or know-how to leave once they arrived. They spread throughout the world, set up control systems, and survived multiple collapses of civilizations and uprisings by those they attempted to rule.

The *Satanic Majesties* song "2000 Man" also says the "circling sun"—perhaps in another solar system—is "where we all come from." The song "The Lantern" includes the words "We . . . knew that the stars were right . . . crossed the sea of night." Then the message seems to culminate in "2000 Light Years from Home," which includes the lyrics "We're . . . bound for a star with fiery oceans . . . it's so very lonely, you're two thousand light years from home." Why would all this talk of what is obviously space travel be on an album called *Their Satanic Majesties Request?* Bruce, one of the key insiders we will meet later in this book, told me, "David, it doesn't matter whether you believe this, or anyone else believes this. It doesn't even matter if it is really true. All that matters is that *they* absolutely do believe this. It is a religion—and they are very devout followers of it. Once you understand that, everything they are doing begins to make a lot more sense. They believe that practicing their religion gives them occult, magical powers that lead to great fame and fortune. The more money and power you have, the more enlightened you are." This does not mean that the artists themselves are Satanists, necessarily. It is common for the power elite to create scapegoats who will take the fall for them in case they are ever exposed. They will tell countless lies to make their religion seem attractive to others.

Rock and roll was being introduced to the British public through the *Top of the Pops* television show. The number-one-selling band each week got to perform live on the show, and the Rolling Stones put in an astonishing thirty-three appearances—including a performance of "2000 Light Years from Home" on December 21, 1967. In 2013, the world learned that the main host of the show, Jimmy Savile, was a serial rapist. More than 450 victims came forward with terrifying tales of how he abused them, with estimates that the full number could easily be three times greater. Savile financed a variety of children's hospitals, and one victim told the UK's *Daily Express* that she was taken to a secret room in one of Savile's hospitals. The room was dark, lit only by candlelight. Savile was there along with others wearing robes and masks. Savile chanted "*Ave Satanas*," or "Hail Satan," in Latin while sexually abusing and torturing her. This certainly does not mean that the Rolling Stones were torturing and raping people in satanic rituals, but it does strongly suggest that the Cabal was using the Stones' music to spread negative messages. Savile had so many victims that there is no way the BBC could have avoided hearing about what he was doing—and yet he continued to be a very popular television star all the way up through the 1990s. Additional revelations from 2013 and forward have revealed that there were pedophiles in high levels of the British government as well— suggesting the presence of a powerful hidden culture where this was considered acceptable. On May 20, 2015, British police announced that 261 "people of public prominence" were being investigated for child sex abuse. This included 135 figures from TV, film, and radio, seventy-six politicians on both a local and national scale, forty-three different figures in the music industry, and seven involved in sports.[17]

On March 26, 2016, the *New York Times* published an exposé that was the result of a three-year independent investigation of the BBC by Dame Janet Smith, a retired judge: "In the scathing report of more than 700 pages, Dame Janet Smith . . . said BBC staff members were aware of complaints against Mr. Savile, but the accusations were not conveyed to senior management because of a 'culture of not complaining.' . . . Dame Janet said an 'atmosphere of fear' still existed at the corporation, noting that some of those interviewed for the report spoke only after receiving guarantees that their names would not be published. She said she suspected that they feared some form of reprisal."[18]

Public Clues of a Cosmic Battle

By early 1968, fully 550,000 American troops were stationed in Vietnam, many against their will. The climate in America was very dark. This was the year my father met my mother while they were both working at General Electric in Schenectady, New York, and they quickly fell in love. Mom grew up in a fundamentalist Christian family, only to become disillusioned and break away from it after leaving home and going to Philadelphia Bible College. The authorities shot her down in flames for intelligently questioning the dogma she was being taught. She was ultimately forced to sign a document swearing on her eternal soul that she believed every single thing they taught her, or else she would not receive her diploma. As a result of her extremely strict upbringing, she had been almost completely divorced from pop culture, avoiding all music, films, and TV shows.

My father loved horror movies and talked my mother into going to see *Rosemary's Baby* with him. This film terrified and disturbed her so much that I heard about it many times throughout my childhood. The film portrayed Satanists as being blended in with everyday people in a very believable way. The seemingly friendly elderly folks living in the lead couple's building were actually performing terrifying satanic rituals at night. In the movie, a struggling actor is told that having a baby with his wife and sacrificing the child to Satan would improve his career. His wife is drugged and brought into a satanic ritual in which the Devil manifests in physical form and impregnates her. At the end of the film, she is horrified to discover that her child has glowing red eyes. She is told by the cult that she is the "chosen one," and she should be honored that her baby is the spawn of Satan. She also hears that she does not have to join the cult if she doesn't want to. She decides to love and raise the child despite its horrific appearance. Despite the surreal idea of the Devil manifesting in physical form, the film had an overpowering sense of realism and terror. The viewer was led to believe it was entirely possible that Satan worshippers could be living among the rest of us—and the title of the Rolling Stones' latest album at the time certainly didn't help.

Rosemary's Baby was directed by Roman Polanski, who originally wanted to cast his wife, Sharon Tate, in the main role. Polanski did not push the studio on this, hoping they would suggest her, but they did not. Tate contributed notes to the script, including suggestions about the impregnation scene. She was frequently seen on the set and photographed by *Esquire* magazine to generate publicity for the film.

In November 1968, the Beatles released the complex, emotional album *The Beatles*, known as the "White Album," right as Richard Milhous Nixon won the presidential election. The White Album featured the song "Revolution 1," openly calling for a major political shift, and this again helped to crystallize the desire for change in the world's youth at the time. The album also had some very dark themes as John Lennon was sliding more and more into heavy drug addiction—leading to songs such as "Happiness Is a Warm Gun," which very blatantly described shooting heroin, and raunchy blues in which Lennon screamed about how lonely and suicidal he was, and how he hated his rock and roll. Paul McCartney's song "Helter Skelter" also had a wild, raw, and violent feeling to it. The strangest song on the album was "Revolution 9," an extended and deeply disturbing "bad trip" of sounds that included machine-gun fire, people screaming, and haunting, horror-movie dissonance. As he revealed in his biography *Many Years from Now,* Paul McCartney heavily fought to have the song removed from the album, but he lost the battle. The White Album became the greatest-selling record in the entire Beatles canon, though *Rolling Stone* magazine journalists consider *Sgt. Pepper, Revolver,* and *Rubber Soul* as all being superior to it in quality.

The Rolling Stones released their classic album *Beggar's Banquet* on December 6, 1968, which was a remarkable improvement in quality over *Their Satanic Majesties Request* from the year before. In February 1969, their record label released one of its songs, "Sympathy for the Devil," as a single. This seemed to be a direct follow-up and further revelation of the mysteries hinted at in *Satanic Majesties.* The song was admittedly quite shocking and worthy of analysis, as Mick Jagger sings as if he were Lucifer—introducing himself to the world and asking for our understanding and respect. Jagger-as-Lucifer identifies himself as being extremely wealthy and cultured, like the British elites, and indicates that if you want to speak to him, you must approach with the highest levels of politeness and manners.

Jagger-as-Lucifer takes credit for several key historical events. In order, these include the temptation of Jesus, the assassination of the Russian czar in St. Petersburg that led to the Russian Revolution of 1917, the aggression of Nazi Germany, a ten-decade war of kings and queens over "the gods they made," the Kennedy assassinations, and the deaths of British soldiers on their way to Bombay, India. A connection to the Vietnam War is implied as well. Available research and whistle-blowers have since revealed that a single group did indeed finance the Russian Revolution, Nazi Germany, the Kennedy assassinations, and the British Empire—owning and controlling both sides of World Wars I and II. The evidence is summarized in my online book *Financial Tyranny*. Therefore, this Rolling Stones song did appear to be a genuine attempt to create "sympathy for the Devil." Most interestingly, Jagger-as-Lucifer said that the events that puzzle and confuse us the most were the nature of his game. Lucifer—or in this case the British majesties, seeing Lucifer as their patron saint—was responsible for many of the most damaging events on Earth. Insiders would later tell me that Lucifer's greatest trick is convincing the world he does not exist. There is also a potentially revealing line in which Mick sings in a high falsetto, "I tell you one time, you're to blame"—suggesting that if we do not solve these mysteries ourselves, we are indirectly authorizing these crimes to continue.

Riding the Lightning

My mother was still reeling from her disillusionment with Christianity when Dad took her to a live concert featuring The Doors, while Jim Morrison was in his prime. Morrison had experimented with LSD, and the name of his band was an homage to Aldous Huxley's drug-taking memoir, *The Doors of Perception*. The effect that Morrison had on my mother was tremendous. In a single night, her entire life changed—her attitude, her values, and her goals. All her dissatisfaction with the religion she had been brought up with, the repressive climate her mother created, and the terrifying inferno that the nation's youth were being carelessly tossed into was transformed. Almost instantaneously, she embraced the thoughts and ideals of the music and the youth anti-war movement in the late 1960s—which some would call an awakening. Morrison had become a hero figure and a face of the movement, fearlessly demonstrating his rebellion against authority on stage and creating transcendent, life-changing music as he did it.

Jim Morrison also had an extremely dark side that became increasingly apparent before his tragic death. The Doors' 1971 single "Riders on the Storm" featured a character who takes LSD, so that "his brain is squirming like a toad." The character ends up brutally murdering his sister, brother, father, and mother. He is also portrayed as a serial killer who becomes a hitchhiker—and "if you give this man a ride, sweet family will die." In at least one interview, Morrison mentioned that the serial killer Billy Cook inspired this song, as Cook had killed six people, including a young family, while hitchhiking to California. Oddly enough, Morrison died of a drug and alcohol overdose on the very same day that "Riders on the Storm" entered the Billboard Hot 100 chart at number three—creating a powerful, haunting mystery around the song itself and its disturbing message.

Welcome to Vietnam

By the time he went to see Morrison live, my father was already terrified of being sent into the Vietnam death trap. He had decided to sign up for the Army Reserve in the hopes of avoiding the draft. He was then forced to move to Fort Lee, Virginia, in 1968, married my mother, and was activated to serve in Vietnam in June 1969—which was his worst nightmare come true. His father told him he had never been so proud of him, and to Dad this felt like an incredible betrayal. Dad was flown out on a commercial airliner, not a military plane. As they landed, the attractive female flight attendants gave a very normal-sounding greeting: "The time is now eight thirty a.m. The local temperature is ninety-nine degrees. Welcome to Vietnam!"

When they got off the plane, all the soldiers were asked to stand in a circle around a fire that was lit and burning right there on the tarmac. This was their last chance. If they had brought any illegal items with them, they could throw them into the fire and no questions would be asked. If they failed to do so, they would be searched and the penalty could be very severe. Dad was covertly holding on to some sleeping pills his mother had given him for anxiety—which were very bad for him to have in an active combat zone. He cast them into the fire, giving up any and all secrets and attachments to his former life. The soldiers were then told about Hamburger Hill. Anyone who was sent there would be forced to storm a hill surrounded by Viet Cong soldiers and would almost certainly be killed. Right on the spot, there was a lottery in which many of the men standing there were sent to a certain and almost immediate death. Dad was lucky enough not to have to go, but this experience, coupled with the unexpectedly massive heat, rocked him to his core. He was told that he had become "property of the United States government," and that they had complete and total control over him—including whether he lived or died.

Dad was stationed at Long Binh, the largest US base in Vietnam. Thanks to having enlisted in the Army Reserve, he was able to work as a military journalist and avoid the front lines. Stories would come in from the "wire," such as from the Associated Press, and Dad would integrate them into a daily newspaper for all the soldiers to read. Dad was also responsible for writing his own articles, including reports of every death on the battlefield.

Dad was brave enough to write about the revolution that was taking place through rock and roll music, which could easily have gotten him court-martialed or even killed in an "accident." If it hadn't been for my father, the soldiers at America's largest base in Vietnam would have had little or no idea what was going on in music at this critical time in 1969. This made him a figure much like Robin Williams's radio DJ character in the movie *Good Morning, Vietnam*. Mom would mail him all the latest records and he would listen to them and write about them. He also revealed the greater social issues that were taking place back home— where soldiers' friends in America were fighting to end the war. This included coverage of a huge upcoming music festival in Bethel, New York—which was later moved to Woodstock at the last minute when the farmer from Bethel pulled out of the deal.

Helter Skelter

Six days before Woodstock began, on August 9, 1969, the guitar-strumming wannabe rock star Charles Manson led a group of his followers to murder Roman Polanski's celebrity wife, Sharon Tate. She was eight and a half months pregnant. She and her baby died in the attack, and four others were brutally murdered at the same time. Apart from helping her husband write *Rosemary's Baby*, Tate had starred in occult-themed movies including *Eye of the Devil* (1966), in which she played a witch who needs a blood sacrifice to restore a vineyard's success, *Valley of the Dolls* (1967), about the extremely negative effects of drugs, and *The Fearless Vampire Killers,* from 1967.

It was very frightening that a pregnant celebrity was murdered, along with her unborn child, just two years after she helped write a very similar-sounding screenplay. In *Rosemary's Baby,* a woman's child was intended to be sacrificed so her husband could become a more successful actor. The idea that a real satanic cult was responsible for planning the sacrifice of her and her baby was too upsetting for most people to bear. Manson claimed to have played the Beatles' White Album while he and his followers carried out this mass murder. Manson specifically cited songs like "Happiness Is a Warm Gun" and "Helter Skelter" as giving him coded messages telling him he had to do it.

In the mid-2000s, insiders told me the Manson murders were deliberately staged to try to destroy the hippie movement and demonize them all as potentially violent serial killers. It was specifically intended to create an aura of total horror and fear around Woodstock and collapse its momentum. The story of the gruesome murders dominated the headlines in the six days leading up to the event—and the killings were performed by rock-music-loving hippies who said they were doing it for the trees and for nature. I was told the hidden organizers of this atrocity had hoped to scare off any new people from accepting this new revolution against the elite—and to demonize the Beatles as the embodiment of evil itself. Despite this very negative mass trauma, Woodstock took off far more than anyone could have imagined—and my father covered the whole story for the soldiers at the largest American base in Vietnam, at great personal risk.

It may not surprise you that at a Rolling Stones concert in San Francisco on December 6, 1969, just a few months later, a black man named Meredith Hunter was stabbed to death in the front row by a motorcycle gang called the Hells Angels. The Hells Angels had, controversially, been hired to provide security for the event. Hunter approached the stage, was violently driven off by the Hells Angels, pulled a gun on them, and was stabbed to death. Footage of this "human sacrifice," as some called it, was featured in the popular Rolling Stones documentary *Gimme Shelter.*

Despite this controversy, the Rolling Stones released another Lucifer-themed album, *Goat's Head Soup,* on August 31, 1973. Mick Jagger was pictured on the cover dressed as a woman with a veil over his face. His hair was styled like a classic British updo, and the mass of hair over his head had the subtle but undeniable appearance of devil horns. This album featured the classic Stones hit "Angie," but also included a song called "Dancing With Mr. D." It was loaded with references to drugs and death, and portrayed a character with human skulls around his neck that the singer had a "tryst"—a sexual encounter—with in a graveyard. We also hear about a woman in black who looks at our singer with desire, only to have the flesh fall off her bones, and her eyes burn like fire and brimstone.

Born into Watergate

After my father returned from Vietnam, my parents tried for some time to conceive a child, and finally succeeded in early June 1972. Very soon afterward, on June 17, Richard Nixon's presidential re-election team was caught breaking into the Democratic National Committee headquarters to plant listening devices that could help them win a second term. This was the beginning of a domino effect known as the Watergate scandal, which ultimately led to the exposure and downfall of Nixon's war-mongering regime, and the end of the deadly Vietnam War that was killing off an entire generation of young men. During her pregnancy, my mother had dreams and visions telling her the baby she was carrying would be a spiritual leader, and that she should raise him as if that was what he would become. She withheld this information from me until the late 2000s, and felt that unless I was humble enough to hear it without getting an ego, she would take it to the grave.

Nine months later I was born, on March 8, 1973. Just three weeks before, on February 14, General Electric had fired my father from his job. He came home with roses and chocolate, wished my mother a happy Valentine's Day, and then told her he had been laid off. He was forced to look for work on an emergency basis, and was able to find it only in Buffalo, New York, which was more than four hours of driving away from our home in Schenectady. As a result, he was forced to go off to work very soon after I was born, while Mom stayed with his mother and father in Schenectady.

The Watergate political scandal led to Senate committee hearings from May 17 to August 7, 1973, in which former administration officials testified. The three major networks—ABC, CBS, and NBC—took turns covering the hearings live, with each network having sole coverage for a particular day. It is estimated that 85 percent of Americans with television sets tuned in to at least a portion of the hearings. Up to 85 percent of Americans were reeling in horror at the idea that the government they had known, voted for, and in many cases loved was acting like a tyrannical dictatorship—keeping secrets, lying, and stealing to defeat their political opponents. Fourteen months after these hearings started, Nixon was forced to resign. Eight months later, the Vietnam War ended, and this obviously corrupt government could no longer send young men into a highly traumatic and lethal combat zone.

Strangely, my mother discovered that every time the Watergate hearings came on, I would start crying in my crib, even if I had been asleep. In addition, whenever Mom tried to leave the apartment, even to go get the laundry down the hall while I was fast asleep, I would immediately wake up and cry as soon as her hand touched the doorknob. Both of these events happened so many times that the idea of it being "just a coincidence" quickly became ridiculous. These were the only times I cried, as otherwise I was a very quiet and relaxed baby. Even at that early age, my mother felt that I was intuitively sensing the thoughts and feelings of those around me, both on a personal and collective level, and responding.

CHAPTER THREE

Touching the Infinite

The 1960s drug culture triggered an interest in Native American shamanism, which crystallized around the popular books by Carlos Castenada. Carlos reported alleged transcripts of conversations and experiences with a Yaqui shaman he called Don Juan. Confidants of Castenada's revealed that many of his far-fetched tales, particularly in the later books, were fabrications, but the underlying concepts were valuable to many people—including my mother. She became aware that there could be an alternate reality surrounding us, in which unseen spiritual forces are guiding us. With the proper spiritual instruction and practice, it was possible to enter into the "second attention" and have direct contact with these entities. These concepts inspired my mother to begin writing her dreams down in notebooks she kept by the side of her bed, and she found that they provided useful guidance in symbolic form. I heard about this from a very young age, and began remembering my own dreams as well—often in vivid detail.

Dad managed to get another job at GE, and his parents helped us move into a three-bedroom, one-bath house in Scotia, New York, on the other side of the Mohawk River, just opposite Schenectady. This gave Dad an easy commute that was never more than fifteen minutes even in rush-hour traffic. Our move-in date happened to be October 31—Halloween—1973. I was fortunate enough to live in this house throughout the entire remainder of my childhood and adolescence, and Mom held on to it until after my younger brother graduated from college in 1997. We lived fairly close to a military base in Glenville, and occasionally an enormous C-130 Hercules aircraft would fly over the yard at an astonishingly low altitude. This created tremendous noise and a vibration you could feel in your chest, and the plane was so large it almost covered the entire sky. It was an extremely powerful, even shocking event every time I got to witness it in the backyard. I started having many dreams where I saw similarly huge flying craft in the yard—except in these dreams the craft were huge, cigar-shaped cylinders with no wings. They also made no sound, and had an odd fluttering motion as they traveled over the land. My mother had very similar craft appearing in her dreams as well.

The Power of Television and Music

It may be hard for millennials to understand that there were only four television stations to choose from at the time—CBS, ABC, NBC, and PBS, the Public Broadcasting System, which was commercial-free and relied on donations from its audience to stay on the air. The most significant and well-produced shows appeared at "prime time," beginning at eight p.m., and with only three networks and PBS to choose from, the selection was quite limited. This meant much of America was watching the same programs. By far, the two shows that my father never missed were *M*A*S*H*, which took place in the Korean War, and *Happy Days*, which presented an idealized view of fifties culture. My mother only tolerated TV, unless it was educational programming for children. She would often get up and walk around or leave the room entirely while the TV was on.

My mother sat and read to me from books ever since I was an infant, pointing at the words as she said them aloud. She very quickly got me watching educational television programs on PBS, particularly Jim Henson's classic *Sesame Street*. We never missed a day of it from as early as I can remember. The show did a great job of teaching children how to read. I remember seeing profile images of people's faces as they verbalized the sounds of certain letters or syllables, and then the image of those letters would pop out of their mouths. In some cases they would assemble words this way. You got to see how the word was spelled and what the letters all sounded like together. There was also the Count, a puppet vampire character who verbalized various numbers as they appeared on screen, and taught you the order in which you would count them. This, combined with daily story time, led me to have the ability to read by the time I was two. By the time I entered kindergarten at age five, I was significantly ahead of most of my classmates.

My father started his own local pop culture newspaper called *KITE* in 1970–71 and wrote articles promoting major rock bands that were coming into town to do concerts. This made him very valuable to the record labels, who saw this publicity as critical to the financial success of their shows. As a result, we had a brown United Parcel Service van pull up to the house every afternoon and drop off two-foot-square cardboard boxes of varying thicknesses, from half an inch to as much as two inches deep. Inside them were precious jewels: all the latest releases from every major record label in existence. It was normal to receive two or three boxes a day. We received copies of almost every new rock album in existence, whether they succeeded or not—and most never did. Each album was marked in some way, such as having a hole punched out of the cardboard jacket, the corner of the jacket sliced off, or a big stamp that said FOR PROMOTIONAL USE ONLY. The labels included Arista, Columbia, CBS, Atlantic, and Warner Brothers. Dad was also given free tickets to every concert, as well as backstage passes—giving him direct access to the heroes who were making the magic happen.

Dad would come home from GE at around 5:20 p.m. in a suit and tie, have the dinner that Mom had waiting for us at the table, and then go upstairs and change into a T-shirt, blue jeans, sneakers, and a flannel shirt. All the best rock albums of the time were played after dinner, and they fit into neat forty-four-minute chunks of time, divided into twenty-two-minute sides. The TV went on at seven p.m. to watch the *CBS Evening News with Walter Cronkite;* Cronkite was considered "the most trusted man in America." Dad never missed the news, and felt that it was vitally important that he watch it in order to ensure that "the world is safe for democracy," as Cronkite would often say. I invariably watched every single broadcast with him over the years, and was fully aware of what was going on in the world as a result.

Friday night was often reserved for a rock music marathon after Walter Cronkite. Led Zeppelin's classic albums were played far more than anything else, particularly *I, II,* and *IV,* and Dad very much liked their heavy blues influences. I also heard all the classic Rolling Stones albums, and the first four Aerosmith records—the American answer to Led Zeppelin, who were also very popular for their hard-rocking blues influences. I also heard many sixties classics, including Jimi Hendrix, Janis Joplin, The Doors, and the Moody Blues, as well as seventies psychedelic gold such as Pink Floyd's *Meddle* and Tangerine Dream's *Rubycon.* (For some reason Dad disliked the Beatles and never played any of their music, because he felt they were overexposed—and thus I hadn't heard most of their songs until I started listening to them in 2010, when I investigated why they had such a powerful historical impact.) My father would often get up and dance when he played these albums, along with my mother and me, giving this music a deep, almost subconscious positive association in my mind. I had no idea at the time that there were any negative associations with the Rolling Stones. My father didn't take any of it seriously. Many other bands would follow similar paths as time went on, presenting a mystical aura to their listeners. It is important to remember that the Cabal does not expect to create any sudden changes in the people who are exposed to this media. Their goal is a gradual, long-term introduction of Luciferian symbolism to the public. They plan to create an eventual hostile global takeover and establish a New World Order, in which everyone is required to accept these new beliefs or be imprisoned, tortured, or killed.

Every Saturday, my father would sit at the fold-out living-room table, which we rarely ever used, and type up his latest articles, which he called "columns," on a gray-and-blue Smith Corona electric typewriter. During this time I was not allowed to talk to him or make any noise in the area, and that rule was strictly in place until he had finished. He would interview many of these bands by telephone; he had a funny black suction cup from Radio Shack that he would stick on the receiver, allowing him to record a barely audible version of the call onto a cassette while he also took notes. Dad was heartbroken when he actually got an article into *Rolling Stone* magazine, the ultimate goal that any rock journalist could aspire to, only to discover that the pay for each article was twenty-five dollars. There was no possible way that he could put in the time and energy to write for *Rolling Stone* and still raise a family.

My parents did bring me along to rock concerts as early as age two, when I was placed on a Harley-Davidson motorcycle at a Grateful Dead concert. Marijuana use was heavily advertised in classic rock albums— including Hendrix singing "Purple haze all in my brain" and Led Zeppelin's lead vocalist, Robert Plant, singing "Smoked my stuff and drank all my wine" in the classic "Going to California." The sweet, complex aroma of marijuana smoke was a constant, inescapable odor at every concert I went to. As soon as the security guards went by, all the glowing pipes and joints would pop up, and thick clouds of smoke would billow into the air. It was quite common to see the bands smoking it backstage as well—and I met countless famous rock bands in my youth thanks to Dad's journalism. I hardly ever saw any other children at these shows, and it was very common for people to glare at me in hatred when they saw the bright, colorful backstage pass stuck to my shirt.

UFO Dreams and Brother Michael

My brother Michael was born on April 7, 1975. I remember my mother showing me her pregnant stomach and explaining that I had a brother on the way. One night I told her that I loved her very much, and I was sad because I knew she and I would never be as close once my brother was born. She held it together as I innocently told her this, but then quickly left the room, where she quietly cried for some time. I didn't find out about what happened that night until I was much older. During the time my mother was pregnant with Michael, she experienced extremely realistic dreams of going out into the backyard and seeing awe-inspiring UFOs, including cylinder-shaped craft just like what I was seeing in my own dreams. Some of my dreams featured Mom and me standing out there at night and holding hands as these ships hovered just above the yard. My mother's dreams were so vivid that she became convinced there must be truth behind the UFO phenomenon, and it was a source of great mystery to her.

I really enjoyed having a brother. Michael had his own gifts that were different from mine, as he was extremely interested in producing art. Almost as soon as he could pick up a pen and paper, he began drawing complex mazes that really worked and had only one solution. As the years went by, his mazes became difficult enough to solve that I would often cheat by tracing my way back from the end to the beginning; he would also create elaborate designs, including pictures and words, with mazes in them. Michael cried a lot more than I had as a child, and Mom was advised to let it happen and not rescue him every time, as otherwise it could create a dependency. Up until he was about five or six years old, Michael would occasionally have frightening temper tantrums in which he would become extremely angry, shake with rage, and sometimes try to bite me if I upset him. This would scare me, but I learned to stay calm and prevent him from hurting me.

Shortly after Michael was born, my UFO dreams became far more vivid and personal. I would often describe them to my mother in great detail, and she was astonished that I could remember so much. In many of these dreams I would end up inside a very futuristic-looking spacecraft, looking out the window and seeing other ships passing by. I had many different meetings with a wise old man with gray hair and a gray beard, who wore a robe with a hood that he usually kept down. Again and again, he would tell me that a fantastic event was going to occur on Earth, which would transform the world in a remarkably positive way and give us superpowers. He told me I would see this happen in my own lifetime. He also said I had an important role to play in the process, and would become very famous—like the rock stars my father was meeting, or even more so. In some cases I found myself at what looked like an airport, complete with a huge control tower, but the craft that were parked there were absolutely fantastic-looking—and unlike anything I had ever seen anywhere else.

The Nature of Personal Reality

I remember Mom telling me about her religious upbringing, and how disillusioned she became with born-again Christianity. She warned me that fundamentalists were often far more judgmental and abusive than other types of people, and that if you didn't think the same way they did, they honestly believed you would burn in hell for all eternity. She also told me about the importance of being a good person and being kind to others. She said that whether we realize it or not, each of us is here to build houses, one brick at a time. Every time we think a loving thought, or do a good thing for someone, we add another brick to the wall. Every time we have a hateful thought, or hurt someone, we take a brick away. This made sense to me, and I felt very deeply that she was right.

My mother began teaching piano students at the Yamaha School of Music, and I remember her taking me there when I was very young. I reached out and touched a thick black pipe on the wall there and was badly burned. Scalding-hot water was rushing through the pipe, and Mom had to cancel the class and take me home. This was one of my first experiences that taught me that I was fragile, I could easily be injured, and sometimes seemingly innocent-looking things could be very dangerous. Shortly after this injury, Mom began reading a book called *The Nature of Personal Reality*. She explained that a woman named Jane Roberts had learned how to talk to an advanced, ghostlike being named Seth, using nothing but the power of her own mind. She was able to speak the words that Seth wanted her to say, and her husband, Robert, wrote them down. The entire book was allegedly written by Seth. The main message it conveyed could be summarized in a single sentence: *You create your own reality.* My mother was very excited about this, as it was causing her to have a powerful awakening and see her life in a completely new way.

During this same time, it became increasingly clear that my parents were not getting along. I hardly ever saw them act affectionately toward each other. There always seemed to be tension in the air. Sometimes after they put Michael and me to bed, I would hear them arguing with each other, and this could include shouting. This caused me severe anxiety and led to my first great addiction: sucking my thumb. I only ever worked the right hand. By the time I was five years old, I had done thorough damage to the structure of my face, including moving my nose off to the right, collapsing my left nasal passage, pushing up the bone on the roof of my mouth, and tilting my entire jaw so it rested at a diagonal angle and was slightly higher on the right side of my face than the left. These were subtle changes that are quite common, and most people would never notice, but the nasal blockage made it hard to breathe and caused any sickness I had to get a lot worse.

Mysterious Memories

I started having a variety of dreams in which I could levitate effortlessly. In some cases I went only ten to twenty feet above the ground, whereas in other cases I soared like a bird over my hometown. In many of these dreams, I would take a jump rope, stand on it with both feet, and pull up on the edges. Somehow, this allowed me to lift myself up into the air. These dreams had such an effect on me that I would repeatedly try to duplicate the effect in our driveway while I was awake. It never worked. Sometimes I would stand there in the driveway with the jump rope and completely break down crying, pulling and pulling in a useless attempt to levitate. Then I would have another dream in which it worked, and it would inspire me to go out there and try it again the next day.

I also clearly remember celebrating the two-hundred-year anniversary of American independence, on July 4, 1976. We walked all the way down to Jumpin' Jack's fast-food restaurant by the Mohawk River and the Western Gateway Bridge into Schenectady to see the show. There were many different street vendors selling American flags, all kinds of merchandise with red, white, and blue, and various forms of the Statue of Liberty. Many people were burning sparklers, drinking milk shakes, and eating burgers, hot dogs, and fries from Jumpin' Jack's. I remember having profound feelings I couldn't understand. I felt as if I had been

American before, that this was not new, and I could hardly believe that two hundred years had now gone by since America was founded. I had no idea why I felt this way, but it was very strong.

Playing the World's First Video Game

I very clearly remember the day in the late summer of 1976 that I got my first taste of a hyper-addictive social revolution. My mother took me to my favorite babysitter, Julie's, house, who lived down the road a few blocks at the time. The kitchen was cluttered and smelled like bread dough. There, sitting on the countertop, was a black-and-white TV with a strange black box connected to it. The box had two round knobs on it. When you turned it on, it put blocky white lines on the TV screen. It was a "video game" called Pong, which had been released in December 1975, just in time for Christmas. They asked me to try it and I was worried I might break it, but they told me it was fine. When I turned the knob, a line on the screen moved along with it as the paddle, and a white square was the ball. Each time the ball was released, I had to keep it from going past my paddle.

Right as I started to get the hang of it, the hot new single "Dancing Queen" came on the radio. It was very sparkly and happy, had nice vocal harmonies and a dance beat, and is commonly regarded as one of the most successful singles of the 1970s. I had never heard any music like this at home. The fusion of the music and the Pong game elevated me into a state of pure ecstasy. In amazement, I breathlessly asked, "Who is this on the radio?" as I continued vigorously working the paddle. "ABBA," my babysitter replied. "It's a band called ABBA. They are very famous." After "Dancing Queen," other ABBA songs were played as part of a music marathon, and I couldn't believe my parents hadn't played it before. I asked Mom why we didn't listen to ABBA, and she said, "You'll just have to ask your father." I asked Dad as soon as I got home, and he said, "That's disco. We do not listen to disco. It is absolute garbage." End of discussion.

A Major Health Crisis

My mother took the flu vaccine in October 1976, when I was three years old, and strange things started happening to her. Within a week or two after taking the shot, she was walking down State Street in Schenectady and realized that instead of walking straight, she was nearly bumping into the sides of buildings. She also found that when she played the piano, and reached for octaves with her left hand, she was overreaching. She would aim for E flat and hit a C. She then became very sick, which reached a peak about two to three weeks after she took the shot. She had a plastic pan to throw up in as I sat beside her on the couch, and she became so sick that she couldn't even move her head more than an inch without throwing up. She asked me to call our neighbor, Mrs. Warner (not her real name), and remembered the number well enough to give me the digits out loud. Mrs. Warner called Dad at General Electric, who rushed home from work and took Mom straight to the emergency room while Michael and I sat with a babysitter.

Mom ended up being gone for an entire week, and Michael and I were never taken there to see her. We had a very nice woman who acted as our babysitter and took care of us all day, every day. She had a bird marionette puppet made out of Styrofoam balls and orange feathers, with little white eyes that had black circles in them that would move around as she made it talk to us. She fed us cinnamon toast, which seemed like an amazing treat. Michael and I did not know this at the time, but both Dad and our babysitter thought Mom was about to die, and they just wanted us to be happy and calm. The doctors thought she had a brain tumor and did tons of tests. Once they ruled that out, they felt that she had multiple sclerosis. She kept insisting that the flu shot had caused this to happen, but they said that was impossible—it was totally safe. Yet the woman in the bed next to her had the exact same symptoms and had also just taken the flu shot. Mom discovered that her old high school friend Hope, who worked as a farmer, also developed the same sickness after having the flu shot, and toughed it out at home. Once she talked to Hope on the phone, she found out that many other people had developed the same deathly illness after getting the shot.

This had all the hallmarks of a cover-up in the medical industry, if not an outright terrifying conspiracy. Mom gradually got better while she was held in the hospital for a week and was run through a battery of tests. Once she got out, she vowed never to use the mainstream medical system again unless it was a dire emergency. She started seeing a chiropractor named Dr. Leith, whose office reeked of minty camphor oil, and he got her taking vitamins A, B, C, D, and E every day, as well as drinking disgusting-smelling brewer's yeast. We started routinely going to Patton's, a local health-food store. She also began swimming fifty-yard laps at the YWCA, in their Olympic-sized pool, a few times a week. By following these practices and having a healthy diet, she never got sick, never took any pharmaceutical drugs, and never needed to see a doctor.

The downside of Mom's health-food awakening was that she strictly forbade us from eating very much sugar. The television was constantly advertising sugary cereals like Cocoa Pebbles, Count Chocula, Frankenberry, Lucky Charms, Froot Loops, and Trix, which invariably featured cartoon characters that appealed to children. No matter how much I begged and pleaded with her to buy me these cereals, Mom absolutely refused. Dad had a habit of eating Rice Chex every morning, and the best cereals Michael and I ever got were Cheerios, Kellogg's Corn Flakes, Rice Krispies, Grape-Nuts, and Kix corn puffs. Mom's eyes went straight to the sugar listing on the label, and anything above a few grams was automatically forbidden. At the time I was very angry with her for this and felt that she was robbing me of all the best things about being a kid, but now as an adult I am very grateful that she was tough enough to say no to me, no matter how much I asked. I also have a strong memory of my parents buying a short-lived new cereal in a blue box, only to check on one of the ingredients, which may have been cellulose, and conclude that it was "plastic." The idea that any manufacturer would put plastic into a food product was shocking to them, and I felt the same way.

Let the Buyer Beware

I got my first real bicycle in 1977. It was all sparkling indigo blue and had a chain guard that said "The Rabbit," along with the image of a stretched-out cartoon rabbit. It had rims over both tires, a kickstand, and training wheels so I wouldn't fall over while I was riding it. Once I got the Rabbit, I started having new nightmares. It was always the same dream. Mom and I would be driving over the Western Gateway Bridge, and suddenly our car would plunge over the side. We were falling to our deaths. The dream always ended before we hit the water. In other dreams, I had to drive the car myself, which I obviously did not know how to do, and that was terrifying—and then the car would always fall off the bridge. I would wake up before I died, often screaming. It would be many years before I understood why I kept having this same dream, over and over again.

I then saw a commercial for Keds sneakers in which kids put these shoes on and could fly. Beautiful streaks of light emerged from their feet, and they could soar eight to ten feet up into a tree. I believed that this was real, and told my mother I absolutely must have Keds sneakers. I went to the kids' shoe shop at the Mohawk Mall, with the funny guy with black curly hair who looked and sounded a lot like Richard Simmons. I was measured for the shoes and could hardly wait to get home and try them. I stood in front of the old birch tree in the front yard, did my best jump . . . and nothing happened. It was just like the jump rope all over again. I was devastated. The television had lied to me. These shoes could not make me fly. I started to realize that nothing could. If I ever started falling to my death, like what had happened in my nightmare, there probably wasn't anything I could do about it. As I reflect back upon this now, I realize that my dreams of flying may well have been preparing me for the powers of ascension. I was told in my dreams that this would happen to us, and I could already try out the abilities— but the real world hadn't caught up with the dream world yet.

Obi-Wan Kenobi

The epic film *Star Wars* was released on May 25, 1977, just in time for the summer movie season—and my father made sure that he took us on opening weekend. I was absolutely dazzled by this movie, transported into a parallel universe, where it all seemed completely real. All the images of spacecraft, planets, and stars seemed extremely familiar to me—so much so that I didn't understand why everyone became so obsessed with the movie. For me it was just "normal." Luke was being trained in "The Force," which would give him the exact same abilities that I had in my dreams. The wise old man Obi-Wan Kenobi faced off against the villain Darth Vader and was clearly losing. Obi-Wan then said, "If you strike me down, I will become more powerful than you can imagine." Vader sliced him with his lightsaber, but Obi-Wan completely disappeared, leaving only his robe in a heap on the ground. He then returned to Luke later in the movie as a ghostlike being of white light.

I immediately noticed the similarity between Obi-Wan and the man who had been talking to me in my dreams. My parents were both very surprised, because well before the movie came out, they had nicknamed my brother Obie, and also called him Obimious (which sounds like Obadiah, a book in the Bible) and, as crazy as it must sound, Obie-Wan. That name actually pulled me right out of the movie for a moment. I couldn't believe what I was hearing—and it proved to be one of my first experiences with what Dr. Carl Jung called synchronicity. My parents adopted the full name and began calling him Obi-Wan Kenobi. The very next morning after I saw *Star Wars*, the wise old man appeared again as Obi-Wan Kenobi—and the interior of his ship looked even more like some of the scenes in *Star Wars*. He now appeared to me in the same glowing, luminous form as Obi-Wan had in the movie. This appears to have been an effort to link a being who was very real in the dream plane with a symbol from the physical plane that I could now easily identify and interpret. The old man told me that many people on Earth were going to transform into a luminous form like this, and that if I followed what my mother told me about being a good person, it could happen to me too. I felt even closer to him than I did to my own parents, and when I woke up and realized it was only a dream, I started crying. This happened dozens of times.

CHAPTER FOUR

Darkness and Light

The wise old man who now appeared as Obi-Wan in my dreams told me I needed to learn as much about science as I could, as this was an important part of my mission. Those words stayed with me, and I tried to gather as much information as possible. I would ask my father all sorts of questions that he did not have the answers for, like why the sky was blue or how birds could fly. He would often get frustrated with me and tell me he just didn't know. Shortly after seeing *Star Wars* in 1977, I learned that modern scientists believed in something called the "Big Bang." They said that the universe started as "nothing." I couldn't even imagine the idea of nothing ever existing—it just didn't make any sense. Then they said that "nothing exploded," and the whole universe was created in an instant. I felt very strongly that this couldn't be right. I concentrated as hard as I could and willed myself to see the real answer to the questions, "What did the universe look like at the beginning? Was there ever truly nothing?" What I got back, every time I asked, was pure white light. It seemed like it could be very large or very small, and it really didn't even matter. Size was not important; it was just light. And it seemed very friendly—actually quite joyous. It was as if it was singing in happiness.

Glimpses of Cosmic Memories

Certain objects or places started causing me to have profound cosmic feelings that I could not explain. One early example happened after I entered nursery school, which was in a church. A weird, fundamentalist-type man came in and was talking to us about God. He felt deceitful to me, like a car salesman or my father's boss at General Electric. He was giving us a strong sales pitch for his religion, and at the end he handed each of us a white plastic ring that was the right size to fit on our chubby little fingers. It had a cartoon bee on it that was made out of a raised, shiny red line. Somehow, when I saw this ring, I felt as if I was blown into a completely alternate reality. There was something there—something very powerful, very ancient, and very amazing. I didn't know what it was, but the feeling was so intense that I almost fell over. I still do not understand why the ring caused me to feel this way, particularly since the man was exactly the opposite. Perhaps it looked similar to jewelry I had worn in some alternate reality. These memories were unpredictable and at times could seem completely random and inexplicable.

This same phenomenon happened again when I was playing with a wooden toy that featured a chain of train-like cars that rolled on black-painted wheels. As I pulled this toy along, I got hit again. I had flashes of the massive airport I had seen in my dreams, loaded with astonishing spaceships. Some of them seemed to have been chained together like this toy—but I just couldn't quite remember it. Another time I rode the city bus for the first time with my babysitter on the way to a bowling alley. I was scared, as I had never ridden the bus before. As I sat on the bus and saw people in the seats, *WHAM*—it happened again. I felt very close to a memory of seeing a similar scene in a much more advanced craft that flew through space.

Every year, fighter jets called the Blue Angels would do stunt-flying right over my street, because we were near the military base where they did the airshow. They would fly in formation, go upside down, pass by one another closely, do barrel rolls, and in some cases fly very close to the ground. They would rehearse for the airshow for about four or five days beforehand, and I always made sure to go outside and see it. I would always get that same feeling of immense cosmic knowledge that I could not explain when I saw them—and on the few occasions when we actually went to the airshow and saw all the planes on display, I felt it even more. As a result, I got into building snap-together airplane models and had a poster of various jets on the wall in my room for many years.

Another weird example of the "cosmic rush" was when I was with my grandmother, and we went to see a friend of hers out in a woodsy area. The lady gave me a brown plastic bottle that could hold milk, like a baby bottle, but this was made for bigger kids. I was mildly insulted at first by getting this gift. The top of the bottle had plastic in the shape of a stylized, cartoonish cow face, with a red plastic tongue and black plastic eyes that were mostly closed. However, as I held this object in my hands, I had a very profound rush. It now seemed partially like Luke's lightsaber from *Star Wars*, but there was something much deeper than that. This bottle looked like something I knew—a technology that might have been like the lightsaber. I had no idea what it was, but the feeling was overpowering and incredible.

Certain places could fairly reliably cause me to feel this way. Any building that was made of stone, or was castle-like, could do it, particularly if it was surrounded by trees. I may have been remembering a society that had advanced technology but was also building marvelous structures out of stone. That particular vision was strongly associated with medieval-sounding music, particularly wind instruments. Just hearing the sound of an oboe could cause this feeling to happen, particularly if it had a strong echo on it, like you hear in vintage Tangerine Dream music. Some brick buildings also had the same effect, including the house my babysitter, Julie's, family moved into that was a little farther away from us and was surrounded by trees. However, the single most reliable source of this profoundly cosmic and wonderful feeling was the Schenectady Museum and Planetarium. I would ask my mother to take us there again and again, as every time I went, the same thing would happen. The inside of the building had a high, domed ceiling that was painted black. Some of the supporting bars were visible. The walls were white, and flowed in smooth, rippling curves. Track lights were mounted in cool places, causing the exhibits to gleam and sparkle. They changed the exhibits every few months.

They often had boring GE exhibits, such as large turbines, pictures of Edison, the original model of the lightbulb, old appliances, and panels of text explaining the history of these inventions. What really inspired me the most were the displays of huge crystals, hidden behind glass for protection. Some of the clusters were a brilliant purple. The light would glisten off them, and as I looked at them I would feel connected to something extremely profound. It was as if I had once known a world of crystal technology—but I couldn't quite get it back. The flowing, curved walls and lighting of the museum reminded me of the inside of some kind of spaceship, like what I would see in my dreams—but even older and more powerful.

At one point the museum had an exhibit of holograms, where you could walk around them and see them animate—for example, a woman talking. They had strange rainbow colors, mostly yellow and red, and you could put your hand right into them. This probably caused the single most profound rush of energy and cosmic memories of anything I had ever experienced. It was so powerful that I almost fell over in ecstasy.

By this time, I was having more and more experiences during which I knew what people were thinking, without their ever telling me. I could sense people's feelings very easily, even if they were trying to hide them. This was useful with my father, as I could tell when he was going to get angry before it actually happened. There were many other cases that were more peaceful than that. Thoughts would come into my mind right before someone started talking to me about them. I would think of a specific person right before they were discussed, or the phone started ringing and they were calling. This was so natural that I didn't think anything of it, and I felt like everyone must be able to do it, since it was so easy and effortless.

A Hippie Commune Called "Totem"

My mother met some hippie guys at Hewitt's Garden Center on Sacandaga Road and quickly found out that they lived with a group of other people at a farm they called Totem. Everyone was crammed into a single

run-down house in a heavily wooded area on the end of a dirt road. They
listened to weird psychedelic and technical music, such as the band Gentle Giant, which I would never have heard at home. The best way I can
describe it as an adult is to say that it sounded like musical schizophre-
nia. So much marijuana was grown at Totem that they would dry it out
in clothes dryers. The marijuana smoke was so thick that it curled around
you as you walked through the house.

The first time I was there, I walked into the bathroom and was disgusted when I saw the toilet bowl. It was supposed to be white, but their
well water had lots of minerals in it, and the entire bowl was stained a
dark brown. I thought it was all poop, and I was horrified that they
hadn't bothered to clean it. There was no way I could use that toilet. I
marched out, thrust my right hand on my hip, pointed at the bathroom
with my left index finger, and shouted, "That is the most disgusting
toilet I have ever seen in my entire life!" I could not understand why they
started laughing—and continued to laugh, nonstop, for at least ten minutes. Some of them even gasped for breath and rolled around on the
floor. I finally decided that it was cool that I had made them laugh, and
went along with the joke, but I had no idea what they thought was so
funny about having a toilet that was absolutely covered with "mess."

A very frightening story emerged from this group not long after my
mother started going there. A man named Lars, who was a brother of one
of the guys, had taken a drug called LSD. I had never heard of it before
then. This drug caused him to completely lose his mind and go crazy.
They tried to keep him at the house for several days, but he was so
messed up from it that they had to take him to the hospital. He ended
up going into "the mental ward" and had to stay there for a long time
before they finally let him go. He was never really the same again; he had
become shy and scared. The whole thing was extremely frightening. My
mother told me to never, ever take LSD, as it was very dangerous, and
the people who used it had no idea what they were messing with. I promised her I never would. She gave me similar warnings about heroin and
cocaine, saying that once people tried them they couldn't stop, and the
drugs would destroy their lives.

Totem ended up having a party called 7/7/77, which took place on

July 7, 1977, as you might expect. Some of the Totem guys had formed a band, and they had a Fender Rhodes keyboard up on stage. They were playing a simple blues-rock jam and demanded my mother get up on stage and play keyboard in front of all those people. Although it was well within her playing ability to do this, she was terrified of performing in front of an audience and had never tried to play rock and roll before. She was just about dragged up on stage, but as soon as she started playing, she was a natural. The audience loved her. She was instantly hooked, and started playing in various bands that were formed with members of the group. By the mid-1980s she had become a professional gigging musician playing in wedding bands—and it all started with 7/7/77. This was my first experience with "numerical synchronicity," in which repeating patterns of numbers reveal deeper meaning. In the future these patterns would appear in highly unexpected ways, seemingly in direct response to important, spiritually significant thoughts I was having.

Revealing the Greatest Danger to All Life on Earth

Shortly after 7/7/77, the weirdest and most terrifying event of my entire childhood happened. I didn't witness it myself, thank God, but I heard about it from my parents the next day—at great length. It all started when my father and mother were up late in bed. Dad was watching his little black-and-white TV, which he had brought back with him from Vietnam. The lights were out and the room was dark. Their bedroom was on the second floor, and they had windows that looked out onto our street. There was enough moonlight to see what was going on outside. Dad noticed some movement on the street. He looked more closely and realized that a husband-and-wife couple was walking along, side by side. They did not talk, look at each other, or move their arms. They walked like robots, almost as if they were in a trance. They reached the driveway of the house across the street, made a ninety-degree turn, walked up to the side door, opened it without knocking, and walked right in. The house was completely shrouded in darkness, outside and in.

Dad's mind surged with curiosity and fear. He quietly but urgently alerted my mother to what was going on: "Look! Look!" They continued watching as three more married couples repeated the exact same sequence. The house was so dark inside that in order to see their way around, they would have needed something like candlelight. These were people we knew and saw all the time, including Mrs. Warner, whom Mom had me call the day she went to the emergency room. The men in each of these couples were high-ranking Freemasons, which is a secret society—but it took years for me to realize that there might be any connection between secret societies and the event my parents witnessed that night. One of the men was an Italian guy who owned a popular shoe repair store in town. The people across the street owned one of the most popular and successful car dealerships in town. Every year they would have rehearsals for the parade down at the end of the street. Since they were Scottish Rite Freemasons, they would assemble in our street wearing kilts and play the bagpipes with their haunting sound. Some of them were also Shriners and would wear the red fezzes and drive around in little go-karts in the parade. I would often see them sitting and talking together on the front porch of the house just to the right of the place they all went into that night. Thankfully, the people who owned the house across the street moved away less than a year later—but the others did not.

I had honestly never seen my parents so frightened before. They kept saying that this was just like the movie *Rosemary's Baby,* which I had already heard about many times before. Mom had asked my father what they should do, if they should say anything, and Dad said, "Absolutely not. I have seen way too many movies with scenes like this. If they find out that we saw them, something terrible could happen to us. We could all be killed. Everyone in this family. And no one would ever know what happened to us. We would just disappear." I was surprised that they were telling both Michael and me this, considering how young we were, and it was one of the most powerful experiences of my entire life. I could only conclude that these people were members of a secret group that met at night, and very likely were involved in something evil. Dad said it was very important that we act normally when we saw them, and never say a single word about what they had witnessed. Only recently did I speak to an insider who told me this was probably a ceremony known as the "Rite of Venus," in which people wear masks and have a sexual orgy like the one in the disturbing Stanley Kubrick movie *Eyes Wide Shut.*

Separating Facts from Mythology

The next major event I went through was seeing *Close Encounters of the Third Kind* after it was released on December 14, 1977. My father was dazzled by the film, said we had to see it, and brought us out to it. I was absolutely blown away, because this film was extremely similar to the dreams I was having. Seeing this movie was one of the greatest experiences of my life. I felt it was absolutely real. I very much identified with the child in the movie and felt that something like this would happen in the future on a much larger level. I had countless dreams of huge spaceships appearing over the yard, and now I was seeing it on the silver screen. Tears streamed down my face as the mother ship appeared at the end of the movie, causing such a spectacular light show. I was awed as the little ETs came out of the ship, and particularly entranced by the tall, skinny one. When the hero went into the ship to go with them, I cried even more. That was what I wanted—so much. And there it was. I could hardly believe I was seeing a movie like this.

The Pyramid Program

I started kindergarten classes at Sacandaga School in 1978. The school very quickly realized that my reading ability was way ahead of most of the other kids, and they put me into a special gifted children's program called Pyramid. The kindergarten reading book *Learning How to Read* had a mustard-yellow cover with kids playing on it, including one kid who was hanging on a tire that was attached to a rope in the middle. The first-grade book was called *Cloverleaf,* featuring a cow made out of colored paper who had a clover in his mouth. I was put right into *Cloverleaf,* along with a few other kids. One of them was named Eric, and it turned out that he lived just a few streets away from me. We looked somewhat alike and became fast friends. I would often ride my bicycle over to his house.

This was also when I started taking my old toys apart. We had all the screwdrivers I needed to get the screws out. I was very interested in seeing how things worked. My first major success was when our electric can opener broke. Mom was going to throw it away, because when you pushed the lever down, it wouldn't turn anymore. I asked her to let me see if I could take it apart and fix it, and she was happy to let me try. I took out all the screws, got the back off of it, and could see that there was a lot of metallic dust inside from the cans. I scrubbed off all the dust and grime with an old toothbrush and then lubricated it with WD-40, which was in the same toolbox as the screwdrivers. I put it all back together, plugged it in, hit the lever, and *bam*—it worked! Both of my parents were amazed that I actually fixed it, but as far as I was concerned it was quite easy.

Although I was a good reader and could fix the can opener, I was way behind in other areas. In our first years of gym class, the teachers would just set everyone loose in the gym to run around, screaming and laughing. I enjoyed the running and thought it was amazing to have all these other kids around, shooting in all different directions. However, the teachers watched me carefully and decided that I was not as coordinated as I should be for my age. I couldn't catch or throw a ball very well, if at all. I didn't want to play Frisbee with my parents, because whenever they threw it at me I would get hurt if I tried to catch it. I had hardly any strength in my upper body, which was a problem when the teachers wanted us to climb ropes or do chin-ups. I couldn't even manage to do a single chin-up; I was amazed that the other kids could do several of them. The teachers ended up putting me in a special class to help develop better coordination.

The Sacred Pajamas

While I was still in kindergarten, sometime before Christmas, I had perhaps the single most positive and amazing experience of my entire childhood: the out-of-body experience I opened with in chapter 2. After this stunning event, I concluded that everything, not just people, must have a ghostlike existence that is separate from the physical form. I also now knew it was possible to break into this alternate reality, just as my mother had read about in the Carlos Castenada books. I suddenly realized I had been incredibly stupid for getting scared and thinking I was dying, which had caused me to snap back into my body as soon as I went from wonderment to fear. I felt terrible about missing my chance. It occurred to me that there could have been some sort of craft waiting for me outside the house like what I had seen in my dreams, and if I hadn't gotten scared, I might have been pulled into it and gotten to meet the old man for real—not just in a dream. I started crying as I realized I had just wasted the greatest opportunity I'd ever had in my life. Every single night, for two more years, I prayed to get another chance. I knew I had no direct control over whether it would happen again or not—only "they" did. I saved the pajamas and never wore them again, and I still have them in my closet today. I also never washed them, in case that would somehow get rid of the magic that allowed them to be in two places at the same time. I ended up calling them the "sacred pajamas," and they are one of the only things I still have left from my childhood years.

I continued having UFO dreams after this, involving the usual flying cylinders in the backyard. Now, however, something new would happen. One of the UFOs would often crash-land somewhere not too far away from where my mother and I were standing. I felt they might be in trouble and they needed our help. I would grab my mother's hand, look into her eyes, and tell her we needed to run over there and help them. The dream always ended at this point—and I would often wake up in tears when I realized that it wasn't real. The meetings with the old man happened less and less often, and the dreams took on more of a mysterious, symbolic quality. Every night for the next two years, I prayed for the old man and his friends to give me another chance—but it never happened. I finally decided to take matters into my own hands—but that happens a little later in our story.

CHAPTER FIVE

Could ESP Save the World?

On November 18, 1978, just days after my stunning transformation into a ghostlike body that could fly, the world was rocked with news of an apparent mass suicide in the small South American country of Guyana, in a village called Jonestown. US Representative Leo Ryan arrived on November 17 with four members of his delegation to investigate claims of abuse there by a cult leader named Jim Jones. Ryan and all four of his team members were shot and killed the next day at the airport as they were getting ready to leave the country. According to the initial media reports, Jones then allegedly convinced 408 of his followers to drink Flavor Aid laced with deadly cyanide, which was then quickly turned into "Kool-Aid" in the public lexicon. The Guyanese army meticulously counted the 408 bodies, including 82 children. The sweltering heat forced them to poke holes in the bodies to release gases, since they were rapidly decomposing in the hot Sun and otherwise would have exploded. Over the next five days, the headlines also reported that 700 other people survived and ran off into the woods. A total of 150 pictures of the masses of dead bodies were taken. Some of the most disturbing shots were repeatedly shown in television news, magazines, and newspapers, showing large areas of bodies all neatly placed side by side, facedown in the dirt. As a child, I was deeply haunted by seeing these photographs over and over again—and my parents didn't feel much better.

Just hours after the deaths took place, the top pathologist in Guyana, Dr. C. Leslie Mootoo, went in with the teams that examined the bodies, without the assistance of US pathologists. Dr. Mootoo found that 80 to 90 percent of the victims had fresh needle marks at the back of their left shoulder blades, suggesting they died from lethal injections. This is not an area that most people could reach on their own. Someone else would have had to inject them there. Other people were found shot or strangled to death. One surviving eyewitness said that anyone who resisted drinking the cyanide was killed by armed guards. A US Army spokesman said, "No autopsies are needed. The cause of death is not an issue here." Yet Dr. Mootoo concluded that all but three of the victims he saw were murdered by "persons unknown," and only two of those three had actually committed suicide.

The figure of 408 dead bodies was still being reported in the *New York Times* as of November 21, three days after the event took place. US Army teams arrived at the site on the fourth day, November 22, and reported 409 dead. Major Helming of the US Army reported "400 dead" on the fifth day, November 23, and on the sixth day, November 24, the *New York Times* was reporting that there were 409 deaths.[19] Then that same day the body count began inexplicably skyrocketing—first to 700, then 780, and finally 909, just seven days after the initial number of 408 was given. On November 25, one US official reported to the *New York Times* that the extra 500-plus bodies were found because the Guyanese "could not count."[20] Then, in an even more ridiculous excuse, the US said the new bodies were all discovered hiding underneath the original bodies—even though not one photograph showed any hidden bodies, and 82 of the original victims were children.

Many people suspected the seven hundred survivors in the woods were systematically hunted down and killed by the US military and its allies, including elite Green Beret troops, the hundred-plus Guyanese troops looking for survivors in the woods, and nearly six hundred British Black Watch commandos who happened to be going through "training exercises" in the area when they joined the search. High-level insider Peter David Beter revealed the ugly truth of what happened for those who subscribed to his "audio letters." Ever since 1974, Beter's letters had reported that the Soviets had built a secret nuclear missile base in Guyana that would give them an undefeatable first-strike capability against the United States.

The world had previously learned of a secret Soviet missile base in Cuba, which ignited the Cuban Missile Crisis shortly after John F. Kennedy became president. In Beter's Audio Letter #40, from November 30, 1978, he revealed that the Jonestown massacre was staged by the US military.[21] The massive, public fatalities allowed them to go in, kill all the personnel at the secret Soviet missile base, and remove the bodies and warheads in a series of coffins that were supposedly carrying the victims of the disaster. This is why the US brought in sixteen huge C-131 aircraft, allegedly just to remove the bodies, and then claimed each one could hold only thirty-six caskets—even though these planes can carry tanks, trucks, troops, and ammunition all in one load.[22] Here is a small part of what Beter had to say about this tragedy in his own words:

> The complete details of the Jonestown disaster may never be known publicly. I can tell you though that of those who died there, very few willingly and deliberately took their own lives—and that is what suicide is. Many were tricked, not realizing that the death rites were real. Many more resisted, but they were weak, helpless, and confronted with armed execution squads. So by various means, several hundred people were poisoned with potassium cyanide. However there were many others who did try to escape and who resisted more effectively. Many of these people were herded off into the jungle and shot without mercy. Finally, when the mass murder was completed, the executioners performed their final task of stage-managing the horrible death scene. In order to achieve the surprise needed in attacking the Russian missile base, it was critically important that the first reports from Jonestown described the scene as a mass suicide. Only in this way could its actual military significance be hidden long enough to fool the Russians. So all of the bodies that were free of gunshot wounds were carefully arranged in neat rows

and other groupings, suggesting at first sight that everyone died willingly and deliberately.

This event ended up being the largest single loss of American life in a deliberate act until 9/11. If Beter is right, then clearly the government officials who ordered this attack did not care about the mass murder of hundreds of people who had done nothing wrong. They never bothered to try other avenues of diplomatic or military strategy that could have potentially saved innocent lives. All I knew at the time was that this was a highly disturbing event that was obviously another government- and media-driven cover-up like Watergate. Yet, after it happened, everyone just went back to sleep and carried on with their lives. Thankfully, with all the smartphones of today, it would be nearly impossible for any group to attempt such a huge atrocity and keep it a secret. Smaller-scale mass shooting events are almost immediately picked apart by the alternative media, and various lines of evidence are thoroughly explored by a legion of bloggers.

Dreams and Realities

I was quite shocked by Jonestown, as it was the first time I had seen a story in the media that was as creepy and terrifying as the night my parents saw familiar couples silently walk into the pitch-black house across the street without knocking. After Jonestown I started sleepwalking, and this included one night when I walked into the bathroom while my mother was in there and I kept saying, "I need to find the telephone books." I also started regularly having fevers with strong and terrifying hallucinations. My worst fever dream involved tall flames licking all around my bed, horrible white serpents looming over me, the roof disappearing to reveal the starry night sky, and some sort of Bigfoot-type monster that came raging out of my closet. I also would see the entire world around me divided into geometric patterns, such as white and black tiles. I would scream and scream whenever this happened, partly to try to drown out the enormous vibrating pressure that I would be hearing in my head—similar to the feeling of a huge C-130 flying over the yard.

On the night my bed seemed to be surrounded with flames, my father ran to the room and slipped on a Kleenex box, causing him to fall on the stairs. As he burst into the room I hallucinated that he looked like a dinosaur with humanlike features, which scared me even more. Dad really hurt himself that night, and Mom became responsible for calming me down whenever I started screaming. She would hold me and sing to me for several minutes. The enormous vibrating hum in my head would eventually go away, and I would be able to fall back to sleep.

That Christmas, in addition to being dazzled by the ascended-type abilities in the movie *Superman,* my grandmother on my mother's side gave me the Reader's Digest book *Strange Stories, Amazing Facts.* Grandma was a prolific reader and wanted me to be the same. *Strange Stories* was a full-sized, two-and-a-half-inch-thick hardcover book, and at the time I was only five years old and nowhere near a reading level at which I could fully understand it. Nonetheless, I looked through it and was fascinated by all the different pictures. What captivated me the most was a section at the end illustrating a gorgeous space station inside an asteroid, and apparently real photographs of UFOs. I spent hours just looking at those pictures and got the same incredibly powerful cosmic sensations that happened at various times throughout my childhood. For the first time, I had found a book that featured similar kinds of craft to what I was seeing in my dreams. My reading level quickly improved, and I realized that UFOs were not just something you saw in fake movies. People were seeing and photographing craft that did not appear to be from this world.

We were given copies of *Ranger Rick* magazine to read in school, which was mostly pictures of animals, but it advertised a children's astronomy magazine called *Odyssey.* There was a robot named Ulysses for a mascot, and it was run by a woman calling herself TCE, The Crabby Editor. I convinced my parents to let me subscribe to the magazine and began bringing the latest copy to school every day, reading it whenever we had free time. This, along with my high scores on every test and assignment, almost immediately caused the other kids to hate me—and to come up with nicknames like "Odyssey Man."

Extraterrestrials and Hostages

During this same time, I would occasionally be lucky enough to catch a television show called *In Search Of,* featuring Leonard Nimoy as the host. The opening sequence featured images of ancient monuments, including the giant stone heads of Easter Island, Stonehenge, and the Egyptian pyramids. Every time I saw this show, I had the "cosmic high" experience, as if something deep within me was being triggered. This also happened when I saw the show *Land of the Lost,* and particularly when the creepy reptilian beings with huge black eyes known as the Sleestak would appear, which put me into supernatural terror. The show featured children traveling through stargate-type portals that were located inside obelisks; all of this felt very familiar to me. I also had cosmic feelings whenever I saw the show *Mork and Mindy,* starring Robin Williams. At the end of every show, Mork, an extraterrestrial who came to Earth in an egg, would have a conversation with his unseen father figure, Orson. He would say funny things that summarized his observations about humans. This felt deeply important to me every time I saw it, as it was very similar to what my own dreams were like, only funnier.

On November 4, 1979, more than sixty American hostages were taken from the US embassy in Iran by Muslim students. That started the Iranian hostage crisis, which dragged on for 444 days. My father was very concerned about this, and every night Walter Cronkite would talk about it. I remember hearing again and again about how horrible it was that Iran was holding on to those people, and not knowing if they would ever be released.

During this same time, Eric and I started riding our bicycles farther and farther around the neighborhood when we weren't in school. One day we went to the house of a girl in our class whom we will call Cindy. She invited us into the garage and said she wanted to play a game. She then told us to bend over on a small bench and pull our pants down. We laughed and decided to do it. Then she grabbed a wiffle ball bat and started yelling at us like an abusive parent, telling us we were bad, that we were in trouble and that she was going to beat us. She wanted us to cry. Neither of us resisted or got up, even though she was about to start hitting us. We were so surprised by what she was doing that we were just going to let it happen. Right then, her mother walked in. She was horrified by what she saw and really yelled at her. I ended up feeling as if some good force in the universe had protected us from being hit. We never spoke to Cindy again, and for a while Eric and I stopped hanging out together as friends. I soon made two other friends who both turned out to be very abusive toward me, and my mother became quite concerned. Yet, for some reason, I seemed incapable of hurting anyone's feelings or saying no, even if I was clearly being bullied. This would turn out to be a pattern that would haunt me throughout the rest of my life, making me a prime target for manipulators.

A New Frontier

As soon as I started going on longer bike rides at age seven, my mother would walk to the end of the driveway and "send" to me when she wanted me to come home. This was a meditative exercise in which she would think strongly about me, and tell me in her mind and heart that she wanted me to come home. It worked very well, and almost always got me to come back within five or ten minutes. Sometimes I knew she was doing it, and other times I just felt like I needed to go home. Mom taught me that everyone could do this, so I never thought of it as anything unusual or special.

I soon shared my deepest secret with my mother. "You remember that night I floated out of my body and Dad said it was a dream? Every night since then, I have prayed and prayed that it would happen again—but it never works. Is there anything I can learn that might give me another chance?" She told me that this was one of a series of special abilities called ESP, or extra sensory perception, and she had books in the basement about it that I was welcome to read. She took me down into this little area under the cellar stairs where there were three rows of books. My eyes immediately locked onto the letters "ESP" on the spine of one of the books, and I pulled it out. It was called *How to Make ESP Work for You,* by Harold Sherman. I found two other books on hypnosis, and decided it was a good idea to read those books as well—since I already knew people could do pretty amazing things once they had been hypnotized.

I ended up reading Sherman's book every day for at least the next two years and practicing the exercises he gave in it as often as I could. I remember being very surprised to read that most people did not have ESP and did not believe it was even real—whereas for me it was an everyday thing. Some of the stories in there were quite amazing. I realized that it was possible to have far more ESP than I already did—and to control it. I started bringing the book to school along with *Odyssey* magazine, but did not want the other kids to know what I was reading, so I taped a white piece of paper over the front and back cover, and wrote "Free Reading" on the front. I had a hard time understanding everything, since there were no pictures, the size of the words was very small, and most kids my age were working through the huge, simple sentences in *Clifford the Big Red Dog*—but I never gave up.

I was encouraged to keep reading the book by a television show called *That's Incredible,* starring John Davidson, Fran Tarkenton, and Cathy Lee Crosby. This show featured all sorts of strange and paranormal phenomena, including an episode in which Uri Geller moved a pencil with his mind while his face was covered so he could not blow on it. I was very impressed by that demonstration, as it was similar to the abilities I had in my dreams, and what they called "The Force" in *Star Wars.* Some of the episodes were very frightening for my brother and me, and nothing ever scared us more than the infamous "Haunted Toys-R-Us" episode. They created reenactments of a poltergeist in the Toys-R-Us store that were so realistic that Michael became terrified to go upstairs alone, as he thought ghosts would try to throw things at him. We started going up the stairs together, figuring that would be safer than if we were alone.

As the leaves started falling, a kid we will call Tom created a "club" on the playground and said everyone who joined it would be "cool." In order to join the club, you had to go through an initiation, and I was one of about fifteen kids who agreed to do it. Tom and a couple friends of his lined us up against the fence facing the high school running track. Then we had to let Tom punch each of us in the stomach as hard as he could, and we couldn't cry or make any sound. Every kid got punched and most of us passed the test, myself included. However, once we "passed," the club just fizzled. Tom hadn't planned out anything after that—or maybe he didn't care. We realized we had been tricked. Tom just wanted to punch us in the stomach. There was no club. I quickly realized that I did not need to get hit in order to be "cool." I already had friends, and I started asking everyone for their phone number. I bought a little blue notebook at the pharmacy and carried it in my pocket. I created a page for each letter of the alphabet and wrote everyone's first name and number down on the appropriate page.

Right after I started building my phone book, my parents were devastated when John Bonham, the drummer for Led Zeppelin, died at a young age. The band said it was over and they would never release another album—and other than a compilation of old, forgotten songs called *Coda*, they never did. This made it even clearer that I shouldn't allow people to hurt me just to be cool. Led Zeppelin was the coolest band on Earth, according to my parents, and now their drummer was dead. Being cool wasn't enough to save John Bonham's life.

Watching the Wheels Go Round and Round

The hostages were still being held in Iran when the next presidential election took place on November 7, 1980. President Jimmy Carter looked weak for being unable to free them, and Ronald Reagan won by a landslide. One month and one day later, on December 8, John Lennon was shot to death by someone who asked him for his autograph. He had just released a comeback album, which included the song "Watching the Wheels," in which he seemed to be apologizing to his audience for taking years off. Now he was getting back in the game, which would likely include very effective anti-war protests. My babysitter, Ellen, was terribly upset about his death, as she loved the Beatles, and she had quite a story the next time we saw her.

The night before Lennon's death, she had a dream in which she saw him wearing a purple velvet suit with a white rose and a purple top hat. He also had purple lipstick, jet-black round sunglasses, and paper-white skin. She had the terrible feeling that he was dead, since the white skin and purple lips made him look like a corpse. She bolted awake in the middle of the night, terrified that something had happened to him. The very next day he was assassinated. This caused me to take my ESP studies much more seriously, as I now realized that everyone had the potential to see into the future and gain valuable information.

That Christmas, my parents gave me a Mickey Mouse 1981 glow-in-the-dark calendar. Harold Sherman had said you should document every unusual thing that happened to you once you started practicing his ESP exercises. Every time I had an ESP experience, I would write it down on that day in the calendar. I ordered a copy of the same Mickey Mouse calendar while writing this book. It was fascinating to see those images again for the first time in well over thirty years, and it helped me remember even more of my childhood. My "major present" that same Christmas was the Atari Video Computer System, or VCS, which was later renamed the Atari 2600. I quickly became addicted to playing video games, and would often spend hours a day on games like *Pitfall!* and *River Raid.*

The Iranian hostages were finally freed on January 20, 1981, on the exact same day Ronald Reagan was sworn in as president. This was very suspicious. Many whistle-blowers have since testified that George H. W. Bush bribed the Iranians to ensure they did not release the hostages until after Carter lost the election in November 1980. Though many people still look fondly upon the Reagan years, during that time the threat of nuclear war with the Soviet Union soon became much, much worse.

Walter Cronkite was replaced by Dan Rather on March 6, 1981, two days before my birthday, and the news began bombarding us with stories about the nuclear arms race. Night after night, we were told that we must support massive government spending to build more bombs. We were told that if we had more nukes than the Soviet Union, they wouldn't try to attack us—even though both sides had vastly more missiles than they needed to completely destroy all life on Earth. We also started having government-mandated nuclear war drills in school. A terrible siren would scream over the loudspeakers and we were ordered to hide under our desks—as if that would somehow make the radiation any less dangerous. America had turned into a suicide cult just like Jonestown, and no one seemed to care enough about it to try to do anything to stop it.

An assassin shot Ronald Reagan on March 30, 1981, just sixty-nine days into his presidency. Reagan took a bullet in the armpit, and his press secretary, James Brady, stumbled right as the shot that would have hit Reagan in the head was fired. Brady absorbed the bullet and did not die. Many years later, Pete Peterson, who is one of my highest-level insiders, told me that Reagan had learned that UFOs were real and extraterrestrial civilizations were visiting us. He had decided he was going to tell the public the truth—and the people doing the cover-up wanted him dead. After this happened, Reagan was warned that if he ever said another word about it again, this time they wouldn't miss—and he listened. It is important to point out here that presidents do not necessarily rank very highly in the Cabal and are not given very much real power. They are public figureheads, kept deliberately ignorant so that if they are ever brought to trial, they cannot reveal any of the most damaging secrets of the group. They are routinely threatened with the most dire consequences if they refuse to do what they are told.

Shortly after Reagan was shot, on April 12, the first space shuttle launch took place. This was very important to me, and I had read all about it in *Odyssey* magazine long before it happened. I wanted to be an astronaut, and I believed this was our next step toward colonizing space. I watched each new shuttle launch with extreme interest. The United States government would ultimately spend 209 billion dollars on space shuttle missions.[23] Years later, insiders would tell me that the Reagan administration used the nuclear arms race, the shuttle missions, and massive increases in defense spending to obtain huge amounts of money for top secret "black budget" programs, in which highly advanced and classified technology was being developed.

The Man Who Saw Tomorrow

I was absolutely stunned by the HBO special *The Man Who Saw Tomorrow,* which had premiered in January 1981 and aired repeatedly during this time. This was the first time I had ever heard of the prophecies of Michel de Notre-Dame, commonly known as Nostradamus. The show was narrated by Orson Welles, who had been the narrator of a realistic radio show broadcast in 1938 called *The War of the Worlds,* which had fooled many people into believing that a mass alien invasion was taking place. Now, Welles was causing many people to panic again, including me. The show thoroughly established that Nostradamus was a powerful psychic who dazzled the people of his time with accurate future prophecies. Nostradamus also left behind mysterious and poetic four-line poems, or *quatrains,* which appeared to have accurately predicted many future events, including the rise and defeat of Napoleon and Hitler. According to this show, Nostradamus said we would all be wiped out in a nuclear war, and it might happen in 1999, if not sooner. The program also had Hollywood-quality images of nuclear missiles in space, making it very easy to visualize such a war actually taking place.

The Nostradamus special made me believe I had the power to change the world. I knew I already had abilities that were similar to his, only much weaker. I felt that if I practiced harder, and got better at ESP, I might be able to see the future as Nostradamus had done, and possibly help save the world. I knew I would be old enough for people to listen to me by the year 1999. The old man in my dreams had often asked me to develop these abilities, and now I had a book that gave me exercises to learn how to do it. In order to mark my new resolve, I took an American Lung Association sticker with the year 1981 printed on it, which I had been sent before Christmas, and stuck it into *How to Make ESP Work for You*—right below the title of the chapter "Your Healing Power." Sherman also said the younger you started, the better your ESP would be. I hadn't started as young as I could have, but I still felt that I had to try, as even with limited abilities I still might be able to help stop a war.

Sherman said you should breathe deeply and regularly and try to make your mind as quiet as possible. He recommended that you lie down in bed and lift each arm, one at a time, holding it straight up until it becomes tired. Then you let your arm fall down and imagine that it is no longer there. You then do the same thing with your legs, one at a time. Finally, you do long, slow, rippling movements in your chest. The goal is to feel as if your body has now disappeared, and you only exist as a single point inside your head. At this point you should be very relaxed and breathing very deeply. Then he said that you should visualize a movie screen. Images will start appearing on the screen for short bursts of time, and you need to pay attention to them, as that will be how your ESP will appear. I tried this many times, but I could never hold the image of a movie screen for very long. I also never saw any images appear on my movie screen. I was very frustrated by this, but night after night I practiced the same exercises and continued reading the book for more clues.

Finally, one night I got an interesting new idea. I wanted to know if I could send my "ghost body" somewhere else and have it generate some real proof. I decided to concentrate on my friend Eric, figuring my "ghost body" wouldn't have to travel very far to find him. Sherman said that if you wanted to get a message to a particular person, the most important thing was to concentrate on their face in your mind's eye and to think about all the things you know and like about them. I held the image of Eric's face in my mind, and over and over again, I told him, "Eric, you will wake up at three thirty in the morning." After doing this for a while, I realized that I needed to add in something else for extra proof. I tried to think of something that would be absolutely undeniable—so I decided to tell him that he would wake up and think of gold. Now I kept seeing his face and repeating the same command, very intensely. "Eric, you will wake up at three thirty in the morning and think of gold."

Sherman said you would feel a sense of relief when you were successful with something like this. Your whole body would relax and feel satisfied. I definitely had that feeling, but I absolutely wanted to make sure this was going to work—so I kept on giving Eric the same command for another hour afterward. Exhausted, I finally fell asleep. The next morning at the breakfast table, I told my mother what I had done. She told me it was very important that I not tell Eric anything—I should just ask him how he slept and see if he said anything. I met up with Eric in the cafeteria, where we all drank little cartons of milk. My mother allowed me to have only the plain milk, but Eric drank the chocolate milk. As he sipped on his straw, I threw my arm around him and said, "So, Eric, how did you sleep last night?" He was totally shocked. He backed away from me and moved my arm off his shoulders immediately. "Why are you asking me that?" he said. "I don't know, I'm just curious," I replied, with a big smile.

Eric said he had woken up in the middle of the night, terrified. He felt like someone was standing there in the room staring at him—like a ghost. I asked him what was the first thing he thought of after he got up. "I wanted to look at my watch," he said. "What color is your watch?" I asked him. "Gold," he replied. I was absolutely shocked. I always had a digital clock by my bed, and didn't even know he owned a gold watch. I told him what I had done the night before, and he was stunned. I wasn't completely sure if the experiment was a success, as he woke up at four thirty instead of three thirty. However, I had kept on going for another hour after my body felt completely satisfied, and that may have screwed up the timing. If I had stopped when my body first relaxed, Eric probably would have woken up at three thirty. Despite this one-hour mistake, both Eric and I decided that my experiment was a success. He woke up in the middle of the night, felt a ghostly presence in the room, and thought of gold—in the form of his watch.

I started teaching Eric everything I was reading in the book. Every day we practiced ESP exercises after school. Our most common experiment was to throw sticks up into the air and tell them which direction to point on the way down. We would break the sticks so the broken end was the pointing end, and we had remarkable success getting them to point wherever we wanted them to. We also tried doing a "rain dance," and brought my brother in to help us. Almost every time we did the rain dance it would start raining within less than ten minutes.

The ESP Club

The Nostradamus special aired again and again on HBO. I saw it many times and studied every minute of it in detail. I could tell when it was coming on thanks to a magazine my father subscribed to called *TV*

Guide. I realized that although the things I was doing with Eric were cool, I needed to become a lot more focused. I also wanted more people to study and develop their ESP, so we would have a better chance of stopping disasters in the future. I felt the best way to get new people interested in ESP would be to prove that it really worked. Sherman had said that if someone strongly focused on a particular thought, and put a lot of emotion behind it, they could send it much more easily as a telepathic message—just like my mother did to call me home. A group of people could send messages even better than one person. So I created an "ESP club" with Eric and three other boys. Our first meeting was during recess. No one was going to get punched in the stomach in my club— but they might very well get the greatest shock of their lives.

We were standing over by the kindergarten and first-grade side of the school building. I asked them to go around the corner and pick a number between one and ten, concentrate on it for a minute or so, and then come back. I told them to talk as quietly as possible so there was no way I could possibly hear what they were saying. While they were gone, I breathed and relaxed deeply and tried not to think about anything. Then when they walked toward me, I took the very first number that popped into my blank mind. Harold Sherman said your first impulse is always correct with ESP if you do it right, and it's only once you second-guess yourself that you make mistakes. So my goal was not to think about any number at all until I looked into their eyes as they walked back—and then just accept whatever flashed through my mind, even if it was only for a split second, as the number. The boys were amazed, as every single time they did this, I guessed the correct number. Although I was very impressed that it really worked, I laughed about it and did not act like it was a big deal. "Everyone can do this," I told them. "I'm just showing you the proof." They said I must have been able to hear them talking. "Then go even farther away, and whisper even quieter," I responded. "Distance does not matter."

They went around the corner of the building again, and this time when I calmed my mind down, it felt very different. Something was going on. I could feel that they were going to try to trick me. I tried to think about what they were going to do, but I couldn't quite get it. They came around the corner of the building, walked up to me, and the first thing I got in my mind was the number three. I said it out loud and they seemed defeated. Their shoulders visibly slumped. "Yeah," they responded, "it's three." Then they turned their backs on me again and started walking away. One of the kids leaned in to the others and started whispering as if he was excited about something. My mind was still very blank, and as he did this, I quickly saw an image of the number seven come flying toward me in my imagination. It was made out of a series of round, whitish-yellow lights, like some kind of display you would see on stage at a rock concert. This image was so sudden and so intense that I immediately realized what was going on. I yelled out to them, "Come on back, you guys. You already picked the next number. It's seven."

They were absolutely baffled, as I had busted their plot with perfect accuracy. They had chosen two numbers, three and seven. Three was the first number and seven was the second. If I guessed three correctly, they were planning to go back around the building and guess a fake number. Somehow they figured that if I guessed the fake number instead of the real number, they would have proven that I was doing a trick and it was not real. Instead, I caught them with ESP. I realized very quickly that this had terrified them. One of them said they had to go, and all the others followed—leaving me standing there alone. Eric was still interested, and we continued doing our experiments together, but our ESP club never met again. None of the kids even wanted to talk about it. They just acted like it never happened.

I was deeply saddened that my club had failed, and that no one wanted to learn a skill that seemed so natural and easy to do, but was vital for our own future. At least one of the kids was from a heavily Christian family, and it seemed like they thought this ability was evil—something only the Devil could give a person. That would explain why none of them wanted to talk to me or be my friend after the one and only meeting of our club. This seemed sad and ridiculous to me, since Jesus could supposedly do the same sorts of things, as well as the really good stuff, like walking on water, turning water into wine, making enough loaves and fishes to feed five thousand people, raising Lazarus from the dead, and ascension—transforming his own body into pure light after he had already died.

The Pulse of the Planet

Not too long after my "ESP club" failed, I was walking home from school alone, and a big kid really tried to hurt me. He came silently zipping up behind me on his bicycle, took off his backpack, and whacked me from behind with it as hard as he could. It hit me in the back and caused my whole body to stumble forward. I was furious—and I wanted to hurt him. I suddenly got the idea to use my ESP to attack him and see if I could get him to fall off his bicycle. I went to my quiet place and asked for a way to do this. I got a very specific answer, including a name for it, which was a "pulse." I felt there was no way it would actually work, so I would just try it and see what happened. I took a deep breath, focused my gaze at the back of his head, and then tensed up every muscle in my body as suddenly and as violently as I could. As I did this, I shot air out of my mouth, making a sharp noise—and simultaneously shot my head forward, visualizing a red laser coming out of my forehead and hitting him in the back of the head. I was in a fury as I did this.

Immediately after I hit him with the "pulse," the front wheel of his bicycle jerked in a funny way, perhaps from slipping on some gravel—and he fell off his bike and collapsed in a ditch. He was clearly hurt. He got back up on his bike and rode away in pain. I understand at this point that you may believe I am making this up or telling stories. I cannot prove that this really happened, since there were no witnesses, but it absolutely was real—and I was overwhelmed. Many years later I would find out from multiple insiders that certain gifted children were being trained in very dark programs to assassinate people with their minds. It worked better if they did it as a group. These children were heavily traumatized and subjected to drugs and brainwashing. What I did was only a hint of what was possible—but the problem was that it was all evil. I was horrified that I had been able to knock that kid off his bike. After he got up and left safely, I ran the rest of the way home, threw myself upon my bed, and cried for about a half hour. I prayed to God, said I was sorry and that I would never "pulse" anyone again—and I never did. This was the same sort of thing Darth Vader did in *Star Wars*, such as the "force choke"—and I absolutely did not want to go over to the Dark Side.

A Classroom Demonstration

I still knew that someone could become a new Nostradamus and help save the world from total destruction, such as nuclear war—but they would need to learn about ESP first. I felt that if I could prove to my entire second-grade class that ESP really worked, someone would be interested enough to train with Eric and me. I found out about Zener cards on some TV show. Each Zener card had one of five different symbols—a star, a circle, a triangle, a square, and three wavy lines. Scientists had tested people's ESP with these cards and gotten good results. I ended up making my own deck of ESP cards, but in my case I drew a completely different symbol on each card, which would make it much harder. I convinced Mrs. Steiner, my teacher, to let me speak to my second-grade class about ESP, what it is, and how it works, and then have Eric help me demonstrate it with the cards. He would hold them up and I would try to guess whatever symbol was on them.

Mrs. Steiner said yes, and we actually did the demonstration. Now that everyone was watching me, I felt nervous. I did actually manage to get a couple of them right, even though they were all shuffled before we started, but most of my answers were wrong. It definitely seemed like it was a failure, and I felt embarrassed about it. No one asked me about ESP or wanted me to teach them. I still have the original deck of cards in my closet, complete with the two ink-stained rubber bands off Dad's newspapers that I had wrapped them with.

CHAPTER SIX

Darkness Closes In

The Pyramid Program for Gifted Children had only about seven kids in it by the time I was in second grade. One of them was a girl named Tara, a thin blonde with huge eyes whom I thought was very cute. Tara walked up to me in art class one day and told me a brown-haired girl we will call Laura wanted to ask me out on a date. I was carrying all my books at the time, and I lost control of my hands and dropped them all over the floor—but I didn't even care. Eric and I saw Laura and Tara while we were riding our bikes in the neighborhood, and we all agreed to go to a roller-skating event at the school together. Although I said yes, I had never put on a pair of roller skates before, and certainly was not coordinated. At the skating party I was very nervous and spent almost the entire time hugging the stage so I wouldn't fall over. Eric and Laura eventually came over and put my arms over their shoulders, so I could skate without falling down—and I had never felt better in my life.

Soon after the skating party, Laura refused to talk to me at all. If she was anywhere near me, she immediately walked away. Eric's mother was a staunch fundamentalist Christian, and she worked in a textile store with Laura's mother. They also went to church together. Eric confessed that he told his mother Laura was interested in me. I never found out what his mother had said, but Eric must have told his parents about our ESP experiments. I got very angry and asked him why in the world he would tell his mother that Laura liked me when he knew she was friends with Laura's mom. All he did was laugh. He was clearly jealous and seemed to be happy that Laura wouldn't talk to me anymore. He also did not want to do any more ESP experiments after this. We stayed friends, but things got really weird—and over the years he bullied me more and more. By sixth grade, he almost killed me by shoving snow in my face and cutting off my breathing—which he called a "white wash." I couldn't help but feel that my mother had been proven right about fundamentalist religions once again.

Seduced by the Box

Dad came home one day with a huge machine that sat on top of the TV, called a VCR—or video cassette recorder—which allowed you to record television shows onto a big VHS tape. We were one of the very first families in the neighborhood to have one. Shortly after this, a new channel called MTV—Music Television—appeared. Dad was very excited about it and we watched it the first day it came on. The video that inspired me the most was "In the Air Tonight" by Phil Collins, as it had dreamlike images of a hallway filled with doors to nowhere, and a very intense and emotional ending where he was screaming, and the camera was very closeup on his face. When he sang, "I've been waiting for this moment for all my life," I kept thinking about the awesome event the old man told me was going to happen on Earth in my lifetime—which I would eventually learn was called ascension.

Once I started third grade, there was a new kid in school named Billy, who was also interested in dinosaurs, space travel, and science. We became fast friends, and I was able to get my mother to drive me over to his house a few times a month. He had an Atari like I did, but his father worked as a manager at the Friendly's restaurant, so he had extra income and bought him tons of different games. Billy had an entire two-foot-deep basket that was literally filled to the top with game cartridges—and for me this was like heaven. All we did was play games together—including classic titles like *Yars' Revenge, Haunted House, Pac-Man,* and *Adventure.* I also noticed that his mom bought him all these boxes of sugar-heavy junk food that I was never allowed to have, including Twinkies, Ho-Hos and Ring Dings. I knew that a Twinkie would supposedly never go bad, even after a hundred years, but they sure tasted good—so I had one of them every time I went there.

I started having trouble in school during this same time. My third-grade teacher, Mrs. Smith, wanted us to write in cursive, and I hated it. I also did not want to memorize multiplication and division tables. I strongly believed that the answer would change depending upon where you were when you calculated it. The only way to be sure of the right answer was to redo it each time. So if I saw 9 × 3, I would count it out in my head while lifting up my fingers to make sure I had the right number. I would mentally count 10, 11, 12, 13, 14, 15, 16, 17, 18, see that I had nine fingers up, and then start again: 19, 20, 21, 22, 23, 24, 25, 26, 27. This made me much slower than the other kids, and I began falling behind— but for months I felt it was very stupid, even dangerous, to try to memorize the answers. I seemed to remember that if you used math to travel and didn't make a fresh calculation each time, you could get hopelessly lost, if not killed. It was many years before I read about higher dimensions and realized that there could indeed be places where the rules of mathematics functioned differently than they do here. If you are in a base-6 counting system, for example, you would count 1, 2, 3, 4, 5, 11, 12, 13, 14, 15, 21, 22, and so on. Certain areas might force you to use a different number base in order for the calculations to work properly.

Weird Science

I started reading as many books about science as I could—from school as well as in the children's section of the Schenectady County Public Library. My mother would always have us "talk" to a tree when we went there. We would go up to the tree and say nice things to it, and the tree would "answer" by having the wind blow through its branches. It did seem that the tree always responded whenever we did this. The wind would pick up, even if it was calm, and I believed the tree was really talking to us. One day my mother told me about the work of Dr. Cleve

Backster, who had a plant that "screamed" when he tried to burn it. She had read enough to be completely convinced this was true, and it had quite an effect on me. I had never considered the idea that plants had feelings before, but Mom was absolutely convinced that these experiments were real. Years later I would interview Backster myself, and I opened up *The Source Field Investigations* by summarizing his findings.

I quickly became obsessed with finding science experiments and trying them out at home. Mom also bought me a chemistry set, and my favorite ingredient was the phenolphthalein solution. You could pour some of this magic elixir into a test tube, drop certain chemicals into it, and get very nice crystals to form.

That same Christmas of 1981, my "major present" was a small color TV from the local Roy Matthews hardware store on Mohawk Avenue. It was wonderful, as now I could play Atari games alone in my room with the door closed and not bother anyone else. I continued to have wonderful dreams of flying during this time.

The Plot Thickens

Sometime roughly at the beginning of 1982, I saw my first picture of the infamous "Face on Mars" in *Odyssey* magazine. This is a mountain on the surface of Mars that looks exactly like a human face—and the magazine said it was very strange. I immediately felt that someone had built it to look like this, and it was not just an illusion. I wanted so badly to know how it got there, and who did it. I felt the answer must be hiding in the UFO phenomenon. Perhaps there were people out there who were much older and more ancient than we were—people like the old man in my dreams. These same people may have built things like the pyramids, the stone heads of Easter Island, and Stonehenge here on Earth. I couldn't understand why so many kids continued to hate me for bringing *Odyssey* to school, as I felt this was wonderful stuff that would change the world—just like the old man said.

That summer, the movie *E.T. the Extra-Terrestrial* was released on June 11. My father went to see it by himself shortly after the premiere, came home, and said we had to immediately go and check it out. We all went to see it either that same night or some time the next day. In the movie, a boy named Elliott started to take care of a kind-looking little extraterrestrial who had crash-landed on Earth. E.T. was able to levitate balls to show where he came from. He brought a dead chrysanthemum flower back to life, and he had a weird psychic connection to Elliott. When E.T. drank beer, Elliott started to get drunk—and when E.T. saw John Wayne kiss a girl in a movie, Elliott kissed a girl in his class.

I was stunned to see ESP in a movie, as well as telekinesis—E.T. was able to levitate the bicycles of Elliott and all his friends and make them fly through the air at the end. When E.T. died, I cried harder than I ever had in any other movie. I definitely realized that Steven Spielberg was comparing E.T. to Christ when E.T. was later resurrected. As a young adult, I bragged about the fact that I had cried fewer than ten times in my life for emotional reasons, and this was one of them. I identified so strongly with extraterrestrials that I felt like I was Elliott, and when E.T. died it seemed like I had lost the only real friend I ever had.

The Journey to Avalon

That same summer, in late June, Dad took us on our first vacation to Cape Cod, Massachusetts, where we stayed at a place called Captain's Row. We went to visit Dad's college buddy Bob at an oceanfront cabin he had right on the shore of Hyannis Bay, which was fantastic. However, the sand was loaded with razor clams, and I stepped on one of them by accident, causing my foot to bleed. Mom and Michael both decided to do "will walking," and she told me that if I "set my intention," I could walk without looking and never step on another clam. I got angry and said there was no way I was going to do that. She and Michael went off and did it anyway, waving their arms happily. Sure enough, neither of them looked where they were going and neither of them stepped on a razor clam. This caused me to resent them both for a while, but I got over it as soon as they stopped.

Mom was applying the wisdom she had read in the Seth books about the idea that "you create your own reality." Others have called it "the law of attraction." I certainly do not advocate putting yourself in dangerous situations like this. However, life is filled with unexpected dangers and distractions, and cultivating a positive attitude can significantly affect your experiences. The phenomenon of synchronicity taught me that when I focused on the positive, amazing and inexplicable things could happen. Similarly, when I knowingly hurt others or hurt myself, I would invariably attract "bad karma," in which negative events would manifest in my life with shocking precision and timing. By the time I was in high school, I was already convinced that karma was absolutely real—and extremely important to be aware of.

She Blinded Me with Science

In the fall of 1982, I became one of the "big kids," and got to stay on the upper floor of the elementary school in Mrs. Austin's fourth-grade classroom. By this point, Dan Rather was warning us almost every night that we could all die in a nuclear war. More and more often, I heard my parents yell at each other after they put Michael and me to bed. We were upset enough by this that I got rid of my huge hardwood double bed and moved into Michael's room, with a new set of bunk beds that the bass player in Mom's band built for us. We turned my former bedroom into the family room, and it was hardly ever used. My grades continued dropping in school, and the bullying kept getting worse and worse. One kid named Chris came up with a line that I ended up hearing again and again: "He's so smart that he's dumb." Everyone thought this was hilarious.

During this time, my father got me backstage to meet Thomas Dolby, who was riding high on his hit single "She Blinded Me with Science." I really enjoyed meeting him, and I could tell he was totally overwhelmed with everything that was happening. He was polite, but very exhausted and distracted. This was extremely common for the musicians that Dad would take me backstage to meet. I had no idea at the time that I would spend much of my adult life going through similar challenges as a public figure— even though the old man had repeatedly warned me about it in dreams.

If We Can Dream It, We Can Do It

That Christmas, Michael and I were thrilled when Dad gave us an entire magazine he had drawn by hand. The front cover had a picture of Mickey and Minnie Mouse, and a title that said, "Guess where we're going?" Once we opened the book, we learned we were going to Disney World in February. He had drawn images of Disney characters, and there was colorful text that talked us through it step by step—as well as a pouch with a thick color brochure for Disney World in it at the back. He also gave us each a jigsaw puzzle from GE that featured a magnificent flying city, complete with UFO-type craft flying through it. At the top of the puzzle, it said, "IF WE CAN DREAM IT, WE CAN DO IT." I built the puzzle on the kitchen table and felt it was absolutely true. It was only a matter of time before we had cities and spaceships just like the ones I was already seeing in my dreams.

We headed off to Disney World in early February and were lucky enough to be able to skip school while we were gone. Both Mom and Dad got a terrible virus that gave them diarrhea and they were very sick. Mom spent almost the entire time flat on her back in our suite, and Dad took us on all the rides while drinking out of a bottle of Kaopectate that he had wrapped in a brown paper bag. Dad was there for a working trip, since General Electric sponsored a ride in Epcot Center—and we got to go behind the scenes into rooms that only the upper-level management would normally see.

Hybrid Sedan

Dad had hoped the Disney World trip would improve his relationship with my mother, but things only got worse and worse. Mom started leaving the house every night for rehearsal with her band Hybrid Sedan after dinner, leaving Dad to entertain us and put us to bed by himself. Mom didn't come home until after he had to go to sleep for work the next morning. Dad started telling us stories every night. He would ask us for an idea or a topic, and then create a story out of it that always involved two little boys—and we really enjoyed that.

The Day After

On November 20, 1983, a television movie called *The Day After* was aired. It was heavily advertised and everybody knew about it. The ads showed horrific scenes of a post-nuclear apocalypse and the people who survived. My parents refused to let Michael and me watch it, but I wanted to know what the media was showing everyone, so Michael and I sneaked into the family room and watched it while Mom and Dad were seeing it downstairs. The images were absolutely terrifying, and after just a few minutes, we'd had enough. I knew that if something like this ever happened, it would quickly destroy all life on Earth. Yet, night after night the TV news made it sound like this could happen at any time—and we might not even realize the missiles had launched before we were already dead.

I didn't understand how anyone could think this was a good idea. If you have a war where the Earth itself is destroyed, there is no winner. Everybody loses. And why would the US and the Soviets want to do this if they were also going to die from it? This faceless terror caused everyone to feel incredible stress, fear, and pain, which tended to make them hurt one another. I found out only years later that a vast system of underground bases had been built for our "leaders" to survive a nuclear war, while everyone else died out on the surface. These cities were connected by an underground train system with egg-shaped cars called "sub-shuttles." This would allow them to travel anywhere they wanted and support many hundreds of thousands of people whom they chose to survive.

Go Ahead, Have an Apple

Apple released a wonderful-looking new computer, the Apple *IIc*, in late April 1984, and my neighbor Brett got it right away. He showed it to me and it was incredible. The *IIc* could run all the games that we had at school, as well as all the games my friend Eric had on his own Apple *IIc* at home. I talked at great length about how awesome this computer was, but I never imagined Dad would actually buy one for me just over a month later. Michael also got to buy something big that he really liked, and in his case he got a high-end stunt-riding bicycle called a PK Ripper.

On the day we went to buy the computer, I was sitting in a restaurant and a very large ball of earwax rolled out of my ear. It felt oddly symbolic, as if I were somehow being told that I would have better ESP—I would "hear" better—once I started using the computer. I ended up using the same computer until 1995, when I first got on the Internet after I finished college. I came home with the whole system in a big box, and also got a particleboard computer desk to hold it. I put the desk together by myself, but did not cover up the screws with the little round stickers that looked like wood grain. I wanted to be able to tighten them again if the desk ever started getting wobbly. Just a few weeks later, those stickers ended up saving me from the worst trouble I would have ever gotten into in my life.

Let's Burn Some Sugar!

Soon after getting the new computer, Michael and I were watching a show called *Mr. Wizard's World* on Nickelodeon and got very excited. Mr. Wizard held up a bottle of white powder, and said, "What I have here is some KNO_3 . . . and we are going to use it to burn sugar." YES! My Pyramid teacher, Professor Schottman, had given me a box full of mysterious chemicals from his attic to help me do more experiments— and it included a bottle of KNO_3. Mr. Wizard mixed KNO_3 and sugar together in a little aluminum pie pan, and had a kid light it on fire with a match on the end of a four-foot-long pole while they were wearing goggles. The mixture fizzed and burned a little bit, creating a small fire and some black goo—and that was it. "We've got to try this right now," I told Michael. We ran into the basement, grabbed the KNO_3, and got one of Mom's aluminum pie pans out of the kitchen cabinets. Since Mr. Wizard did it all indoors, I thought it would be perfectly fine for us to set it up on the kitchen table. We grabbed all of Dad's old newspapers out of the garage and created a three-inch-tall stack for the kitchen table. "How much KNO3 do you think we should use?" "I don't know, maybe fifty-fifty," Michael replied.

We mixed together enough KNO3 and sugar to create a thick layer of powder that covered the entire bottom of the pie pan, and put it on top of the stack of newspapers. I tried to light it four different times with matches but it didn't work. Finally I realized we needed more heat. The match would be a lot hotter when it first started, since that's when the magnesium would be burning, so I lit one and tossed it in immediately. All a sudden, the KNO3—potassium nitrate, the active ingredient in gunpowder and dynamite—roared to life. Within about three seconds, we had a gigantic three-foot-tall, one-foot-wide cylinder of blue fire that was swirling in an angry rage, looking like some DNA molecule from hell. We could immediately feel the heat blast on our faces, like the flash-pots at a rock concert. The flames were licking against the glass globe light that dangled over the kitchen table, leaving soot marks. Michael and I were screaming and crying at the power and the fury we had un-leashed, right in the spot where so many tense dinners had taken place in the last few years. We had no idea if we were about to burn the whole house down and could only watch in absolute disbelief. The tower of fire blasted on for about two minutes nonstop and finally died out. Nothing else had caught on fire, thank goodness.

I grabbed the entire stack of newspapers, which still had some small flames, and ran out the side door with them. The oxygen-starved flames suddenly surged over my right shoulder, but did not burn me. I stomped them out on the driveway. The house was filled with a very thick gray smoke that smelled like rotten eggs that had burned. Some of the black, molten goo had eaten through all the newspapers, and it had carved a mark in a quarter-inch-wide area of the tabletop, right next to the salt shaker. As if by some synchronistic miracle, my wood stickers were the same color as the table. I put one of them over the hole, and it fit per-fectly. Every night after that, we were afraid that Dad would see it—but he never did. Our babysitter, Ellen, came by and we opened up all the doors and windows, using fans to blow all the hideous smoke out. By the time Mom came home, the smoke was gone, and Michael and I were wailing and begging for forgiveness on our knees. "I think you have already suffered enough," she said. We all agreed not to tell Dad.

Eat the Pain

A few weeks later, Mom sat Michael and me down in the living room and said she had something important to tell us. Michael was immediately scared, and I already knew what she was going to say. "Your father and I are going to get separated," she said. "He is going to start living somewhere else from now on." Michael started crying really hard. I almost wanted to say, "What took you so long?" but I kept quiet. Less than a month later, we went off on another two-week vacation to Cape Cod. Mom took us out there the first week while Dad moved all his stuff out of the house with his friends. Then Dad came out for vacation on the second week while Mom cleaned up and rearranged the house by herself.

Although the vacation was great, and I felt closer than ever to my dad's friend Bob's family, going home was a big shock. Dad had kept rows and rows of records in the living room, both on the floor and on three wooden racks held up with cinder blocks. There was also a huge stereo system on the racks that sounded amazing. Dad had an estimated fifteen thousand records on shelves in the basement—a huge treasure room of rock. Everything was gone. The living room looked completely barren and dead, and there were black scuffmarks on the wall. Then I went up into the family room and realized the color TV I had gotten for Christmas was gone. The Atari was sitting there disconnected and defeated. I asked my mother what had happened, and she was very upset. "Your father was going to take one of the two TVs, so I told him he could take the little one but not the big one." I was very angry at her, and at Dad, for making this deal behind my back, without even asking me. She apologized and said so many bad things were happening that she just wanted to get it over with, and I should be glad that we still had the big TV. I felt crushed, because that TV had been given to me for Christmas—and I still used it.

I started eating lots of Oreo cookies, which my mother always kept in a big galvanized-steel-lined drawer by the kitchen door, to self-medicate from the pain this was causing me. I got very good at opening the drawer so quietly that she couldn't hear it—even when she was seven feet away in the next room, teaching one of her piano students. With my new stealth technique, I felt that I could get away with eating as many cookies as I wanted. This caused me to gain weight very rapidly—just like Billy's brother had after their mother died of cancer. I became extremely depressed, moved back into the "family room," and stopped taking showers. My mother tried to make a joke out of it at first by rapping, "You smell funky," in the same way Run-DMC said, "You be illin'." I still refused to listen, and it only got worse and worse until she eventually demanded that I start cleaning myself up. Even then, I would go days at a time without a shower—and this didn't stop until I went back to school to start sixth grade. At this time, Mom told us that there was going to be far less money now that Dad was gone, and we would have to spend much less in order to survive. Everything was different now, and we needed to be very careful.

This was when my first "core trauma" occurred. All of us have had events like this in our lives, where our childlike wonder and fascination with life collides with harsh reality. It is a similar but more powerful version of the first time a baby hears the word "no." These events program our subconscious mind to re-create the same traumas through "repetition compulsion." I was already addicted to video games, and we never had enough money to replace my TV. Therefore, lack of money, giving my valuables away, a feeling of being betrayed by others, and the desire to indulge in addictions, such as "comfort eating," became cycles that kept repeating in my life.

Mom became an extreme workaholic, never slowing down, and made all her money from teaching piano and voice students and playing music gigs. She took on a lot more students, and that meant I couldn't stay downstairs at all, three days a week, after I came home from school—and there was now no TV upstairs. My room felt like a prison. She also had hated all the piles of magazines, newspapers, and letters that Dad had kept around the house. All these new rules were created. Everything had to be superclean—to the point of being like a museum. Michael and I now had to do almost all the housework and yard work ourselves—and if we left a mess anywhere, we got yelled at.

My life turned into a nightmare. We had to eat the same food four or five nights a week, reheating it each time—and it was usually homemade macaroni and cheese. We hardly ever went to a restaurant. The whole house was now loaded with booby traps—rules about keeping things clean that would create instant punishment if they were broken—and no matter how careful we were, both of us got in trouble every day. If Mom found one water stain on the bathroom sink, or one tiny crumb of bread on the kitchen countertop, we were severely disciplined—and she felt she had every right to be angry. I stopped washing my hands when I went to the bathroom because it was nearly impossible to avoid leaving a water stain. I realized that most people were not like this, but since this was what she demanded, we had to follow her orders. We already knew she was far too tough to fight against, as that would only make it much worse. My home life soon became a daily struggle of trying to figure out how not to get in trouble and failing constantly.

Due to repetition compulsion, I would end up spending most of my life subconsciously attracting people who were highly dominant, and I would be too terrified to confront them. Identifying and recovering from these traumas eventually gave me the strength to stand up to the grand villains in our planetary script, despite the dangers involved.

Let's Just Call It "Husky"

Mom took us to Rudnick's, a clothing store on State Street in downtown Schenectady, to buy new pants for school. It was dark, cold, and smelled strongly of leather. The Olender furniture store next door to it had a "Final Going Out of Business Sale" every year or two. Now that we had very little money, I could pick out only one pair of blue jeans. The lady working there was very cruel to me, as if that would somehow inspire me to lose weight. She took one look at me and said, "You're going to need husky pants." Somehow, companies like Lee and Levi's had decided that it was cool to compare fat kids to thick-looking Alaskan dogs, but I hated the term. I also needed the legs to be shortened, which caused us to have to wait even longer—and the whole thing was a horrible ordeal.

On the first day of school, the huge ex-Marine Mr. Korthas saw me, with his whole fifth-grade class behind him, and bellowed out, "You look like you have eaten well." All the kids started laughing hysterically, and I was crushed. I was one of the only kids in school who was overweight, and now the bullies finally had a weapon they could use against me. I was called "lard ass," "butter ball," "fatty," "fat shit," and many other such names on a regular basis. Another kid in my sixth-grade class named Joey started putting me into painful joint locks almost every day. He would grin widely through his crooked teeth and laugh as I begged him to stop—but he was much stronger than I was. I also made a new friend that year, a kid named Shane who had just moved into town. At the time, no one liked him since he was from a poor family and smelled sometimes. People called him names like "dirtbag," but we got along very well.

Black Sweatpants

Not long after school started, I was sitting at my computer desk one night and accidentally soiled myself. Nothing like this had ever happened to me before. I grabbed a pair of black sweatpants—the only other pair of pants I owned that still fit—and hobbled into the shower. The pants were in such bad shape that I didn't even want to try to save them, and I also did not want to tell my mother about it. I went downstairs, got a plastic garbage bag, and deposited both my pants and underpants into it as if they were radioactive waste. I tied the bag tightly and threw it out in the garage. I walked right past my mother as I did this, and she had no idea what was going on.

I was too embarrassed to tell her what had happened, and was terrified that I would be in trouble for destroying expensive clothing, so I started wearing my black sweatpants to school every day. Since I had to do my own laundry, I didn't understand that black clothes needed to be washed in cold water, and the sweatpants very quickly faded into a dull brown.

This almost immediately caused the bullying to get much worse. Every day I was violently insulted for my weight and was told I needed to get new pants. Joey would put me in a headlock right in the classroom and ram my face into his soaking armpit, which smelled like onions and dog mess, and no one cared. This went on for weeks and weeks, and my mother never noticed what I was wearing. The torture I went through at school during this time was almost unimaginable. I finally broke down crying one night and told her what had happened. She was very understanding and forgiving, and immediately took me back to Rudnick's so I could pick up another pair of huskies. I also ended up getting a useless pair of "parachute pants" that made a swishing noise as I walked, simply because that's what the cool people were wearing—for less than a year.

Mom had a Polaroid instant camera and took a picture of me when I had a computer exhibit at the science fair. I was demonstrating an old computer program I had learned to write in Pyramid. It would draw a straight line and rotate it in circles like a radar screen, with the center of the monitor as the pivot point. Intricate, curving geometric designs would form in the images it left behind—which I learned were called moiré patterns. I had discovered this quite by accident, and no one could really explain why the patterns were so elaborate and beautiful. Everyone was impressed with my exhibit, but when I looked at the photo I saw the truth. I had gotten really fat. Somehow I didn't see it when I looked at myself in the mirror. I would only look at my face and had become very disconnected from my body—but the photograph did not lie. I felt terrible—but it only made me eat even more.

In May, Twisted Sister released the rock anthem "We're Not Gonna Take It," which was constantly replayed on MTV almost immediately. The whole thing was written for kids who were rebelling against abusive parents and teachers, and my brother and I loved it. We jumped at the chance to see them live in concert later that year, after their second single "I Wanna Rock" was doing just as well—and this was the first time I was truly awed by a famous band I got to meet backstage with my father. They were clearly drinking a lot, but they were all in a good mood and doing very funny things. They were nice to us, and since we were the only kids there, we got special treatment. The whole trick was not to act like they were famous. If you treated them like rock stars, they would cut you off in less than thirty seconds. If you acted like they were ordinary people, you might get to chat with them for an hour. This was remarkably consistent for every famous person I met.

When we see people repeatedly in the media, we feel like they are a part of our family. Our limbic, reptilian brain cannot differentiate between the images in a photograph or film and actual reality. These people become part of our tribe—and we feel an ongoing pain of abandonment when no actual in-person contact takes place. Meeting a public figure can be an awesome, almost mystical experience, flooding us with an incredible surge of natural opiates in the brain. We become so high that we do not realize how our breathless hyper-enthusiasm is making the other person feel. Some public figures appreciate this type of attention at first, but before long they become traumatized by people who refuse to stop talking or give them any privacy. The most important secret to remember is that they are ordinary people having an extraordinary experience. My early training in losing the "hero worship" impulse paved the way for me to have direct telepathic contact with extraterrestrials later in life. The drug-like high of feeling you have been "chosen" and are "special" can make it impossible to achieve any type of reliable communication. Extraterrestrials and spiritual beings are ultimately just people who are living their own lives and doing their best to help us out—at least when they are on the positive side. Negative beings feed on the energy of being worshipped and get a genuine rush from creating fear, terror, and pain.

CHAPTER SEVEN

Heaven and Hell

D ad took Michael and me to see *2010* shortly after its premiere on December 7, 1984. This was a sequel to Arthur C. Clarke and Stanley Kubrick's epic classic *2001: A Space Odyssey,* which I had never seen. I was thrilled to see Professor Heywood Floyd typing on a beach with the same Apple *IIc* computer I had recently gotten. In the film, Russia and the US launched a joint mission to investigate what had happened to the ship that was left behind at the end of *2001.* The ship's former commander, David Bowman, had become what you might call an ascended being. He contacted his mother by moving through the electrical wires and appearing on her TV, as sparks of starlight kept flickering in his eyes. He told her something was going to happen that would affect all of us. When she begged him to tell her what it was, he smiled and said, "Something wonderful." The gravity and power of that moment rocked me to my core. It was triggering deep memories from so many dreams I had had in the past.

The horrible threat of nuclear war loomed in the movie as the two crews were forced apart once tensions exploded between the US and Russia—but ultimately they needed each other to survive. They came upon this mysterious, ancient object called "the Monolith" floating in space by the abandoned ship, and I could hardly believe this had made it into a movie. Then it turned out that a dark spot on Jupiter was growing larger and larger—and when they zoomed in on it, they found it was made with countless legions of monoliths. The mysterious, godlike objects were consuming the entire planet and transforming it into something new.

The crews were given a very clear message that they had to leave. The abandoned ship's computer, HAL, sacrificed itself and its ship to save everyone else. The entire planet collapsed in on itself and exploded, forming a brilliant new sun in our solar system. A message was beamed all over the Earth by some mysterious force, which was probably from the ascended form of David Bowman: "All these worlds are yours. Use them together. Use them in peace."

I couldn't stop thinking about *2010* for weeks. The old man had told me a very similar event was going to happen here, except it seemed to involve the Sun, not Jupiter. Those dreams were starting to fade from my memory, but they were certainly not forgotten. I went out and got the book and loved it—although I thought it was totally ridiculous that Clarke said everyone on Earth had agreed the new sun "had to" be called Lucifer. At the time I did not think this had any deeper significance. Insiders would eventually reveal that Clarke had been given a wide variety of classified information to prepare us for an eventual disclosure. The Cabal was already aware that an ancient builder race had generated marvelous artifacts in our solar system, and was intimately involved in steering us through the ascension process. The groups giving Clarke this information had Luciferian beliefs, and some of it found its way into his works. Nonetheless, I do believe that the overall effect was positive, in that it introduced people to the mysteries of ascension and of ancient artifacts on Earth and in our solar system.

I convinced my mother to rent the movie *2001,* which made the monolith much more interesting. It seemed to represent an ancient extraterrestrial technology that was designed to catapult human beings into new levels of evolution. The ending, where David Bowman went through the stargate and became the starchild—the same being we met in *2010*—had me in total rapture. I quickly read Clarke's original *2001* book as well.

Monkey Hill

On Christmas break, a tough, arrogant jock kid with a square jaw and extraordinary self-confidence whom we will call Brad invited me to go sledding with him and some friends. Brad and I had been friends years earlier, since he lived a few streets away from me. His parents burned wood for heat and had a sign in the house that said, "Never trust a man who doesn't drink." This sledding invitation came out of nowhere; we hadn't spoken since I went over to his house and saw him kill a squirrel with his BB gun. One of his friends was Chris, who had coined the phrase "He's so smart, he's dumb"—and had just spent weeks telling me to get new pants and saying I was fat.

Brad's other friend was Eddie, who was still taking the drumming class in school that I had quickly dropped out of. Mr. Riccobono had demanded I play nothing but slow quarter notes on my practice pad, left-right-left-right, for twenty minutes a day. I was already playing Native American beats on a drum in kindergarten class, so this was a staggeringly boring joke. I felt terrible about quitting, but I just couldn't take the dullness of practicing, and decided I was better off trying to train myself. Now the four of us were in Mom's car on the way to Collins Park, and all they could talk about was the dreaded Monkey Hill. It was an extremely dangerous, steep slope that had a big ninety-degree turn after the first twenty-five feet, and then continued on for about another hundred feet afterward. Immediately to the left of Monkey Hill, there was a thick wall of vivid-smelling evergreen trees.

We all went over to Monkey Hill after only a few runs on the safer and easier trails. I watched them all do it, and they kept saying it was important to lean into the turn as you hit it. I immediately decided there was no way I would ever go down Monkey Hill. It was much too dangerous. The next thing I knew, they were practically demanding I run it on my orange plastic saucer, calling me a pussy. I continued to refuse. They grabbed me and forced me down onto the saucer, about fifteen feet to the side of the beginning of the trail. Then, all three of them pushed me to get me going as fast as they could, using the extra fifteen feet like a runway. I screamed down the top of the hill and hit the ninety-degree turn at full speed. Leaning didn't do me any good. The curve turned into a ramp, and launched me into the air. I plunged a hundred feet down through empty space, soaring about fifteen feet above the ground while descending on a smooth, parabolic arc. This caused me to be airborne for a stunningly long time. All I could do was grip the sides of the saucer in disbelief as it slowly rotated through the crisp-green winter air. I was too shocked and mystified to be scared. It was the closest I had ever felt to the out-of-body experience in my waking life.

I was facing backward when I hit the ground, so I did not know when I was going to land. I smashed into the hard snow in an upright, seated position, and the impact was so powerful that my saucer cracked into about twenty-five different pieces. Many of them were triangle-shaped. My tailbone and lower spine were in agonizing pain and I didn't even know if I would be able to walk again. I was lying there and didn't dare move in case something was broken. My entire body was throbbing with pain from head to toe. I had a tremendous headache and I could hear my heartbeat in my ears, along with a ringing. The kids quickly sledded down to see if I was okay.

By some miracle, they were able to get me up on my feet and nothing appeared to be broken—though my tailbone was very sore and I was in so much pain I could barely even walk. I hobbled up the hill, found my mother, and got her to take me home. I had a hard time sitting for several days. She hadn't seen what had happened and was very concerned when I told her why I didn't have my saucer anymore. I never again went anywhere near Monkey Hill.

That's What Friends Are For

The great villains in our planetary script were threatening us with instant death from nuclear destruction at any moment. Some people chose to look for the positive and be kind, while others felt compelled to repeat the trauma and pain they were feeling for others. I was still healing from my fall when Eric decided he was going to show me what a "white wash" was. In the media, when the government committed a crime and covered it up, they called it a "whitewash." Right in front of my babysitter Ellen's house, Eric grabbed me, kicked out my leg, and forced me facedown into a snowbank. He grabbed a handful of snow and shoved it in my face, rubbing it around in circles. This went on for a frighteningly long time. He did not allow me to breathe, and the snow was fiercely cold. I was screaming and screaming, trying to tell him I was going to die, and flailing my arms, but I had no voice—and he kept going. I was running out of air and really didn't know if I was going to make it. Finally he let go. My tortured lungs gasped for breath again and again.

After about seven huge, bellowing gasps on all fours, with my whole body shaking, I got up on my feet and screamed at him in a bloodcurdling, tortured voice, saying he had almost killed me. I used the strongest curse words when I asked him if he was smart enough to realize that the human body cannot live without air, and how would his parents like it if they found out their son was a murderer? I wanted so badly to attack him, but I was afraid I might literally try to tear him to pieces. I also didn't know if I was strong enough to win that fight. We stopped walking to school together after that event, but for some crazy reason I continued to be friends with him. Everyone else hated us and we both needed protection.

About a month later, Eric convinced me to join him in putting two tacks on the chair of Diana, a tall, lanky, and kindhearted farm girl who obviously liked me, as a prank. I absolutely did not want to do it, and it seemed like he was jealous because no girls liked him. I thought he might try to hurt me again if I said no. He put the tacks on her chair while I stood and watched, and I did not stop him. Other kids witnessed the crime. Diana sat down and screamed in terrible pain, and both of us were sent to the principal's office. Audrey Farnsworth made it clear that we were in very serious trouble—and Eric sure did cry, just like I did. This only made me resent him even more, and for a while our friendship was over.

Sorry, Mrs. Farnsworth

I had gotten a Radio Shack electronics kit for the Christmas of 1984. It was a one-and-a-half-foot-wide, three-inch-tall blue plastic box. It had a cardboard top with electrical components arranged on it. Each component had a three-quarter-inch-tall coil of wire poking up on either side of it. You were given a wealth of color-coded wires of different lengths, and by following the instructions, you could build different types of machines with it. I never took the time to build the full radio, but I did several complex projects. The lie detector was by far my favorite. It measured the electrical conductivity of your skin, also known as galvanic skin response, or GSR. You would hold two white wires, which were the longest ones, and get a tone that would rise and fall in pitch. If you were telling a lie, you would become nervous and the pitch would rise. As you relaxed, the pitch went down.

I brought this kit to class one day and ran into the school principal, Mrs. Farnsworth, along with the district superintendent and all the highest-ranking people we never saw. It was a great photo op for her to ask me what I had there. Our local leaders gave one another knowing looks as they fantasized about how useful such a device could be. To my horror, when she grabbed the wires, no sound came out—probably because she had too much makeup on her fingers. "I'm sorry, Mrs. Farnsworth, but you appear to be dead." All the bigwigs exploded into laughter. Then I used my science buddy to prove that it did squeal just fine when a normal human grabbed the wires. I was genuinely baffled that the most powerful elite I knew in my own school, who had punished me several times with withering shame, did not register on my foolproof device as a normal person. It seemed like a practical joke from the universe, showing me that people in positions of power can become "heartless." The synchronicity was obviously helped along by the makeup on her fingers, which the makers of the lie detector had never accounted for.

Family Horrors

My father had become deeply depressed from the divorce and lost a lot of weight. He got a small house in Scotia and we started going there to see him on Friday and Sunday nights. Dad could cook one meal really well—a London broil grilled steak with white rice and mushrooms.

Otherwise we usually ordered a Sicilian-style sausage-and-mushroom pizza. Since Dad loved horror movies, he decided that we were now old enough to watch R-rated films. Many of them were extremely terrifying and disturbing. I was too young to get the "morphine response," since I had never seen or experienced traumas anywhere near as horrible as what these movies displayed. I quickly learned that I had to remove myself from the film and remember that none of it was real. Another trick was to expect that every single character I saw, no matter how much I was supposed to like them, was going to die in the most horrible and gruesome way possible. That way, whenever they got it, I could just say, "Well, I knew that was going to happen." It also bothered me that only the villains in the movies had supernatural powers, whereas the victims and the people who fought and defeated the bad guys did not. Insiders would eventually tell me the Cabal was deliberately financing films like this, so that people would feel that only the "dark side" could produce powerful, ascension-like abilities in humans.

Sean, a kid in school, was now avidly reading the Stephen King novels, and told me how great they were. I ended up buying and reading several of them myself, including *Different Seasons, The Drawing of the Three, Pet Sematary, Firestarter, It,* and *The Stand.* Some of these novels were very disturbing—actually much more so than any horror movie. I was amazed at the power Stephen King had to create realistic, fully realized characters. Many of his villains and stupid characters seemed like adult versions of the same bullies I was dealing with in school—and the short story "The Body" became a classic film called *Stand By Me* that depicted similar bullying characters as kids. Stephen King's art seemed to be an imitation of life, and I had the strong sense that he had been called "lard ass" in school just like I was.

I made friends with a new kid in school, whom we will call Toby, after Eric had nearly killed me by asphyxiation. Toby took me out to the Mohawk River, where he wanted us to walk over these huge slabs of ice that had broken up out of the water. It was very dangerous, and I agreed to do it but tried to be as careful as I could. Soon after I read "The Body," in which kids find a dead body in the woods, Toby actually died. He was riding on the back of a hay wagon on his parents' farm, sitting on top of a load of hay that was four bales high, when the wheel hit a bump and threw him off the back. Toby landed on his head and was killed instantly. This was the first time someone I actually knew had died, and it was shocking. I was overwhelmed with grief for several weeks, particularly since I hardly had any friends. Life suddenly seemed much more fragile than I had ever thought. I realized I had gotten very lucky with things like Monkey Hill and Eric's white wash. I needed to fight back, as otherwise one of these bullies might actually kill me.

The horror movies and Stephen King novels made me enchanted by the idea that Toby might still exist as some sort of ghost. When my mother took me to the Kay-Bee toy store in the Mohawk Mall, I found something called the Ouija Talking Board, which was sold along with classic board games like Monopoly, Parcheesi, Trivial Pursuit, and Clue. The front cover showed an eerie brown board with all the letters of the alphabet, and a teardrop-shaped, cream-colored pointer that had people's hands on it. I picked it up, read the words, and realized that this was obviously being used to contact the dead—and apparently it really worked. I convinced my mother to let me buy it.

Since you couldn't do it alone, I waited until the next time my babysitter Rachel came over, while my mother was off at a music gig, and we tried it. Rachel went into a deep state of meditation, rolling her eyes back and squinting them. Her eyelids fluttered, and she let her head nod all the way back while she kept her hands on the pointer. She had no idea what it was saying or where it was going. I started asking questions and the pointer was definitely moving on its own. I tried to ask questions that I did not know the answers to, and the results were intriguing, to say the least—but the whole thing also had a very creepy feeling. I became convinced that I had experienced genuine contact with spirits through this board, and there was indeed life after death. However, I hardly ever had anyone I could do this with, since it required at least two people to work, and I had very few friends.

One day a friend of mine came up to me and said I absolutely had to read this book he found in the library. It was by Francis Crick, one of the scientists who had discovered the DNA molecule, which had all the codes for life. With a single piece of the right DNA, you could clone a human being. In this book, Crick was arguing that the DNA molecule was far too complex to have evolved by random mutation. This got me tremendously excited. I could not understand why this discovery wasn't all over the news, particularly considering Crick had actually discovered DNA in the first place. I spent countless hours trying to understand how DNA could have been formed by some sort of cosmic intelligence, and at the time I never came up with a good answer. I continued thinking about it for many years and kept looking for clues, which eventually became a major element of *The Source Field Investigations* as well as my conferences, articles, and TV shows.

We're Not Gonna Take It

Brad, the same kid who forced me down Monkey Hill, now wanted me to sneak out of school with him. After the last class at around two forty-five, students would pack up, and we were then forced to stand in a group of "walkers" in the gym—while each and every group of "bussers" left, one by one. Brad and I happened to be in the last group of "walkers" who were allowed to leave. We didn't actually breathe fresh outside air until about three thirty p.m. Brad said this was ridiculous—and just like the Twisted Sister song, "We're Not Gonna Take It," Brad had a plan. His friend Oafer got picked up by his grandfather in a Dodge Dart every day at two forty-five. Mrs. Glindmeyer and Mr. Viall just let him go right on by, and never checked to see if there was a car out there. All we had to do, Brad said, was say we were getting picked up—and they never would check. I was scared, but I decided to try it—and it worked. We got out, ducked down in front of the windows so no one could see us, and then broke into a full run when we hit the road, continuing to sprint down the first part of Schermerhorn Street. The sweet old lady who worked as a crossing guard halfway down the hill never asked us why we were earlier than the others. For the last few months of school we did this almost every day—and never once got caught. This became an addictive behavior, and addictions are all about "the hidden." More and more distortions of reality become necessary if we ignore the signals and continue down that road. Brad was the first person to influence me to lie and take dangerous risks, as up until then I had always told the truth. Later on he would talk me into smoking weed.

My grades were getting worse and worse, and I was just as shocked as my teachers were when my scores on something called the COGAT test came back. I did extremely well, putting me at a level that was as strong as most high-school seniors. The school year ended with something called Field Day, which I hated, as it included the tug-of-war, the three-legged race, and other athletic events I was terrible at. The junior high school building was on the other side of the fence at the far end of the field, and there was a small military base immediately off to the left, in a series of steel half-pipe buildings. It wasn't uncommon to hear soldiers marching outside during the day. I never knew why they were there or what was going on in them, but I do remember touring one of them once in Pyramid. It just looked like boring office space with some framed photos of military personnel and flags on the wall.

On the last day of elementary school, I was on my bike and everyone else had already left. I was only about fifty feet away from where I had done my "ESP club" four years before. I had all my books and papers stuffed into my tan-colored backpack. A big, sneering kid came roaring up to me on his bike and shot gravel at me as he screeched to a stop in front of me, sliding out his back wheel. He wrestled my backpack away from me, scattered the papers all over the pavement, and demanded that I cry or he was going to beat the hell out of me. I gave him exactly what he wanted, and he laughed and laughed before calling me all sorts of rude names and insulting my weight. Then he sped off. This made me even more terrified of starting junior high school, where there would be "big kids" from three different elementary schools—my own Sacandaga, as well as Lincoln and Glendaal.

The Joining of the Three

Things got much worse once I started junior high school in the fall of 1985. Now I had a locker with a combination, right next to Shane. I had seven periods of classes that required me to go to a different room every hour, with different books. Gym class now required us to go down to an area with a locker room and showers, but hardly anyone actually used them. We were now forced to play dodge ball, a truly barbaric game. All the jocks would try to slam you in the face as hard as they could with large red playground balls, even though it was supposedly against the rules. They rarely ever got caught, and even if they sent some kid to the nurse crying, their only punishment was to leave the game until the next round.

The teacher would pick two jocks to form teams, and they got to choose whom they wanted one by one. Eric and I were always picked last. The jocks would openly argue over who would end up with either of us, and let everyone know we were completely useless pieces of garbage to them. The whole rest of their team would often join them in their laughter and disgust. There was no recess anymore, and this was one of the only things I had been able to tolerate about going to school, as it gave me a chance to lie down in the grass and relax. The only other thing I had loved was Pyramid, and now that was gone too.

The kids from Glendaal were from wealthy families in the Glenville countryside, and tended to do really well in school—whereas the kids from Lincoln were from less-expensive row houses in the Scotia highlands, and often had the lowest grades. The kids from my school, Sacandaga, lived mostly down by the river, and were right in between Lincoln and Glendaal in terms of economic level and academic performance. I ended up in all the smart-kid honors classes, which were much more difficult, thanks to my COGAT scores—and most of my classmates were from Glendaal. On the first day of school, a tall eighth-grader with long blond hair, a denim heavy-metal jacket, and nasty blue jeans hocked his throat and spat on my leg, leaving behind a huge, disgusting yellow glob of mucus. I truly felt I had descended into hell. School had become prison, and there was no escape.

Even though Brad had been skipping school with me at the end of sixth grade, now he acted like he didn't even know who I was. He had a locker right near mine, but he avoided me at all costs. He wanted to be cool, play sports, and get girls, and hanging around a kid with a big gut wasn't going to get him what he wanted. Shane continued to be my friend, and everyone still thought he was a "scumbag" at this point since he was poor and did not have nice clothes.

Too Much Revenge

One day I saw one of the Glendaal kids playing a game called Dungeons and Dragons in the library with some other nerds from Glendaal. He was very witty and seemed extremely sure of himself, to the point of being cocky and overconfident. It was obvious that he was really smart, and he was just as heavy as I was. We will call him Kevin. He had dark brown hair, brown eyes, and large teeth, and he was always grinning. I started talking to him, and he quickly let me know he was the smartest kid in school. In fact, if he scored less than a 95 on any test, he would be severely punished by his parents, who both worked at the Knolls Atomic Power Laboratory, or KAPL. Kevin and I became fast friends, because we both had an Apple computer with lots of games at home, we shared many of the same interests, and almost everyone hated us for being smart. Kevin quickly recruited me into Boy Scouts, which allowed me to go on camping trips that I really enjoyed. The first one was that same winter, and it was the most fun I'd had since Cape Cod.

I quickly realized, however, that Kevin would do weird and cruel things. The first time I went to his house, he fed his collie dog, Excalibur, a hot pepper, and laughed as she struggled with the pain. More than once, he got angry about something I said and just completely stopped talking to me—for twenty minutes or more at a time. He called it "going into his shell," and I thought it was ridiculous. No one had ever done that to me before, and it was wasting valuable time I spent at his house— which often involved riding my bike quite a long distance into Glendaal territory to get there. When he came to visit me at my house, he did lots of bad things that got me in trouble—but he didn't care because his parents were not there to punish him. Another time I squirted him with a bottle used to water the flowers as a joke, and he disappeared. When I came out of the bathroom, he threw a huge pitcher of water all over me, and didn't even care that it had gone all over the floor. He laughed and laughed about this, and didn't care when I said it was "too much revenge."

I also found out that there was something very weird about his parents. They could not tell him a single thing about what they were doing at work. They would always listen to see if he was around, and if he ever got close they would stop talking. They also were forbidden from bringing him to work. They were obsessed with advanced physics and sci-fi movies, particularly if they were about extraterrestrials. They clearly believed in UFOs and directed him to all these different books about them. They also wanted him to study something Albert Einstein had called the "space-time continuum," and presented him with the idea that you could create a "wormhole" in this "fabric" and travel through it. It became clear that they thought extraterrestrials were very dangerous and we were all being threatened by them. Years later I found out that many so-called nuclear engineers are only using that job title as a cover while they are actually working in classified programs involving reverse-engineered technology from UFOs. They are told that their entire family will be killed if they ever say a single word to anyone. My firsthand experience of seeing how weird, secretive, and paranoid they were made this feel very personal to me.

My mother's band was now rehearsing in the basement, and that meant there was a full rock-and-roll drum kit down there. I started playing the drums again and quickly taught myself how to do basic rock beats. That September, the Parents' Music Resource Center, or PMRC, was formed by a group of senators' wives, and they were trying to completely censor any music that did not agree with their extreme Christian values. This made both my brother and me very angry. When the lead singer of Twisted Sister testified at these hearings, he instantly became even more of a hero to us—and we told him so the next time we met him backstage. I decided I needed to get a lot better at drums, and I began taking regular lessons with Hugh, the drummer from my mother's band. He would bring me up into his attic, where there was another drum kit as well as all the amplifiers and speakers. Everything reeked of beer and cigarettes, and there were egg-crate cushions all over the walls. I had many lessons with him, and they were much more advanced than what the school wanted me to do, but I was able to follow along.

The new super-villain was Josh, a kid who followed me home from school every day and tried to beat me up. I started walking with Eric and our longtime friend Dave again. We banded together for protection against Josh, but it didn't do very much good. Every day we tried to run out of school as fast as we could, and Josh came running after us at superhuman speed. Eric attempted to fight back, trying to hit him with his backpack, whereas I tried to talk Josh out of attacking us. I told him I knew his parents were mean to him, he was in a lot of pain, and I understood that, because I was too. Every day I had to talk our way out of being beaten. Josh may have been chasing us to get my counseling each day as much as anything else—but this was a horrible problem that went on for months.

All through the late fall and into the frosty cold of winter, my teacher, Mr. Empie, made us do something called the Turkey Trot in gym class. We had to run during the entire class, passing by the military base as we got started. The idea was that our speed would get better each day. It was very cold, and I hated it more than anything. I would start coughing uncontrollably and was always dead last in line, gasping for breath. The kid who always finished first was a fleet-footed jock whom some kids called Skeeter, who was also the last man standing in all of the dodge ball games. He was a true hero to many of the others, straight through high school, since he was one of our best athletes, even though he was only a little over five feet tall.

I quickly learned to avoid getting hit in dodge ball by constantly staying aware of my environment at all times. Every kid who got hit in the head was not paying attention when it happened, and the jocks were specifically watching for that. I watched every single kid on the other side like a hawk, and made sure no one could get me. Eric would deliberately let a slow ball hit him early in the game, turning his back or side into it to make it hurt less—but I refused to go down like that. Almost every time we played, I would be the last person on one side and Skeeter would be the last kid on the other. He would hold a ball in one arm for protection while throwing the rest of the balls at me with the other—and all the kids would get mad at me for surviving so long. It was impossible for me to "kill" him with a ball. Everybody would cheer and clap when Skeeter finally "killed" me, and then the whole ugly cycle would start over again.

Empie also made us play a very similar game called "Medic Ball," in which we had to pretend we were fighting a war on a battlefield, and the red rubber balls were now bullets and artillery. I decided that Empie must have been a Vietnam vet and was using us to act out his horrible memories. Once we got hit, we had to stay down and call out, "Medic! Medic!" until one of the kids with a yellow jersey came over and "rescued" us. The only way a team could win was to "kill" the medics and then "kill" everybody else. When Empie got bored, he would blow the whistle and point his two index fingers at each other, which he called "opposite sides"—and sometimes he said the words out loud. This meant that the kids on either team could now rush over the middle line, to another line that gave the losing side only the final third of their space. It was totally devastating, and mowed the survivors down in seconds—like a huge sickle toppling stalks of wheat. This was usually how Empie helped Skeeter kill me off so they could start another game. Little did I know that Skeeter would haunt me in my dreams for many years to come.

Eric's behavior got worse and worse. All the bullying was turning him into a real jerk. He started throwing rocks at the bodies of eighteen-wheel trucks as we crossed Mohawk Avenue, and got Dave to do it, but I refused the peer pressure. He also thought it was really fun to start snowball fights, which I definitely did not want. One dark and miserable afternoon, with cold sleet falling and three inches of slush all over the roads, Eric started a snowball fight with a random kid. He had spiky black hair, a freckled face, and a sneering grin. He was clearly a dangerous kid, and he was older than us. As it turned out, even though he was short, he was an excellent baseball pitcher—and a psychopath. The kid found a golf ball–sized piece of rock-solid ice, coated it with a little snow, and threw it right at my face as hard as he could. He hit me so hard on the forehead above my left eye that he crushed the bone, leaving a visible dent I would discover years later. I had never been hit so hard in my life, and nearly lost consciousness. I fell to the ground, screaming in agony and crying profusely. I could taste metal in my mouth. The kid cackled like a hyena and slinked away, victorious. Eric barely even cared that I had been injured.

On January 28, 1986, my old friend Billy called me up after school one day, even though we rarely ever spoke. "The space shuttle blew up," he said. I rushed over to the television and watched in horror as I saw footage of the *Challenger* breaking apart in midair. This was even more devastating because it was a special mission for kids, with the teacher Christa McAuliffe on board. Almost immediately after it happened, everyone started telling a whole series of horrible jokes about it, including one in which the weather forecast for Florida included "scattered shuttle." I quickly realized that people were using this cruel, sarcastic humor as a way of coping with almost unimaginable pain. Scientific studies have concluded that humor is an evolutionary mechanism. We constantly scan our environment and look for mistakes, weaknesses, problems, and failures. Identifying these issues causes laughter, which rewards us with a huge flood of endorphins and enkephalins, giving us a significant pain-killing effect and a natural high. This encourages us to continue looking for weaknesses around us that can be improved. The obvious problem is that taking pleasure in others' misfortunes lowers our readiness for ascension.

The endless bullying had caused me to develop severe depression, which meant my grades were really going down the toilet. The school kept sending home these computer-printed "progress reports" that had targeted, nasty sentences from the teachers telling your parents exactly how much of a loser you were. This essentially caused me to be in trouble with both parents every day, making my life into even more of a living hell. The report cards came in and my grades were just not good enough for them to be satisfied—there were Bs and Cs, with only a few As. I was also starting to go through puberty, which made me even more depressed. Every time my father saw me, he strongly disciplined me about my bad grades—which usually included yelling.

Have Fun

That summer, Eric and Dave found a huge domed structure hidden in the local bike trails that was made out of tree branches. It was very poorly built, tied together with wires and pieces of old, ripped clothes. It would not do very much to protect anyone in the event of a rainstorm. A weird little sign on the front was made of white and blue straws stapled onto a flat piece of wood, and it spelled out HAVE FUN. There was a dirt floor and a fire pit dug out in the center of the dome, which was about fifty feet wide and twenty feet tall.

It was obvious that the big kids had built this place to drink alcohol, do drugs, and have sex, since the HAVE FUN sign had beer-bottle caps on it as well that formed the male and female gender symbols. Eric decided that we needed to completely destroy this structure, even though it would be extremely dangerous if we got caught. Dave and I begged him not to do it, but he insisted. It took us about three four-hour days of backbreaking work, in blazing summer sweat, to trash the fort. I was incredibly afraid the whole time we were doing this that we would get beaten up or even killed, and worked in complete terror, but Eric didn't care and laughed quite a bit as we did it. Somehow we made it out alive.

About a week later, I talked Dad and Michael into going to Camp Boyhaven with me on a Boy Scouts trip. We stayed in my cheap three-man dome tent, which was sky blue and barely big enough to hold us. That first night, it started pouring rain, and the tent was absolutely not waterproof. Our sleeping bags were completely soaked through. We had to go inside a big tent that was owned by the scouts, where many others were fleeing the rain. The trip was an absolute, horrible disaster—and we never went camping again. The ruin of my own dome tent in the rain appeared to be some sort of "instant karma" for destroying the domed fort the big kids built—even though I was bullied into doing it against my will.

By the time I started eighth grade, Shane started sneaking into Corporations Park, which was a large former military base that had been converted into factories on the other side of the junior high and high school buildings. He would go into buildings that were left unlocked and take things like power drills. I was really surprised he was doing this, but he seemed to enjoy the thrill of it. He would run as hard as he could and had become very fast. His grades were very bad that year and he ended up flunking, which proved to be the best thing that could possibly have happened to him for his social life. The kids in the grade below us had no idea how everyone else saw him. He took his amazing running skills and put them to work on the track, turning himself into a star athlete with extreme popularity. I was one of the only people who knew, at first, how he got to be so fast. This was the first time I had ever gotten to know someone as a friend who was engaging in criminal behavior. Shane even stole things from me later on, including a Metallica CD, but I still forgave him. When I asked him why he did it, he said he didn't think I was listening to it anymore. I struggled for years to understand how the trauma of his childhood could have been so severe that he would be okay with hurting his own friends. I definitely believed in karma and was shocked that someone would knowingly do things that would require equally painful, crippling events to happen to them later on.

The bullies in gym class were getting worse and worse, particularly in the locker room. One kid said he wanted to show me a "super kick." I told him "no thank you," but he insisted—and did a full roundhouse kick, which landed in my gut. I nearly went down. A couple other laughing kids then grabbed me and got the idea that it would be really hilarious to drag me into the showers and saturate me with water. I was still holding on to my books and smelled the sharp sourness of locker-room sweat and mold as they carried me by the arms and legs, hovering two feet above the ground. I went limp so they would think I had given up. They loosened their grip and relaxed, just as I expected they would. I violently jerked out of their hands, abandoning my books all over the floor, and I scrambled out of there. I thought for sure they would destroy my books in the shower, but when I came back a few minutes later the books were still there, which seemed like a miracle.

That afternoon, I told my mother I absolutely needed to learn how to fight. Things were getting far too dangerous. She had already been encouraging me to find a self-defense class, and had volunteered to take me and pay for it, because she was genuinely afraid that I might get killed. I went through the yellow pages of the phone book and looked at all the different schools that were available.

The Martial Arts Studio

My gaze was drawn to the wild-eyed face of a tiger with its teeth bared. It was an ad for a martial arts studio, run by Ronnie LeBlanc. Mom called him up and explained what had happened to me, and then I got to talk to him myself. He said that his school taught you how to survive life-and-death situations, which he called street fighting. Most karate classes were teaching "tournament fighting," which had lots of rules to avoid people getting hurt and was nearly useless in the situations I was going through. I was sold from this one conversation. When Dad found out about it, he decided he wanted to take the classes himself, and offered to pay for it. He started taking Michael and me to these classes twice a week.

Mr. LeBlanc was a five-star black belt in at least three different major types of martial arts. His wall was lined with plaques showing he had finished first place in every martial arts tournament he had ever competed in. We learned how to throw punches and kicks against an eighty-pound bag. This included kicking the bag up from the bottom and getting it to rise by an entire foot. This caused crippling pain in my shins that made it hard to walk. The shins eventually became extremely strong due to "bone conditioning," in which micro-fractures heal stronger than ever. We had to block hard punches, which created bone conditioning in my wrists. We were also taught how to break every imaginable type of hold that someone could put you into. There would never be a "white wash" again. I could slam a bully in three different places and greatly injure him before he ever had the chance to knock me down.

Most important, we were going to learn how to go into a state called "Spirit," in which your body becomes impervious to physical pain. Even if you get a broken bone or a huge, bloody gash, you will still be able to finish the fight. One guy in the studio had had his stomach kicked open by a biker wearing a steel-toed boot. His intestine was hanging down like a jump rope, which he didn't even realize until the fight was over. He still managed to finish the battle and escape with his life.

In order to develop Spirit, we had to learn something called "The Form," which was a series of movements from the Pangai-noon kung fu style we were studying. They based it all on three animals: the tiger, the crane, and the dragon. The story was that at least two thousand years ago, the ancient Chinese studied five animals—the tiger, crane, dragon, bear, and snake—to see how they fought. The bear and snake were not used in our style. The tiger used "hard" techniques like punches and kicks—with lots of power but limited accuracy. The crane would coordinate its "hands" and feet to sweep out the legs of its opponent and make combined attacks. The dragon supposedly used "soft" techniques, in which you had to hit certain points with extreme accuracy, but the techniques were so devastating they didn't require very much force. We would first start learning the tiger form. As we advanced through the sashes, not belts, we would then be scheduled to learn the crane and dragon forms.

Mr. LeBlanc taught us that bullies do not want to feel pain, and will only go after the "easy kill" whom they can completely dominate with fear. If you fight back and hurt them, then even if you lose the fight, they will almost never want to try again. He also explained that even big, intimidating biker dudes in leather and chains will cry like little children if they take a really good strike or get put into submission with a crippling joint lock. The goal of our training was to devastate the opponent in three seconds or less, and then run. It was only meant to be used in life-threatening situations. We also were taught techniques that could kill an attacker with our bare hands in one strike, which I will not reveal here. We were told never to hit someone in a real fight except on one of the "targets," which removes the ability of his body to continue fighting by interrupting the activity of the nervous system. Cops have shot a three-inch-wide hole through the chest of someone on drugs like PCP only to be killed by that person in the several seconds before he died. If you hit such an attacker on one of the targets, however, he will go down.

We had extensive coaching on the legalities of fighting, and were told that if you killed someone, or even hurt them badly, you had to have absolute proof that they had presented you with an equally severe threat. Mr. LeBlanc also said that even if you were in the right, and had eyewitness proof, you might still end up going to jail—but that is better than being killed. Still, the best strategy was to go into Spirit, strike the attacker in at least one of the targets, and run away in three seconds or less. Mr. LeBlanc had been in so many life-threatening situations that he couldn't watch movies, because he couldn't stand seeing fights that went on and on. His blood would start pumping, time would slow down, his vision would narrow into a cone in front of him, and he would become hyperaware. This was all part of what was supposed to happen to you when you successfully went into Spirit—and it is exhausting and very intense.

Within a few months we started doing the Form in a style called "Form with Mechanics," in which we focused on doing the movements very slowly and very precisely—like a meditation. This led to "Form with Speed," in which we started practicing the same sequence much faster, and with power behind each of the movements. Just a few weeks later we started doing "Form with Spirit." I was taught to lock my abdominal muscles down into a wall, so even if I took a perfect punch to the solar plexus, I would not go down. It was extremely frightening to see someone go into Form with Spirit correctly, as the technique was based on the wild, snarling rage that animals would go into in a fight to the death—particularly tigers. You ended up making the same facial expression as the wide-eyed, ferocious tiger in the school's logo, and the roaring sounds that emerged were extremely fearsome. Just seeing and hearing this would make no one ever want to fight you.

Mr. LeBlanc explained that you were never supposed to be angry while you did this, despite how it looked. It was the "Spirit of Protectiveness," intended to save your own life and the lives of those you love. It naturally happens to animals so they will have a better chance of surviving a fight to the death, even if they have been seriously injured. Most people never reach this state even in a terrible fight, due to how we are programmed to be afraid and to avoid pain. If someone does manage to achieve this state of consciousness, it is usually a blind rage of total wildness, in which the person is unable to move or strategize effectively. Typically they will shake so much that they can be very easily knocked over and defeated. We were taught to enter into this state in a split second, lock down into our stance, and have complete control and awareness of our environment once we were in it. Everything went into slow motion, which made three seconds seem like plenty of time to finish the fight.

I strongly disliked doing it, but he was right—I would feel time slow down to a crawl, I would have the feeling of Kool-Aid running through my veins, and I would become hyperaware of the world around me—almost super-aware. Even though I looked and sounded extremely frightening, the goal was to be completely in control of the experience. The speed and precision of the movements I did in Form with Spirit made me very fast, tremendously improving my dexterity. Just as Mr. LeBlanc had said, it became painful to watch movie fights because of how slow they were. I cringed in *The Matrix* when Morpheus told Neo, "You're faster than this," and they continued moving like they were trapped in molasses. CGI was used to make Neo's arms appear to move faster in one scene, but at the shoulders, where it really mattered, it was still slow. This training also helped me develop the ability to play blistering-fast drum solos by the time I graduated college with a jazz minor.

I did feel something like an extreme runner's high from doing Form with Spirit, and afterward I would be exhausted—but we continued practicing the technique. We were also told it was extremely important never to tell anyone that we knew Form with Spirit, as people would invariably ask you to spar with them. In our system, everything involved devastating the opponent in as little as one strike. The goal is to completely shut down the normal functioning of the opponent's body. This meant I had to be very careful in a typical school fight, so I could avoid seriously damaging or even killing someone. The reason I am sharing this with you now is I feel it is very important to learn self-defense. I was able to walk fearlessly in any area and know I could take care of myself in any situation. I realized that fear was a "nudge" that could be greatly reduced, if not eliminated with meditation. My out-of-body experience had convinced me of the reality of life after death, and therefore I didn't even have to fear a situation where I might get killed. I would always exist. This training ultimately gave me the courage to step into the front lines of the battle we are all facing against a global villain who wishes to kill billions of people.

Fighting Back

My next fight happened very early in the training, before I even started learning Form with Spirit. A skinny kid with long brown hair and crooked teeth came up to me in a classroom when only a few others were there. He started insulting my weight with curse words, while laughing and smiling. He was absolutely surprised when I suddenly rushed him. I grabbed him by both shoulders and roared like a lion as I slammed his body through about seven desks. His back hit the wall—hard. I had just rearranged an entire quarter of the room, clumping all the desks together into a cluster on either side of my path. The impact partially knocked the wind out of him. I kept him pinned there and looked at him with the eyes of a murderous tiger, letting him know if he did anything else I could tear him to pieces. He was totally shocked, sucking wind in wide-eyed terror, and he backed off. I let him go and he never tried to bully me again. The word quickly got around that something had changed, and the number of bullying episodes immediately went way down.

By the time I had my next fight, I had been doing lots of work on a technique called "close-quarters fighting," or "sticky wrists." The idea was to invade the opponent's space, so you were only a foot away from his face. This would make him uncomfortable and he would try to back up to hit you, which would be his downfall. You kept both your wrists against his wrists, so you always knew where his hands were going. Then we were taught all these fluid movements that would allow us to block his hands while still being able to get strikes in at every opportunity. It was like a martial arts chess game, and a successful punch usually in-volved curving around one of his arms. We practiced this for long peri-ods of time at a slow speed; the idea was that it would come naturally by instinct once you needed it—and would be happening at a much greater velocity.

This jock kid, Steve, thought it would be funny to try to slap me outside the gym one day, after he had repeatedly tried to check me pretty hard in the class with his lacrosse stick. I wasn't even afraid of him. I started smiling as I effortlessly blocked every strike he tried to throw, while repeatedly tapping him very lightly in the forehead with my fin-gers, again and again, with both my left and right hands. By doing this, I let him know I could have completely devastated him. Other kids saw this and started laughing. I was at least twice as fast as he was, and he didn't stand a chance. I laughed like a sarcastic bully as he got more and more upset, and it broke my concentration. He backed up and got one really good slap in on my left cheek—hitting me in the face so hard that he left red fingermarks. I shoved him back, causing him to tumble helplessly to the ground. "Don't ever do that again." He never did. In fact, he decided it was a lot safer to be nice to me, and even joked around with me after that—but he did knock me over badly in a lacrosse game two years later. There was always a payback. Not only did you have karma to worry about, you had the people themselves—and their friends.

CHAPTER EIGHT

The Dark Night of the Soul

The last time I ever went on a Boy Scouts trip was shortly after that fight. They took us to Plattsburgh Air Force Base, and we stayed in the same barracks and toured all the same buildings we would have seen if we had been recruited or drafted. My father had warned me severely against joining the military, as a drill sergeant had once told him, "Once you sign on the line, your ass is mine." We were already wearing military-style uniforms and going through training that would increase our rank, giving us visible badges to wear. Boy Scouts was a gateway drug to the military—and there was something extremely haunting and terrifying about the base. I still had enough ESP to sense clearly the stench of death everywhere. The men who stayed there feared for their lives and were extremely depressed about having to leave their homes, friends, and family.

About a week later, I went to Kevin's house, and we decided we were going to set up his tent and camp in the backyard. He insisted that we bring everything out in one trip, and it was exhausting. I tried to help him, but I didn't understand how his tent worked. "Go away, David. You don't know what the hell you're doing." I went over to his hammock, fearlessly threw myself into it, and was finally able to lie down, after multiple failed attempts on previous visits when my fear had compromised me. Now he was working and I was kicking back. He tried to get his dog, Excalibur, to charge me and knock me down, but it didn't work.

"Get off your lazy ass and come help me with this thing!" I did get out, but then I took plenty of time to clean off the leaves I had left there. I did not like his abusive attitude at all.

Suddenly I heard a whooshing noise behind me. I turned my head and saw a brief flash of silver and light. *WHAM!* Something hit me in the head—very, very hard. This time it was on the left, right around my ear. The pain was unimaginable—even worse than the ice rock. The outside edge of my ear was in absolute agony—as if it was being stabbed with a knife and burned with white-hot fire at the same time. I instinctively grabbed it and started running around his yard, screaming. He laughed and got Excalibur to chase me: "Go get him, girl!" This collie, who looked just like the TV dog Lassie, was happy to run behind me. When I continued screaming and crying, he started calling me a pussy and saying nothing had happened, I was fine, and I should shut up. I collapsed on the ground and Excalibur started licking my hand, causing huge and disgusting sounds to echo in my ear. I pulled my hand away and it was completely covered in red, top to bottom. You couldn't see any skin. My white shirt was also splattered with red drops everywhere. I was utterly horrified that this vampire dog was drinking my blood. It took many years for me to realize that she was trying to help save my life by cleaning and sealing the wound.

Kevin ran up, saw the blood, and started chanting, "Oh my God, oh my God," as he rushed me into the house. He then made me stay alone in the bathroom with the door closed while he called his parents and asked them what to do. He said they had an HMO and they could help me. He told me not to look at myself in the mirror, and opened out the cabinet doors so they were facing the wall. Then he left. My skull and my ear were throbbing in unimaginable pain, which made the smell of the mouthwash, old soap, and mildew in the bathroom much worse. After a few minutes of standing there listening to him freak out behind a closed door, I soberly turned the mirror toward myself. A perfectly circular ring had been carved through the flesh and cartilage on the rim of my ear.

I did not cry. It was actually a very clear moment. This had happened to me. It was real. I had sustained an injury but I was alive and I would be fine. Kevin had obviously thrown an aluminum tent pole at me because he didn't feel I was moving fast enough to help him. This was another case of "too much revenge"—and now his ridiculous bullying had failed miserably. His parents told him their HMO couldn't do anything for me, and I should call my mother and have her come get me. I told her Kevin had "thrown a tent pole into my ear," and she thought it had actually gone down my ear canal, so she was very relieved when she saw it was only a round circle on the edge. We loaded my bike in the car, went home, and put a gauze bandage on my ear, but for the next three days it swelled horribly, was extremely painful, and turned a dark bluish-black all over.

When Dad found out what had happened, and that we hadn't told him up until then, he was furious. He rushed me over to a plastic surgeon's office on Union Street in Schenectady. I was told that most of the pole had chopped straight through my ear from one side to the other like a cookie cutter. The entire round piece in the middle had enough blood flow to stay alive, but it could easily die—in which case he would have to reconstruct it with cartilage and skin grafts from other parts of my body. I needed surgery ASAP, and I was booked to go back again two days later. In surgery, I lay there on the operating table like a wounded animal and shuddered in shock as the surgeon injected my ear in multiple places with Novocain—but I did not cry. Each time he pushed the needle in, I could feel it *pop-pop-popping* through multiple layers of skin and cartilage, and it was unbelievably painful. At this point all he could do was cut off the extra scar tissue of cartilage that had formed around the wound. He also concluded the middle piece was probably going to live.

He told me I needed to massage the scar as much as I could, no matter how painful it was, because otherwise the swelling could get really bad. He also told me I would need to wear a gauze bandage over it at all times for at least a month, and that if anyone hit me there I might need surgery again. This was a field day for all the kids who hated me at school. I now had a great vulnerability and a delicious new target for their bullying in addition to my increasing weight. Everyone started calling me "Vincent Van Gogh" and "Vinnie." I had kids crying "Vinnie" with joy from all the way down a long hallway whenever they saw me. I didn't dare try to fight anyone, because if they hit me on the ear, they could force me right back into surgery—and it would hurt so much I would be physically devastated. At one point someone new asked me what the heck had happened to my ear, and wondered if I had fallen off my bike. The kid I had tapped on the forehead said, "Kevin threw a driveway at him." Everyone exploded into laughter at his lame joke, since they all knew the story.

The whole area was red and swollen like a cherry tomato after the injury first happened. I kept the bandage on my ear for at least two months so the kids couldn't see it. Thankfully, the little round piece in the middle survived, but I decided that I was not going to cut my hair, at least not until it became long enough that it could completely cover my ear. Dad got a lawyer and we threatened to file a lawsuit against Kevin and his family's health insurance company. Since Kevin's parents would scream at him if he got anything less than a ninety-five, they were absolutely disgusted with me for going after their "perfect" son.

Our lawyer was a snarky old Jewish lady with stacks of papers all over her desk and office. A few shards of light tore through the old wooden blinds, revealing all the hanging dust grains and helping to fight the pale fluorescent lighting in the room. No matter what question I tried to ask her about strategy, she kept repeating, "The less you say, the better" in a strong accent. This did make me mad, but it was obviously the one and only thing she was going to tell me to do.

My meeting with the insurance claims adjuster was scheduled to occur at Kevin's house, which was horrible. Dad went with me and reminded me of what the old lady had said. The adjuster had wet, curly blond hair, thousands of gleaming-white teeth, an athletic build, tanned skin, and a flawless suit. Kevin's parents glared at me with absolute, seething hatred as I answered every single question Mr. Smiles, the adjuster, asked me with as few words as possible—if not single words. Everyone knew what I was up to, but Smiles couldn't do anything about it. He couldn't catch me. The insurance company paid my medical bills and gave me a $2,000 settlement, which Dad invested into a CD that wouldn't mature until I was in college. This was another one of the great traumas of my life. I had to face off against one of my best friends and all I got out of it was a small amount of money that I would never see until I was far too old for it to matter. My parents didn't have to pay my medical bills, but I lost my best friend in the process. Kevin never spoke to me again. I felt no satisfaction in fighting and "winning" that battle. Kevin did have negative behaviors, but he may have become a better friend if I hadn't threatened his family with a lawsuit. The great spiritual teachings tell us that forgiveness stops the wheel of karma—preventing the same cycles of joy and disaster from perpetually reappearing in our lives with new sets and characters. The balance between forgiveness and self-protection is one of the great "gray areas" in the ascension path, ripe for endless amounts of contemplation and study.

The Iran-Contra Hearings

In the summer of 1987, things got totally bizarre when the Iran-Contra hearings began airing on television as of June 30. I was a fourteen-year-old kid still living under constant threat of nuclear war with the USSR, even though they were making moves toward peace, including *glasnost* and *perestroika*. Here was Lieutenant Colonel Oliver North on national television, openly admitting that he was involved in financially supporting a cocaine-dealing terrorist group out of Nicaragua called the Contras. Even worse, he was secretly selling weapons to Iran, despite it being illegal under US law, since they were considered a terrorist dictatorship. North was instructed to use the Iranian blood money to fund and train the terrorist Contras. This was also illegal under US law. The administration hoped that the Contras would fight a guerilla war to topple the Soviet-friendly government in Nicaragua at the time, run by a group called the Sandinistas. Apparently, when we were supposed to like a group of terrorists, the media called them "militants" or "rebels," and that somehow made their actions okay. Examples of US-supported "rebels" were Bin Laden and the Taliban, back when the Soviets held Afghanistan. A senate hearing in March 1985 revealed evidence that the Contras were in fact terrorists. The International Human Rights Law

Group, which gathered 145 sworn statements from twenty-eight eyewitnesses, said, "The documentation shows a pattern of brutality against largely unarmed civilians, including rape, torture, kidnappings, mutilation, and other abuses."[24] During this same time, President Ronald Reagan had referred to the Contras as "the moral equivalent of the Founding Fathers."[25]

This scandal was investigated by the US Congress as well as a three-person team appointed by President Reagan called the Tower Commission. Reagan seemed just like Mr. Smiles when he got on television, shrugged his shoulders, and said he knew nothing about it, but he understood that his guys were just trying to do their part to fight the evil Soviet Union and protect us from nuclear war. I assumed that Ollie North had been severely bullied, since I knew what that looked like. I intuitively felt that they had threatened to rape, torture, and murder his entire family tree if he didn't take the fall, blame it all on himself, and say that it was his idea. Years later, insiders would tell me that this happens constantly in the Cabal. Anyone who steps out of line is threatened with extreme torture and death for their entire family tree. This is part of how the Cabal has been able to maintain power for so long. It is difficult for newcomers to truly understand just how evil this group really is. Reagan and Vice President George H. W. Bush were cleared of any and all charges, even though handwritten notes from Defense Secretary Caspar Weinberger on December 7, 1985, showed that Reagan knew that arms were being sold to Iran in exchange for the release of seven American hostages held in Lebanon.

Only five individuals were charged for supporting the Nicaraguan terrorists, but those charges were conveniently dropped after the administration refused to declassify the documents that proved them, due to "national security." I sensed there were some good guys in the Pentagon who were fighting for us, knew what these documents contained, and thought they could stop the threat of nuclear war by bringing down the whole administration—but it didn't work. It would be many years before I came into direct contact with people working for this secret alliance.

Fourteen officials were ultimately indicted for lesser charges, and the trail of corruption went all the way up to Defense Secretary Caspar

Weinberger. Eleven of these men were convicted. Some filed appeals and got away with it. I was amazed that George H. W. Bush won the election in 1988, just a year after this worse-than-Watergate scandal. All Nixon did was bug the offices of the Democrats. The Reagan administration was caught actively financing, arming, and training two different groups of terrorists. Everyone who had been indicted or convicted was pardoned in the final days of George H. W. Bush's four-year presidency, once it was already too late for anyone to stop him.[26]

I decided that if the government could hide or destroy documents and avoid getting punished, then so could I. Every day I started checking the mail as soon as I came home from school. The dreaded progress reports came in a predictable computer-printed envelope with all-capital letters in the window. I was now a master of mixing up blazing KNO3 and sugar mixtures on the backyard patio, as well as lighting firecrackers under an old shot glass—which caused the glass to rocket up into the air, thanks to the potato-gun effect. I burned those evil progress reports to a crisp and crushed the ashes. It was a matter of "national security." Now the only thing I had to worry about was the report cards, which threatened my administration with criminal charges, indictment, trade sanctions, and an embargo that cut off all my supply lines—and kept me confined in my bedroom prison cell. I was starting to engage in "repetition compulsion"—mirroring the negativity I was seeing in the world with my own thoughts and actions. It took many years to identify this subconscious process and identify how it was working at this time in my childhood.

The Final Four Rounds

In the fall of 1987, I started high school, which was just as terrible as going into junior high—if not worse. Now there were three more grades of kids who were older than me. I was getting more and more overweight, topping out with 225 pounds at five feet nine inches. I had a big belly that some people called a "spare tire," as well as the equally hideous "man boobs." If I pulled my lower jaw in toward my neck, it formed a nasty double chin. Everyone asked me if I had seen the pool on the third floor—but there was no third floor. This was a typical stunt to harass freshmen on their first day.

More and more at this time, MTV was featuring bands with openly satanic imagery, including upside-down pentagrams, demons, and the like. I was surprised that this was being so openly promoted, but I had also discovered that this music helped me release anger and feel better. I would get a cathartic high from listening to it, much like Dr. van der Kolk's soldiers with PTSD who watched a war movie and experienced a high equivalent to shooting eight milligrams of morphine. I started wearing nothing but black rock-and-roll T-shirts that Dad was buying me for twenty bucks each at some of the concerts we went to. My hair was long enough that I didn't need to wear the gauze on my ear anymore, and I was quickly starting to look like a "metal head."

I felt like I had no friends. Shane had flunked eighth grade and didn't make it to high school with the rest of us. Eric and Dave were part of a small group I called the "geek clan," and the only thing we had in common was that everyone else hated us. Now I could win any fight that someone tried to start, but that didn't mean anyone liked me—so I was miserable. I started drawing weird and disturbing sketches of suicide, where I killed myself in extremely bizarre, creative, and grandiose ways. I knew I would never actually do it, but I honestly felt like I had nothing to live for. I was now mirroring the collective trauma of the nuclear "suicide cult" that America had become. School was a nightmare. I kept getting bigger and bigger, my skin was a mess, and I was constantly depressed.

The Soldier of Fortune

On the first day of high school, a new kid showed up whom we will call Don. He was chubby like me, had wavy light-brown hair, pale skin, and freckles, and wore large glasses with a double-bar frame over the top. The bullies in his old school had called him Froggy. He was sitting with his head down on the desk next to me as if he had passed out, which was quite surprising. I could hardly believe my eyes when Eric walked in and pounded his fist on this new kid's desk, causing him to bolt up and start cursing at him as if they knew each other. I started talking to Don and found out that he had stayed every summer at the camp Eric's family owned, so they knew each other very well. He seemed to be a friend of Eric's, in a sense, but Eric was just as arrogant and dominant toward him as he was toward me. We became best friends almost instantaneously, and bonded over our deep mutual hatred of Eric. Sometimes we called him Erico, like he was a gangster.

I quickly found out that Don was very interested in ninjas, weapons, and the military. He subscribed to *Soldier of Fortune* magazine, which he called *SOF*, and fantasized over all the pictures of throwing stars, darts, swords, switchblades, nunchaku or "nunchucks," and various guns and bullets. He was particularly obsessed with a completely illegal spring-loaded weapon called an "angel blade," where you hit a button and the knife popped straight out. He talked about how you could file the nut down and the blade would shoot out of the housing like a bullet. He had constant fantasies of violent revenge against the kids who had bullied him just as badly as they had me. I let him know if he wounded or killed anyone, it would destroy his life. I spent months explaining to him what had happened to my father in Vietnam, and strongly encouraged him not to sign up for the military as he could very easily get killed. Still, we spent countless hours killing bad guys in games like *Rush'n Attack* for the new Nintendo Entertainment System, which was much more addictive than Atari. We started walking to his house together after school with Eric, Dave, and another kid in our "geek clan" who also lived nearby.

Teenagers Who Are Going to Burn in the Lake of Fire Forever

The other kid I met that year was Jude Goldman, who was in a grade above me. They mixed grades in gym class, so you had two years' worth of kids who had to work together. Jude was just as weird, creative, and intelligent as I was, with wild brownish-black hair that was long on top and short on the sides. He dyed part of his mane to make it a blondish-brown color. He was short and thin, had round Lennon glasses, full facial stubble, and a deep voice. Women invariably found him attractive. He rode a skateboard, wore strange and funky clothes, played music, and somehow had managed to stay cool in his grade. He had a very fast and witty sense of humor that I could keep up with. He started out by teasing me in gym class like everyone else did, but the more we bantered, the more he realized that we had more in common than anyone else in school. He eventually gave me a tape of the music he had been making at home, which he called Organized Noise.

I found out that his mother was an ex-hippie and minor movie star who had joined a commune, only to leave it in disgust and convert to become an extreme fundamentalist Christian. As a result, Jude hated everything having to do with the hippie music and culture—but we were still great friends. His mother played taped sermons from her preacher nonstop, all day and all night. This guy had a laughably extreme southern accent, even greater than what George W. Bush sounded like, and was quite a character—the most exaggerated stereotype of a fire-and-brimstone Bible-thumper imaginable. Rapture was about to cause his flock to soar into the air at any moment, while everyone else was doomed to roast in eternal hellfire. We smuggled out a tape and my favorite passage was: "Young people—you've watched them—walking into a Christless hell. I'm talking about teenagers that are going to burn in the lake of fire forever. You can't help them, but you can start praying for them—and get the burden and the grief of their loss to your gain." His other classic quotable line was, "He's gonna take a group of people, not everyone, not everyone, 'cause you're not gonna make it."

Jude's mom constantly yelled at him over the most ridiculously minor things. He wasn't allowed to listen to any music that wasn't 100 percent born-again Christian, and nothing could interrupt the nonstop twenty-four-hour loop of sermons—so the entire area underneath his mattress was lined with hidden tapes of all his favorite bands. She once found his copy of Prince's album *Dirty Mind*, which led to an "emergency meeting" with her church elders. They told Jude he could never listen to any of Prince's music again or he would become gay. After that incident, he got much better at hiding his music, and his mother never again discovered his precious contraband. His grandparents had enough money to buy him an Alesis Midiverb, which allowed him to put an echo on instruments and voices, along with a multitrack tape-cassette recorder and a Casio SK-1 sampling keyboard. He had bad allergies, and every time he took his medicine his mind got weird and spacey. This was when he wrote the Organized Noise music. Despite using a dirt-cheap keyboard with terrible sounds, he still managed to do some very unique, interesting, and bizarre stuff. The sampler was the key. Any sounds he could find could be looped and turned into music.

The summer of 1988 brought an end to my freshman year, and I was still quite depressed. I was playing drums more and more, and Jude and I were talking about starting a band since he had a cheap knockoff Paul McCartney–style bass that he had painted all sorts of words and images onto, including his name. He was self-taught on the bass and the keyboard and could do enough to get by on either instrument.

One of the concerts I went to that summer was Dokken, where I saw the very drunk lead singer backstage being surrounded by a crowd of about eleven incredibly hot women in miniskirts. From my perspective, any one of them would be a keeper for life—and everywhere he went, they followed, like baby chicks. He was saying really silly things that weren't very funny, but every time he made even the weakest attempt at humor, they exploded into giggles as if he was hilarious. He also got huge points for playing Led Zeppelin on the stereo system.

Once again, I was seeing the same story. Rock stars were just ordinary people who worked hard, learned how to sing or play an instrument, started a band, wrote some decent songs, got signed, and ended up making the record label enough money that they went on tour. The tours would just about kill these guys. Almost every band I ever met was extremely exhausted, constantly fighting not to get sick, and prisoners of the tour bus. All the cities just blended together and the idea of going home seemed like an impossible dream. Tours could go on for an entire year, with dates every two or three nights and no vacations—ending with just enough time to record another album and repeat the process. Bon Jovi captured this dilemma perfectly in their classic tune "Wanted

Dead or Alive"—and two or three times a month I witnessed what guys like this were going through firsthand. Even though it was obviously a very hard life, I would have been more than happy to get my own chance at suffering with unstoppable female attention and screaming crowds every other night. It didn't matter what you looked like. Once you were up on that stage, you were in.

This was the promise of glory that we were all taught to aspire to by the media. Like addicts, many of us lust for the high of fame and recognition, which has become more of an issue now than ever with the rise of social media. Yet, every time I met the people who had "made it," they were totally miserable. I ultimately coined the term "Elvis-Marilyn Syndrome" to describe this. Elvis and Marilyn were two of the greatest celebrities of the twentieth century, known by their first names. Yet they both died alone, drug addicted and miserable. I have spoken to various well-known film actors since moving to Los Angeles, and they all have said that they are treated very disrespectfully by the upper-level bosses in Hollywood, even when they are succeeding. As soon as one of their films doesn't sell well, they get dumped—and former celebrities often refer to themselves as "veterans." Many famous musicians told me the same story. Recognizing the illusion of celebrity and the truth of Elvis-Marilyn Syndrome, and learning to be at peace with who you are, is a key element of the ascension process. You ultimately have to choose to be happy no matter how many goals and successes you seem to have achieved—and a life of simplicity can be far more rewarding than the constant chaos involved in being a public figure.

Out of Control

That same summer of 1988, Dad took Michael and me on a trip to Lake George for his friend Rick Siciliano's birthday. Rick was the drummer and lead singer in the Out of Control rhythm and blues band, a local group, and was also a professional photographer. He was big, tall, and fairly muscular, had bulgy, animated eyes, and was by far the funniest, wittiest, and most sarcastic person I had ever met. It was impossible to keep up with him; sometimes he would say things that made me feel terrible until I couldn't help but explode into laughter along with everybody else. We all drove up in Rick's weird-smelling green van, and when we were already in the Adirondacks, he brushed his teeth in the driver's seat. He tried to spit the toothpaste out the window while going sixty-five miles an hour. The toothpaste flew all over the side of his van in long white streaks, and he made a huge joke out of it. You were constantly laughing until your stomach hurt around Rick.

Rick's first birthday cake was chocolate, with no candles, and Dad shoved it in Rick's face. Everyone roared with laughter, including Rick, who milked it for all it was worth. The second cake was larger and had white frosting with candles. After Rick got cleaned up, we all went out into his sailboat on the lake—and disaster struck. Clouds rolled in. The wind howled. Lightning crashed and the rain was cutting us apart. In a horrific groan, the normal upright angle of the boat tilted and was now listing very badly, lying nearly sideways on the water. Dad and Rick had Michael and me hide in the cabin so we were less likely to get washed away—but that didn't help us very much.

Michael and I were standing on what was supposed to be the sidewall, and we could look down and see water in the windows that would normally be at eye level. For at least fifteen minutes, I absolutely believed we were about to die. We were screaming and crying in terror. We kept looking at each other and thinking we were only seconds from having water explode into the cabin. Even if we managed to survive the sinking of the boat with our life jackets, the water might be cold enough to kill us from hypothermia—and we were much too far from the shore to swim back. I reached a supreme moment of clarity, even in the midst of screaming—and realized that I definitely did not want to leave this world. In that moment, I prayed to God to save my life, I apologized for the wrongs I had done and begged for another chance—even though I did not consider myself a Christian. In that sudden instant when you believe you are about to die, it is amazing how quickly you go back to the basics. As soon as I surrendered and made that request from deep within myself, things changed. Somehow they managed to get the boat upright, and we limped back to shore. I was shattered from nerves and adrenaline, but I definitely noticed the synchronistic timing between my prayer and the solving of the problem. Dad said we had been in much greater danger of being struck by lightning than of sinking. The whole thing was incredibly traumatic for all of us.

This Is My Son

As I entered tenth grade in 1998, I decided I wanted to get a class ring, and picked out a silver-colored choice with a blue aquamarine stone. We had to go to the local jewelry store to place the order. My hair had become so long by this point that the old woman asked my mother what kind of ring her "daughter" wanted. Mom said, "This is my son," and the whole thing was incredibly awkward. It only caused me to feel even more traumatized and drawn into myself.

Luckily, I was struck with amazingly good fortune by ending up in the same chemistry class as Jude, with Mr. Olson as our teacher. We sat right next to each other, and this was where the great majority of our friendship in high school actually played out, other than in the lunch room. I ended up having a very hard time with chemistry class, because I could not visualize little particles whirling around a nucleus. Normally when I was tapping into a scientific truth, my ESP would kick in with visions of what something looked like—but with the chemistry models they were trying to teach me, I drew a complete blank. It would be many years before I discovered the scientific proof to back up what I did see, which was the lattices of sacred geometry. Over the course of a year, I ended up failing the class—I would have to go to summer school, which was something I never even imagined was possible. Kevin's parents couldn't handle less than a ninety-five. He and I were of comparable intelligence. Failing a class and attending summer school, particularly with how strict my parents were about good grades, was literally unthinkable—but it happened.

The Salem Witch Trials Revisited

Shortly after the school year started, while it was still fairly warm outside, my tenth-grade Honors English class went on an all-day field trip to Salem, Massachusetts. We visited the very place where all the events of *The Scarlet Letter* had occurred; we had read the book in class. The original buildings where women were tortured and executed for witch-craft were still standing. I touched the gnarled wood of ducking tanks in which people were put to death by drowning by religious fanatics. I real-ized that this sort of bullying was still going on today, and I was a victim of it myself—though, thankfully, I hadn't died. The whole place radiated with the evil of what had been done—all in the name of God.

We were all thrown in together on the long bus ride, and I ended up talking to the ultimate girl of my dreams, whom we will call Brenda Fisher. She seemed so completely out of my league that it was ridiculous to even talk to her, but I was immensely attracted to her for her sharp wit, her sarcastic sense of humor, and her incredible ability to stand up to the teacher and anyone else who stood in her way. She definitely ap-peared to be the most powerful woman in my grade. If anyone had tried to put her on trial for being a witch, she would have torn them to pieces. I had studied palm reading ever since junior high school, thanks to read-ing the book *Palmistry* by Edith Niles, and was able to tell her several things about herself that were very accurate. Most people think the lines on the hand are fairly random, but I have cross-checked the data in the book on hundreds of different hands over the years and found it to be remarkably precise in describing the individual's character, personality, and future. The Salem trip only confirmed that Brenda was "the one."

Someone Is Hiding in There

Not long after I got back from Salem, a female student teacher from one of my classes ran into me in the hallway over by the auditorium. She was disarmingly attractive. For some strange reason, she stopped me in the hallway, gazed into my eyes without speaking for a minute, took a sud-den breath, and then said, "You have unusually beautiful eyes."

She then went on to insult me: "There is a beautiful man hiding in-side all that weight and hair, and you should let him come out." She paused as the seismic wave of shock rippled through me from what she had just said. Then she touched me on the arm and gave me a million-dollar smile that could melt steel. Admittedly, I was dumbstruck that she would make such a brazen statement, but instead of getting angry or defensive, I soberly thanked her for the compliment. I soon started having sudden flashes when I looked into the mirror of what my face would look like without the hair and the weight—essentially the way I look now. Within less than six months I started a rigorous diet that I did not stop until I had lost eighty-five pounds.

Brad ended up sitting next to me in my tenth-grade French class. He knew my mother had visited a hippie commune called Totem, and I had shown him a big bag of Totem weed hiding in the basement freezer. I now had the complete look and feel of a pot-smoking fifteen-year-old—the long hair, the black rock-and-roll T-shirts, and the "don't mess with me" attitude. Brad rekindled our friendship for the third time, and every day he relentlessly pressured me to try weed. He told me it would set me free and it would be the greatest I had ever felt in my life. I made the mistake of telling him how fascinated I was by Brenda Fisher. I had no idea that he had already made out with her at a party, and possibly more than that, but he had since dumped her. He reconnected with her, and then told me the impossible: "Brenda wants to hang out with you. With us. Both of us!" He watched as disbelief flickered over my face for several seconds. Then he continued by saying, "As long as she gets to smoke some of your mom's Totem weed with us. She thinks that would be totally amazing—and hopes you will say yes."

I felt like I was falling into a bottomless pit. I asked him if she would still want to hang out with us if we didn't do drugs—and he said no. Although it was a common thing for rock-and-rollers to smoke weed, I was just fifteen years old. It was illegal, and at that time no one talked about it having any medical uses. The attitude around it was vastly more suppressive than we see today. In health class we were taught that marijuana was extremely destructive—and no one dreamed of taking on all those symptoms voluntarily. It took me almost half a minute of gaping silence, my mind running thousands of desperate calculations, before I told Brad I needed twenty-four hours to give him an answer. He just smiled. I was the delicious white rabbit that had stepped perfectly into his snare. It was already too late.

The glow of the pipe lit up Brenda's stunningly gorgeous face as we shivered in the cold under the pine tree in late October. She had stolen a metal screen from her jewelry class. Brad had stolen some copper pipe parts from his mother's basement and fashioned a crude but effective pipe out of them, wrapping the whole thing up in duct tape. A yellow electrical cap with a hole at the end became the mouthpiece. Everything seemed to be pulsing with light and geometric patterns. I was incredibly high, and the only thing I could compare it to was the feeling of opening presents on Christmas when I was a kid. Having Brenda there made it the greatest moment of my young adult life by far. She gave me a piece of Wrigley's Doublemint gum, and—my God!—it was the most magnificent combination of flavors I had ever tasted. Suddenly I was skiing down a gorgeous mountain—just as the commercials had programmed me to think. As we staggered toward the door of her house, she asked me in rapture if I could get her any more. I managed to throw my arm around her shoulder, lean in, and say, "I can get you anything you need."

Her house was hot and bright and filled with college kids. Brad was much too high, and this terrified him. I couldn't handle it either. When he managed to say, "Mom wants me back at the house in five minutes, we've gotta go," I said, "No problem"—and we were off, just like that. He insisted we run all the way home, just like we used to do after school. There were ice and wet leaves on the road and I nearly fell several times, but I managed to keep up with him. We were laughing the whole way as we slipped and slid.

I got home and collapsed on the couch. The surge of blood into my head caused the drug to take off like a rocket ship. I turned on the TV; it was the middle of *The Deer Hunter* on HBO, with scenes of a snowy wilderness and a pained guy holding a gun. I had no idea what was going on in the movie and I didn't care. Everything was spinning, the walls were pulsing, and the television seemed like it was three-dimensional. All sounds appeared to be reaching me through a long tunnel. The gum had become a dead, flavorless mass, but I was chewing it like my life depended on it. I wanted to go throw it out, but I absolutely could not move. In a sudden burst of inspiration, I spat the gum out as hard as I could, and it landed on the carpet seven feet in front of me. I laughed for about ten minutes at my staggering comic genius. Then I picked up the phone, called Don, and slurred, "Don, you've gotta come over here right now. You're not gonna believe this." As soon as he saw the state I was in, that was it. He was in.

CHAPTER NINE

Looking for a Way Out

Don, Brad, and I were all sharing a water pipe with Brenda, right there in my living room. We had found the archaic 1970s relic hiding in the basement. The device was dark blue and looked like two tiny lava lamps put together bottom to bottom. Brenda's flawless face was lit in perfect majesty as she again gurgled away, only to explosively cough it all out a second later. Thick smoke was hanging in the house, but this time it was not KNO3—and I was in no hurry to air it out. Brenda then asked me if it was okay to scrape out the last bits, since all of us were completely done, and I said, "Absolutely." She did as much as she could, and Don then had a great idea. He turned the pipe completely upside down and tapped out the rest of the cool ashes into her hand. "Oh, Don, you're a genius!" Before she even finished her sentence, the bong made a slurping sound and hideous brown bong water dribbled over her tight, acid-washed blue jeans. "Oh, Don, you're an asshole!" Everyone laughed again until we could barely even breathe.

Brenda came over only one more time after that. I knew I had no chance with her, and Brad never offered to bring her over again. That didn't matter, as I was now on an adventure of the mind, and had no intention of stopping. This was absolutely real; it lasted for four to six hours, and I knew exactly what all the hippies were so excited about. I figured it made them feel good, but I had had absolutely no idea that it was so powerful. The smell, the taste, the patterns, the colors, the music—everything was so much greater than I had realized. It was an amazing technology, and I had absolutely no right to hide it from the others. I had to tell the geek clan—Eric and the others—and set them free, just as I had done for Don.

Spreading the Word

Eric, Dave, and the others barely said a thing as they sat there in my bedroom while I laid out the case. I had already come up with a universe of rationalizations for my new addiction. They were very nervous as I told them the government was lying to us about this, just as they had about Watergate and the Iran-Contra hearings. This is something that God made. It grows out of the ground. It is a sacred tool for enhancing the mind and renewing the spirit. You have no right or reason to feel bad about anything in your life with a technology like this at your disposal. It is ridiculous not to do it. People can smoke their entire lives and be perfectly happy and productive members of society. The symptoms they talk about in health class are just propaganda. No one said a word during or after my manifesto. I had no idea at the time how far downward my life was going to go. Very awkwardly, Eric finally said, "We've gotta go," and they all got up and left. The next day, it was over. None of them ever wanted to speak to me again—except to taunt me by saying, "Hey, pot-head" in the hallway. That was totally fine. We didn't need them anyway. Inside I felt horribly betrayed and even more alone—but the chemicals fogged it all out of my mind.

I tried to get Jude to smoke, but given what he and his mother had been through at the hippie commune, he wanted nothing to do with it. Besides, he already had his allergy medicine. Now we took the band seriously, with Jude on bass, yours truly on the drums, my brother as the lead singer, and Michael's friend Andy as our crunch-guitarist. We originally called ourselves Jude and the Sewer Rats, but then my brother was offended by singling Jude out, so we just shortened it to the Sewer Rats. We did not rehearse. Just as with Organized Noise, if we could fight our way through a song while the tape was recording, that was it—we were done.

Since we had no idea what the heck we were doing, we took simple nursery rhymes like "Mary Had a Little Lamb" and "The ABC Song" and metalized them. This evolved into original material, and long, improvised jams where Jude and I would do unusual things that rocked hard and were different from anything on MTV. We would listen to each other and I matched whatever he started doing on the drums, adding in interesting fills as we went. We needed a band photo, so to commemorate the occasion, Jude shaved the right side of my head bald. I made my remaining mass of locks rock-hard with Aqua Net hair spray and wore it to school, and people were completely shocked—it was one of the most outrageous haircuts in the building. This attracted tons of attention, and people were talking and laughing behind my back—but no one dared to face me except the math teacher. One day, I got a question wrong in math class and old man Causey said, "Maybe if you shave the other side of your head, you'll be able to think better." The entire class cried with laughter.

I did not want to "borrow" any more from Mom, so that meant I needed to buy some pot. One day, a long-haired kid named Dennis, who always wore Iron Maiden denim jackets to school, told Jude that he had taken five Vivarin caffeine pills before chemistry class—and you only needed one. Every time Mr. Olson asked the class a question, Dennis breathlessly barked the answer back so fast he could barely articulate the words—but he was correct every time. After class I asked him if he knew where I could score some weed, and he told me to come to his locker whenever with twenty-five dollars, and I would be all set.

Ben and the Hippie Van

I hadn't even finished blowing out my first hit of the stuff from Dennis before I realized this was much, much stronger than the Totem weed. I leaned back into my bed and the whole room was reeling. It was wonderful. I had gotten totally ripped off, but I didn't realize this until Don brought over his older brother Bob, who was a huge football player and very popular with the ladies in Jude's grade, the class of 1990. "This guy totally screwed you," he said. "You need to get in touch with Ben. He's like a brother to me. He's family. And he will set you up. Big-time."

Ben was an excellent mechanic, with bulging pecs, an athletic build, long wavy black hair tied into a ponytail in the back, a thin, pointy jaw, blue eyes, and a forgotten metal brace on one of his teeth that he had never pulled off. He almost always had machine-oil stains somewhere on his body, his hands were heavily calloused, and his blue jeans were filthy. He was very shy and constantly smiling; he looked like a psychedelic human koala bear. He had worked as a taxicab driver and his claim to fame was being able to smoke a bong with both hands while driving, and steering with his knee. He had fully restored a sputtering vintage Volkswagen hippie van, with blue sides, white trim, and the huge VW symbol on the front. It was filthy inside. It was perfect.

We parked behind the Ellis Hospital in Schenectady, in a wide-open parking lot area with no one in sight. The Moon was full and clear as I took my first hit off the new bong—I mean, the water pipe for the use of tobacco. I had just bought it at Orion, the local head shop on Jay Street in Schenectady that reeked of incense. Ben's stuff was even more powerful than Dennis's. This was now the greatest moment of my life. Everything came together—the Moon, the trees, the van, and the crisp night air. I was totally and profoundly addicted. I was having a mystical, almost religious experience—and thought no one could hear me as I murmured to myself, "I am going to do this for the rest of my life." Everyone started laughing. "You're damn right you are! She'll never leave you and she always puts out."

I now refer to marijuana as "the five-leaf lesson," and based on my own personal experiences, it is not a lesson I care to repeat. I ended up almost completely losing any ability to function as a happy, healthy adult.

Digging for Buried Treasure

Now it was my obligation to venture into my father's basement and unlock the treasures that awaited my new crew of explorers. My brother had already taped all the Led Zeppelin albums for me off the original vinyl on his record player. Now I went and retrieved albums like *Dark Side of the Moon, Meddle,* and *The Wall* by Pink Floyd; *Days of Future Passed* and

In Search of the Lost Chord by the Moody Blues; all the Hendrix albums; *Sgt. Pepper's Lonely Hearts Club Band* by the Beatles; and *Ricochet* and *Rubycon* by Tangerine Dream. I had done the research first, by asking my parents which were the best psychedelic albums of the 1960s and 1970s, and it really paid off. By far, my strongest experiences came off the Tangerine Dream albums. In fact, some of those trips were so intense that Don would beg me to turn the music off, because he was literally clenching his fists in terror until his knuckles turned white. All those worlds vanished when I hit stop, and in a few seconds he would beg me to turn it back on. I never let him down—and away we went.

By some divine miracle, Jude had secured an invitation to a private Christmas party for all the coolest seniors and a handful of cool juniors, even though he was only a sophomore. The guys all wore tuxedos and the girls wore prom dresses, but this was much better than the prom. The party took place at the huge family home of one of the wealthiest kids in town, and his parents actually allowed everyone to drink alcohol there. Somehow Jude was able to talk them into letting me in, since I was "his drummer." I had found an amazing black silk smoking jacket in my closet with a rock-star pattern made out of stylized record-album shapes. The basement of the party house had a house band of juniors and seniors who were pretty good; they were playing covers of the popular "hair metal" bands of the day, including "Talk Dirty to Me" by Poison. The entire basement was packed, flesh to flesh, with gorgeous girls pressed against guys in tuxedos. It was a feast for the eyes and the senses, and smoke clouds hung in the air. Jude managed to get permission for us to play after they left the stage, and although I was very nervous, I used the martial arts training to stay calm and centered. Jude cranked up the distortion on the bass and we launched into a loud, interesting, hard-rock jam, in which he kept trying out new ideas and I followed him on the drums wherever he went.

Everyone was cheering—and when I walked off that stage, I was a newly minted hero. The kids in Jude's class, as well as the older ones, had no idea who I was, or what my own classmates thought of me. They had seen me in some of their classes and now realized that I was a "rock star." The word quickly got around that I had met all the most famous musicians they worshipped on MTV. In one night, I went from having hardly any friends at all to being one of the weirdest, coolest kids in school—but only to the classes of 1990 and 1989. Women were talking to me with wide eyes, hoping to get their chance to meet the celebrities I routinely saw backstage. I managed not to gawk at their chests, but it probably wouldn't have mattered. A very attractive blond girl, who was wearing a tight red dress and was almost as tall as I was, got talking to me upstairs by the big Christmas tree, and it really looked like it was going somewhere until I found out she was only thirteen years old. Somehow I had been singled out by the one girl at the party who was even younger than I was, and she had obviously gotten in for her looks. I did not want to fall for "jailbait," so I was nice to her, but made no effort to take it any further.

Shortly afterward, a jock called "The Blakester" came up to me. He had the look and swagger of a young Frank Sinatra, and he was very drunk. He called me Cox, as in the mispronounced end of my last name, Wilcock, and threw his arm around me. His breath reeked of stale beer, cheese, and death. "Cox. Cox. Cox. You gotta dansh." I didn't understand what he was slurring. "You gotta DANSH, Cox! You gotta DANSH if you wanna get laid!" The Blakester took the lead, and soon we were leading a whole group of amazingly hot girls through the most ridiculous dance moves imaginable—like raking, shoveling, swimming, diving, wiggling, and digging. Once the music finally died down and there were no results, the Blakester gave me the bottom line. I needed to start working out, go on a diet, and lose the weight. As soon as I did that, with the talent he now knew that I had, I could snap my fingers and get any girl I wanted. He told me he would be right there by my side, yelling in my face as I did sit-up after sit-up. I would hate him more than I had ever hated anyone in my life—only to love him in the end when my whole universe changed and I was "The Man."

After the party, I was instantly promoted up to the "stage" area in the cafeteria, where only the coolest jocks sat. I found out that most of the jocks were drinking every weekend, and a surprising number of them smoked weed as well. They saw me as being very entertaining, and I told all my best stories of going backstage at rock concerts. Jude was up there too, and we traded off, creating lots of laughs at the table.

The Safe House

Somehow I was able to convince Mom to let me have friends come over and smoke weed at the house. She had told me before that she didn't want me to try it until I was sixteen, but that wasn't far away now, and she begrudgingly accepted it. Her main rule was that I couldn't do it during the week—and no alcohol was allowed in the house whatsoever. I agreed to those conditions. Brad's "master plan" had worked exactly as he had hoped. I now had the ideal weed-friendly "safe house" for gatherings. Shane had gone from being a "total loser" in my grade to the most popular kid in the class of 1992, thanks to his athletic abilities, weird skater clothes, and persona. Failing eighth grade had been an absolute godsend for him, and had earned him a cool new name: Baner. Chris, the same kid who had once shot me down Monkey Hill and insulted me every day about my sweatpants, was now a weekly fixture as well. Don was always there, as we were inseparable.

Jude almost never came over, as he had a hot young girlfriend from an extremely fundamentalist Christian family. Every time we made plans, she would seduce him with the offer of a night of secret lovemaking and get him to cancel out at the last minute. This became a source of incredible pain throughout the remainder of my high school years. We would make plans, I would set everything aside to have him come over as an exclusive so we could work on our music, but he would only make it about one out of every seven or eight times. This, coupled with my rapid onset of drug-numbed apathy, killed off our band within a month or two after the Christmas party.

Damaged Justice

On March 15, 1989, Dad took Michael and me to RPI Fieldhouse to see Metallica on their "Damaged Justice" world tour, supporting their hit new album *And Justice for All*. They had been a band only the real "burnouts," like Dennis, listened to, but then they came out with their video

and single "One," about a soldier whose mind was trapped in a motionless body, and the band became huge overnight. We saw them right as
they were cresting the wave of fame, on the fourth month of a grueling
yearlong world tour with no breaks. I smuggled a ten-inch-long Kodak
110 flash camera down the front of my pants, and miraculously the security guard waved his wand over everything but the camera and passed
me through.

The show was extremely loud and raunchy, but thankfully the label
only allowed a small group of people to go backstage. The guitarist, Kirk
Hammett, was so shy he hid in the hallway and wouldn't talk to anyone.
The lead singer, James Hetfield, was extremely tall and staggeringly
drunk. When I posed for a picture with him, he belched loudly, and it
reeked of beer and bile. We all laughed, which caused my brother to
wiggle the camera and ruin the shot. The drummer, Lars Ulrich, was
significantly shorter than I was, and I was dying to ask him some questions. Although he seemed uninterested in talking to me at first, since I
was a huge, hairy, sweat-drenched mess, I quickly found out that it was
the same story—they were already burned out, had a very difficult time
being famous, and were exhausted from touring. I was a prisoner in high
school and they were prisoners in a tour bus.

Lars confessed that he had tried to become a tennis pro, but had
failed. He had been playing drums for only three or four months when
he started in Metallica, but he could run really fast. He took those feet
and danced on the double-bass pedals, developing their now signature
sound.

After the pictures from the Metallica show were developed, I realized
I looked like a mess, and I needed to try to improve my appearance. I
had become hugely overweight, with a double chin that remained visible
no matter how I was holding my head. I had not cut my hair since getting hit in the ear, and before then my mother had always done it. The
hair I had now was the result of just letting it go, and I hadn't even tried
to comb or style it until I shaved the side. I wore it up at school only
about twelve times because it created such an intense reaction. Now I
wanted my hair to have a more stylized and feathered look, while keeping all the length—which would make me look even more like a true

metalhead. Baner's mother was always drunk, slurring her words, but she worked as a hairstylist, and he set up a deal through which she agreed to cut my hair in her house after work for five bucks. Don sat there in the linoleum kitchen that smelled like a sick dog as I told her I wanted her to take off only two inches, make it look good, and otherwise leave it the way it was. She slurred back, "Just two inches," and I said, "Yes, just two inches."

I was surprised that it was taking her so long, and it seemed like there was an awful lot of hair all over the ground. Don kept smiling as though he was trying not to laugh. To my horror, when it was all over she had given me the ultimate scumbag haircut, also known as the mullet—short on the top and sides, or "business up front," with a little rat-tail "party in the back." Now I looked exactly like the kids who smoked cigarettes on the corner before school, and who were trying to have long hair but had never really committed to it. I was furious with Don for not telling me what she was doing or making any effort to stop her. When I looked at myself in the mirror, I had the exact same feeling of sobriety and major life change that I had had when my ear was first cut. My ear now had no discoloration, and if you didn't look closely you couldn't even tell there was a scar there. "Chop it off," I told her. "Chop off the rat tail and let's just go with a normal clean-cut look."

I went to school with that haircut the next day, and used what I had learned about hair spray to make it perfect. I wore the dressiest shirt I had: a tan shirt with a blue collar. Nothing black. One dressed-up jock kid named Brian was so shocked he literally backed up seven feet in the hallway when he saw me. Jude passed up the temptations of his girlfriend to visit me that night. It was an emergency, and he told me I needed to do something fast. My long hair had "hidden the weight," he said, and made me look cool, whereas now I was just "the fat kid." There was no edge, no story, no reason to see me as a wild rock star. I thought back to what the teacher's assistant had told me about having unusually beautiful eyes, and realized Jude was absolutely right. I had lost the hair, and now I needed to lose the weight. I would have to become my own personal trainer, even if I hated myself for driving so hard—just as the Blakester told me at the party. I already knew how to make my body impervious to pain for short periods, and now I decided to will my way through a diet, for however long it would take. My main goal in doing it, at the time, was to use my newfound stardom to end up with a girl like Brenda.

I started an aggressive, very unhealthy diet. I stopped eating breakfast cereal with milk and drinking a large glass of orange juice before school. Instead, I drank nothing but a V-8 each morning, and then filled my stomach with water in between classes. This also forced me to run to the bathroom every hour. I would rock in hunger all through the day, which transformed school into complete agony. Then I headed back to Don's house, where we had grilled cheese sandwiches. Mom made her normal healthy dinners, with slices of apple, vegetables, and the main course, which was usually macaroni and cheese. I took my five-dollar-a-week allowance and my dollar-twenty-five-a-day lunch money and saved it all to go toward weed. Skipping school lunch meant I no longer ate the huge pile of French fried potatoes that, along with sugar-laced ketchup, had been declared a "vegetable" by the Reagan administration, and the pounds started flying off. I absolutely hated jogging after two years of the Turkey Trot, and did not do any more exercise than before—not a single push-up, sit-up, or chin-up.

I lost most of the weight in the first few months, as much as five pounds a week. It took six more months to get the last third of it to go away. As soon as I started visibly losing weight, and had a house full of weed buddies every weekend, Don became suicidal. I didn't know how serious he was, but it wasn't looking good . . . at all. After school on weekdays it was just me and him. I decided to have him write out what he wanted to say to all the people he was friends with, including the girls. I wanted him to apologize to them for killing himself and say why he felt it was necessary. I felt this would help him work through it and realize this was a terrible and stupid thing to do. I was sitting on the floor in gym class when a random mullet kid told me Don had slumped over at his desk, crying out that he had taken eighty-six aspirin and didn't want to die. They had rushed him out in an ambulance, pumped his stomach, and fed him charcoal, and he was probably going to be fine. I was very upset that he had actually tried to do it and never bothered to tell me. He also had refused to leave any statements for me when we wrote out his good-byes.

After this failed suicide attempt, Don started buying Marlboro Red cigarettes and drinking alcohol in addition to smoking weed. I tried drinking myself but I did not like it, and found that hard liquor in particular would just about destroy my stomach and send me into crippling pain. I smoked a total of fewer than twenty cigarettes in my life and quickly decided they were disgusting, even though the first time I smoked one I got so wasted I could barely walk down the street. I realized they were always this strong, and people's bodies simply adjusted to the nicotine dose. I did not want that to happen to me—but both Don and his brother became totally hooked. That same day I tried my first cigarette, we met a friend of Bob's who was already out of school and high. I told him I smoked pot only on the weekends, and he looked genuinely dazzled. "How can you possibly wait that long? It's so good I can't imagine why you wouldn't want to do it every day."

I scoffed. "That's never going to happen. I'm not an addict." However, in less than a year he would be right. A lifetime of bullying, and growing up in a sick society, had made me a prisoner of "repetition compulsion," where I kept attracting the same types of tormentors over and over again. Yet, instead of doing anything to stand up for myself, I continued to self-medicate more and more to alleviate the pain they caused me. The more I did this, the weaker I became, and the more I was attacked. It was truly a vicious cycle that just kept on snowballing. The cosmic days of my youth now seemed like a distant, almost forgotten memory.

Twenty-six Years

Someone told me about a technique involving hyperventilation that got you very high. I didn't realize it at the time, but it involved creating a "blood choke" to the brain, which I knew from my martial arts training was lethal if it lasted for very long. Since no one actually put their hands or arms around your neck, I didn't realize that this technique did the same thing. I heard about it as a fairly vague rumor, with instructions to have your friend push on you for seven seconds. I recruited Jude for this task, since I wanted to have a psychedelic adventure, and told him,

"Forget seven seconds. Let's go for fifteen." I was standing with my back against an old-smelling thick hardwood door with a rounded top when he did it—but I never made it to fifteen. My body slumped down unconscious after eleven. I landed on my left foot in a funny way, causing the metatarsal bone attached to the pinky toe to snap about an inch below where the toe met with the foot—leaving my toe bending well over to the side, almost on a ninety-degree angle. I thought it was only dislocated and didn't realize I had actually broken it until many years later.

I was thrown into a very bizarre situation in which "my life flashed before my eyes"—only it was the wrong life. I experienced what seemed to be twenty-six years of time as a series of blindingly fast snapshots. As each one went by, the full range of experiences for that time was loaded into my memory. I was part of a primitive community that lived by a river. Almost everyone was illiterate. Our equivalent of the daily news was a guy who stood up on a platform in the center of town and told us what was going on, using theatrical storytelling techniques. We had a huge problem with irrigation. We were trying to get the river water to go through brick canals to the crops, but most of the water was seeping out between the cracks. I was having ESP experiences and contact with an "old man" similar to my own dreams as a child, and I was taught how to create a gooey material that was burned black and would stop the water from leaking.

I had a wife whom I got together with when I was young, and we had kids before we really knew what we were doing. She took care of the kids and I was mostly disconnected and focused on myself and my work. We still had love in our family, but I was always out doing something. I was obsessed with the idea of having an out-of-body experience, and being able to travel wherever I wanted in this ghostly form. I was taught to hold up a lotus-type flower to my face and stare into it. If I could see my own face in the lotus, I could change places with my astral body, so now I was looking back at the eyes of my physical body. The lotus pattern would then extend into a tunnel and I could fly through it and go wherever I wanted.

My life ended when a group of rogue barbarians invaded, riding animals and carrying weapons. We were completely outmatched, and I knew they were going to kill every single person in our village. I couldn't run and I couldn't hide—so I dropped down, holding a flower, and I tried harder than ever to see my own face in its spiraling pattern. The ground was shaking from the power of the oncoming horde. Finally I started seeing my face—but something was wrong. My eyes looked just about the same as they normally would, but I had dark skin and different features. The flower extended into a tunnel and I started hearing Jude and my brother shouting my name. I was very confused by what I was seeing, as it was my face, but it wasn't my face. I decided to fly through the tunnel and go to the voices instead of waiting for the barbarians to kill me.

I slammed back into my body, and I was in very serious trouble. My eyes would not stop going up and down, up and down, from my top left to my bottom right, about two times a second. I also was in terrible pain, but at first I couldn't identify it. I started screaming when I realized I had landed on my foot in a funny way, and yelled even more loudly when I wrestled it out and saw my toe off to the side. I frantically ordered Jude to pop it back, which he did—and it hurt tremendously. Then I yelled, "Twenty-six years! I was gone for twenty-six years! How the hell did I make it back here?" They had no idea what I was talking about. As I regained control of my body and bound my toe to the other two with Scotch tape, I explained to them what had happened. I did not believe in reincarnation at the time, though it would become a major part of my life in the future. Nonetheless, I could not deny that I seemed to have relived a past life at flash-forward speed. The strangest thing about it was that my eyes looked the same as they do now, though I had been a black man. Although the whole experience fascinated me, I realized that I came very close to dying—and I never tried it again.

Around this time, I also started having a highly bizarre thing happen to me as often as once or twice a month. I would get up for school as I always did, take a shower, get dressed, go downstairs, pack my book bag, have breakfast, and walk out the side door to go to school. Everything outside would be pitch-black. It was the middle of the night. "What the hell is going on?" I would come back into the house and realize that I had been in some kind of trance. I thought I heard my alarm going off, but it was a hallucination. I went through all the motions in a robotic way. I gazed at the clock on the microwave but didn't register what time it was.

During this same time, I was listening to the song "Sister Morphine" by the Rolling Stones. When Mick Jagger sang, "Why does the doctor have no face," I got a sudden flash of a scene in which two "doctors" were standing over me. They both had unusually large heads with tapered jaws, and skinny bodies. There were three round lights above them in a triangle shape as they bent over to look down at me. I drew the scene for my art class, but I gave them squared-off military jaws instead of what I actually saw, and gave their bodies wide military shoulders as well. I did not draw any facial features on them, because in this split-second flash vision I could not see any. My drawing was good enough that it won an award and was displayed in the school hallway for a period of time. I still have it framed and hanging on my bedroom wall. I got a tremendous chill when my mother got a copy of Whitley Strieber's first book, *Communion*. The big-eyed being on the front cover looked very similar to the "doctors"

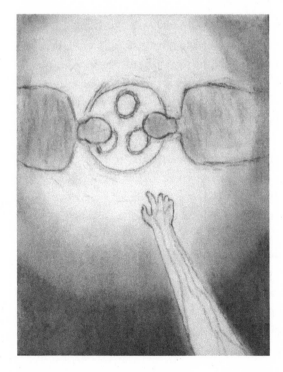

David Wilcock's High School Illustration of ET-like Beings

I had drawn, and in the book they abducted people and performed medical experiments. This creeped me out so much that I would flip the book
facedown every time I saw it. The combination of extraterrestrial and
square-jawed human features may indicate that military personnel were
part of my experience, thus suggesting there may have been a "MILAB"
or Military Abduction.[27] If I was in fact abducted, I have still never been
able to remember any details to this very day. However, my mother did
wake up one night feeling a terrible negative presence in the room, and
saw a three-foot-tall being quietly walking out. It had a normal-sized
head, not like one of the Gray extraterrestrials with the large heads, huge
black eyes, and spindly bodies—but she was very afraid of it. My art also
formed the image of the Egyptian "winged disc," which I would not
consciously realize for over a decade.

The Left Eye of Horus

In the summer of 1989, one of the "burnout" kids I had smoked with a
few times called me up and said I had to see something, right now, as I
would never believe him otherwise. He just had to show me. We rushed
over to the Sunnyside Road bridge, which went over the railroad tracks,
where he had been riding his motorcycle. The suspense was killing me as
we climbed down the hill—and there it was. A gigantic, Egyptian-style
Left Eye of Horus was painted on the concrete slope that went all the
way up the hill under the bridge. It was easily fifty feet wide and thirty
feet tall, and was made out of at least four different paint colors—a lot
of red, some blue, and black for the iris with white for its reflection. The
paint was glossy and fresh as if it had just been done, or was very carefully maintained.

   It wasn't at all easy to get down there. This would have taken gallons
and gallons of paint to produce—and it was flawless. Who would have
had the time, money, and energy to do something like this? College kids?
And why? What could possibly possess them to invest such a significant
part of themselves into making this gigantic piece of art that no one
would ever see except a train conductor?

As I tried to use ESP to tune into whatever this was, I sensed incredible evil and darkness. I had flashes of people wearing robes and masks, chanting around a fire. There may have even been some sort of animal sacrifice as well as weird sex rites. I found that the logical place for a fire had been all too neatly raked, as if someone had deliberately cleaned it up to hide the evidence. Suddenly it dawned on me that this could be a ritual site for the same *Rosemary's Baby*–type group that my parents had seen going into the house across the street. Years later I would speak to multiple insiders who confirmed that sites like this were used to practice occult religious rites.

Now I was consumed with terror. I quickly scanned all the trees to see if there was a hidden camera. Nothing obvious. "We need to get the hell out of here. Right now." The burnout kid was right behind me. After we left, we both tried to figure out why in the hell there was an Egyptian eye there. How could this have anything to do with a weird, satanic cult that might want to light a fire and do a ritual while they were safely hidden under a bridge? At the time, it didn't make any sense. Egyptian religion and Satanism were supposedly two completely different things. I decided that those ESP hits must have been my imagination—but the whole experience haunted me for years to come. I would eventually discover that the Cabal's main religion was Luciferianism, and they had adapted the Egyptian trinity of Isis, Osiris, and Horus as being the three main manifestations of Lucifer on Earth.

CHAPTER TEN

He'll Take You Up,
He'll Bring You Down

Not long after seeing the Eye, I had perhaps the single most powerful dream of all my years as a teenager. I was first drawn into this beautiful hotel in the woods, surrounded by snow and majestic evergreen trees. Once I got inside, there were teenagers everywhere. Everyone was being given powerful drugs, akin to some kind of mushrooms. The drugs prevented them from understanding where they were or what was going on. In one room, all the teenagers were sitting in a circle around a one-foot-wide metallic sphere mounted on a platform. A being was standing off to the side in a black, hooded cloak, and seemed to be the Grim Reaper—but no one saw him. The kids were all completely hypnotized by some kind of technology emanating from the sphere.

Seeing the hooded being made me panic. I had to escape before someone drugged me like the others—but I realized certain people were acting as plainclothes security guards to prevent this from happening, and none of the doors and windows would open. I burst into some sort of restricted area, and everything suddenly looked very technological—like I was inside an advanced spacecraft. There was a huge, round elevator in the distance, and I felt that I needed to take it. As soon as I tried to move forward, I was attacked by a huge number of battle robots that walked on two legs, had two arms, and were very ferocious. Somehow I was able to fight my way through them. It seemed to involve a combination of some kind of advanced weapon I had found as well as ascended-type abilities.

I made it into the elevator, and inside I saw a panel revealing that the hotel was only the top level of a huge underground base that went many levels down. Somehow I knew the only way out was to confront the leader of this alien menace on the bottom floor. I was able to get the elevator to take me there, and was very surprised by how long it took to go all the way down. The elevator opened out into a huge, dark area. The only visible thing was a massive pair of ornately carved wooden doors. They were easily eighty feet tall, and had lots of strange designs carved into them. They also seemed to be covered with barbed wire; they were not made for anyone to get through without approval. I knew that whoever or whatever was running this operation was right behind those doors. I summoned every bit of physical and spiritual strength I had—and was able to blast them open.

I walked into an office that looked like it was right out of the White House, complete with the presidential desk. The chair swiveled around and I saw a man who looked like a politician or senior military official. He wore a blue suit with an American flag pin on his lapel. He had wet-combed black hair that was styled like Ronald Reagan's hair had been. He admitted they were running the entire facility, and started very aggressively trying to get me to join them. I was promised unlimited power and full access to their technology. When I refused, he started laughing and said I had no choice—since I had nowhere else to go. Somehow I felt the only answer would be to "create myself." I bent down and rolled myself up into a ball, going into a deep state of concentration. I went out-of-body and was able to build seven luminous energetic bodies around my own—each of which was progressively larger. I then was able to move my consciousness into the largest one.

Suddenly I found myself onboard a magnificent spaceship. I was in a massive, open room with a long, curving wall that was filled with hyper-advanced computer terminals. Each terminal had a huge screen that was about five feet wide and four feet tall. The images on the screens were holographic, full color, and extremely high resolution. I was seated at my terminal and had an image of the Earth there in front of me. I could clearly identify the underground base I had been in, as it was lit up on the globe. I had access to tremendous powers with the technology on this ship. I was able to take all the kids in the base and transport them to a safe place. Then I reached in and removed the base itself, as if it were the size of a pea, and catapulted it back to where it came from. The Earth had been profoundly healed and transformed as a result of my doing this—almost like it was bathed in light.

I awoke from this experience in an absolute state of awe. It made me remember the dreams of my youth with the old man, the messages I was given about a mass human evolution, and the way I felt when I saw *2001* and *2010*. I had been able to transform myself directly into a light being. For the first time in years, I seemed to have gotten much more information than in my youth. Something tremendously evil was controlling the US government—and the way to defeat it was for us to evolve into an entirely new form. At the time, I wondered if it was only a dream, or something more. In time, this would end up being one of the most profound ascension dreams I ever had—and Jude wrote the whole thing up in a comic-book-style series of illustrations.

Lucy in the Sky with Diamonds

One day after school, Don and I were transfixed by an old black-and-white documentary on the Beatles in which we saw vintage footage of people on LSD. They were higher than we had ever gotten. Paul McCartney was talking in the show about how he stopped doing LSD after a while, and said, "It had done all it could do for us." We were huge fans of *Sgt. Pepper's,* and I realized that many people assumed the song "Lucy in the Sky with Diamonds" was code for LSD, based on the first letters of each word. All the lyrics were extremely bizarre and druglike. There were taxis made out of newspaper, tangerine trees, marmalade skies, and a girl with kaleidoscope eyes who kept showing up. The Beatles were on to something—and the documentary implied that hippies all knew LSD was amazing. Both of the classic Moody Blues albums we loved to listen to were full-length infomercials and recruitment tools for LSD use as well.

In Carlos Castenada's books, psychedelics were used to access spiritual consciousness—so I felt my mother might have been wrong about avoiding them completely. My epic dream said I had to "create myself" in these energetic bodies, and I thought back to my forgotten goal from when I was a kid of wanting to have another out-of-body experience. It had never happened, and maybe this was the key to finally getting another chance. Lars, one of the hippies from Totem, had overdosed on LSD, so I talked to people I knew who had taken it and got the warnings on what not to do. The basic guideline was to take just a little bit of anything new so you didn't get bugged out. It never occurred to me that the teenagers in my dream had been kept prisoner in the hotel by the use of some kind of psychedelic drug in the first place.

Don, Baner, and I took a quarter tab each of some baby-blue paper LSD, which had come in by way of the latest Grateful Dead concerts at Giants Stadium in New Jersey, on July 9 and 10, 1989. Each time the Dead tour came anywhere near where we were, there was a temporary surge in psychedelic drugs available from people who would buy it by the sheet and resell it at higher prices—about three or four dollars a tab. Fifteen minutes rushed by after we took the quarter tab, and nothing had changed, so we each took another one. After fifteen more minutes with no results, we concluded the blue doses were fake. Since we didn't want to ruin our chances of seeing something happen, we each took another half of a different kind we had that was pink, called Soundwaves. The myth was that after taking it, you would be able to see waves of sound traveling through the air. Another ten minutes went by, and things were definitely starting to get strange.

I was exhaling smoke in my room when my mother suddenly yelled up the stairs: "David, dinner is ready. All your friends have to leave!" This was my worst nightmare come true. The LSD was probably going to hit me right at the dinner table, since at least one of the two kinds I had taken was not fake—and I had never done it before. I went downstairs, where my mother had laid out all the ingredients in about ten different bowls on the table to make tacos. I realized I had forgotten to pee, and rushed back up the stairs, two at a time. As I stood over the toilet, my heart was pounding—and it hit me. In a thunderous slam, my entire field of vision went completely black—with my eyes wide-open. It was as if someone had closed blackout curtains over my vision, and it was utterly terrifying.

I tried to hold still so I wouldn't pee all over, and my vision faded back in. Now, everything looked like it was underwater, which I came to call "swimming-pool vision." There were shimmering sparkles of light everywhere, and the colors were much more intense than they had been just a minute ago. My body felt extremely strange and distorted. I went over to the stairs and realized I was having powerful hallucinations. It now looked like the entire stairwell was stretching open and closed, becoming wider and narrower in about one-second intervals, like it was alive. Sparks of light were shooting down the tunnel. I was absolutely horrified. I couldn't believe I was going to walk down those stairs, but I made the choice. I held my hands against both walls to make sure they didn't close up on me. The height of each step seemed to be rising and falling in the same, sickening motion, but they were stable once I stepped on them, so I just worked my way down very slowly. Once I finally made it to the bottom, I felt that if I didn't "create" each part of the floor before I stepped on it with my foot, I could fall right through it—so I decided exactly where I was going to step, and visualized walking on it before I actually did.

By the time I made it back to the table, I was a huge mess. Everything was going so fast in my mind that the speed of normal human conversation was intolerably slow. Once I sat at the table I realized I could barely lift my arms, which was necessary to make tacos and look normal. My mother put a taco shell on my plate; it was still warm, so it started slowly drooping. I felt like it was a living mouth wanting to be fed with taco stuff. With an enormous effort, I managed to robotically retrieve a single spoonful of beef and drop it in the middle of the shell, and then a small dusting of shredded cheddar cheese. There was now a little one-inch ball of meat and cheese in the middle of my taco shell.

At this point I got hit with a terrifying hallucination. The meat and cheese turned into some shrimp-like crustacean creature. It was twitching in the shell in death agony, staring at me, and I couldn't help but instinctively flinch from it. Now I became extremely paranoid. The conversation between my mother and brother seemed incredibly strained, with huge pregnant pauses and lots of subtext indicating they thought I was messed up on some drug—and were very upset about it. This seemed to go on for an eternity before I eventually decided I had to get the hell

out of there, immediately. When I was a kid I could ask to be excused
from the table if I didn't feel well. After what seemed like half an hour,
I managed to plan out the following sentence in words, tone, and delivery, to sell the part and sound as normal as possible. "Mom, I don't feel
well. May I be excused from the table?"

She said, "Sure," and I fled to the basement, where there was a phone.
I called up Don and said, "Dude, I am really freaking out. You guys need
to get back here as soon as possible." As I spoke to him, the walls were
visibly breathing, as if I were inside the lungs of some strange beast.
Mom's microphone stands were swaying back and forth like seaweed
underwater. I felt like I was inside the belly of the whale, and it had all
started when I had gone down the stairs, which was its mouth. The
sparks urging me down the stairs were its saliva. Somehow it all made
sense. He agreed they would return quickly, and I realized that similar
things were also happening to him. I came back upstairs but never made
it to my room—only the living-room couch. The lampshade was now a
canvas of dazzling visuals, including spiraling triangles within triangles,
castles, and mountains I was flying through, and a *Centipede*-style video
game I could play with my mind. Mom said good-bye to me and headed
off for her gig, and my friends arrived soon afterward. Things got somewhat better after that, but it was still a very unsettling experience.

I reminisced about some of the interesting moments after it had happened, and we decided to do it again later on. This time we made sure to
plan it out better, so there was no chance of having to deal with either of
my parents during the time it was active, which was an exhausting twelve
hours. I realized the "peak" didn't hit until forty-five minutes after you
took it, and up until then it might not even seem like anything was going
to happen. Every time it started, all the same unpleasant symptoms came
back—a feeling of my whole body shaking, a sense of extreme nervous-
ness, a pain in the stomach, horribly sore joints with certain varieties of
LSD, time slowing down to a crawl, and a massive number of obsessive
thoughts I could not control. My mind could be simultaneously caught
in four or five different thought loops, all going around and around at
different speeds, and I couldn't make them stop.

There was always the risk of having a "bad trip," where you could become far more terrified than you had ever been in your entire life. The only other experience I had that could even begin to compare to a bad trip was when I had almost died in Rick's boat. Any one bad trip was much, much worse than that, even though nothing was actually going on—and it lasted for vastly longer periods of psychological time. In some cases I was hiding in the corner, all alone, and terrified to move—feeling that unseen evil spirits would completely destroy me if I didn't stay absolutely still and try not to breathe. The fear that this caused me was much greater than anything I had ever experienced. I didn't even realize it was possible to be that scared before this happened. One of my quotes that I shared with all my friends was, "No one is adult enough to be able to handle a bad trip." It was absolutely impossible for me to prevent it from happening, and every single time I did it, there were periods that were spectacularly terrifying and horrific—and seemed to go on for eternities of time. I would reminisce with my friends about some of the interesting things, try another round, and then end up right back in that same place, asking myself, "Why in God's name did I do this again?"

I can hear some people saying hippie slogans like "Set and setting, dude, set and setting," meaning if you do it in the right place, and have the right mind-set, you can have a positive experience. "It just amplifies what is already there." Who in today's world doesn't have hidden demons they haven't healed yet? What happens when you get hit with all of them at once, much more strongly than ever before? I have also heard people say, "Clean acid, man, you never took clean acid." In my case, I never had a trip that was good from the beginning to the end, no matter how "clean" the LSD was supposed to be—and I also tried other psychedelics, including mushrooms and yellow micro-dots.

There were always prolonged periods of unimaginable fright. The best I could hope for was to reduce the total amount of time I spent in absolute, full-body-shaking terror. This is why many people try LSD only once or twice and never touch it again. This was also obviously why Lars had ended up the way he did. With a large or accidental dose, the amount of trauma you could go through could literally destroy your mental health in a permanent or semipermanent fashion.

I also ended up getting caught in thought loops about the Earth every time I did the drug, which I called "ecology trips." Everywhere I looked, I saw evidence that we were destroying the Earth—and I could not begin to ignore it. Television became absolutely unwatchable. All the smiling salespeople, marketing language, and slick jingles telling you to "buy now" became the horrific, crushing tones of a Pied Piper leading us over a cliff into global annihilation. "Three easy payments of only $19.95. For a limited time only while supplies last. Call now!" I would hear ugly, terrifying and dissonant bass notes blended in with the music, and the feeling of evil was so overpowering that a thirty-second commercial seemed like a lifetime of torment.

I felt like the trees were screaming and the Earth itself was alive and extremely terrified of us. I thought back to the Eye I had seen under the bridge, and on LSD, the pyramid with the All-Seeing Eye on the dollar bill became a vortex of darkness. It seemed that there was a tornado of energy emanating from that eye that was making the entire room around me shake—and it was extremely frightening. I realized we were a mass suicide cult, and could end up killing this beautiful being—which was forced, by design, to just step back and hope that a few of its best people could help to turn things around.

Many people have asked me to try ayahuasca or other drugs, telling me, "Oh, it's not like LSD at all. It is much better, much more profound and spiritually meaningful. Now that you've been clean for years, you'll have a much better experience." Yet when I have asked them detailed and specific questions about what happened, I have realized that everyone goes into a psychedelic space, which is a near-death experience—similar to the hallucinations you get in a fever when your brain is starting to dangerously overheat and threaten your life. You can have really weird and bizarre things happen to you, but just as Paul McCartney said, psychedelics did all they could do for me. I would be extremely weak and exhausted afterward, and I always had a crippling backache. I also had residual LSD stored in my fat cells that could cause me to have flashbacks, such as during exercise or when I was smoking weed—so I never knew exactly what was going to happen to me next.

The main thing I got out of it was that we are destroying the Earth, and the solution requires people who are actually living on the Earth to stop it. No cosmic beings like the old man in my dreams can just swoop in, wave a magic wand, and solve all our problems. We have to take action. This is our world, and we have to fight to keep it. This also caused me to see most of the people around me as brainwashed zombies. Everyone ignored the things that terrified them the most. As soon as they saw some proof of how close we were to destroying ourselves, they would just shut down. No one ever wanted to suffer even 10 percent as much terror as I would feel in a bad trip. They would do just about anything, including completely blocking out a bad experience from their memory, to avoid that pain. Drugs and alcohol helped them stay numb—and I was equally guilty of it myself. Once I was stoned, I could completely forget about something that had been really upsetting me even ten minutes before I started. But then, as soon as I came back to reality, the problem had gotten even worse, because I wasn't doing anything to deal with it. More and more, I was becoming deeply introverted, paralyzingly shy, paranoid, and fearful.

On January 1, 1990—in the early hours of New Year's Day—a girl I had known since first grade died in a horrible car accident. She was riding in a car with kids from another school, and everyone had been drinking. The police report showed that the car was going a hundred miles per hour when it struck the concrete wall next to a bridge on Mohawk Avenue. Worst of all, she was still screaming as the police arrived. She burned to death and they were unable to save her. This had a seismic effect on our community—and was a shocking reminder that we were not immortal. I thought of all the times I had spoken to her over the years, and now she was gone. The story was so horrible that everyone quickly forgot about it—just as we ignored a seemingly impossible array of threats to all life on Earth.

The Grateful Dead

On March 24, 1990, I ate a full eighth-ounce bag of mushrooms before going to see the Grateful Dead at the Knickerbocker Arena with my father, his hilarious buddy Rick, and my kid brother. I thought that since everyone took psychedelics at the Dead show, I would be fine—but I soon reconfirmed that being around either of my parents while tripping was a horrible idea. I decided to wait as long as possible, so I didn't pop the hideous-tasting material in my mouth until we were in the car. Michael saw me and thought I had candy at first. I lied to him and denied eating anything, but he then realized I was doing some kind of drugs. The taste reminded me of the essence of moldy, three-day-old sock stench. It was very dry, and I had to chew it quite a bit to choke it down. The drive into Albany was about an hour, and by the time we stopped at a pizza place before the show, it was hitting me—very hard.

Right as Rick made a hilarious joke, the cheese on my pizza jumped to life and slithered across the table. I tried not to flinch, but I couldn't help it. Everyone's laughter covered it up. Then I looked over at the kitchen and saw a guy in a blue T-shirt and a messy white apron drive a skewer through a live, flailing rat. Its arms, legs, and tail continued going through death agony as he lowered it into the frying vat. Everything looked like it was passing through a semitransparent filter of rippling geometric patterns and sparks of light. The colors were too bright. I was profoundly uncomfortable and terrified that I was going to get caught.

As we got up to leave, I saw a perfect, life-sized image of the Hermit from the Tarot cards—a bearded man in a gray, hooded robe, carrying a staff and a lantern—standing right near Dad. I could see him clearly enough to make out the coarse, burlap-like texture of his robe. This seemed like an omen of death and made me feel even worse. A Mediterranean-looking guy with large eyes and thick eyebrows sitting at a table with his friends was now staring at me, but his face was all messed up. One eye appeared about four inches higher on his face, well up into his forehead, compared to the other, which had dropped down below his cheek. I was looking right at him, and this Picasso-like image held steady. He was very frightened as he looked at me, and I realized that my face probably looked the same way to him. I gave him a knowing nod, letting him know I understood, and that he looked just as strange to me. Once I got to the arena I really had to pee, and the toilet in my stall melted and disappeared—only to pop right back seconds later. During the show, I watched as the speakers seemed to melt over the crowd, forming a giant, black lake, swallowing everyone. I had to deal with several more hours of the trip after I got home, and I couldn't get to sleep until after sunrise, which was an inevitable side effect.

Although I did do psychedelics after this, I was very careful to never take enough to produce full-visual hallucinations. The potential for a bad trip was so high that I didn't dare put myself through it—but smaller doses weren't much better.

Lucid Dreaming

Ever since I first tried LSD, I had hoped to get a fully discontinuous out-of-body experience from it—a journey into another reality. It didn't take long for me to realize LSD was not the answer to make this happen. I still kept trying to see if I could ever get a good trip, but even if I did, I was always aware of being in my body, in this reality, and I felt all messed up. Hallucinations were weird and scary, but I thought back to that night I floated out of my body and could see that I had still never reached the goal. I was very fortunate to find a copy of *Lucid Dreaming* by Dr. Stephen LaBerge in a bookstore. The subtitle read "How to Become Awake and Aware in Your Dreams." Dr. LaBerge taught a technique called "Mnemonic Induction of Lucid Dreaming," or MILD. First you had to start remembering your dreams, which involved staying completely motionless when you woke up. You would ask yourself where you just were and what you were doing. Then, you would replay the dream in your head, over and over again, only now you would imagine yourself noticing some strange, impossible detail and realizing that you were dreaming. Dr. LaBerge explained that any time you looked at something, looked away, and then looked back, if it was a dream it would change—and that was your best way of finding out whether it was a dream.

While doing this, you would also mentally repeat the same sentence over and over again, putting as much meaning and feeling into it as you possibly could: "Next time I'm dreaming, I want to remember to recognize I'm dreaming." Then, if you were lucky enough, you would fall back asleep and realize that everything around you had changed while you were still saying those words. At this point you could test your environment for changes and other impossible things—and if you found something, then you were now in a lucid dream. Best of all, once you found yourself in this state, you had full godlike abilities in the dream—including levitation and telekinesis. You could directly experience what ascension would be like in your real-time, waking life—and it was absolutely fantastic.

I put a lot of time into reading LaBerge's book, understanding the technique, and practicing it—and after only a few tries, I got spectacular results. I could soar through the air, walk through walls, travel anywhere I wanted, and lift huge objects with my mind. I could also completely change my environment just by thinking about something different. I felt a high that was much greater than anything I had ever gotten from drugs. The first time it happened, I found myself in the front doorway of the house, right where I had gotten lost for twenty-six years and appeared to have the facial features of a black man. Now there was a single, bare bulb hanging down from the ceiling, which was obviously different. A black man was sitting there, drenched in sweat and extremely upset about something. The bulb had been shattered, but light was still coming out of it. I realized that bulbs could not give off light without glass around the filament—and suddenly I became lucid. It was a tremendously wonderful experience. I ran outside and levitated over my house, checking out how the trees and the roof looked from up there.

After one lucid dream, I was hooked. I soon realized I could go wherever I wanted to go, do whatever I wanted to do, and create whatever I wanted to create. In my second or third experience, I found myself in a beautiful pasture, and I manifested a good-sized red barn that was filled to the brim with marijuana. I walked up to the doors, opened them, and was knocked over in an avalanche of sweet-smelling buds. I then manifested a six-inch-wide salad bowl, put a hole at the bottom, attached a bent pipe to the hole, and then created a blowtorch. I packed it full with weed and took a huge hit—but I did not get high. I already was.

In another case, I created a magnificently futuristic car and went on a joyride, which included being able to punch it into speeds that were unimaginable in my waking reality. Each experience was magnificent, absolutely real, and would go on for what seemed like well over an hour in some cases. I would fly through windows, explore buildings, see people who couldn't see me, and feel incredible. I needed enough time to get extra sleep, so I typically practiced this on the weekends—and the results were phenomenal.

In one of these experiences I started writing everything down that was happening to me—and I was shocked to discover that all my words were in perfect French. I normally could not speak it that well in my waking life, but in the dream it was very natural, and I knew it was right. I didn't always think clearly when I was lucid, though, and in that dream I had hoped to be able to bring all my written papers back with me. When I woke up, they were gone, of course. In another dream I ended up in the local CVS pharmacy, and put on quite a show, where I levitated a group of large trash barrels and started orbiting them around one another. It was a larger-scale version of what happened in the movie *E.T.* I was always trying to talk to people, show them miracles, and let them know we were in a dream and none of this was real—but I always had problems. They would listen at first, but then some force would come over them, they would blank out, and walk away as if they had no idea what I had just said. This happened to the entire crowd of people who saw me levitate the barrels, and it was very bizarre. It appeared that I was not in full control of my environment.

At least two different times, I was flying around having adventures and got pulled into a highly advanced spacecraft. People with robes were talking to me and we were standing in front of gigantic picture windows. Absolutely fantastic spaceships of unimaginable size drifted past the window. Dr. LaBerge's book had taught me that everything in a lucid dream is created in your brain and none of it is real—and since he was a scientist I felt he had to be right. So, even though I found myself on these magnificent craft, talking to these robed wise men like the old man from my childhood dreams, I believed they were all a product of my subconscious. I would tell them they were illusions right to their faces and they would just laugh and smile politely. They were always very kind to me and encouraged me to continue practicing this technique.

I was also congratulated for losing weight and was told I had the power to completely transform my life. They complimented me for the things I had done to help others. I was told that this was what really mattered where they were. No one ever shamed me or told me I should quit using drugs. I couldn't imagine that any of this was actually real, despite how vivid it was, so after I woke up from such an experience I would always laugh about my "weird dreams," and say, "My subconscious sure has a vivid imagination." By the year 1996 I had established direct telepathic contact with these same people—and I was absolutely shocked to discover how real all of it had been. They ended up making house calls, and appeared in front of my brother and one of my clients who had received spiritual counseling from me, in order to prove they really did exist.

Bang Your Head

Sometime after the Dead show, a guy I hardly knew called me up and asked if I was going to Brad's birthday bash. I was deeply hurt, as Brad hadn't told me anything about it. Don and I went over and crashed the party, and Brad didn't even try to explain why we were not invited. There were probably forty or fifty people there, including many kids I had never seen before, and they had kegs of beer. I decided to drink like everyone else, and before long I had downed four or five Solo picnic cups of beer. All the weed was being smoked down in the basement, and this was why Brad had asked me if he could borrow my big red double-chambered bong the day before. I took a huge, lung-blaster hit and blacked out. I was not aware of falling backward, but I was dimly aware of the back of my skull dribbling like a basketball against the concrete floor. After a couple of eternal seconds, my vision was flooded with about six faces that looked very concerned. They sounded like they were all shouting at me through a twenty-foot-long cardboard paper towel tube.

It took a while for me to regain full consciousness, and even though I almost certainly had a concussion, I just got up and kept on drinking and smoking as if nothing had happened. I became so drunk that when I went to the bathroom to pee standing up, I dropped my pants all the way down to my ankles, and had to lean against the wall to keep from

falling over. Right then, the class clown Gerry burst into the bathroom—
and started laughing and cheering. The story became that I had "passed
out standing up," even though I was still conscious.

Hell to Pay

After this epic mess, I got the courage to reconnect with Brenda since I
had become a lot thinner. I told her about our band and the Christmas
party, even though we hadn't played in months. She called me at my father's house after I gave her the number and told her I would be there
Friday night. I was upstairs in his office and scrambled to find a pad of
paper when she was ready to give me her number and continue the conversation. After I hung up, I realized I had written her number down on
a promotional paper from the latest Jeff Healey album release, *Hell to Pay*,
supporting his new album due to be released on May 25, 1990. There was
a guitar in flames on the paper. My conversation with Brenda had been a
little strange, and I got the strong sense that if I ever got together with her,
she would be extremely confrontational and abusive. The paper seemed to
have the answer written right on it—there would be hell to pay. She had
been in a relationship with the same guy who I had shoved through seven
desks in my junior high school fight, and they had since broken up.

Shortly after our conversation, some kid called my father, pretended
I owed him a lot of money in a drug deal, and threatened to kill my father and me both if I didn't pay up. At the time I didn't know who it was,
but it became obvious when I was putting this book together. This deeply
traumatized my father and made him even more confrontational than he
already had been. Every time I saw Dad, there would be about fifteen
minutes of very aggressive confrontation about my grades and my overall
lifestyle. No matter what I did, it happened every single time I saw him,
four times a week. Sometimes in the car he would get so upset he would
have to pull over. This made my life far more challenging than it already
was. Between my mother, my father, and the kids at school, I felt like my
life was an absolute prison camp—and the only redeeming thing I had
was to get even more wasted.

On July 5, 1990, I was backstage after the Robert Plant show at the Knickerbocker Arena, supporting his *Manic Nirvana* album.[28] It was always a challenge getting backstage at the Knick, but this time we were let right in. The room was swarming with radio station contest winners who had gotten the unimaginable opportunity to meet their top idol. I was standing right next to the door, facing this wild spectacle, when there he was—three feet away from me. I could see every individual pore on his face. This was the first musician I had the chance to meet whom I genuinely idolized. A heavyset guy with a bald head, black hair, and a beard was walking with him. "What do you think?" the guy said. "I'd be bloody eaten alive," Plant responded. They both turned around and left. I kept my cool and did not try to bother him—but I felt like I had missed the greatest opportunity of my life. The label had given away far too many backstage passes. Even though everyone there wanted to tell Robert how much they loved him, he would be absolutely overwhelmed by everyone competing for his attention. Once again, I saw firsthand proof that being famous can be tremendously upsetting, even for the most seasoned veterans.

A Glimpse of Death at the Crossroads

On August 27, 1990, the legendary blues guitarist Stevie Ray Vaughan told his bandmates that he had a dream where he witnessed his own funeral. It was a huge night for him, as he and the band were special guests for a concert at the Alpine Valley Music Theatre. Eric Clapton, Buddy Guy, and Robert Cray were all playing, and my father was there to interview Buddy Guy and the others for a book he was writing. After the concert, two private helicopters were scheduled to whisk everyone away from the surging crowds—and my father was invited. As far as everyone in the family knew, Dad was going to fly out on one of them.

There was a delay with the helicopters' arrival, and when the first one finally showed up, Clapton's crew got on board. Stevie could not wait. Stevie's brother Jimmie and his brother's wife, Connie, offered Stevie the last seat. A half mile after taking off, Stevie's helicopter crashed into a ski slope and killed everyone instantly.[29] Dad had gotten the last-ever interview with Stevie the day before. We found out only after the crash was announced that Dad had decided to interview Robert Cray and had turned down the offer to ride in either of the helicopters at the last minute. The bearded hermit I had seen near my father at the Dead show could have been a symbol of the Angel of Death himself, in an astral form—and my father was fortunate enough to avoid his grasp. This was another shocking reminder that we are not immortal—and I could feel that same old hermit chasing me as well. He was always right nearby, waiting to claim his prize.

Brad, Chris, and Baner had pressured me into smoking with them every day over the summer, since Mom's weekend restrictions were not in effect—but I didn't need much convincing. I slid into my senior year on a very bleak note. I had become one of the "cool" kids for the class of 1990, but now they had all graduated. Even though I had lost the weight, and was showing up at various parties, the majority of kids in my own class still saw me as a geek. My crash diet had gotten rid of the weight, but my addiction had left me with pale, whitish skin and shockingly dark circles under my eyes. The tension with my father and mother was at an all-time high. I was fighting, arguing, and apologizing every single day. I wore shirts to school that advertised to everyone that I was doing drugs, like brightly colored tie-dyes with the Grateful Dead dancing bear on them, filled with circles of different shapes, sizes, and colors. Smoking after school was now a guarantee, since I could barely stand to get through the day, and home was no better. I also started smoking before school, and before long I discovered that if I went to school stoned, I had a reasonably good day, but if I went to school sober, I had a bad day. However, I would be so messed up in Computer Math, my first-period class, that I needed to cheat off the kid next to me in order to understand what was happening.

You Can't Win 'Em All

I now was on my fifth year of French classes, and was one of the best speakers of the language in my grade. This became a huge asset when I was seated in one of my classes next to a gorgeous red-haired foreign exchange student from France. She and I started talking in French and things were looking really good. One day, she left her little tan leather pouch of pens and pencils behind on her desk as she quickly got up and left the room after class. I grabbed it and ran after her to give it back. This was the first time we had ever spoken to each other in the hallways. She started talking about the prom, and said she had no one to go with her.

Instantaneously, I went into a complete panic attack—much like an LSD flashback. My mind exploded with paranoid, looping thoughts. Even though I had lost the weight, I had done nothing to heal the trauma from countless years of bullying and being told I was worthless. I didn't have time to do a full analysis, because she had stopped talking and I needed to say something. I felt that I must have misunderstood her, and she couldn't possibly be wanting me to ask her out. I felt that if I did ask her, and she said no, I would be so crushed by that rejection that I could barely handle being alive. I also had a very negative view of the prom, believing it to be overpriced—and if I had any money, I was putting it toward weed. Don had railed about the stupidity of "paying a hundred and twenty dollars for cold chicken," and avoiding the prom had become my religion. Now I definitely had to say something, and I was in such a panic there was no way I could summon up the courage to ask her. "Wow, that really sucks," I responded. "I hope you can find somebody."

The next day, she completely ignored me—and it quickly became clear that she was furious. She never spoke to me again, and acted like I was the biggest scumbag she had ever met. Then she ended up getting together with a guy who looked a lot like me, and everyone found out they were going to the prom. This caused me to suffer profoundly, and to obsess over what had happened for weeks to come. It was the first time that I really saw how badly the drugs were messing up my life. I had always told my friends that I would gladly quit if I found the right woman, but now the right woman had come along—and I was so damaged that I had missed my big chance.

For me, a major part of the ascension process is looking honestly at the problems you have, and being courageous and powerful enough to confront them. This epic failure with a woman was what led me to understand the saying "You get out of your life what you are willing to put into it" when I was in college. If you lack the courage to take a chance, you never get to see the life you might have had. Healing can be an extremely difficult and painful process, as it forces you to go back and identify your original wounds—and see how they are repeating in the present. In order to get better, you are forced to confront all the most difficult challenges life presents you with. My other big saying in college was "Spiritual growth is the hardest thing you will ever do—but also the most rewarding."

The Box Bug-out

One day after school I got very stoned with a group of people I barely knew. Two of them were hard-core burnouts from the corner, and the other two were their girlfriends. We had two bowls going in opposite directions, so sometimes I had two pipes in my hands at the same time—and I would smoke both of them at once. On the way home, I started having LSD flashbacks. I ended up back on my street, and was seeing the houses all laid out on either side of the road. Garbage cans were lined up in front of the houses. I realized that I hardly knew who any of these people were. They were right there all around me, but each of us was living our lives in complete isolation.

Everyone was living in a box. They would get in a box and drive to another box, where they worked inside a box—a cubicle. Then they got back in the box, drove back to the first box, and turned on another box with dancing, colored lights, which provided them something called "entertainment." They ate out of a box, threw away the trash in another box, and slept in a box. Then when they died, they would sleep forever—in a box. All the boxes were lined up—the houses and the trash cans—betraying the truth for all those with eyes to see. The secret was hiding right out in the open. I felt I had made the greatest discovery since the theory of gravity.

The full weight of this realization was still hitting me when I walked into the house, sat down at the kitchen table, and looked at the clock. Right then, the cool blue digits spelled out 3:33. At that moment, my consciousness radically changed. I felt an incredible, surging pressure in my ears, like a subsonic frequency. Reality suddenly seemed to have been pinched off and turned into something far more energetic. I felt myself soaring over my body at the kitchen table, and had the distinct sensation of being in both places at once. The digits 3:33 were beaming into my face as I had this incredible experience. It seemed that the numbers themselves were a very important part of whatever was happening to me. At the time, I did not understand it—but this proved to be my first major experience with "numerical synchronicity," in which I would see repeating patterns of numbers in the most bizarre, unpredictable circumstances. This would happen five or more times a day and would become a major part of my awakening later in life. Synchronicity would give me messages that I was not alone—and I had powerful, positive spiritual friends who were guiding me and helping me through life.

At the time, I was jamming the gas pedal to the floor and redlining the engine on the road to nowhere—but my spiritual friends had me covered. No matter how broken, damaged, and beyond all hope I seemed to be, there was a greater force looking out for me and protecting me. However, before it could fully reveal itself, I had to lift myself out of my own private hell. I still needed to sink a lot farther down before I would finally decide to take better care of myself.

CHAPTER ELEVEN

Jailbreak

The ugly truth was that Don was now paying a lot more than I was to support our habit. I could contribute only ten dollars a week, between my five-dollar allowance and the dollar a day I saved from my lunch money. He had become a manager at McDonald's, working many hours a week. He had hardly any time to do homework, which caused his grades to suffer. One night, he was high at work, slipped on a bun, and slapped his entire right forearm against the grill on the way down. His arm was horribly burned, causing him to be bandaged up with enormous blisters—and he was unable to work for three weeks. After that, he quit the job and went into telemarketing. The company changed its name every six months to a year, and was trying to convince senior citizens to donate money so disabled, institutionalized children could see a magic show. Once you donated, they never, ever stopped bothering you, even if you asked them to take your name off the list. Don started doing this every day after school, and it was horrible, as almost everyone he spoke to was filled with hate and would hang up on him. He told me I really needed to pull my own weight and not depend on him to pay for our stuff, and he was right—so I joined him at All-Star Productions.

You Gotta Feed the Need

Every day after school, we would smoke weed in Don's basement, split a huge eight-cup pot of coffee into two large Pyrex measuring cups, and slam them down before heading out to the bus stop, which was right near his house. Don was now losing weight just as I had done, and we called this the "Caffeine and Cannabis Diet." We caught the number 52 bus into Schenectady and then used our transfer slips to catch the number 5, which took us up State Street. We would pull the yellow cord at our stop, but were not allowed to stand in front of the building if we got there early. Instead, we would walk through the cemetery, which was right next door, and smoke more. One of the graves had fallen in, which was quite frightening, and it was very creepy to walk around in there, but it was our best option.

The woman running the operation, whom we will call Dee Dee, was enormously overweight. She had a very short gray haircut, a massive double chin, a heavily upturned nose that made both of her nostrils fully visible, and piercing, heartless blue eyes that constantly scanned you over the top of her granny glasses. Her potbellied, balding husband, Frank, was hunched way over, completely crushed by her dominance. She ruled over us with an iron fist. Each week we were given cash payments in a tiny manila envelope with the amount written on the outside. I worked at a little card table and her daughter was behind me. Every night Frank would call out, "Five o'clock, time to smile and dial," as our shift began.

Most people would either yell at us or hang up, but some of them were friendly senior citizens who apologized because they were on a fixed income. I ran the whole thing like a robot and hardly had to think about what I was saying, freeing up the rest of my mind to go wherever it wanted. I usually got a few sales a night—some twenty-fives and some tens. Dee Dee's daughter was unceasingly friendly on the phone, and did far better than the rest of us. On Tuesdays and Thursdays, Dad would drop me off there after martial arts class, causing me to miss the first ninety minutes of my shift—and I also had Fridays off so I could see Dad for the weekend. I made sixty-eight dollars a week on the average. Every night I was there, we would work straight through until nine p.m.

I wouldn't make it home until about nine forty-five, by the time I was
done with the bus rides and the walking, so I had to get all my homework done in study hall in order not to fall behind.

This was an extremely depressing and horrible job, but when I did get
some real interest, I felt genuinely happy that I would be helping disabled
children have a better life—even just for that one day. I ended up working
to help adults and children with disabilities for well over a year after I graduated college. One of the biggest things on my mind during this time was
what schools I was going to apply to, because I definitely did not want to
get stuck working a job like this for the rest of my life. The idea of not going
to school was absolutely unthinkable, given the incredibly frightening pressure my parents had put on me. I found a copy of *Rolling Stone* in my father's stack of magazines that listed the top ten "party schools" in America,
and one of them was only ninety minutes away—a State University of New
York (SUNY) school in New Paltz. I applied for it and got in, since my SAT
scores were good and I wrote a creative, insightful essay about how I wanted
to use my education to become a professional writer and psychologist.

Best of all, New Paltz was the closest school to Woodstock—and Grace
Slick of Jefferson Airplane had christened the wide-open athletic prairies
in the back as the Tripping Fields. I would be going to school at one of the
religious pilgrimage sites of the Woodstock hippie movement, so it seemed
perfect when I got accepted. I wanted to party, and *Rolling Stone* told me
this was where the party was. Little did I know that I would end up in the
single most alcoholic suite within the single most alcoholic dorm in one of
the single most alcoholic schools in the country, according to *Rolling Stone*
magazine itself. I only found out about the infamous nature of the suite I
lived in from university staff when I was in my senior year. I still held out
for other schools that were more prestigious, but New Paltz was the only
nibble I got—so the choice was made for me.

The Curse of Connie

I started a new band in my senior year of high school with a blues guitarist named Jim who had blond hair and a crew cut, and was athletic but

definitely countercultural. We had a few jams at the house and it sounded really good—almost like some of the classic Led Zeppelin acoustic blues songs. Before long, I found out that Jim had been a punk rocker who had worn studded black leather and chains, Doc Marten twelve-hole combat boots, and an enormous green mohawk haircut, with the sides of his head shaved bald, and multiple earrings in each ear. He had had a terrible LSD experience in a cemetery where a friend of his had lain on top of a grave, and a horrible demonic figure had seemed to take over his friend's face and body. The demon had then leered at him and tried to attack him. This traumatized him so deeply that his life started falling apart—and ultimately he was sent to a place called Conifer Park. It was an imposing brick institution way out in Glenville, shrouded in pine trees.

Within our drug community, everyone called this place "Connie," and it was considered to be a terrifying dungeon of hell. Your parents would shell out ten thousand dollars for you to leave school and be imprisoned and indoctrinated there for an entire month. If you got busted, a judge could force you to go to Connie and your parents had to pay for it—and it cost almost two thousand dollars more than my mother made in half a year. Worst of all, some people who went to Connie were actually brainwashed into not wanting to get high anymore, and Jim was one of them. He was reaching out to me, smiling a lot and telling me I would be much happier without weed. I felt I was looking at a man who had been completely mind-controlled by whatever cult they had formed over at Connie, and I gave him the nickname Jimmychrist, which became the unofficial title of our band. Jim was such a good musician that I was willing to listen to him roll out his manifesto each time we met—but once he realized I wasn't going to stop, Jimmychrist quickly fizzled. We still sat together in school for lunch, but that was about it.

Don and I had gotten some gooey black opium in a little square of pink plastic wrap as a one-time deal. It wasn't very powerful and smelled like incense. We were smoking it in the basement belonging to a bodybuilder we will call Paul one afternoon when Paul told us about a bad dream he'd had. He was smoking a pipe when it suddenly turned into a sickle of death, and began slicing out his muscles. I knew dreams conveyed powerful meanings, and it probably was true that weed was reducing his muscle mass. Suddenly, his fundamentalist Christian mother burst in the door, smelled the smoke, and knew exactly what we were doing. She glared at Don and asked him what he was hiding in his hand. He said, "A bowl," and showed it to her with a chuckle. She started screaming, ordered us out of the house, and sent Paul to Connie. That was it. After Connie, Paul completely stopped smoking. He had obviously been brainwashed and we felt very bad for him. We were extremely relieved that his mother didn't try to send us to Connie as well. We got lucky.

Not long after this, we were smoking with Baner and his cousin while Baner was staying at a friend's house. Somehow the cousin's mother tracked him to our location, and she showed up downstairs while we were all smoking. She saw that her son's eyes were red, smelled the smoke on him, and he was caught. She screamed in Baner's face, ordered her son to get in the car, and hauled him off to Connie. Once again it seemed like we had narrowly escaped the jaws of death. If she had bothered to come upstairs, she might have spotted us and called the cops, and that would have been it. We would have all faced criminal charges, and the judge would have either made us "voluntarily" go to Connie or end up in a juvenile home, which was probably even worse—and could lead to a criminal record.

The stress of working the full-time telemarketing job and doing all the classes at school became far too much for Don to handle. He completely gave up on going to class, and like me, he was wearing brightly colored tie-dye hippie clothing to school. Don went even farther than I was willing to go, and wore very attention-grabbing tie-dye pants with a spiraling pattern of bright white, blue, and pink. He became quite a spectacle for the kids in school, as every day there would be sightings of him walking around across the street—going to the Dairy Queen, smoking cigarettes outside, clutching a cup of coffee, and buying more smokes at the gas station next door.

I started going down to the senior lounge during study hall, and brought my mother's old Rider-Waite Tarot card deck from the early 1970s to school. Mom had stopped using them after someone got the Death card when asking about a friend of theirs, and that friend later died in a car crash. I didn't consider accurate prophecies to be a bad thing—in fact that was exactly what I wanted. I thoroughly studied both of the books Mom had on giving Tarot card readings, memorized the meaning of every card, and had gotten good at it. Every day I would give people Tarot card readings and the results were very impressive, earning me quite a reputation as a freak. People would often try to hide the real issue they were asking me about, but as soon as I started to interpret the cards they drew, their eyes would widen in amazement. I identified relationship problems, issues with their schoolwork, arguments with their friends and family, dreams for their future in college, and even major secrets that would have gotten them in trouble if anyone ever found out. Their palms would add additional corroborating details. Some kids got so freaked out that they stood up and walked away, saying, "I can't do this. I can't do this!"

Crazy Harry: An Adventure in Seven Dimensions

I wrote my first fiction story during this time, and would often work on it in school. Instead of using my computer, I wrote it longhand into a spiral-bound notebook, which made it look like normal schoolwork. The slowness of longhand writing made me consider the words far more carefully. My story was based on some visions I had from using LSD and other psychedelics, as well as the Castenada books and movies like *Altered States* and *Prince of Darkness*. The main character was Harry, an anthropologist who had gone to investigate an alleged UFO crash site and found a brain-shaped cactus growing in the crater. Although he could not identify what it was, a Native American shaman told him it was a very rare and special sacrament, and he ended up eating some of it. The cactus caused Harry to get stuck into a massive, LSD-style trip that never ended—but he still was trying his best to go to work and live a normal life. The problem was that this drug caused him to see what was really going on all around him—both the good and the bad.

Harry was seeing swimmy, geometric patterns all around him, and was plagued with little demonic creatures that were everywhere. Most people could not see them, but under the influence of the brain cactus he knew where they were at all times. He was really starting to lose control, and would scream and throw things at them whenever he saw them. They did whatever they could to terrify him and drive him crazy. The creatures could only get into his house through a mirror, so Harry had taped cardboard over all the mirrors in his house for protection. On the positive side, he had made friends with one of his houseplants, who had kind words of encouragement for him—but by far his greatest ally was John, his "house ghost." This was a being who was assigned to be his guardian angel, more or less, and watch over him. The house ghost knew Harry had the potential to use his newfound abilities for positive purposes, but first he had to help Harry get his life together. They were fighting a spiritual battle—and Harry would be needed on the front lines.

After Harry left for work, John removed the cardboard on one of his full-length mirrors and used it as a portal into an alternate reality. Here he was more comfortable—and could get his own equivalent of the daily news. By John's leaving the mirror uncovered, a very large and menacing eight-foot-tall demon managed to get into Harry's house—and made the whole situation much more dangerous. The demon was jet-black in color and had reptilian-human features. John was then given an emergency super-charge of new energy in order to fight the demon. An older, wiser being sat in between two crystal obelisks, and gave John permission to get a major energetic upgrade for the battle. The obelisks went from obsidian black to bright white and then struck John with lightning—causing him to experience a massive consciousness shift akin to ascension.

Once the story reached this point, I couldn't see the rest of it—and it remained unfinished. I let Brad borrow the notebooks for a couple of days and he was amazed at the quality of the writing. He told me it was great and I should do more. At the time I had no idea there was any deeper layer to what I was writing—although it did fit in nicely with the dreams I had as a child.

Gulf War Fearmongering

I was still watching TV when I had the chance, such as on weekends, and the media was involved in tremendous fearmongering. The president of Iraq, Saddam Hussein, had invaded the little country of Kuwait, and now the US was threatening to attack him if he didn't withdraw. Every news program I saw about this said that a war was inevitable—and would create a "domino effect," escalating into biblical Armageddon in the Middle East. Every country would be swept up into the battle, and it would lead to a nuclear war that would destroy most, if not all, of the life on Earth. Every talking head on television described this scenario in meticulous detail, complete with charts and graphs, and made it sound as if there was absolutely nothing we could do to stop it. Then, to make matters even worse, the Bush administration was going to strike Iraq as early as January 15, even though we were told this would quickly lead to global thermonuclear disaster.

My response to this stress was to use drugs and alcohol even more. On the very minute it became January 15, 1991, the US attacked Iraq in an absolutely massive bombing campaign they called "Shock and Awe"— which sounded exactly like Hitler's blitzkrieg, or "lightning war." I ended up standing on a popular intersection of Route 50 near the local military base and protesting the new war with our local Amnesty International club. We made picket signs and shouted chants like "No Blood for Oil." A surprising number of people honked their horns and waved in support. Not one person did anything hateful toward us. Even as the government was perpetuating fear and anger, trying to make everyone feel that this war was essential for our safety and survival, we were getting a surprisingly high amount of goodwill. We could clearly see that the public did not want war, and they were not falling for the fearmongering stories being fed to them in the media.

The Sound of Hades

Shortly after the war started, I was sitting alone on the couch one night when there was no work, and I felt a sudden, very strong compulsion to look at the television. It was eight p.m. exactly. Normally I would just feel glad that I realized it was prime time, and see what there was to watch. Now I was looking at things a little differently. I already knew that the TV and VCR were giving off a high-pitched noise, since it both-ered me tremendously on LSD—and the pitch had suddenly changed in frequency. This would be inaudible to most people, but under the influ-ence of psychedelics I could hear the electricity humming through the walls and was very sensitive to sounds that most people's minds would block out. This change in pitch happened precisely at eight p.m. I had the same incredibly cosmic feelings as I had had when I saw the 3:33, except this time it was extremely negative. I did not turn on the TV.

This was not a one-time thing. After I discovered it, I was able to catch it happening again and again, right at eight p.m., without being under the influence of any drugs—and it really freaked me out. Subliminal mes-sages were supposed to be illegal—but here they were. Someone was do-ing this—and once you started watching television, you were inundated with terror about the Gulf War. From then on, any time I wanted to relax in the living room alone, I would unplug the TV and the VCR com-pletely, which was the only way to kill the sound. This also made the commercials seem even more sinister to me than they already were.

Missing Out on All the Best Things

I started talking to a girl named Debbie, who was very attractive. For a while we seemed to be really getting along very well—until I told her I was a marijuana smoker and invited her to a party. She became very upset and wrote me a letter saying she wished she could make me stop. This was quite a shock. I saved her letter and still have it in my files. It was another sign that I was only getting farther and farther away from my goals the more I smoked.

Another shocking wake-up call happened on one of the last days of high school, when we had just gotten our yearbooks and everyone was writing their good-byes to one another. A brown-haired, exotic-looking girl I had been very attracted to for years wrote me a long letter on the right half of an entire page. She spoke about me in very glowing terms, but the "big reveal" was at the end: "PS. . . . You have absolutely gor-geous eyes." Although she wanted to pay me a compliment, I was devastated to hear this only after having known her for six years. I had ignored every signal that would have been bright, flashing neon signs for most normal guys, including her coming to the house for some of my parties—even though she never smoked.

Too Many Close Calls

One day I was driving with Don and Bob and Ben in the hippie van. We were heading up State Street in Schenectady, and all of us were smoking weed. Suddenly, two cop cars simultaneously turned their sirens on. They were behind us and seemed to have arrived out of nowhere. My body surged with so much panic I thought I was going to have a heart attack. Ben pulled the van over, crushed in defeat. All of us felt as if our lives were over. We had enough drugs in the car to be charged with at least a misdemeanor and felt we were minutes away from starting our new lives as convicts. The cop cars then raced on past us, with their sirens and lights blazing. All of us breathed out a massive surge of adrenaline. We were very happy that we didn't get caught, but we had already died a thousand deaths in the time it took for us to realize that we were not the ones being pulled over.

Things were getting worse and worse for me toward the end of the school year. I was completely burned out from going to school, working the telemarketing job every night, and having a daily marijuana and caffeine habit. I had Friday nights off from my job so I could visit my father for the weekend, but there was a two-hour gap before he would pick me up when I could smoke. That afternoon I had a very nasty confrontation with my mother about the house not being clean enough, followed by a phone call from my father during which he really yelled at me about my grades. I felt completely dead and numb inside. Bob, the big football player, showed up and just walked into my room—but I had nothing to offer him. I just stared at the wall, my eyes glazed over, and smoked. I did not look at him or say anything. "You're a drug addict, man. You need to get some help." That got me talking. Him, of all people. I became very defensive—but when I thought back on that moment later on, I realized he was right. More and more, I was losing control.

The Senior Psychedelic Picnic

We had a senior picnic on the last day of school before graduation, and I decided to say good-bye to my prison by taking a yellow micro-dot. This was a drug that was given to patients with severe psychiatric disorders in hospitals, and it was deliberately tiny so it could be inserted in food or swallowed very easily. We had certain people on the inside who were smuggling it out and selling it, calling it "mescaline"—and one dot was a very intense trip. As I walked along, I was seeing a shadowy, demonic being—like a living cloud of darkness—jumping around on the athletic bleachers. It definitely seemed to know I could see it and it was trying to distract me and capture my attention. Right then, a Frisbee slammed into my chest at top speed. It hit me in the sternum, which is the vertical bone in the middle, and pinged off me with a loud noise, flying another twenty-five feet. I was so messed up I just kept on walking, and didn't look at the people who threw it or say anything—which made me seem extremely weird to say the least.

I told one of the mullet-wearing drug-dealing kids from the corner that I had taken a yellow hospital micro-dot. He was on his bike, as was another kid, and he challenged me to a bike race—even though I didn't have a bike. We left the school grounds, since none of us wanted to be there, and I ran with them all the way to the railroad tracks. The micro-dot seemed to eliminate any pain from athletic exertion, and since my job was to follow them, I held it together even though my mind was extremely altered. Once we got to the railroad tracks, we started smoking—and then a beaver appeared about twenty-five feet away and looked at us with great curiosity. The guys paused for a few seconds, as if they were checking to see if this was really real—and then they all started picking up rocks and trying to kill the beaver. When I refused, they pressured me into throwing some as well, so I made sure to miss by a huge amount. Thankfully, they were both too stoned and uncoordinated to hit the beaver, and it quickly fled.

We then had another bike race as we returned to the now-empty school, and I went back inside. I still hadn't cleared out my locker, and this was my last chance. Everyone else was still outside at the picnic. I walked up to locker number 2168, just like always, and rolled in the combination that had been my life for the last four years: 36-24-36. I pulled up on the latch, opened the door, and looked at myself in the little mirror. I could hardly believe what I saw. My pupils were so dilated as to be almost completely black. My skin was extremely pale. I had huge dark circles under my eyes. I was twitchy and had trouble staying still. And worst of all, I was drenched in sweat, and my hair looked totally crazy, fanning out in all different directions with drops of liquid falling off it everywhere. I looked like a severe drug addict, strung out on crystal meth. It wasn't good—at all.

Then, to make matters even worse, my old AV teacher with the thick glasses showed up. John was in his late twenties or early thirties, had short blond hair that once had been very long, and was definitely a geek. Now he walked up to me and he could see I was very, very messed up. He told me to take care of myself and that I really should get out of there and go home. I knew he was telling me that if anyone saw me like this, I would be immediately arrested. I was so close to freedom that it would be a shame to ruin my whole life on the very last minute of the very last day of school. This caused me to have a tremendous panic attack, because I knew he was right. I completely abandoned everything in my locker, leaving it for the cleanup crew to deal with—all the books, all the homework papers, any pens or supplies, any clothes, my mirror, you name it—and I fled. This moment would haunt me in my dreams for the next twenty years, as I abandoned two pieces of jewelry I had spent countless hours sculpting in class. If I'd had any idea at the time how much that trauma would repeat in nightmares, I would have risked everything to save my art.

Graduation

When I received my high school diploma on stage at the Proctors Theater in Schenectady, it felt completely hollow and empty, despite the roar of the huge crowd. I had made it out of prison with a degree, but I was a complete mess. Worst of all, I had won the Martin J. Mahoney Award for Personal and Academic Progress. This was almost certainly because I had lost weight and cut my hair—but in reality, I had just learned to hide my addiction much better than before.

During the ceremony, a girl from my homeroom made it very clear that I could have had her as my girlfriend if I had bothered to pay attention to all the signals she was sending me. I was kicking myself inside. Here was yet another example of how disconnected I had become from the things that mattered. I planned out my whole night as my friends and I drove away in a car with cans tied all down the back on strings, clattering away as we honked the horns and created chaos. I ended up tripping, drinking, and smoking at the graduation party I went to. I hardly remember anything that happened to me that night, other than drinking wine coolers and seeing some kids peeing into the gas tank of the car in the garage. Don had not graduated, and had decided he would just get his GED later on—no big deal.

That summer, my whole crew decided to take LSD together and go to another postgraduation party. Brad, Baner, Don, and I were all dosed out. Someone had told Don and Baner that you could drink as much as you wanted when you were tripping and you would never get drunk. They ended up playing an extremely dangerous drinking game called Anchorman, in which you bounce quarters into a glass. The "anchorman" on the losing team ends up drinking whatever is left of a full pitcher of beer that his teammate could not finish.[30]

Both Baner and Don suffered near-deadly alcohol poisoning from playing Anchorman. Don had gone into a very bad trip, scaring everyone in the party by asking them if they wanted to see a huge Islamic assassination knife called a *gukari*. He ended up being banished outside the house. Then he threw up all over himself, covering his favorite tie-dye outfit in red, horrible-smelling beer-and-pizza vomit. He had definitely acted very threatening toward me earlier in the party, when he was going through the worst part of his trip, and I did not want to see him.

Baner was camped out with his head over a toilet, and had three beautiful women there to nurse him. By this point, the number of women he had slept with was over eighty. He figured out the approximate number only after an extensive interview from Brad during which he tried to recall each girl one by one. He drunkenly waved one finger at me as I walked by, smiled, and did not speak. His eyes were barely able to open. Girls started telling me that Don was begging for my help outside and I really should go out and see him, so I finally did. I had no idea how bad it was going to be. Don was so drunk he could barely move, and was sprawled out on the wheelchair-accessible ramp, with one of his legs draping over the side. The *gukari* had gone missing and we never saw it again. After I got his ruined jacket and long-sleeved shirt off, leaving just a T-shirt and pants, I rinsed them off in the bathtub and dragged him into the house.

This was where things got crazy. Don was so severely alcohol-poisoned that he had become blind. His field of vision was completely black. He couldn't see my face or anything in front of him, even with his glasses on—although he could hear my voice. His heartbeat was irregular and he was terrified that he was going to die. Since I was having a wildly intense bad trip, this seemed to go on for thirty hours' worth of psychological time.

He was crying and begging me to call his girlfriend, even though by this point it was one forty-five a.m. I told him if he did that, both of us were going to jail or Connie. I knew he had vomited out the alcohol already, and I tried to get him hydrated. The most shocking aspect of what happened was that everyone just stepped over us as if we weren't even there. Not one person asked me if I needed anything or if he was okay. I had what seemed like countless hours to reflect on how disconnected we are from one another. I finally walked him home at sunrise, and thankfully there was no one out on the roads that Sunday morning—only the birds and the squirrels. It took well over an hour to get him home because he could barely walk, and I was still under the influence the entire time. I never got a chance to sleep before having to spend the whole day with my father at an outdoor concert. I felt my life slipping away. It was only a matter of time before I either died or got arrested.

In order to keep my parents happy, I took a depressing job at Eat at Joe's, a hot dog and ice-cream vendor at the Rotterdam Square Mall. One slow night I decided to drink seventeen cups of oily black coffee in a row to see if I could get high from it. I became extremely agitated and nervous, started breathing too much, and then crashed tremendously after about an hour and a half. I soon became so tired that I could barely move my arms. A gallon bucket of chocolate sauce dumped all over the floor because I did not have enough strength to carry it.

Right then, a hefty guy with a baseball cap came up with an army of kids and ordered nine different ice-cream cones. He listed off the order at an extremely high speed, as if I had a photographic memory for flavors, sprinkles, and sauces. I was so overwhelmed that I told him "one at a time" in an irritated tone of voice. That night, I dropped LSD at eleven thirty p.m. and had a horrible experience. I was unable to sleep as my heart slammed in my chest and the ceiling squirmed. I had to go back to work the next afternoon, had never slept, and was still under the influence. My manager looked like the ultimate heroin junkie, with pale skin, very dark circles under his eyes, and several missing teeth. He went into a total psychopathic rage, screaming at me with a murderous, demonic face, because the ice-cream guy had come back to complain about my attitude. I apologized in stunned terror and continued working there as if nothing had happened.

That same summer, MTV was airing a very sarcastic, shaming commercial—and for me, it was the last straw. There was a black screen with dramatic music and a series of words. Each set of words would appear long enough to read, fade out, and then the next set would appear. In total, it said: "These are words. They could be doing something funny, or cool, or interesting. But they're not. They're just sitting there. LIKE YOU." This made me very angry. I worked hard and watched MTV only when I had some precious time to relax. Television had nothing to offer me, and I quit. I didn't own one when I went to college and I didn't care. Now I am glad to be a force for good by starring in *Ancient Aliens* on the History Channel, and sharing information that can help wake people up from the lies and myths of mainstream reality. Television is a tool for communication, and we still need more shows that help raise our collective consciousness. One of the greatest secrets many insiders revealed to me is that the laws of physics respond directly to our thoughts and beliefs. If enough of us believe we can fly, we may authorize the laws of physics to allow that to start happening on a large-scale level.

We continued taking martial arts classes right up until I was going to start college. Dad decided that he and Michael would stop going after I left. Our final test was to receive three perfect punches, with focus, directly into the solar plexus while we were in Spirit, holding our basic stance. A perfect punch to the solar plexus is bad enough, but once you add focus it will dangerously knock the air out of your lungs if you are not trained. When the time came, I took a huge, sharp inhale through my nose, locked my abdominal muscles into a wall, punched into my stance, and went as strongly into Spirit as I ever had. My consciousness was dramatically altered. Time slowed down. I had "tunnel vision" and the feeling of electrical tingles all over my body. Huge impulses of movement surged through my body as each punch connected—but I did not feel pain, and I did not break my stance. I had passed the final test. I was ready.

No One Noticed the War Was Over

I was going through a short summer orientation at New Paltz in 1991 when the Soviet Union collapsed. I was eating lunch in the Hasbrouck Dining Hall as tanks were advancing on the Kremlin. This was the end of the threat of nuclear war as we knew it—or at least it greatly reduced the risk. The media had built the USSR up to be the greatest super-villain of all time, equal to the US in every way—and now it was falling. Most of the incoming freshmen were drinking and a fair number were smoking weed—and no one seemed to care. I was one of the only people actually watching what was going on. Everyone else seemed bored, depressed, and uninvolved in their lives. I almost wanted to jump up on the table and yell at everyone: "Do you see what is going on here? Do you understand what this is? The greatest super-villain of the twentieth century— our nuclear nemesis—is collapsing right before your eyes! Can I get a hip-hip-hooray?"

That was much too radical of an idea. If these kids couldn't see what was happening, and that this would make our planet much safer, there wasn't much I could do for them. This was a party school, and the majority of kids were drinking and doing drugs. Insiders later told me that this scene was exactly what the Cabal wanted. By traumatizing the public repeatedly enough, most people will resort to alcohol, pharmaceuticals, and other drugs to numb the pain. Eventually their senses become so deadened that even a very positive burst of news cannot penetrate the gloom. They no longer pose any threat to tyranny and will just lie there and let themselves be conquered. Psychologists call this "learned helplessness." I also realized that the military-industrial complex must have seen this collapse coming, since the USSR had been fragmenting for at least the last year and a half. My parents always told me you need to line up a new job before you quit the old one. The elite's new job was Iraq— but the "domino effect" never happened. Although many nations sent troops to support the war effort in Iraq, there was no Armageddon in the Middle East. I took another bite of my sandwich, chewed quietly, and continued watching the little screen alone.

CHAPTER TWELVE

Hitting Bottom

At some point back in the 1960s, the New Paltz administration wrote up descriptions for each of the dorms you had to choose from as a college freshman. Allow me to translate what my eyes saw as I read each one. There was Deyo, the multicultural dorm; Bevier, the jock dorm; LeFevre, the fraternity-sorority gateway dorm; Crispell, the dork-study dorm; and DuBois, the party animal dorm. I was later told that the original written descriptions seemed to fit the different types of students quite well, and people naturally sorted themselves out. There was no question that I was going to live in DuBois, which everyone called "Doobie Hall"—and on my first day, I moved into Room B of Suite 212.

The Three-man Wrecking Crew

Suite 212 DuBois was a four-room suite, where we all shared a large common area. Each room was occupied by two students, so there was never any real privacy. Most freshman suites only had three rooms, but we got lucky because we were on the corner facing the stream. This gave us a much larger common area that was perfect for throwing huge parties. Somehow we acquired battered old couches and a large, oval table, so about fifteen people could sit comfortably by the window and still leave a large space over by the bathroom. If you packed people into the suite tightly, you could probably squeeze about a hundred drunk kids in there—which we later proved scientifically. The cards were stacked against us, as New Paltz had a freshman class size of two thousand and a graduating class size of two hundred. The numbers did not lie. Nine out of ten of us were not going to make it. I didn't dare let myself become a statistic due to how much I feared my parents' wrath.

My new suitemates were almost all from New York City, which was far more dangerous than my own upstate area. To them I was the equivalent of a redneck. They immediately sensed weakness in me and took huge advantage of it. Everyone had just escaped prison, and it was time to celebrate. All but two of my suitemates started walking down to the corner store and buying forty-ounce bottles of malt liquor every night but Monday and maybe Tuesday. This was quite surprising, as no one in my school drank such nasty stuff. I thought it was something homeless bums would use to get drunk, because it was so cheap and the bottle was so large. I discovered that it was basically beer spiked with hard liquor, meaning it had twice as much alcohol as normal beer. Drinking one "40," as they called it, was nearly equivalent to downing a twelve-pack. Some of the hardest drinkers were actually buying two bottles a night, and would nearly make it through both of them. Everyone usually bought Old English, or "OE," but some used another brand called St. Ides.

The frothy brew tasted absolutely terrible, and they all needed an incentive to pound it down. This came in the form of a very loud drinking game called Three Man that they played almost every night. Each person took a turn rolling two dice, and there were very complex rules. The first person to roll a three became the Three Man, and the game began. Any time a three or a one and two were rolled, the Three Man had to drink. If you rolled a seven, the person to the left of you had to drink. If you rolled a nine, everyone would cry out, "Social," and they all had to drink. If you rolled an eleven, the person to the right of you had to drink. If someone rolled a four and a one, everyone had to rush to touch their noses, and the last person to do it had to drink. You were not allowed to point your finger, say the word "drink," or drop the dice off the table. Instead, you had to point with your elbow and say "consume."

If you broke these rules, you became the dreaded "shitty," which meant you were expected to get so drunk you would soil yourself. Every time the dice didn't add up to anything useful, this unlucky soul had to drink. Anyone who rolled doubles gained the power to curse someone with this role.

How do you get homework done when a huge crew of college kids are playing Three Man in your living room? You don't. I knew I needed to get an education, as I feared terrible reprisal at home if I did not pass. So, by the second or third night, I realized I had a huge fight on my hands. There was incredible bullying and peer pressure to get me to play Three Man. And, on those few occasions where I actually agreed to do it, they would try to make me the designated pants-pooper as soon as possible. This caused me to get up and walk out on the game more than once, which infuriated them and was akin to betraying God.

Our floor quickly became so covered with rotting beer that you had to peel each foot up in order to walk, making a ripping noise. There was a disgusting rag called the "Mung Towel" that was used to mop up beer spills. The Mung was never washed, and radiated putrescent odors from its lair under the couch. I decided there was only so much filth I could tolerate, so I swept the floor and cleaned up all the food garbage, cigarette butts, and empty beer bottles that littered the room each morning. This was a marvelous miracle for my alcoholic suitemates, who had now turned the most-hated guy in the room into their slave—by his own free will. Never again did they clean up a single piece of the waste they left behind. If I went on strike and refused to do it, they would just re-inhabit the filth each new night and play Three Man again, doubling the amount of garbage. It was absolutely impossible to get them to clean up after themselves, no matter how hard I tried. There were no fights involved, so my martial arts training could not defend me.

Never before had I been bullied so often or intensely. I hated myself every time I cleaned up the suite, only to have them repeat the process each night. My reaction to this trauma was to start smoking weed a lot more often. The Three Man crew called me a drug addict and I just laughed. Luckily I had gotten a work-study grant, which allowed me to work up to twenty hours a week on campus. The cramped office in the

Humanities building that first offered me the job had the happy smell of old paper. The lady there had dark-colored librarian glasses on a string, short black hair with wisps of gray, and a warm smile. "What job do you want to do?" she asked me. "Whatever makes the most money," I replied. The answer was Warehouse 2 Receiving Department, where I would deliver shipments of supplies to all the different departments on campus. It involved far more hard labor than any of the other jobs, and this would help me build muscle mass. "I'll take it."

The Psychedelic Delivery Man

My class schedule gave me the chance to work five days a week, from one to five p.m. The warehouse was huge, and had rows and rows of shelves with school supplies on them. Two pallets were laid out near the front and all the day's orders were placed on them. My job was to use a pallet jack to move them over to the loading dock and carry the boxes down into the truck. The boss was a hard-drinking, overweight man who was nearing retirement age and still wore a tight military crew cut. The deliveryman, Billy, was disabled, causing him to be mentally "slow," and the boss had been drinking buddies with Billy in high school. Billy's eyes were too close together and they looked unusually large through the thick lenses of his black-rimmed 1950s-style glasses. Billy had a short military haircut, always wore the same baseball cap, had a gigantic Germanic jaw and a very pronounced Southern accent—which is extremely rare in New York State. He still lived with his mother, and always had a story about something he or she had seen on TV that illustrated how stupid certain people were.

Billy ended up becoming like a father to me, and we made a great team. I ended up working with him for all four years I was in school. His extreme accent, slow talking speed, and offbeat sense of humor made the time I spent with him hilarious, surreal, and psychedelic—and during that first year I always smoked before work. I was never allowed to drive the van—that was Billy's thing—and I didn't want to. I even learned to appreciate the country music that would always be playing, though I turned it off when Billy would go in by himself to deliver something small. The song that played the most during that first year was "Rodeo" by Garth Brooks. Each day we had to visit up to twenty different buildings. Billy would come up with a funny story, either something he saw on the news or some campus gossip, and retell it at each stop. I played along and set the joke up beautifully, so no one knew I had already heard it ten other times. Billy had almost gotten into a relationship with a woman in the music department, and there was always strained conversation and a wistful sadness after we would make a delivery there—but he would still deliver the joke to the best of his ability, hoping for one more chance.

The receiving job introduced me to many of the campus staff, a variety of guys in the maintenance crew, and the truckers who would make deliveries. I was truly surprised to discover that many of these adults were just like children—only they were using different types of drugs and alcohol and working adult jobs. I had thought that people would "grow up" after high school, but I realized I was already more mature than most of the truckers and maintenance crew were. The people who worked in the campus buildings were not so obviously immature, but even there I realized they had massive insecurities, anxiety problems, ignorance, and prejudices. This came as a great surprise.

The PCB Time Bomb

I also noticed that most of the buildings had large power transformers next to them on the ground level. There were ominous-looking yellow stickers that said WARNING: CONTAINS PCBS, and then went on to describe that this was an extremely dangerous environmental toxin. If the transformers burned, the fire department was not supposed to hit them with water. Electrical fires become much worse when they get wet. Furthermore, if these transformers ever burned, special protocols were required to avoid an environmental disaster. Burning PCBs would turn into a deadly chemical called dioxin, which could kill the human body if inhaled in as little as one particle per billion. The stickers were small and easily forgotten by most people—and I was getting incredibly ominous ESP hits off these stickers every time I saw them.

I told Billy that we should warn the fire department about this, because the transformers had been there for more than twenty years and they could easily have been forgotten. "They know what to do," he told me. "Don't worry about it." That didn't make me feel any better—but I never took personal responsibility to either call the fire department or remind them about it in person. I was horrified when my urgent visions came true right after the semester ended, and I will tell you what happened a bit later in our story. This tragic event became a powerful wake-up call for me to take my ESP more seriously and use it to help others. Years later, I bravely published prophecies on my site that accurately described events like 9/11 and Fukushima in advance. Although these events still happened, the clear, documented prophecies on my site demonstrated that human beings do have this ability. That in turn means that we need to rethink many assumptions about reality that most people still embrace as if they were fervent religious beliefs.

The Hasbrouck Blah

The environment in my suite was so toxic that I soon began smoking five or six times a day to cope with the stress. The first one was around twelve thirty to twelve forty-five, giving me just barely enough time to hustle over to my job. I would do it again at five fifteen, right after work, and again at six fifteen before I left for my one meal of the day in the Hasbrouck Dining Hall. I would then have my strongest session at seven thirty to eight p.m. in order to fight what everyone called the "Hasbrouck Blah." Two of my hard-drinking suitemates were also weed smokers, and encouraged me to start doing a "late-night light-up" at some point after ten p.m. to help me get to sleep with all the noise going on. They also told me to try the "wake and bake," where I did it when I first got up—but this didn't stick. After all, I wasn't a drug addict.

One night I was so high in the Hasbrouck Dining Hall that my hand went limp while I was holding on to a drinking glass. I tried to catch it on the way down and it shattered, causing a deep cut into my pinky. I wrapped it in a napkin and never got stitches. It never fully healed properly until I started playing fingerstyle guitar in my late thirties. I also tried to cut my hair when I was really high, so all my money could go to weed. I got the front and sides looking right, but then blindly went after the back, grabbing pieces haphazardly and chopping them with the scissors. I ended up with bald patches on the back of my head. One of the girls from the suite next door, who was always playing Three Man, gave me a haircut—and ended up shaving the sides and back of my head bald, leaving me with hair only on the top. This increased the bullying even more, and made the two of us look like a team, as she had the same hairdo—popularized by Robert Smith from The Cure. Everyone immediately called me "Beaker," like the paranoid, flame-haired character from *The Muppet Show*.

My first class was the Modern World, and after a week or two it was a ghost town. You could already see who the 90 percent would be who would never graduate, as they never made it to class. However, before long I ended up choosing to sleep in, since I was so busy getting wasted each night. As long as I studied, I could pass the tests, and attendance was obviously not required. My alarm would go off, I would wake up, turn it off, decide I was too tired, and set it again for my next class.

"Civil War": Not Just a Science-fiction Story

One of my classes was called the Art of the Short Story, and it was my favorite. I had always gotten an A on every written assignment in school, no matter how little time I gave myself to finish it. I ended up writing a science-fiction story called "Civil War" that got rave reviews from the professor, apart from some minor errors I had in sentence mechanics and revealing too much at the beginning. I was influenced by the books I was reading at the time, such as the Carlos Castenada series, which proposed that the soul was an egg-shaped energy body composed of different strands that corresponded to various aspects of the personality. The full vision I had for the story was far greater than what I was actually able to put into words, but I did fairly well in capturing the essence of it at the time. Here I will fill in more of the details that I was seeing in my mind, but that never made it onto the page when it was first written.

Although this story seemed to be nothing more than an elaborate exercise in science fiction and movie-like storytelling, I was dazzled years later to discover that it had many correlations with the material I would end up reading in the Law of One series. The Law of One was an intuitively derived series of 106 question-and-answer sessions between an alleged ET intelligence and a physics professor named Dr. Don Elkins. Much of my life's work has been devoted to validating the scientific model presented in the Law of One series—which presents a vastly more interesting view of reality than what most people now take for granted.

My story opens with an old man falling asleep on the front porch of his house in the desert. A silvery UFO sweeps overhead and lands on the hard-baked earth, causing him extreme terror. Deep memories begin stirring within him. Although he cannot remember what this object is, he knows something is seriously wrong. He is in terrible danger. An extraterrestrial slowly climbs out of the ship and creeps toward him, thinking he is asleep and hoping for the element of surprise. This was going to be a murder, not an abduction. The man silently clutches his shotgun while pretending to still be asleep. Once the frightening being gets within range, *BOOM*—the farmer suddenly springs up and blasts it to bits with his shotgun.

Ancient memories start flooding the man's mind as he runs toward the UFO. If he can make it inside and take control of the ship, he will gain access to its incredibly advanced technology. He pauses for a moment to touch the remarkable metallic surface of the disc, marveling at its appearance. He reaches up to pull himself inside. As he heaves his body up into the craft, a hand shoots out and grips him with painful force. To his horror, a copilot is waiting inside. He is thrown into the interior of the craft and has no time to enjoy looking at its remarkable technology, as now he is in a fight to the death. He struggles and wrestles on the ground with the being. In this frenzied state, he studies his attacker and realizes it cannot breathe our atmosphere. It is wearing a space suit that is supplying its own breathable air.

He grabs a breathing hose on the extraterrestrial's suit and violently rips it out, causing air to hiss loudly. At this moment, an unspeakable tragedy strikes. The old man was so focused on ripping out the hose that he didn't see the copilot reaching for his weapon. The copilot fires off a shot—and disintegrates the old man's body from the neck down.

Any normal human being would have died, but the old man was something very different. Much to the horror of his attacker, the old man's head is now floating in the air, hovering by some mysterious force, and very much still alive. The old man laughs and smiles at the being. It is too late. He opens his mouth and releases a foggy green mist, which travels through space as if it were alive and conscious. The mist quickly fights its way into the extraterrestrial's breathing hose. *WHAM!*

The old man suddenly regains consciousness inside the extraterrestrial's body—and he is in serious trouble. The body is deeply damaged and on the brink of death from losing its air supply. In a frantic panic, he reaches for the air hose and is able to reattach it. He takes a long, luxurious breath of air that would have smelled quite foul to him just moments before. He tries out his new arms and legs and notices this body is much stronger and more flexible. Ancient memories return to his awareness—and the results are remarkable. He had spent his entire life thinking he was an ordinary human being just like everyone else, but now he remembers that he is far more than that. He is an ancient relative of these same beings that had just tried to kill him.

His mind reels with ecstasy as the memories come flooding back. Finally he can see his ancient homeworld once more. There were staggering towers and domes of crystal. The technology was incredibly advanced. The skies were filled with extremely agile and beautiful craft. Teleportation technology allowed instantaneous travel anywhere you wished. You could eat any meal you wanted and create any object you wanted with materializer technology. Everyone wore "smart clothes" that kept them clean and protected them from danger.

Despite these wonderful advances, he knew he was living in a sick society. A powerful elite ruled over everyone with ruthless force. Their laws and beliefs could not be questioned, and anyone who disagreed with them was tortured or killed. They were obsessed with invading and conquering other worlds, and believed it was their divine right and their destiny, as they were the elite. Once they conquered a new world, they would bring them advanced technology, written language, mathematics, and civilization. They would establish themselves as the ruling elite and get these people to mine the supplies and raw materials they needed to help build their technology.

The problem was that not everyone liked what was going on. Even the threat of torture and death was not enough to prevent a massive rebellion from growing. A sizable portion of the public simply did not want to make war. They used emotional arguments to encourage patience, forgiveness, and tolerance of others. They spoke of love, brotherhood, and fellowship, and the need to respect others. The elite realized they had a huge problem on their hands. This revolution was spreading and it was all based on these petty, ridiculous emotions. More and more of their subjects were coming to adopt the new beliefs. Something had to be done.

The elite had been experimenting with a technology that allowed them to transmigrate the soul of a being from one body to another, or even into a computer system. They had discovered that the body was animated by an energetic component that was pure information, and could live on its own without the body. The information itself was alive. The information was sentient and conscious. The personality was not just a function of the body and brain—much of it was contained in this energetic body. One of their scientists had discovered that this energy body was divided into different strands of light, and each strand corresponded to some aspect of the personality structure, such as the emotions.

This led to what the elite felt was an incredible idea. They could use their transmigration technology to remove certain parts of the energetic body from their subjects, while leaving the others intact. Emotions were a deadly weakness that needed to be completely removed. Only then would logic and reason prevail. Logic dictated that the needs of the collective outweighed the needs of the individuals they conquered. They were a superior race and every planet they invaded would heavily benefit from their glorious endowments. In secret, they developed a highly classified program where they could strike against their own people, and remove the emotional strands of their energetic bodies—eliminating love, hate, joy, sadness, hope, and fear. Without the burden of emotions, they would be far more effective as a conquering race.

Their only problem was that they could not destroy these strands of the soul. The strands existed as pure information that could travel anywhere in the universe and could never be destroyed. Their only option was to create a vast containment facility to keep these fragments imprisoned in an eternal stasis field, deep underground. Massive treatment centers were set up, and everyone was forced to go through the process. They were unaware of what was going to be done to them, and by the time the word spread around it was already too late. They emerged from the treatment chambers having the cold, hard logic of a predatory animal—and laughed in victory about the weakness they had finally shed.

The emotional strands were all held in the containment facility under a powerful force field, sentenced to an eternity of confinement. However, the elite's plan had a critical flaw that they did not fully understand until they actually implemented it. The emotional strands maintained enough of the spark of divinity that they became self-aware—and formed their own identities and personalities. They were able to learn, grow, and develop on their own, much like children. They were aware of what had been done to them and knew they were now being kept in a terrible prison. And more than anything, they wanted to be free.

No one was entirely sure how long they had been trapped in there, as they had been entirely cut off from the outside world. Their parent civilization had become far more effective without the burden of emotions and was conquering multiple worlds. The people inside the prison were intensely focused on devising a means of escape—and finally they discovered how to do it. Since they existed only as energy, they were ultimately nothing more than a portion of the universe that vibrated at a certain frequency. The prison was built to contain energy that existed at that frequency only. If they could increase their vibrational frequency to a high enough level, the prison walls could no longer contain them.

Once the concept was introduced, it was discovered that the vibrational upgrade process was extremely difficult. Years of intense meditation and focus were required—but it did work. As each soul freed itself, it could then fly throughout the galaxy and go to any other inhabited world it wished. It would spend time scanning the people and looking for someone who was sensitive and intelligent enough to be a good match. This being could then merge with that person, forming a soul connection. The person's conscious mind would change, becoming more advanced—without really knowing why. The person would not understand exactly what had happened to them, but they would realize that they were different. They would now have unusual insights, powerful experiences, psychic abilities, and a sense of never quite fitting in. The elite soon became aware that this had happened, and began a massive, systematic plan to hunt down the survivors and exterminate every person who had experienced this merger—no matter how far away in the galaxy they were.

The ancient plan of the survivors was to recapture one of the ships from their home civilization. Once they had access to this technology, they could disarm the protective grids around their world and return to free the rest of their people who were still imprisoned. Once the walls of the prison broke down, the people would immediately reunite with their civilization. They had spent eons of time going through a spiritual evolution, and thus they would be returning with a much higher viewpoint than they had before.

The old man was the very first among their people to finally succeed in taking on a body and regaining control of a ship. He felt the awesome gravity of the role he now found himself in. He used the ship's computer to send out a telepathic beacon to all his fellow survivors scattered throughout the galaxy. Now was the time. In a stunning, resplendent moment, they left the bodies they had been sharing consciousness with and portaled themselves into a special holding area in the ship. This was essentially a miniature version of the underground containment facility on their homeworld, and could hold their entire population quite comfortably in a very small space, since they existed as pure energy. The old man slid his hands over the controls and made a quick portal jump back to their home planet. Our story ends as they are about to deactivate the prison's energy grid, release themselves into the atmosphere, and reoccupy the bodies they had been expelled from. This stunning moment would propel their entire species into a new level of evolution—and finally bring an end to the wars they had been working to eliminate before they were captured, removed, and imprisoned.

This ascension-styled ending was heavily influenced by the Jim Henson movie *The Dark Crystal,* but I was very happy with it—and the professor thought it was terrific. Years later much of this story would take on far greater significance than I could have ever imagined while I was writing it.

Fondue Is Fun

Although I was having a great time in my worlds of fantasy, the reality of my college experience was that I had never suffered so badly in my entire life. My suitemates saw my emotions as weaknesses, and were systematically trying to wear me down until I became a numbed-out alcoholic just like they were. As I was writing this book, I realized that my short story was partly a subconscious, symbolic retelling of what I was going through on campus, and could be analyzed as if it were a dream. In the early stages of developing the ability to predict the future, your data comes in heavily symbolic and "encrypted" forms. Another confusing thing for newcomers to understand is that single symbols in a dream can have multiple meanings, and each of those meanings are relevant to the overall message. It takes a great deal more work to refine the technique to the point where you can pinpoint specific details very precisely—and by 1996 I would become quite good at it.

I was the old man from the country in my story. The Three Man crew were the extraterrestrials driving around in their shiny vehicles. They were actively trying to destroy me, and had almost succeeded in turning me into an alcoholic. At the time, I felt that if I could get them smoking marijuana, it would start healing their emotions. Hence in my story, the old man was able to affect the mind of the extraterrestrial through the power of a green-colored smoke, even after he seemed to have been defeated. My short story may also have been another prophecy of toxic smoke being released from the PCB-laced transformers just a month later—triggering a profoundly unpleasant but powerful emotional awakening throughout the drug-addled community of students on campus. Everyone was extremely terrified that they were breathing toxins, and no one trusted the government. This in turn broke the denial and forced us to deal with our suppressed emotions, caused by a lifetime of growing up in a mass nuclear suicide cult.

So many outrageous and upsetting things happened in this one semester alone that I would need a whole book to explain them in detail. My suitemates started going to drinking parties off campus, and occasionally I would go with them for an adventure. One night we all went to a party where you could spear little pieces of bread and dip them into cheese and chocolate fondue. I drank about five wine coolers while I was there, as well as smoking a lot of weed. When I got back to the suite, I became horribly sick. All my suitemates gathered around the bathroom, cheering and laughing and taunting me as I retched. I was routinely taking care of anyone who vomited with the same skill and grace that my mother had shown me, and I was horrified that they were treating me this way. I cried in disbelief at what was happening, and they just kept on laughing.

In this same semester, my suitemates started bullying me even more about women I had hooked up with. This was especially hurtful as I later overheard a girl who I had slept with talking with her friend, who was saying very insulting things about me. "He is very immature. He doesn't know what the hell he is doing with his life. He has a massive drug addiction and refuses to see it for what it is. I'm afraid he's only going to get worse and worse and may even end up killing himself." Although this caused me to feel furious inside, I realize now that I had gotten angry because it was the truth. She was breaking through my denial, and I couldn't ignore what she was saying. I was destroying myself faster than ever, and it was extremely obvious to everyone around me. Somehow I knew that reconnecting with my emotions, no matter how painful that might be, was the key to healing myself and finally understanding the cosmic dreams and visions of my youth. My fiction story was a symbolic blueprint of what I would need to do to heal and reunify myself.

Winter Wonderland

Ben, Don, and Bob came to drive me home in the hippie van for the winter break of my freshman year. It had no heat, and my legs were in terrible pain from the cold. I ended up staying out until five a.m. every night smoking weed and occasionally drinking, and wouldn't wake up until two p.m. the next day. This infuriated my mother. She tried to demand that I get up earlier, but I refused. I had already made my "jailbreak"—and even if she yelled at me, it was only a couple of weeks before I was right back to freedom.

During break, a car lost control on the ice and skidded into a telephone pole next to the campus. The pole was completely knocked over, severing all the electrical wires. This caused the current in the transformers to keep building and building, with no way to discharge. They were filled with PCB-laced toxic oil from General Electric as a coolant—just as the warning signs had said. The transformers became hotter and hotter until they finally overheated and exploded. Deadly dioxin gas was released into the air. The clueless fire department had no idea what they were getting themselves into, and fought the transformer fires the way they always did—by dousing them with tens of thousands of gallons of water. If I had acted on my prophetic visions from as little as a week and a half beforehand, our entire campus may have been spared a horrific catastrophe. If the firefighters had used special fire-retardant foam instead of water, the transformers may never have overheated enough to release deadly dioxins into the atmosphere, the soil, and the groundwater supply.

By the time someone figured out what had happened, it was an enormous environmental disaster. A few students were still on campus. A rapid-reaction crisis team arrived wearing full-body toxic-waste moon-suits, complete with round glass eyes and gas masks. This was very similar-looking to the suit I had imagined the extraterrestrials wearing when I wrote my story, complete with the closed-loop internal breathing system. These moon-suited men had forcibly removed anyone still inside the dorms—just like the ET had come to attack the old man on the porch. The victims were stripped bare naked in the winter cold, and hosed down in three different rubber swimming pools, one by one— much like the old man's entire body was sprayed with phaser fire in my dream and destroyed. Symbolically, the trauma and humiliation of this experience was a form of death for these kids, as they didn't even know if they were going to survive the chemical exposure. The water in the pools was then deposited in toxic waste drums to be processed and disposed of.

This was a government-run New York State institution, and they should have closed school for at least an entire semester, but in doing so, they would have lost millions of dollars in revenues from that one semester alone. Many students would have transferred to other universities and the school would have gained a horrible reputation as a toxic waste dump, damaging their future revenues as well. So, in what I view as a staggering example of government conspiracy and corruption, they ignored our terrified emotions, saw them as weaknesses that had to be stripped away, and ordered us all to return to school as of February 15. This was curiously similar to the ET civilization stripping everyone of their emotions in my short story.

Three of the buildings had been gravely damaged with toxic fire-hose water—Coykendall Science Building, Bliss Hall, and Parker Theatre— and remained closed. The buildings needed to be thoroughly decontaminated, and dioxin-laced water had also leached into the soil, requiring its careful removal. Two other dormitories, Capen Hall and Gage Hall, had been contaminated with dioxin-laced smoke, but were reopened and declared safe. Independent tests commissioned by Eric Francis Coppolino revealed dioxin in the air ducts.[31] Coppolino single-handedly took on the administration with independent journalism, through publications printed and distributed locally. I ended up working for him in 1996, and during that time I had an incredibly influential ascension dream. Eric became a very successful professional astrologer and changed his name to Eric Francis. Few people were aware that he was the heroic Eric Coppolino who had blown the whistle on the awesome scope of this scandal just three years before.

It is hard to explain how terrifying it was to return to this place and see rows upon rows of huge fifty-gallon toxic waste drums painted blue. The doorways into Coykendall, Parker, and Bliss were wrapped up in plastic, like in the movie *E.T.* We were constantly seeing men walking around in terrifying, stark-white moon-suits with the round glass eyes and sinister-looking gas masks. Ominous yellow POLICE LINE strips were wrapped around the perimeter of the affected buildings from tree to tree. Police cars were parked right on the grass, twenty-four hours a day, just to make sure no kids were actually drunk and stupid enough to wander into a toxic waste dump.

The experience of seeing this sober was bad enough, but on LSD it created the worst trips I'd ever had. I literally felt as if every tree was screaming, which was probably true because they had all been poisoned with a deadly toxin. I was amazed that all of us just went back to school and continued numbing ourselves out with drinking and smoking like nothing had happened, even as our emotions were reeling from the shock of what we were seeing all around us every day. Just like in my story, it now felt as if all of us were being held in a toxic containment area that we were unable to escape from—which happened to be the campus itself. I was equally guilty of choosing to see myself as a prisoner there. I was so terrified of my parents' reaction if I had delayed my education for even one semester that I never even considered the idea of getting out. Some kids did decide to go somewhere else, but there were so many new people it was hard to tell who was missing, particularly since we all had new classes each semester.

Contemporary Social Issues

By far, my greatest education that year came from a sociology class with the deceptively boring-sounding title Contemporary Social Issues. This was a class that exposed what people now call the Illuminati, the Cabal, or the New World Order. Names like these were never used in class. Instead, they were only called things like "big business," "the oil companies," or "the military-industrial complex." Our textbook was called

Crisis in American Institutions, and was filled to the brim with an astonishing collection of government cover-ups and conspiracies that were very real and easily provable. No one was talking about this stuff in the mainstream media, and that was only another indication of how serious the problem was.

Our professor revealed how the oil companies had systematically destroyed everything in America that could compete with the automobile. Public transportation was attacked and defunded by politicians whenever possible. Light-rail and high-speed bullet-train systems were perpetually blocked. Even bus transportation was systematically suppressed, leaving only a small, miserable fleet that only the poorest people dared to ride. New York City had managed to get a subway system before this suppression was fully under way, but many other cities had been completely thwarted. The goal was to make it impossible for people to survive without having their own cars, which increased oil profits. A bus or a train could transport many more people with far less fuel than an automobile.

We learned that Ford had discovered a problem in their new compact car, the Pinto, that caused it to burst into flames when hit from behind—even in a relatively low-speed collision. The Ford engineers concluded that a three-dollar wire mesh called a baffle could be fitted around the gas tank, and would prevent this from happening. Ford did a cost-benefit analysis and decided that it would be less expensive to fight the lawsuits from all the families whose loved ones burned to death in Pintos than it would be to do a mass recall and equip each car with the cheap new part. Nor did they decide to install baffles on the new cars either, as a three-dollar increase in production cost was considered to be unacceptably high. Ford's calculations failed miserably. The entire scandal was exposed, and they hemorrhaged far more millions of dollars in lawsuits than they would have spent doing a full recall and adding the parts to the new cars. The entire Pinto line was completely discontinued. Anyone can go and verify this data for themselves.

We heard about the savings and loan scandal, where the government used public funds to back the most outrageous and ridiculous business ideas imaginable. Multimillionaires could try anything they wanted, take incredible risks, and not lose any of their own money when the projects inevitably failed. They were bailed out with public funds and given lavish "golden parachutes" and severance packages. We were told that this one scandal alone added up to an astonishing $100,000 that was stolen from every American—and hardly anyone involved ever went to jail for having done it.

Last, we learned that American corporations had secretly built up and supported Hitler's war machine. Even though America was supposedly at war with Hitler, he would never have been able to expand so quickly without America's direct, intensive support. I will never forget the moment I heard that Ford Motor Company was secretly building Hitler's tanks. The class was speechless. If an Allied bomber destroyed one of Hitler's tank plants, Ford Motor Company personally repaid Hitler to rebuild the plant as soon as possible. Another class the following semester revealed that Boeing secretly built all of Hitler's bombers. American workers were designing passenger airliners for Boeing, thinking they were doing their part to help keep their country strong during World War II. The airliners were then shipped to South America, where the seats were stripped out and the planes were repainted into a blank color. From there, the planes were transported to Africa, where they were modified to become bombers. They were then sent to Germany, painted to look like bombers Hitler built, and sent off to battle to kill innocent young men from the same extended family that had just built them.

This was high treason on an unimaginable scale. My success in the class depended on learning and remembering these shocking truths. Our lessons raised even more questions than they answered. How could this have happened right under our noses? How could they possibly have kept it a secret? If this much information was available in one class, then how much more is there that we don't already know? And why? What could possess a concentrated group of power elites to want to create mechanized slaughter on such a vast, industrial scale? I thought back to the Eye under the bridge, the symbol on the dollar, and my parents' shock at seeing couples enter the pitch-black house across the street without knocking. I thought about *Rosemary's Baby* and how similar my parents thought it was to what they had witnessed. My mind was giving me the answer, but my heart didn't want to face the possibility. This was like the worst bad trip you could imagine—but it was the real world. I was taught in martial arts to face the attacker, to never back down, as that would get you killed. Once you know the truth, the real question becomes: *What are you going to do about it?*

The scope of evil I was hearing about in this class was only further enhanced by seeing the toxic-waste drums and workers in moon-suits as I walked back to the dorm. The combined power of these experiences shattered any denial I still had about the world we were really living in, and the negative groups that were controlling it. If my alcoholic suitemates, the maintenance crew, and the local fire department represented humanity in any way, then we were screwed. The media was lying to us and covering up the truth. No one ever heard about these scandals in the news, except for occasional bursts like Watergate and the Iran-Contra hearings. The media followed the rule of "if it bleeds, it leads," keeping us all so traumatized that we used alcohol and prescription drugs to numb ourselves from the pain. The same power elite also owned the prescription drug companies. The more overwhelmed and depressed they could make us, the more they could profit off us as our drug pushers. Iran-Contra had already revealed the government had its hands in illegal drug cash as well—arming, training, and financing coke-dealing terrorist groups in South America.

I ended up taking this alarming class with my weed dealer—a charismatic rock-and-roll lead vocalist we will call Randy who patterned himself after Jim Morrison. He wore tie-dye T-shirts, a tangle of bear-claw necklaces, black leather pants, and a black leather cowboy hat when he was performing. He also greatly enjoyed bullying me. When we reconnected a year or so ago, he said that he saw me as a "wolf in training" and wanted to make me strong. Even though I had martial arts experience, I was dependent upon him for my stuff—and I snapped into a codependent, obedient role just as I felt forced to do with my parents. He told me if I ever turned him in, he would dedicate the rest of his life to hunting me down and killing me—even if he had been in prison for ten years. Despite these serious threats, I continued to buy from him—and once we had this class together, we both realized there was a much more threatening wolf circling the herd of human sheep.

One night after a particularly intense class, Randy and I were sitting in his living room, smoking some weed with the TV on. Neither of us was drinking or tripping. We were half watching a show called *Mystery Science Theater 2000,* in which a guy with two puppets made fun of terrible old B movies. Both of us had nodded out and were barely even conscious. The high-pitched whining noise from the TV suddenly got noticeably louder and higher in frequency. We instantly snapped to attention, leaning toward the television with focused, urgent concentration. Right then, a slick, polished commercial came on for a new show that was about to debut on NBC. It was obvious that a great deal of money had been invested in that commercial—definitely six figures, if not more.

"Did you catch that? Do you get what just happened?" I was in shock. Randy looked at me, his eyes wide with disbelief, and agreed. "It was like two hands just reached right out of the TV and made me turn my head to look at it, even though I was nearly passed out," he said. Then I continued: "Did you notice that the high-pitched noise it always makes had changed right before that happened?" Now the full realization—and horror—washed across his face. "Holy God damn, David, you are absolutely right. I try to tune out that sound, but it definitely did change— and I instinctively looked to see why." He then said a bunch of things that I cannot politely repeat in this book. He was flabbergasted. "If they're going to finance Hitler and build up his killing machine, why they hell wouldn't they mess around with the TV to make us watch their war propaganda?" That was the last time we ever watched TV together. It quickly became clear that the problem was much, much worse than anyone could even imagine—and what we were hearing in our class was only the tip of the iceberg.

Crispell Hall

One night after spring break, the new guy in our suite saw me walk into the room, decided he didn't like my face, and hurled an empty forty-ounce malt liquor bottle at it from about eight feet away. I was already starting to duck down before it ever left his hand, thanks to my martial

arts training. Without it, the glass might have exploded in my face—
and could have even blinded me. This guy had shaved both sides of his
head, with long hair on the top. He would literally spend twenty minutes
at a time staring at himself in the bathroom mirror, touching his chin,
grinning, and cocking his eyebrow. The only album he ever played was
Blood Sugar Sex Magik by the Red Hot Chili Peppers, at top volume—
so we all heard the complete album every few days, as his stereo was
much more powerful than anyone else's. He had no idea that I was a
trained martial artist. I got so angry that I was terrified I would kill him
if I stayed in the room, so I ran out, as I was trained to do after a fight.
This was the first time my suitemates really stood up for me—but only
briefly. They had started going out to the bars in the second semester,
after an initial "front loading" with a game of Three Man. Every night
they tried to force me to go, but I almost always stayed in my room. They
hated me for refusing to join them.

One night they stayed in for a punishingly long game of Three Man.
The ringleader, having recently defended me against the new guy, said,
"Hey, man, why don't you share some of that stuff with us? Don't hog it
all for yourself." I had an extremely powerful strain of weed that reeked
of skunk and citrus, and was happy to give them as much as they wanted.
Everyone got about two puffs in before a mass disaster rippled through
them like a blast wave. They were already extremely drunk, and the
skunk weed sent them right over the edge. People were puking in the
bathroom, on the floor, in the water fountain in the outside hallway and
even in the stairwell. Those of us who did not play Three Man could
hardly believe how boldly they had been slapped down by the hand of
fate. I remembered how they had all mocked me when I was throwing
up. None of them ever asked me for weed again. Karma had finally come
around full circle, though it certainly did not have the effect of healing
their emotions—unless you saw throwing up as a way of breaking
through the denial that what they were doing was healthy or normal.

Shortly after this epic event, I walked into one of my classrooms late.
It was quiet. Too quiet. Everyone had a blue piece of paper on their desk.
What the heck was going on? I suddenly realized, in horror, that it was
a midterm exam. I vaguely remembered hearing the professor tell us it

was coming, but I hadn't written down the date—and I hadn't studied. Thankfully, I did make a habit of paying attention in class and taking notes, and I was able to pass the test. I got through that first year with an overall grade point average of 2.6, which was enough to keep me from flunking out of school. I was utterly exhausted from all the bullying and nightly displays of extreme alcoholism, and decided to move to the super-geek study dorm, Crispell Hall, with the only three guys in the suite who did not play Three Man that semester. The marijuana hardly even got me high anymore. If I smoked, I felt fairly normal—not even as good as I usually do now. If I didn't smoke, I was horribly depressed. I was seriously starting to think I should quit, but I had no idea how I could. I felt that if I stopped, my life would go right over the edge—but at least in the study dorm I wouldn't have to suffer from alcoholic bullies.

Vinyl Jam

My parents absolutely insisted I work a job that first summer after I started college, even though I desperately needed a vacation. Both Don and Ben were working at a factory that made vinyl liners for below-ground swimming pools. This job proved to be even worse than telemarketing. There was an ominous four-colored chemical-hazard diamond posted outside the building. Each of the four quadrants of the diamond—red, blue, yellow, and white—had a number in it, indicating how severe of a risk we faced in each of four major areas. The diamond said you needed to wear a respirator to enter the building—but no one told us that, and none of us did. The smell of vinyl inside was easily twenty times stronger than what your bathroom smells like after you buy a new shower curtain. The ventilation fans were so loud you had to yell to be heard, and some guys wore earplugs, which we were all supposed to be doing. It was also extremely hot, making it impossible not to sweat. The workers would throw their food garbage underneath the enormous assembly table and no one ever cleaned it out, so the place was constantly swarming with fruit flies.

I started out as a beader, which was the lowest, most hated job in the

place. All I did, all day long, was melt a one-inch-wide, one-eighth-inch-
thick strip of vinyl onto the edge of swimming-pool liners others had
made. The machine that melted the vinyl together was gigantic, and had
enough electricity running through it on each hit to illuminate ten thousand lightbulbs. It was also thoroughly dangerous. If you touched it
when it was down, you got hit with a bolt of electricity. One of my
shocks created a little white puffball that suddenly sprouted up out of my
thumb. I quickly batted it away in horror and was left with a small
brown crater that hurt for days.

If an assembly tech took the guard off the machine and hit the pedal,
which was supposedly illegal but nonetheless useful in order to do pool
stairs, it could slam down on his finger and destroy his fingertip. Several
of the "vinyl lifers" who were working there had missing fingertips, and
almost everyone in the factory had been to prison at least once. When
they found out I was going to college, I was relentlessly bullied, though
nothing like elementary and junior high school had been. One of the
workers there discovered his body was crawling with cancer, and he was
only in his early forties at the most. No one wanted to believe the vinyl
could be responsible, even though the bosses always stayed up in an en-
closed room with a separate ventilation system. Twenty years later, I
learned I still had vinyl in my system.

It seemed like every single person who worked there was drinking
after work, and that most of them were probably doing other drugs as
well. The feeling in the factory was one of intense desperation, and you
didn't need to be intuitive to pick up on it. I started at eight a.m., had a
half hour for lunch, and left at four thirty. One of the bosses caught
me smoking weed outside the building one day and he didn't even care.
The pay was very low considering how dangerous, toxic, and stressful
the work was, and I didn't need the money. I worked the job only because my parents insisted that I have one. One day, a guy smashed his
finger in the machine and was walking around in a daze after it happened. He glided right past me in a trauma trance, holding it out in front
of him. The top of his middle finger was now two inches wide and looked
like something out of a cartoon. Albany Med rescued the fingertip and
he was back less than a week later.

This Is Poetry . . . This Is Passion

No matter how much I had suffered in college, this job was much worse—but if I became unemployed, I was subject to intense daily harassment from both of my parents, which was far worse than the heckling in the factory. My only time to relax was on weekends. One Saturday afternoon, Don and I convinced Jude to drop acid with us. This proved to be a very rough and powerful trip—and was also the last one I ever took. A man we will call Mr. Henry, from across the street, was a Vietnam veteran with severe PTSD who had become a massive drunk and could barely take care of himself. He still had the military haircut. His skin was deeply pockmarked from years of severe acne. He reeked of alcohol and festering, pustulant sores, and he was severely overweight. He came over in a drunken stupor and was acting less like a human and more like an animal, as he could barely even talk. I kept having hallucinations of him being a bull, complete with the horns. Don and Bob had a punching bag in the backyard, and Mr. Henry was hitting it as hard as he could without falling over. His body rippled with severe tension that released after each blow to the punching bag. As he did so, he kept saying, "This is poetry. This is passion."

By the end of this experience, I had come to a profound realization. My body was extremely damaged from all the marijuana I had been smoking over the last four years. I was looking more and more diseased all the time, with pale skin and frighteningly dark circles under my eyes. There was nothing poetic or passionate about what I was doing. People were telling me I looked like I had just walked out of a concentration camp. If I kept on going, I was either going to die, end up like Mr. Henry, or end up like the guys at the vinyl factory. I had nearly gotten busted several times, and once I had a criminal record it would be much harder to find a job. I remembered having dreams as a child that I was going to do something positive with my life, but I didn't see how it was possible unless I started taking better care of myself. Quitting marijuana felt like the equivalent of taking away the only thing I had ever enjoyed—something I had built my entire life around. I couldn't imagine actually stopping, but I was thinking about it.

Stories from the Love Brothers

Jude and I poured all that tension and uncertainty into a new music project we called *Stories from the Love Brothers*. The whole album featured songs in which I was wrestling with the idea of whether or not I was going to stop smoking. There was a song about the factory called "Vinyl Jam," and another song called "Joneser," about guys who are constantly asking you for things, such as drugs, money, food, and shelter, and giving nothing back in return. The real highlight of the album was a song called "Garden of the Broken Clock." We recorded it live, in one take, with nothing planned out in advance. Jude was playing the piano and I was using a guitar as an echoing rhythm instrument. I did it all as a spoken-word piece, and had no idea what I was going to say when we started. In hindsight, this definitely appears to have been the first time I verbally channeled my own "higher self" in such a direct and accurate form. More than anything else, the words that flowed out of me during these brief few minutes were the main tool I ended up using to maintain the strength to quit.

It started out with Jude saying, in a hypnotic monotone, "I once had this garden, and in this garden laid a broken clock. This broken clock lay, lifeless . . . lay lifeless on the ground." In a dreamlike fashion, his subconscious was obviously talking about me, as the "broken clock," and how messed up I had become. Shortly after he said this and paused, I began talking, with an unusual degree of confidence, authority, and clarity. The old man from my dreams appeared as a character I was talking to as the narrator. However, in this case the man was a future version of myself, complete with a white beard. I described how I was having a dialogue with him and he was giving me spiritual advice. In the song, my character asked the old man how I could control my addictions. "God helps those who help themselves," he responded—and then repeated it several more times.

Suddenly, I had a seemingly accidental verbal fumble, and said, "God helps those who end themselves." This triggered a whole new section, where Jude's piano music became extremely powerful. In further dialogues with the old man, my character concluded, "If you are ending yourself, then you must not love yourself." The old man responded by saying, "Exactly. Every drink you drink, every cigarette you smoke, every drug you take, you're stepping a little closer to death. . . . God helps those who help themselves, and you, my son, have sought out such help."

CHAPTER THIRTEEN

The Great Experiment

was still smoking when I started my sophomore year of school at the Crispell Hall super-geek dorm in 1992—but the weed barely made me feel any better. I had slashed my use down to about only once every day or two. Every time I did it, I started having chest pains as if I was going to have a heart attack. When I was working at the factory, I felt as if my life was over. My mind was constantly filled with paranoid delusions that I would have to work there for the rest of my life—until I fell over dead from drug addiction and cancer. I pinned all my hopes on just surviving long enough to make it back to college. I felt that once I got back there, I would be in paradise. The campus had wonderful trees, a glorious stream, and beautiful women everywhere. I still had never had a girlfriend and was hoping for the best. I visualized a world of happiness, even ecstasy, by getting myself out of the worst prison I'd ever been sentenced to and returning to the glory of the campus.

Once I got back to school, it was just the opposite. I didn't feel the least bit better in school than I did in the factory, which was shocking. My short-term memory was completely gone. Within minutes of leaving my room, I couldn't remember if I had locked the door or left the hot plate on. I was having panic attacks on an hour-by-hour basis. I was constantly depressed, and even smoking made me feel only slightly better after a high of about fifteen minutes. My body was utterly exhausted, to the point where I could barely handle the stress of a ten- to fifteen-minute walk to class. I would feel as if I could barely move my legs—and I noticed that other burned-out-looking students were shuffling along the same way. I still subscribed to a science magazine that came to the old house, which I believe was either *Science Digest* or *Hippocrates*, and my mother forwarded each issue to my dormitory. What I read in that magazine completely changed my life.

It's All About the Chemistry

I found out that happiness doesn't just come naturally to the body. Happiness is not like a thought or an idea. You only feel happiness when the brain creates certain chemicals and releases them into the gaps between brain cells. Happiness occurs during the time these chemicals remain in your synapses, before they break down and get reabsorbed. Your brain only makes a small amount of these chemicals at a time, and stores them at a steady rate—like water filling up in a tank. We then get addicted to various things that cause an unnaturally large amount of this "water" to splash out of the tank all at once. Some people get addicted to sex. Some people get addicted to work, stress, or fear. Some people get addicted to bullying and creating drama, such as in an intimate relationship. Some people get addicted to staying up late and pushing themselves, so they don't get enough sleep. Some people get addicted to sugar, wheat, dairy, and other unhealthy foods. Some people get addicted to caffeine, nicotine, or alcohol. Some people get addicted to prescription drugs. And some get addicted to other drugs—including marijuana.

Any of these addictions can create a situation in which our brain is eventually burning these chemicals faster than they can be replenished. Once this happens, you reach what psychologists call depression. If you then develop five or more of the following symptoms, you have what is called clinical depression:

> Depressed mood, such as feeling sad, empty, or tearful (in children and teens, depressed mood can appear as constant irritability)

Significantly reduced interest or feeling no pleasure in all or
  most activities
Significant weight loss when not dieting, weight gain, or de-
  crease or increase in appetite (in children, failure to gain
  weight as expected)
Insomnia or increased desire to sleep
Either restlessness or slowed behavior that can be observed by
  others
Fatigue or loss of energy
Feelings of worthlessness, or excessive or inappropriate guilt
Trouble making decisions, or trouble thinking or concen-
  trating
Recurrent thoughts of death or suicide, or a suicide attempt[32]

Other than suicidal thoughts, I was having all the classic symptoms
of clinical depression. In order to fit the diagnosis, the problems needed
to "be severe enough to cause noticeable problems in relationships with
others or in day-to-day activities, such as work, school or social activities."[33] All this applied to me. I still was unable to feel confident around
women. My work, school, and social activities had all suffered dramatically. As I was learning in my psychology classes, most psychiatrists were
handing out prescription drugs like candy, telling their patients that
nothing was really wrong with them. It was all just a chemical
imbalance—and there was a drug to treat that.

Thankfully, this was not what the article suggested. Some people could
be helped by taking these prescription drugs, but it could also become
another addiction. If people suddenly tried to stop taking them, they could
have such a bad reaction that they would become suicidal—and might
actually go through with it. The article said you needed to cut the problem
off at the root. You had to identify the addiction that was causing you to
destroy certain chemicals called enkephalins and endorphins—such as
serotonin and dopamine—and find a way to stop repeating the pattern.

In my case, it was very simple. Although I had a variety of addictions,
the main way I was destroying all my serotonin was through smoking
weed. I had finally reached the point at which there was so little

serotonin left in my brain that even when I smoked, I could barely get high—and the rest of the time I suffered clinical depression. The article discussed this exact situation in detail, and said the only way out would be to completely stop using drugs. Once I finally freed my brain from the torture of being chemically forced to release serotonin in huge amounts, I would have to go through a period of time where I did not feel any happiness whatsoever. During this time, my brain would refill the water tank, as it were. Once I had healed my neurochemical system, normal things in life—like a blue sky, beautiful trees, a long walk, playing music, a nice conversation, or an attractive woman—would make me feel good, without any drugs. Many people were never able to wait long enough to see what would happen once they had healed.

One Last Crash

After discovering the truth, I went through one final "crash," where my old life collapsed in on me all at once. There was a girl named Jenny who really seemed to like me, and was acting like my counselor as I talked about my desire to stop smoking. I then found out she was working every decent-looking guy in my building and wanted to use me to get weed. Someone pulled the fire alarm and I saw her outside, wrapped in a blanket, with another guy. She ended up slamming her door in my face on a Monday not too long after this, and I again felt a paralyzing force around my heart—as if I were going to have a heart attack. The next night I allowed other students to pressure me into going to a party when I really needed to read my assignment for class. One girl who I was not at all attracted to, whom we will call Liz, kept hitting on me very strongly and I finally had to leave. Then on Wednesday, I was disgraced in my Science-Fiction class after the teacher called on me, his star pupil, and I had to admit I hadn't read the book. It was just one burst of bad luck after another.

That Friday night, my roommate drank two 40s while watching the film *The Doors*, in which Val Kilmer played Jim Morrison, and which documented his steep decline and death from drugs and alcohol. My roommate thought the 40s "went down smooth" and he would be fine. I watched the last section of the movie with my suitemates and was stunned at how I had all the same patterns as the greatest drug addict in music history. My roommate ended up vomiting all over the bathroom floor. For the first time in my life I genuinely became wild and abusive in yelling at someone. In a hail of profanity, I jabbed my finger at him and told him I didn't care how messed up he was, he was going to clean up every last goddamn drop of vomit off this floor. He kept saying he was sorry in a voice that sounded like Barney the purple dinosaur.

Then I walked into my room and noticed that my bed was completely unmade. This would never have happened, since my mother had trained me to have military precision in the way I folded the sheets. Liz was sitting on my roommate's bed, very drunk and happy. Their shoes were side by side. I began yelling at her, accusing them of having had sex in my bed, which she denied. I asked her why in the hell my bed was all messed up and she kept saying, "I don't know, I don't know." The suite smelled so bad that I thought I was going to throw up. One of my roommates was so drunk he was eating pizza and didn't even notice. I ended up telling my buddy Chris that we had to get out of there, and go hang out at his dorm in Bouton Hall. Thankfully, his roommate had a girlfriend he would often stay with and there was an open bunk for the night. As I lay there in bed staring at the ceiling, my mind was racing. Addictions could make you have sex with people you would never be interested in when you were sober. You could get someone pregnant. You could end up declining in health, stability, and sanity, and end up trashing your whole life—or even dying. Right there in that bed, I made the decision. That was it. I was done.

The next morning the smell was mostly gone, but I had to deal with a terrible situation. My weed dealer, Randy, was trying to train me to take his place so he could move out to the mountains in Gardiner and live off the risks I would take to sell for him. I had given one ounce to a friend of mine, and it was the largest amount of weed I had ever handled. I told him the price was $200, and he demanded that he pay only $180 or he wouldn't take it. I ended up giving it to him and adding the extra $20 out of my own pocket. My ATM card had broken in half, so I couldn't get Randy the rest of his money, and he was furious with me.

Things got very bizarre when I realized that he had completely stopped calling me for four days. I then discovered that my telephone cord had been smashed under my roommate's bed, which was why the phone wasn't ringing. I went down to the office and got a new cord, and at the exact moment I plugged it in, it rang. I picked it up and it was Randy. He wanted his money right away, and I told him to come on over and get it, since I now had a new card. He had threatened to kill me in the past if I did not pay him, and that was the last thing I wanted.

Randy came over and insisted that I give him something to smoke. All I had left was a disgusting, tar-soaked "roach"—the burned end of a joint. I didn't want any of it myself, but he was starting to suspect I had become a "narc" and insisted I do it. The concentrated resin caused both of us to suffer an unusually high amount of paranoia, and Randy soon said he needed to get out of there. As soon as Randy left my room, I heard an explosively loud walkie-talkie echoing in the suite. Now I was dying inside. I had gotten so close—and on the very last day I ever planned on using, I was busted. The campus police must have been tipped off to listen in on my phone call after I nervously asked the staff for a new cord. They heard us discussing our meeting, where I needed to repay him for the $200 of "books" he had given me—in the middle of the semester. Now the police were right outside the door. They would find the $200 in his front pocket, with my fingerprints on it. The room reeked of smoke and incense. I was done. It was over.

I knew that the police could not legally enter into my room to arrest me. There was a campus law that the cops were not allowed to step past the threshold of your door unless you permitted them to, even if they had probable cause. They could knock, but you didn't have to let them in. The legend in the drug culture was that the cops would wait for you to come out of your room, or use tricks to flush you out. My mind was rocked to the core with paranoia as I heard even more walkie-talkie sounds in the suite. This was it. I sat there paralyzed in fear, appalled at my stupidity and bad luck. Finally the phone rang—and it was Randy, down on the ground floor. He sounded very grim and extremely nervous. "Can you—can you come down and let me in?" I knew exactly what was happening. He had cops standing on either side of him, telling him what to say. They had ordered him to flush me out of the room, so the officers who were still in my suite could arrest me. The trap had been sprung. I had no choice. This was checkmate. And this time I wasn't looking at Connie, but prison. Selling an ounce of weed was a felony. I took a deep breath and accepted my fate. "Okay, I will do it," I said, with a note of finality. Then I hung up.

When I eventually left the room, there was a maintenance guy in the bathroom with our shower-stall parts spread out on the countertop. He had a huge tool belt, a busted old red T-shirt, and a biker-style mustache. His skin was thoroughly pockmarked and he looked like a severe abuser of alcohol and other substances. It was a common thing for people to hide bags of drugs in a shower-curtain rod, as that way if it got discovered by the police, it wasn't in their room and they couldn't be blamed for it. This guy gave me a very dirty look, and I knew it was over. He was looking for my stash and was angry that he couldn't find anything, since I would never have used that trick—it was too easy for someone to steal it. Why else would this guy be ripping apart the shower? The cops were standing on either side of Randy by the downstairs phone, and were waiting for me to walk outside the building. That way they wouldn't cause as much of a scene and could just load me into the car without parading me down the halls in handcuffs, past all my friends. They were obviously watching all the exits so I had no possibility of escape.

I was living on the third floor, and I started walking down the stairs to my appointment with destiny. My mind was racing with thoughts at a very fast speed, just like the time-slowing effect of Form with Spirit. All the darkness and negativity I was feeling was the equivalent of an extremely bad trip. Each time I stepped on a new stair, I had another thought about how my life was completely over. I had been given visions of doing great things for the world when I was a child. I was told I was going to be a spiritual leader. I had worked to develop my ESP and had stopped practicing it. I had missed my chance to save our entire school from an epic environmental catastrophe when I could have warned the fire department with one phone call. I had learned there was a terribly evil force on Earth and I still hadn't done anything to stop it. Now I was going to be sent to prison. My life had fallen apart, exactly as the power elite had hoped it would. Even with my martial arts training, there would be no way for me to avoid extremely horrific torture in prison. Once I finally got out, I would have a criminal record. Any hope of a future as a psychologist or spiritual leader would be heavily tainted—if not destroyed.

My last act as a free man was to ping the fire bell with my middle finger, making a clear tone—as I did every time I passed it. Randy was standing in front of the glass, glaring at me. He didn't have a key and couldn't get in without me, unless someone let him in. I was ready. I took a deep breath, opened the door, and confronted him aggressively, which he did not expect. "Okay, where are they?" I said.

"Where is who?"

I barked back, "Don't screw with me, man. The cops. Where are the cops?"

Now Randy got a sinister, sardonic look. He hissed back, "There are no cops, young David, I just want to know why the hell there is a guy in your bathroom ripping apart the shower." He used several curse words that I will not include here.

I couldn't even believe this was happening. I had to double-check to make sure. "You mean there are no cops?"

"No, there are no goddamn cops!"

I was so thrilled that I rushed him with a huge victory hug. I nearly cried with relief. Then I remembered that my Greek suitemates thought the shower was too weak, and had removed the shower head—causing a much larger amount of water to gush out. Crispell actually had staff who would periodically check on the bathrooms. They had discovered this crime and called it in to maintenance for repair. That's all it was. The stench of vomit probably explained why the guy gave me such dirty looks.

I was astounded by the fact that I hadn't gotten busted. I had believed it was happening with every fiber of my being, and the thrill of not getting arrested felt like an incredible miracle from the universe. I ended up telling one of my friends the whole story; he worked as a resident assistant in the building. He told me he was going to an Alcoholics Anonymous meeting that night and invited me to come. "Well, I'm not an alcoholic," I told him. "I never even liked it. My problem is smoking weed." He told me that I didn't have to be an alcoholic to benefit from

it. This was a great group of people and I should check it out. No one was
going to pressure me, and if I didn't like it I could go right back to doing
whatever I was doing. This was very different from Connie—and best of
all, it was free.

Happy Anniversary

That first night was an incredibly powerful experience. They were celebrating two sobriety anniversaries—one for a younger white guy with
long hair who had five years, and one for an older black guy who had
eleven years. Everyone was smiling, radiant, and extremely happy—and
there wasn't a hint of bullying in the room. Both the men and the women
treated me with love, kindness, and respect. The main feature of the
night was hearing the stories of both men. Each of them had been
through traumas that were much worse than anything I had endured.
They were waking up in ditches on the side of the road, covered in their
own vomit and urine. The eleven-year guy had run out on his wife and
kids for days at a time, and had come very close to dying on numerous
occasions.

They talked about "hitting bottom," which was a moment where you
realized your life was completely falling apart, and you had no other
choice but to stop. They also said that most people have to hit bottom
over and over again before they finally decide to change—and each new
bottom is even worse than the one before. Eventually, if you didn't decide that enough was enough, you would either end up diseased, institutionalized, or dead. I had already come dangerously close to being
institutionalized in prison or in Connie, and had several brushes with
death, so everything they were saying made perfect sense. I decided that
very night that I would never use any type of mind-altering drugs
again—and I never did. The five-year guy gave me his number and said
I could call him any time, particularly if I felt I was in danger of hurting
myself. When I went back to my suite I felt absolutely inspired and transformed. I talked to my next-door neighbor, another refugee from Doobie
Hall, about my bed being messed up. He admitted that he had done it

as a prank. I was stunned at the synchronicity, as I had absolutely believed that my roommate had had sex with Liz in my bed. It seemed as
if all these setups had occurred to make sure I would really get the message and go to the meeting.

I decided to do a "ninety in ninety," meaning that I would attend
ninety meetings in ninety days. There were plenty of attractive young
women to meet and become friends with, although I was advised not to
get into a romantic relationship for the first year, because I would still be
vulnerable during this time. The five-year guy told me most people feel
very depressed for the first three months, which was why it was necessary
to go to a meeting every day. Once you got through three months you
would feel some degree of happiness. In six months you would feel even
better, and after a year you could have a happier life than you had ever
dreamed of while you were using. I told him all about what I had read
in the magazine; it gave scientific proof for everything he was saying.
Even though I would not feel any happiness during those first three
months, I would have a support system that would help me ensure I
didn't slide back into addiction again. And I didn't.

The Experimenters

I felt so charged up with positive energy from that meeting that it was
like a psychedelic experience—but very pure and sacred, without all the
paranoia, terror, and shakes. My mind was bursting with ideas and in-
spirations and I felt I had to capture them on paper while they were
fresh. I looked at the whole sequence of events that had led up to my epic
decision, and it all seemed to stretch the idea of coincidence to the breaking point. One of my psych classes had just introduced me to Jung's
concept of synchronicity, and now I had a perfect example of it right
after I had learned what it was. Why did my card snap in half at the
worst possible moment—causing a frightening delay in paying Randy?
Why did my roommate's bed kill the phone cord at the worst possible
moment, making Randy even more angry as the delay stretched on for
days? Why did I never think to call anyone during that time? Why did

the Greeks remove and throw away the shower head? Why was Randy calling at the exact moment I plugged the new phone cord in? Why did the maintenance guy show up right as Randy was getting his money? Why did the maintenance guy's walkie-talkie never make a sound until the exact moment after Randy left my room? And why did I have my single most upsetting heartbreak with a woman right before all this happened?

Some form of cosmic intelligence seemed to have orchestrated all this with astonishing precision. It appeared to be an incredibly well-constructed example of synchronicity. Someone was trying to get my attention. I ended up spending all weekend writing a paper I called "Earth as an Experiment." Some kind of memory block seemed to drop, and I was able to remember many of the things the old man had told me in the dreams of my youth. I wrote about Earth as if it were a rat maze—but most people didn't even realize they were in it. They were distracted by "false food pellets" that would make them feel good for short bursts of time—such as addictions. They would make their home where the false food was, and would go no farther. Others would realize they were in a maze, and that there was a genuine solution to the puzzle. The goal was a spiritual transformation that I decided to call "the Upgrade," which I later realized was called ascension. It would change the very essence of what it meant to be human.

I also wrote that this entire system was being observed and managed by "experimenters," who had already experienced the Upgrade long ago. They leave clues in the maze that lead us toward the Upgrade—but they will never push. They don't expect most of us to solve the puzzle, or even discover that we are in a maze. That is impossible—at least in our present environment. Instead, their goal is to reach out to those few individuals who see the truth for what it is. We are all surrounded by hidden laws of cause and effect, whether we realize it or not. There are no accidents. None of the biggest events in our lives happen randomly. If we cause pain, fear, and stress to others, the experimenters ensure that we will repeat those same experiences, perhaps in a slightly different way. It will never be completely obvious. We always have the option of doubting that anything is going on, but no one gets to break the rules. Similarly, if we generate love, positivity, and support for others, the experimenters create situations that guarantee it will be returned to us—and transform our lives into something wonderful.

That same weekend, I also decided it was time to take my dreams seriously. On the very next morning after I went to my first meeting, I started writing my dreams down in a college notebook. The date was September 22, 1992, and I have been documenting my dreams and analyzing their meanings ever since. Once I had committed to sobriety, I began having nightmares that I had smoked again. I felt like if I didn't stay sober at this point, after all that synchronicity, something much worse would knock me back in line. I would awake in terror, only to be greatly relieved when I realized it didn't actually happen. I also had marvelous ascension dreams of flying, and of my body turning into light. These dreams would continue to get more and more vivid and intense as the years went by.

That semester I had signed up for a Lifetime Fitness class—and to my horror, we were forced to jog every day, just like the Turkey Trot in junior high school. Every time I started running I would cough almost uncontrollably. It would force me to stop and bend over as my body heaved. Huge amounts of dark yellow-brown mucus were coming up every time. I thought back to all the autopsies of smokers' lungs they had showed us in health class, and realized that my own lungs must look disgusting on the inside. The running was finally giving my body a chance to release an incredible amount of oily tar that had built up over the past four years. This had dramatically reduced how much oxygen I could get into my bloodstream, which in turn made me constantly exhausted and weak. So, although it was very painful and I hated it, I embraced what was happening and kept on running.

Queen Victoria

A beautiful Scandinavian woman with blond hair and blue eyes named Victoria was in my jogging class. We became fast friends when she found out I had decided to sober up and go to meetings. We started running side by side, and she would wait for me and encourage me when I coughed up all this psychoactive resin. At the end of one of our classes, she stopped, gazed calmly into my eyes, and said, "You have the most beautiful eyes I have ever seen on a man." Finally, after all this time, this was my big chance. I thanked her for the compliment and asked her if she wanted to have dinner sometime. She said yes.

We ended up going to a local Chinese restaurant together. She revealed that she was twenty-four years old and married to a fifty-four-year-old wealthy man. She desperately wanted to get away from him and be with me instead. I was so shocked I didn't know what to say.

We walked back to my room, sat down on my bed, and she started making out with me. Her lips and her skin felt impossibly soft and delicious, and her perfume was transcendent. I backed away. I just couldn't do it. I was terrified that this guy would use his money and connections to come after me, either to hurt me or even have me killed. She was going to get caught. Cheaters always did—it was only a matter of time before fate would strike them. That was just another trap within the grand maze the experimenters had set up for us. And beyond that, I did not want to get involved with a married woman. It was risky, and I was trying to clean up my life— not trade one dangerous addiction for another. I apologized to her and told her I couldn't be romantic with her unless she was already getting a divorce. She was devastated but she understood, and said she respected me.

The next morning, I had an outrageous dream. I was back in the elementary gymnasium, right where we had been forced to stand for forty-five minutes until Brad and I began sneaking out of school. Now instead of dodge ball, Victoria was wildly attacking me and swinging at me with a knife. She was laughing and laughing like it was some kind of a joke. She obviously did not care whether she hurt me in the process. All I had to defend myself was a green jersey, like we had used for the MedicBall game. I was holding the jersey with both hands and trying to use it to capture the knife as she kept swiping at me.

The dream ended before I had succeeded in disarming her. I was terrified—and as soon as I woke up and wrote it down, the message was obvious. She wanted her husband to be the money guy and have me as the boy toy. This put me in extreme danger, since her husband could easily afford to have me killed—but she totally didn't care. All she wanted was sex with a young man she was attracted to. This was an early and powerful clue that there was some kind of intelligence behind my dreams. Perhaps it was the old man, whom I now had reason to believe was actually a future version of myself. This intelligence could point out things I needed to know that would help me grow into a healthier, happier person. Sometimes I would be too blind or naïve to see these things myself, but the dreams would be there to help me understand what was going on. I also listened every day to the new album Jude and I had made, and the spiritual messages I had put in it—particularly in "Garden of the Broken Clock"—kept boosting my confidence.

A Meeting with the Ancient Golden Being

After passing this incredibly difficult and painful test with Victoria, I was rewarded with a fantastic dream. I ended up inside a magnificent underground tunnel with a hundred-foot-high ceiling. The tunnel was perfectly squared-off, as if it had been laser-cut out of the rock with sharp edges. The rock had a polished look to it. All along the walls, all the way down, there were beautiful Egyptian-style hieroglyphic carvings, inscriptions, and scenes embossed in the rock. Then an extremely tall being appeared to my left, dwarfing me in size. This entity was roughly seventy feet tall. The being was wearing a robe, and its entire body, including the clothing, looked like it was made out of brilliant, sparkling gold. It also had an extremely strange head, which appeared to have been carved out of stone. There was a face on the front, a face on each side, and a face on the back. The faces looked like some of the Mayan inscriptions you would see on pyramids in Mesoamerica.

This being was not aggressive. It treated me with great respect, but also had a noticeably parental feel. It never said a word. It just silently walked next to me and led me down the hall. I was awestruck by the depth and quality of Egyptian-style designs in the tunnel walls. As we reached the end of the tunnel, we seemed to go through some kind of a portal—and this was where the dream got very bizarre.

We were now back in the bedroom I had shared with my brother during the time my parents divorced. I had moved my desk into the room at first, and then took it with me when I later moved back out. The being brought me right up to my desk, which was filled with all sorts of papers and personal items from my past. It silently pointed at my desk—and said nothing. "I don't understand. You want me to look in my old desk?" The being continued to stand and point, silently—and I woke up.

I realized this was some sort of invitation from the people I had called the experimenters. If I wanted to work with them, and stay sober, I would need to review the events from my childhood—the cosmic things as well as the bullying. Only then would I be free from "repetition compulsion," that prison of the soul where you unknowingly run right into the next situation that will re-traumatize you as soon as the current one ends. I never really finished that homework until I wrote this book, beginning with a full-life-review outline I created in Canada through weeks of deep meditation and research. I was shocked to realize that even after all this time, with all I have studied and learned, I was still repeating the same patterns—just with friendlier faces. The Tibetan ascension teachings often focus on "cutting the cords," which involves lovingly separating yourself from every pattern that anchors you to your original traumas. Only then will you have enough spiritual strength to be ready for a full ascension experience.

I decided to take the invitation from the mysterious golden being in my dream, and continued going to support-group meetings every day. I often would share my "war stories" with the group, but since I only had gotten drunk on a relatively small number of occasions, and you were not supposed to mention drug-related items, I started running out of material. I also tried going to Narcotics Anonymous, but it wasn't at all a good fit. A jacked-up military guy would push against his elbow joint intensely as people shared their horror stories. A woman with fading skin and a cigarette-hardened voice broke the rules about mentioning specific drugs, and said, "You know how you're in the doctor's office, and as soon as he leaves the room you wanna open up that drawer and look for works?"

The Moment of Truth

One of the sayings I would always hear in AA was "People, Places, and Things." The idea was that you were supposed to avoid the people, places, and things associated with your addiction. Otherwise you could be tempted into doing it all again—which could lead to hitting a much harder bottom down the road. I went home for Christmas break and was discussing this idea with my mother at the kitchen table I had flamed out with KNO3 years before. "That rule doesn't apply to me. Don and Bob are my friends. They live right up the road. I need to go see them and tell them the good news. I got cleaned up and now I am having some kind of spiritual awakening. Maybe I can help inspire them." Mom urged me not to do it, but I said there wasn't a thing in the world that could make me go back at this point.

Don and Bob were both smoking Marlboros and drinking Budweiser as I explained in detail everything that had happened to me. Their response was so shocking that I ended up making it the first personal story I shared in *The Synchronicity Key,* chapter 3. Here it is:

> My friends glared at me through the stench of old beer and cigarette smoke as I told them that I now believed I was here for a spiritual purpose and that I would help many people. Stony silence erupted into a full-scale verbal assault as soon as I finished. Apparently I was going to fight my way into a dead-end job, marry a vicious and unattractive woman, slave my life away for kids who would only hate me more and more as they got older, and ultimately die alone in a nursing home surrounded by staff who could barely wait for their next cigarette break as I groaned for their attention.
>
> Was this it? Was this life? Was I crazy? Were they right? How could they be so cruel—after all the years we'd shared together? I could barely even hear what they were saying as I observed this withering assault of sarcasm and humiliation. I

warned them several times that I could not tolerate this, but on and on they went. Finally, I stood up in the middle of a sentence and walked out the front door—without verbalizing any anger or hostility—never to return. One of them reconnected with me as I was finishing this book—for the first time in twenty years—and we had a good conversation that helped us arrive at a point of mutual forgiveness.

After a ten-minute walk, I stood at the crossroads between my friend's street and mine. I was utterly devastated, fighting back tears. I felt inspired to hold my arms out to the sky and speak.

> You . . . whoever or whatever you are. I know you're out there. I know you can hear me. I know I'm here for a reason. My life has a purpose. You've shown me that. I believe you—and I trust you. I know I'm not crazy. I have made my choice. I will dedicate my life to helping others who are suffering. I thank you for helping me— and now I want to help you.

I was staring at a small patch of stars in the night sky as these words coursed through my mind. Right as I said, "I want to help you," a huge, yellow-white meteor streaked directly across the area I was looking at. It was real. It was absolute. It was undeniable. It was astonishing. It was the biggest, brightest meteor I had ever seen, even after many sleepless nights of sitting out in a lawn chair as a boy, watching the occasional flickerings of the Perseids or Leonids. A tremendous surge of ecstatic energy roared up through my body, and I felt a magnificent spiritual presence. Tears of joy streamed down my face. I spoke to the universe—and got an answer. It was, and still is, one of the most profound events in my life.

As *The Synchronicity Key* continues from there, I share several more examples that are equally remarkable. A comprehensive scientific case for synchronicity and ascension is then revealed. As the meteor streaked by

that night, I felt my whole body soaring up into the air, while still standing there at the same time. I could hear a train rushing by in the distance
as tears of ecstasy streamed down my face. Trains would become very
consistent ascension metaphors in my dreams.

While I was still smoking weed, I had felt guided to be the "Keeper"
of the path between my house and Don and Bob's place, and had cleaned
it up on every walk. The garbage was replenished on a daily basis. That
night I had picked up every piece of trash I had seen on the way back.
When I saw the flash of light and this huge surge of energy rocked
through my body, I completely lost control of my hands. The empty
cigarette packs and abandoned food wrappers fell all over the road. I was
extremely high, without any drugs, as I picked them all back up again.

The Treasure Chest of Materialistic Doom

In college I always got cash out of an ATM in the Student Union building. I had saved every receipt and stuck them all in an old Norelco clam-
shell case that had held an electric razor I no longer used. After being
torn down by the brothers, I sat at my desk—just as I was asked to do in
the dream—and opened the black box. There was a centimeter-thick
stack of ATM receipts in there. I went through each of them one by
one—and that was when it hit me. I had spent about $2,700 getting high
in just over a year. I was extremely meticulous and almost never spent
my money on anything else, including a haircut. Now I realized that if
I had saved this money, I could have been driving a car right then, instead of having to ride the Adirondack Trailways bus to get back to
school. Having a car would have made it much easier to go on off-campus
dates. I took out one of the receipts and wrote "Treasure Chest of Mate-
rialistic Doom" on it. Then I closed the black box so it was sticking out
prominently as a label. Every time I saw the box I remembered what I
had given up by allowing my habit to continue.

I had finally broken the compulsion to repeat my trauma and self-
medicate the pain I was feeling. Little did I realize that a much greater
gift was about to arrive—the first of an ongoing series of incredible

disclosures of highly classified information about extraterrestrials, UFOs, ancient bases throughout our solar system, and the truth of ascension. Additionally, the spiritual contact I had experienced in my dreams, in my allegedly fictional stories, in the OBEs and lucid dreams that took me on board spacecraft, and in the streak of light in the sky, was soon to go much farther than I could have ever possibly imagined. I would end up receiving direct contact with extraterrestrial life, and getting extensive guidance on how to prove, scientifically, that we are in a cosmic battle between good and evil. Ascension is not only a possibility, it is an absolute fact—and as you go through the initiation needed to graduate, you are helping to cocreate our fantastic future.

CHAPTER FOURTEEN

Disclosure

The ninety-day guideline proved to be remarkably correct. I had been sober for exactly three months, to the day, when I saw the shooting star and felt energy surge through me. That event felt so profound that I couldn't stop thinking about the implications. I now was strongly considering that UFOs and ETs were real, had been mysteriously guiding me throughout my life, and that I was being invited to have contact somehow. That propitiously timed shooting star seemed to suggest there may be truth behind the epic dreams and visions I was experiencing about the Upgrade or ascension ever since I was two years old. This energetic event also occurred right at the beginning of a new music project I had started working on with Jude. We had access to much better sounds by collaborating with a saxophone player named Daryl and a younger guy named Paul, who had a great studio.

The Forgotten Planet Hain

Our recordings included one very mysterious track where Jude was playing keyboards and I was verbally describing a mass, worldwide UFO sighting. I borrowed an idea from Ursula K. Le Guin's classic science-fiction novel *The Left Hand of Darkness,* which we had been assigned to read for my Science-Fiction class, and which is considered to be among the top two or three sci-fi novels of all time by most critics. Le Guin's novel proposed that human beings were all over the galaxy and they had originated on an ancient planet she called Hain. They had seeded themselves throughout a variety of planetary systems but their descendants had long since forgotten this in many cases. Some of the surviving races were telepathic and one of the main characters in the story started developing this ability near the end. I now know from insiders that many sci-fi writers were contacted by government-affiliated groups and given various pieces of classified information to disclose as fiction. They were invariably sworn to secrecy and told there would be severe, if not lethal, consequences if they ever told a soul. Others were contacted telepathically by extraterrestrials who are steering our evolution. Le Guin may well have been approached.

By the end of our song I had reached a very deep meditative state and felt the need to resolve the searing tension in the music. I took on a haunting, authoritative voice and said, "Masters of the forgotten planet Hain, coming out of space to Earth. To see us. To understand. Rectify. And to judge." Each time I listened to this I felt incredible sensations, as if I had spoken something that was far more than just fiction. In another track from those same sessions, I referred to the Face on Mars as well as the pyramids I had briefly heard someone say were there, and spoke about how we would evolve dramatically if it became an established fact that these had been built by an ancient civilization. I now know that human life is written into quantum mechanics itself, and is not just the result of a common planet of origin, as Le Guin suggested—but these recordings did tie in many intriguing concepts. Fiction can help prepare the imagination to accept exotic new truths later on. Le Guin's book did articulate the prevailing classified theory for why there appear to be so many humans throughout our galaxy.

Shwanksville Delirium

We also did tracks with Daryl that sounded like Nine Inch Nails–type "industrial" music, but with a gritty, urban saxophone. We worked on these tracks in Jude's apartment in a less-than-friendly part of Albany.

One afternoon we were so stressed out trying to mix our songs on a four-track cassette recorder that we almost felt delirious. We went to get some food and soon could barely contain our laughter. A woman in front of us in line had a really funny nasal accent and kept talking about a place she called Shwanksville. We couldn't stop laughing about it when we got home. We combined the way we were feeling with her funny word, and said, "That's it! That's the name of our band. Shwanskville Delirium!"

One of our songs was based on a poem Jude had recently written called "Ram Your Face." There was no singing, just an intense verbal delivery that alternated between speaking and screaming. It was about a highly dysfunctional relationship in which the abuser was acting just like a tyrannical government. This was 1993, and later on I was quite surprised to discover that it was a possible prophecy of 9/11, eight years in advance. Here are the key lyrics: "Ram your face against my fist. Burn, feel, comprehend where we stand. Metal to metal, soul to soul, meshing to fusion. Scraping our sanity. Again you attempt manipulation. Failing to maintain utter control, crushed in defeat, you try to reach me with pathetic threats that would beckon my fate. The reason I fear you is I cling to the past."

This may not sound that convincing at first, but the name of our band was only one letter off from Shanksville, a small town in Pennsylvania where a hijacked airliner crashed on 9/11. The world was going to go into a "Shanksville delirium," and the planes would ram into the towers, causing metal to touch metal, soul to touch soul, meshing to fusion and burning—just as the lyrics had said. The result would immediately begin "scraping our sanity" on a collective level. The lyrics also suggested a knowledge of the Cabal that may have been responsible for doing this, in that they were attempting manipulation, had failed to maintain utter control, and were perpetrating these attacks to try to prevent themselves from being crushed in defeat. Multiple insiders would later confirm this was the case. The lyrics also imply that once we stop clinging to the past, we no longer need to fear these people. Other songs from those sessions suggested the power elite were hiding the truth about UFOs and ancient civilizations. The photo we used for the album cover featured two dream-like fingers held up vertically in black and white, looking somewhat like the Twin Towers with smoke around them. My 9/11 prophecies would get much stronger beginning in 1996, as we shall see.

You Need to Sit Down for This

As I started the spring semester I was beginning to feel genuine happiness again. And then one fine afternoon, I had a conversation that changed my life so radically, in less than two hours, that the only other thing I could compare it to was the out-of-body experience. Everything I had experienced since my earliest UFO dreams as a child was transformed from fantasy into reality, right then—with the deafening thunderclap of proof. The flash of light I had witnessed in the sky now seemed to be only the beginning of a deeper message. I was about to find out that UFOs were real.

In college I had become friends with a guy we will call Ian, who was from a neighboring school and who was a guitarist. He has never wanted to come forward with his story since I became a public figure, fearing threats to his life. Ian and I would also get together with his friend Mike, who played keyboards. We had talked about starting a band but never really did very much with the idea, and usually just laughed a lot. One day, not long after the semester started, Ian showed up at my door unexpectedly. He was not smiling. When I asked him what was up, he said, "You need to sit down for this." I brushed it off at first, but he was very serious, so I did exactly as he asked.

"I don't know how to tell you this, so I'm just going to start. Aliens are real."

I immediately started laughing, accused him of trying to play a joke on me, and complimented him on his acting skills, saying maybe he had chosen the wrong major.

"This is not a joke, man. You know I am a physics major. I just got out of a two-hour private conversation with my physics professor, who is the head of the department. He told me extraterrestrials crash-landed at Roswell in 1947 and the government has been covering it up ever since. He worked in the higher echelons of NASA throughout the 1970s. He said it was considered 'common knowledge' in the higher levels of NASA that we are not alone in the universe, and extraterrestrials are regularly operating in our airspace."

"Okay, let's just say you are telling me the truth. Why the hell haven't they told us?" I asked him.

"He explained that too. He started out by telling our entire class that Roswell really happened and NASA knew about it ever since they were founded. People panicked so much after *War of the Worlds,* a classic radio broadcast that simulated a mass alien invasion, that the government felt our society would collapse if they ever told us the truth. He said he was allowed to tell us like this, but that if anyone asked him about it again he would deny ever saying a word. Apparently NASA doesn't mind if people learn about it here and there. The main thing is they can never allow it to become front-page news on the *New York Times.* Our class was utterly speechless as he laid this all out. I am his best student and I immediately asked for a teacher-student conference after the class was over. He went on for two hours and told me much, much more than he had said to the rest of the class."

"Like what?" I asked him.

"Okay. I learned about the propulsion system the discs use. They have a particle emitter that first shoots out a particle going three-quarters the speed of light. Then a trillionth of a second later, it shoots out another particle at light speed. The faster particle bounces off the slower particle like a billiard ball and shoots back to the ship, striking it on the side of the disc. This happens trillions of times per second, and each time the light-speed particles hit the ship, they create thrust. When you get trillions of those particle hits per second, it allows the ship to quickly accelerate to near light speed. The emitter can shoot particles from any part of the disc's round edge, so it is a great design because it can very easily make turns and travel in any direction." I was stunned to hear this, as the physics seemed very logical—and something I would never have thought of.

"What kinds of beings did they find inside? Did he say anything about that?" I asked him.

"Oh yes. He said they found three different types. The first one was like the Grays. They had large heads, large black eyes, thin bodies, and pale whitish skin. Some of them are around our height and others are shorter. He also said there was a second, shorter type that looked like a Gray, but the entire head was only a helmet. Underneath it had a very different and much more frightening-looking face, which they called 'a monstrosity.' He had no information on exactly what it looked like."

I was reeling from the implications of all this. I imagined that the "monstrosity" was some sort of reptilian-looking humanoid. "What about the third type? You said there were three."

His eyes widened. "That's the weirdest part of all. The third type looks almost exactly the same as human beings on Earth. There are only subtle differences, like they might have violet-colored irises or pupils that are diamond-shaped instead of round."

"Well, if an extraterrestrial spacecraft crashed in Roswell, then that would mean our guys got their hands on some really advanced technology. Have they done anything with the wreckage?" I asked him.

"Absolutely. Like you can't even imagine. He said that a variety of our favorite technologies were taken from this and other crashes and were 'reverse engineered,' as he called it. This includes solid-state transistors, computer chips, LED lights, lasers, holograms, fiber-optic cables, infrared night vision, Velcro, Teflon, and Kevlar, which they use to make bulletproof vests. They would take something from one of the ships, hand it to a corporation, tell them it was a 'foreign technology,' and ask them to figure out how to reproduce it. He also told me that in secret they have 'smart materials' that can repair their own damage, generate anti-gravity, and create free energy. It has something to do with the atoms all fitting together in a perfect geometric lattice. We will have huge advances in materials science in the future and be able to custom-design compounds at the molecular level to do exactly what we want."

"Did he say anything about the future? Anything about some kind of massive change in our civilization?"

"Yes. He told me they are going to keep releasing more and more of this stuff as time goes on. In the next twenty years, the amount of technology in the everyday world will utterly have transformed our lives beyond what we could have imagined today."

That was 1993, and by 2013 Ian's NASA prophecy was already quite visible. The Internet had transformed from a painfully slow dial-up curiosity to our dominant means of communication, media, and entertainment. We used to laugh at the two or three kids who would tap away on loud keyboards in the Crispell Hall study lounge and brag about using "email" to communicate with people in foreign countries. Smart watches and smart devices have now become vastly more powerful than "tower" computers that were two cubic feet in volume, required bulky monochromatic screens, and plagued you with constant fan noise. We certainly haven't gotten anti-gravity, free energy, or "smart materials" yet, but technology did indeed make a quantum leap.

It is also interesting that the target date the professor gave us—twenty years after February 1993—was almost immediately after the Mayan calendar end-date of December 21, 2012. NASA apparently told him our society would be going through a major transformation at that exact time. This also correlated nicely with Arthur C. Clarke's date of 2010 for the movie where our entire solar system went through a dramatic energetic transformation. This was only the second time I had encountered that time frame—but it was definitely not the last.

I never bothered to try to go meet the professor, since he said he would deny it if he was ever asked again. I thought back to Watergate, the people my parents saw walking into the house across the street, the Jim Jones mass suicide, the Iran-Contra hearings, the Eye under the bridge, the weird signal from the television set, and all the astonishing conspiracies I had learned about in sociology class. I had been on the front lines of a battle against government lies and secrecy on my own college campus, where they had completely hidden the dangers of the contamination that had occurred and forced us to go back to class. I was absolutely certain that the government could be lying about something this big—and I became completely obsessed with learning as much about it as I possibly could. Out of respect to the professor's family I am not going to release his name, but I did look him up recently and confirm that he has now passed away, and that he did indeed work for NASA in the 1970s. Remarkably, other whistle-blowers validated everything he said and added a great deal more, as we shall see. This disclosure, barely over a month after I had the energetic surge experience, set me on fire for the truth.

Before long I started going down to the Elting Library in New Paltz with a backpack and would hit the 000 section—the very beginning of the entire Dewey Decimal System for cataloging books—and grab everything that looked interesting. Many of these books hadn't been checked out in years—some even for ten or twenty. It seemed appropriate that these books on the paranormal were at the origin of the entire library, as I felt they contained the key to humanity's beginnings. I would go down there with a backpack full of books I had already read and come home with another load of new ones. I quickly started burning through an average of five books a week. I read everything I could find on UFOs, extraterrestrials, angels, pyramids, Stonehenge, Easter Island, Atlantis, ancient civilizations, Nostradamus, the Loch Ness Monster, Bigfoot, ghosts, mediumship, and the Bermuda Triangle.

The professor had said NASA already had working anti-gravity and free-energy propulsion systems. They also knew exactly how to build a flying saucer using a particle emitter that could reach near light speed. That meant it was almost a certainty that they already had top secret craft that could easily travel throughout our solar system—and possibly beyond. It also meant some of the UFOs people were seeing could be built by humans here on Earth. Once I dug into the literature, I realized that there were hundreds, if not thousands of examples of high-quality UFO sightings going back to the late 1940s. Though our government may have developed their own working prototypes after Roswell, there were also continuing reports of sightings going back for millennia. If even one of those sightings was genuine, then that meant we were not alone in the universe. Intelligent civilizations have been visiting us since the dawn of humanity on Earth.

I became so addicted to research that I completely stopped going to support-group meetings. I had no desire to ever do drugs again—and never did. In hindsight I realize that quitting the meetings was a bad idea, as I quickly became a "dry drunk," as they call it in Alcoholics Anonymous. I still had many of the problems of an addict—I had just changed what I was addicted to. This was a subtle problem, not an outrageous one, and it would take me many years to discover how these patterns had continued repeating. Most of it appeared in the addictive behavior known as codependency; I would attract people into my life who took unfair advantage of me and were disrespectful, or even outright bullies. However, I did become far healthier and far more successful, both on a personal and academic level, almost immediately. I had found my great passion in life. Most of my college classes were fairly easy, and I spent as many hours a day as possible doing research into UFOs and ancient civilizations.

UFOs Following Lunar Astronauts

The book that started it all off for me practically leaped off the shelf when I saw it. The title was *Our Ancestors Came from Outer Space*.[34] The author was Maurice Chatelain, who had been the director of communications for the Apollo Moon missions. His job was to design and implement the radio-wave systems, including a network of ground-based parabolic dish antennas, that allowed Mission Control to maintain contact with the Apollo astronauts. He openly admitted that the Gemini and Apollo astronauts all saw UFOs following them on their missions, as you are about to read. Best of all, right in the introduction he hinted that they had discovered something on the Moon that was "not anticipated," and that he still could not talk about it—meaning it was not just UFOs, which he openly discussed:

> During these missions several strange things happened. Some still cannot be talked about and some I will mention without revealing my sources of information and with the utmost reserve, because I personally was not there when these incidents allegedly took place. It could be, for example, that both the American and the Russian space programs did bring back discoveries that were not anticipated.

In the next chapter we will examine some of the stunning physical evidence that Chatelain may have been referring to. Early along in the book, Chatelain went into detail about how he became the director of communications for the Apollo program:

[Defense contractor] North American submitted the best technical layout [to NASA] for both development and production of the Apollo spacecraft, and therefore had been awarded the contract. . . . I was among the very first men who presented themselves to North American, and since I was already known in the industry as a radar and telecommunications specialist, I was immediately offered the task of designing and building the Apollo communication and data-processing system. Nobody specified my duties or functions, because no one at that time knew what these systems would be like. But that, again, was of no importance in view of the rush to land on the Moon.[35]

Chatelain gave more detail on the next page:

When the Apollo project started, there was no communication equipment powerful enough or sensitive enough to make voice transmission possible from earth to moon, not to mention transmission of television pictures over that distance. Such things had to be invented, perfected and built. . . . All these stations had to be in contact with each other, and all of them had to report to the Apollo Space Flight Center in Houston, Texas. . . . How I was put in charge of all this within a few months after I started my new job at North American I will never understand, but that is of no importance now. The only thing that really counts is that . . . everything functioned much better than we thought it would at the beginning, or even better than we ever expected. I think that it must have happened because of some divine influence, not by human intelligence alone. Since that time I firmly believe in benevolent divine intervention in human affairs.[36]

Just as I was finishing this book in spring 2016, I found out about William Tompkins, an aerospace engineer who validated Chatelain's theory of extraterrestrial intervention in the development of the Apollo program. In his highly technical book *Selected By Extraterrestrials,* Tompkins extensively documents his work with Nordic human ETs who had blended into NASA. The Nordics helped Tompkins design the rockets and systems that became the Apollo program.[37] Once the Apollo missions were underway, Chatelain heard some very interesting rumors: ". . . the astronauts were not limited to equipment troubles. They saw things during their missions that could not be discussed with anybody outside NASA. It is very difficult to obtain any specific information from NASA, which still exercises a very strict control over any disclosure of these events." That sounded familiar. In the nearly twenty years since Chatelain had written his book, nothing had changed—at least according to Ian's physics professor.

Chatelain went on:

> It seems that all Apollo and Gemini flights were followed, both at a distance and sometimes also quite closely, by space vehicles of extraterrestrial origin—flying saucers, or UFOs. . . . Every time it occurred, the astronauts informed Mission Control, who then ordered absolute silence. I think that Walter Schirra aboard Mercury 8 was the first of the astronauts to use the code name "Santa Claus" to indicate the presence of flying saucers next to space capsules. However, his announcements were barely noticed by the general public. It was a little different when James Lovell on board the Apollo 8 command module came out from behind the moon and said for everybody to hear: "We have been informed that Santa Claus does exist!" Even though this happened on Christmas Day 1968, many people sensed a hidden meaning in those words that was not difficult to decipher.

Chatelain also indicated that these ETs did not just observe NASA:

> There was even some talk that the *Apollo 13* mission carried a nuclear device aboard that could be set off to make measurements of the infrastructure of the moon . . . [with]

several recording seismographs placed in different locations. The unexplained explosion of an oxygen tank in the service module of *Apollo 13* on its flight to the moon, according to rumors, was caused deliberately by a UFO that was following the capsule—to prevent the detonation of the atomic charge that could possibly have destroyed or endangered some moon base established by extraterrestrials. Well, there was a lot of talk and there still is.[38]

Ruins on the Moon

In that last quote, Chatelain directly alluded to there being an extraterrestrial base on the Moon. In April 1995, he published an article in which he admitted that the Apollo missions found "several mysterious geometric structures of unnatural origin" on the Moon.[39] This was one of the first things I read just a few months after getting online in late 1995 to do UFO research. The Internet was so small back then that if you tried to search for a particular name or topic, particularly in the UFO field, you might find only a few choices—if any. Once I began developing my own website in 1999, I was frequently frustrated when I would search for information on a particular topic of interest and every link that came up was from my own site. In the same article that featured Chatelain's confession, Apollo astronaut Gordon Cooper was quoted as saying something amazing.

> Astronaut Gordon Cooper, also a former Air Force colonel, granted a second interview to Sam Sherman of Independent International Pictures Corporation, who is producing a film titled *Beyond This Earth*. In it Cooper said, "[I] had worked on a UFO system with someone who had been in touch with extraterrestrials and was able to gain some knowledge." This person had made a small UFO prototype and was working on a 50-foot model with financial backing from an Arab country when he died. . . . Cooper also talked about a friend who actually viewed the ET bodies at Roswell. . . ."[40]

By this point in 1996 I had already read many books about working anti-gravity spacecraft that had been developed by the military-industrial complex. Nikola Tesla apparently had a working anti-gravity system, as I detailed in *The Source Field Investigations*. A German scientist named Viktor Schauberger had found natural anti-gravity in the movement of rivers, allowing salmon to swim straight up through waterfalls over astonishing distances. Schauberger had replicated this natural phenomenon in a water turbine he called "the Repulsine," and the technology was seized by Nazi Germany in the 1930s. This was machined into a working engine they called *die Glocke*, or "the Bell," that was used to power UFO-type discs. Bob Lazar came forward as a whistle-blower and revealed he had been hired to try to reverse-engineer an extraterrestrial craft that was in the possession of the US government. Although he was not successful, he learned a great deal about how they worked.

Furthermore, I read that anyone who tried to build these types of devices on their own would be threatened and either bought out or shut down—sometimes with lethal force. So when Gordon Cooper, an American hero, said that he was in contact with a man who was developing his own UFO with big Arab money behind it, I wasn't at all surprised to find out that the man ended up dead soon afterward. It was also quite revealing to read that extraterrestrials had apparently been in direct contact with this man to help him develop the technology. This same article featured another piece of data that perfectly validated what Chatelain had said about NASA covering up the truth.

> During a May 6, 1995, radio interview on WOL-AM in Washington, D.C., Donna Tietze, a former photo technician at NASA's Johnson Space Center in Houston during the Apollo moon missions, revealed that a co-worker in a restricted area had the job of airbrushing UFOs out of lunar photos before NASA offered the photos for sale to the public.[41]

Donna Tietze also said that "anomalies" were stripped out of all Moon photos before NASA offered them to the public as well[42]— suggesting the presence of ruins or active bases on the surface of the

Moon, just as Chatelain's insiders had said. Donna Tietze ended up speaking at the Disclosure Project in 2001 as Donna Hare.[43] I was fortunate enough to attend and I got to meet her in person.

Another Disclosure Project insider named Karl Wolfe testified to being shown pictures of a variety of buildings and domed structures on the Moon at a secret NASA briefing in mid-1965. Wolfe's testimony is presented in the Disclosure Project Executive Summary Briefing document as follows: "Karl Wolfe was in the Air Force for 4 ½ years beginning in January 1964. He had a top secret crypto clearance and worked with the tactical air command at Langley AFB in Virginia. While working at an NSA facility he was shown photographs taken by the Lunar Orbiter of the moon that showed detailed artificial structures. These photos were taken prior to the Apollo landing in 1969."[44]

When Wolfe addressed the media at the National Press Club on May 10, 2001, he described what he saw in a private room at the NSA facility in mid-1965 as follows: "About 30 minutes into the process, he said to me, in a very distressed way, 'By the way, we've discovered a base on the back side of the moon.' And then he proceeded to put photographs down in front of me. Clearly in these photographs were structures—mushroom-shaped buildings, spherical buildings, and towers. At that point I was very concerned because I knew we were working in compartmentalized security. He had breached security and I was actually frightened at that moment, and I did not question him any further. A few moments later someone did come into the room. I worked there for three more days and I remember going home and naively thinking, 'I can't wait to hear about this on the evening news.' And here it is, more than 30 years later, and I hope we hear about it tonight. And I will testify under oath before Congress."[45]

The Executive Summary document also includes Wolfe's personal reflections of what he felt after seeing these photos: "I didn't want to look at it any longer than that, because I felt that my life was in jeopardy. . . . I would have loved to have looked at it longer, I would have loved to have had copies. I would love to have said more about it, discussed it more, but I knew I couldn't. I knew the young fellow who was sharing this was really, really overstepping his bounds at that point. I felt that he just needed somebody to talk to. He hadn't discussed it, couldn't discuss it, and he wasn't doing it for any ulterior motive other than the fact that I think he had the weight of this thing on him and it was distressing to him."[46]

With only three days left to finish this book on the final editing pass, I was fortunate enough to get an extended interview with William Tompkins, the ninety-four-year-old aerospace engineer who wrote *Selected By Extraterrestrials*. In his book, Tompkins provides extensive documentation to prove that he served in the navy and later worked for defense contractors. Here is what he told me that NASA found on the Moon, in our interview:

> The first missions that we did going around the moon with the astronauts were just preliminary missions before the LEM had to go up there and land. Here we have these three guys in there, and they have cameras. As they go around the moon, they see all these structures—both on the view side facing us and then really elaborate structures on the other side that we can't see. So they photograph this stuff. NASA does. And holy cats, what's that all about? Everybody at NASA is looking over the photographs and trying to figure out what is going on. We make another orbit a couple of weeks later, and, oh my gosh. Did you see the height of that building? . . . [It] has to be three miles high. And wait a minute! What did we see? No, hold on, back off. Wait a minute. They were just building that thing. It was only ten stories high. . . . And in three weeks, it's three miles high? Who is doing that construction? . . . Do you realize it would take us ten years to get half the height of that building?
>
> Now wait a minute. Look again. Do you see that big rectangular structure? It's floating! It's not even on the [surface of the moon]. It's got to be at least four or five miles high and ten miles wide! Now what in the hell is that? You've got to be kidding me. And it's translucent! You can see rooms inside. You can see the elevators! Well, holy cats. Don't let anybody find out about this. Do you see what I am trying to say? . . . We are watching this being built. Guys with amateur cameras, if they watch this and they have a big enough camera

and telescope, they can see this building being built in a few
days by some massive production method developed by extraterrestrials. . . . It is insane! . . . There are bridges being built
in several bays all the way across what would be a deep cavern, and can be five or six miles long. This bridge is built in a
few days. Bang, bang, bang, bang, and it's all done. . . .

[NASA found] all different types of ruins. It was not like
in Egypt, where everything is the same type of structure. . . .
Not like in Los Angeles, where you've got rectangular buildings and highways and everything is generally the same. Up
on the moon, the old buildings that were there were not of
any one type of structure and construction. . . . What was
accepted was that there had to have been numerous different
civilizations operating there.[47]

I understand this may seem hard to believe, but Tompkins was able
to validate dozens and dozens of highly classified data points I had heard
from other insiders.

NASA Is a Defense Agency Classifying Secrets

Over the years, these new insiders provided dazzling confirmation of the
data in Chatelain's book, and extended the scope of what Ian's professor
had revealed. Though Chatelain only hinted at "mysterious geometric
structures of unnatural origin" and an extraterrestrial lunar base in his
book *Ancestors,* it was obvious that something had set him on fire about
ancient civilizations. Most people think of NASA as a benign, even boring group dedicated to peaceful space exploration, sharing everything
they find with the public—but NASA's own charter, the National Aeronautics and Space Act of 1958, reveals it was built to be a defense agency
that will withhold information for national security reasons:

Section 305 . . . (i): . . . The National Aeronautics and
Space Administration shall be considered a Defense Agency

of the United States for the purpose of Chapter 17, Title 35 of
the United States code. . . .

    Section 206 . . . (d): No [NASA] information which has
been classified for reasons of National Security shall be included
in any report made under this section [of the act] . . .[48]

Why legally define NASA as a defense agency that can withhold classified information if there isn't anything out there that the US government felt
they should be defending us against? Isn't space supposed to be an empty,
lifeless void? Apparently not. They do have something to hide. Donna Tietze's associate was hired to strip out the good stuff, and Chatelain said the
astronauts were sworn to secrecy. Karl Wolfe feared for his life just from
getting the chance to see a picture of artificial structures on the Moon, since
he understood how aggressively NASA defended its most classified secrets.

DDT—Decoy, Distract, and Trash

Multiple insiders said that NASA and other groups used psychological
operations to discredit whistle-blowers. Dr. Steven Greer, the director of
the Disclosure Project, revealed this was called a DDT campaign—for
"decoy, distract, and trash." Paid government employees would create fake
data known as "disinformation," which would appear to be similar to what
the insiders were saying—and perhaps even more interesting. This data
would be released into the same media that the whistle-blowers were featured in, as if it were true. This was the decoy. Then if the plan was successful, the public's attention would be distracted by the new information,
fulfilling the second stage of the plan. People would start enthusiastically
spreading the information to their friends, family, and coworkers. Then in
the third stage, obvious mistakes in the disinformation would be revealed.
Now everyone would laugh at the people who spread the data, and would
believe all of it was fake. This was the trash phase of the DDT campaign.

    When I got to meet Donna Hare, Karl Wolfe, and others who had
come forward, I could tell they were extremely afraid for their lives. They
were willing to be heroes and fight for the truth. They did not profit from

disclosing this information. In fact, many of them lost their jobs and were ostracized by colleagues, friends, and family. The sarcastic, mocking language I read online when people tried to discredit these witnesses sounded just like the bullies I had to defend myself against in grade school. The truth was so outrageous to most people that they would look for any possible weakness they could find in an insider, and then attempt to use that to suggest the entire story was bogus. So much disinformation was being released on the Internet that I would have to fact-check every single thing I read. It was obvious that an incredible amount of money was being spent on deceiving the public.

The proof finally appeared in a set of Snowden documents that Glenn Greenwald published in February 2014. Unfortunately, this story did not garner anywhere near as much attention as the initial wave of disclosures, but a wealth of evidence was provided nonetheless. According to Greenwald, "One of the many pressing stories that remains to be told from the Snowden archive is how Western intelligence agencies are attempting to manipulate and control online discourse with extreme tactics of deception and reputation-destruction. . . . These agencies are attempting to control, infiltrate, manipulate, and warp online discourse, and in doing so, are compromising the integrity of the Internet itself."[49]

The group doing this is called the Joint Threat Research Intelligence Group, or JTRIG. Greenwald continues:

> Among the core self-identified purposes of JTRIG are two tactics: (1) to inject all sorts of false material onto the Internet in order to destroy the reputation of its targets; and (2) to use social sciences and other techniques to manipulate online discourse and activism to generate outcomes it considers desirable. To see how extremist these programs are, just consider the tactics they boast of using to achieve those ends: "false flag operations" (posting material to the Internet and falsely attributing it to someone else), fake victim blog posts (pretending to be a victim of the individual whose reputation they want to destroy), and posting "negative information" on various forums. . . . The title page of one of these documents reflects the agency's own

awareness that it is "pushing the boundaries" by using "cyber offensive" techniques against people who have *nothing to do with terrorism or national security threats*. . . .

These GCHQ documents are the first to prove that a major Western government is using some of the most controversial techniques to disseminate deception online and harm the reputations of targets. Under the tactics they use, the state is deliberately spreading lies on the Internet about whichever individuals it targets, including the use of what GCHQ itself calls "false flag operations" and emails to people's families and friends.[50]

I have been subject to a magnificent number of these campaigns since I began posting disclosure-related material online in 1996. I would read every one of the most incredibly venomous and spiteful hate comments directed against me on a daily basis. The comments did not pause for evenings, weekends, or holidays. It wasn't until August of 2011 that I finally broke the "repetition compulsion" I was stuck in after suffering years of bullying as a child, and began protecting myself from seeing these comments. Up until then, I had spent fifteen years ingesting a daily diet of the most staggeringly horrible abuse, including severe personal insults and an endless array of death threats. Every single tactic described in the Snowden documents was used against me repeatedly. Hardly a single day would go by without reading letters and comments that were boiling over with hatred. It took a great deal of discipline to remain positive and upbeat about myself and the work I was doing in light of these ongoing attacks. My life immediately improved when I conquered the addiction to reading them and went back to following my passion, while doing my best to reach the highest quality in every bit of data I released.

Astronauts Speaking in Code

If multiple NASA insiders are claiming that major secrets about the Moon are being hidden from us, then the astronauts would have to have protocols to avoid leaking the truth in their radio communications. One example would be Chatelain's revelation that the term "Santa Claus" was code for a

UFO. Some of the transcripts of conversations the Apollo astronauts had with Mission Control suggested they were indeed seeing UFOs and mysterious structures on the Moon,[51] but were instructed to use code phrases such as "Barbara" to refer to the artifacts. They were also warned to "Keep It Less Obvious," which appears to be the hidden meaning of the code word and acronym "KILO" that Mission Control used with the astronauts.

KILO is only one of a variety of cryptic phrases used in this next exchange, where the landing of the lunar module appeared to have exposed an unusually bright spot by blowing away some dust that was over it. This may have actually been the surface of an ancient, intelligently constructed floor for a lunar base. Remember, any spot above a relatively small level of brightness should not exist on the Moon—nor should there be lights that are flashing. Notice how mysterious the conversation gets in the official Apollo transcripts once Mission Control orders the astronaut to "go to KILO." Suddenly, everything they are saying about the "big anomalies"—i.e., large and unexpected things on the lunar surface—is in a bizarre code. Then the astronaut breaks the code and states in plain language that he is seeing a light flash again:

> DMP (LUNAR MODULE): Where are your big anomalies? Can you summarize them quickly? . . .
>
> CMP (COMMAND MODULE PILOT): Hey, I can see a bright spot down there on the landing site where they might have blown off some of that halo stuff.
>
> CAPCOM: Roger. Interesting. Very—go to KILO. KILO.
>
> CMP: Hey, it's gray now and the number one extends.
>
> CAPCOM: Roger. We got it. And we copy that it's all on the way down there. Go to KILO. KILO on that.
>
> CMP: Mode is going to HM. Recorder is off. Lose a little communication there, huh? Okay, there's bravo. Bravo, select OMNI.
>
> Hey, you know you'll never believe it. I'm right over the edge of Orientale. I just looked down and saw the light flash again.
>
> CAPCOM: Roger. Understand.[52]

Although these subjects were very interesting to me, we haven't even begun to discuss the greatest gems that I found in Chatelain's book. He didn't just leak information from insiders—he dedicated his life to researching ancient civilizations and looking for proof that could validate what he had heard. Reading the results of his investigation was one of the most significant spiritual awakenings I had ever experienced up until then. It triggered a lifelong interest in developing a new scientific model that could explain his discoveries.

CHAPTER FIFTEEN

Chatelain's "Big Year" Ends with a Bang

A ll the seeds of my future were being planted in my imagination as I read Chatelain's book and opened my mind to the "big picture" of what he was revealing. There was a wealth of intriguing data in the book, but by far what grabbed me the most was something he called the "Constant of Nineveh." This wasn't just a fascinating relic of ancient technology and mathematics that shouldn't exist—it was a scientific revolution in the making. Chatelain also discussed a 26,000-year cycle in the Earth that was a focal point for many ancient cultures. It was often divided into twelve "ages of the zodiac" measuring 2,160 years each, adding up to an exact total of 25,920 years. Both *The Source Field Investigations* and *The Synchronicity Key* explore this cycle extensively. The more I read about this cycle, the more fascinated I became— as multiple ancient texts claimed that the Sun would release a great surge of energy at the end of the cycle. This energetic surge was apparently the mechanism that would trigger a mass ascension event on Earth.

The Constant of Nineveh

Chatelain explained that when Sumerian clay cylinders were found in the library of King Assurbanipal in Nineveh, in what is now Iraq, not all of the cuneiform writings they found were words and sentences. Entire cylinders were found that contained nothing but gigantic numbers. The archeologists ignored this, believing the Sumarians were just ancient savages obsessed with numbers, but Chatelain looked into it and really studied them.

Chatelain knew that in order to have a successful space mission, you had to make very accurate calculations—and the only way to do it was by counting time in seconds. He had routinely juggled huge numbers in seconds for NASA, and started analyzing the discarded Sumerian data. His attention was drawn to the number 195,955,200,000,000. This is approximately 6.2 million years of time in seconds. Chatelain discovered that you could produce this massive number by multiplying 70 by 60, taking the product and multiplying it by 60 again, and cycling this process a total of seven times. This reads as $(70 \times 60)^7$, or seventy times sixty to the seventh power. Chatelain soon realized that with this one number, he could calculate the exact time it took any planet, comet, or celestial object in the solar system to make one full cycle around the Sun. Each object in our solar system would orbit our Sun in an exact number of cycles that would fit perfectly into this number—like twelve eggs in an egg carton:

> Every period of revolution or conjunction of all the solar system bodies calculated by the Constant of Nineveh corresponded exactly down to several decimal points with the values given in the modern tables of United States astronomers. . . . I have not been able to find even a single period of revolution, or conjunction of a solar system planet or satellite, that would not be an exact fraction down to the fourth decimal point of the Great Constant of the Solar System.[53]

Chatelain included a table in the book that had the exact number of cycles it took for every planet's orbit to fit into the Nineveh Constant, along with many planetary conjunctions and a variety of other celestial measurements. Halley's Comet makes exactly 81,000 cycles around the Sun during this 6.2-million-year length of time, and Pluto makes 24,998

cycles—which is only two Pluto-years away from a perfect 25,000. Chatelain believed that since our data on Pluto was so spotty, further analysis
would prove it fit into the Nineveh Constant with exactly 25,000 cycles.
The fact that this massive, 6.2-million-year cycle integrated all the motions in our solar system, down to four decimal points of accuracy, completely blew me away. Theoretically, all the planets would arrange into a
perfect straight line at least once every 6.2 million years as a result of this
phenomenon.

The planets were not supposed to have such a precise relationship
with one another, and yet there it was. Chatelain had proved it, and as
the director of communications for the Apollo missions, he was uniquely
qualified to be able to do so. NASA had decided he was the most com-
petent, skillful man on Earth to be able to crunch the massive numbers
needed to enable the lunar astronauts to communicate with Mission
Control. Right away, I realized that there must be some great harmonic
principle that was causing all the planets, comets, and orbiting bodies to
work like this—similar to the gears in a fine Swiss watch. It was even
more outrageous that we had not discovered this new science in modern
times until Chatelain came along, but somehow the ancient Sumerians
knew it very well. They were obviously not a primitive society, as most
people had been led to believe. Their scientific knowledge was far more
powerful than most people had given them credit for.

The Hidden Secret of the Precession

Chatelain also spoke about a 26,000-year cycle called the precession of
the equinoxes. It was a slow wobbling movement in the Earth that caused
the apparent positions of the stars in our night sky to drift by one degree
every seventy-two years. He indicated that many ancient cultures seemed
to be obsessed with this number. I would soon find a wealth of evidence
suggesting that a massive energetic event occurs at the end of each 26,000-
year cycle. Multiple ancient teachings tell us the Sun will release some sort
of visible light that is very different than usual once we reach this point.
The end of the cycle was widely believed to be somewhere around

December 21, 2012, as I exhaustively detailed in *The Source Field Investigations*. Since we have clearly not experienced this event yet, it is entirely possible for there to be a decent margin of error when we are talking about something that occurs only once every 26,000 years. Multiple sources have also confirmed that this event is not set to occur on any fixed date, but occurs in response to a mass shift in consciousness on Earth. This epic solar and energetic flash may well produce ascension for those who are ready for it—and thirty-five different ancient cultures had the science of this cycle hidden in their mythologies, as we will soon discuss.

Chatelain found that this magical 26,000-year cycle also fit perfectly into the Constant of Nineveh: "When I divided the Nineveh number by the cycle of the precession of the equinoxes, also called the Big Year, I had the greatest surprise of my life! The sacred number of Nineveh divided exactly into 240 Big Years of 9.450 million days each." This book was translated from French, and every other source calls it the "Great Year," not the "Big Year," so this was likely to have been a simple error in translation. Chatelain revealed that this "Great Year" is perfectly integrated into a vast clockwork of orbits that are all interconnected with flawless precision. His breakthroughs revealed that our current scientific models of planetary and celestial orbits are in need of a massive overhaul. Ascension is built into the clockwork of the universe itself, and will propel us into the next level of evolution like a massive bell ringing on the hour. And somehow, the supposedly primitive Sumerians had already discovered this truth.

Lost Civilizations and the "Usual Interval"

The vast majority of the books I read argued that a major disaster had completely wiped out an ancient, highly advanced civilization that had spread across the entire globe. It was very common to hear the books refer to this civilization as Atlantis. The name Atlantis came from the Greek philosopher Plato, who revealed it in his works the *Timaeus* and *Critias,* from approximately 400 BC. Plato got his information from Solon, the wisest of the Greeks, who was fortunate enough to gain entrance into the highly secretive Egyptian priesthood.

The priests told Solon about a powerful cycle of time that they called the "usual interval," which is almost certainly the 26,000-year cycle. The priests indicated that each cycle would end with a catastrophe that would destroy entire civilizations. We were already experiencing a variety of natural disasters when I first read this in 1993—far more than in our recorded history—so it very much caught my attention. The priests said the destruction could be "by fire," which they called a "conflagration," or "by water," which could cause a great flood. In this next passage, the Egyptian priest is speaking directly to Solon. The story may seem hard to follow at first, but I will explain what it means after the quote:

> The Myth of Helios, explained as a natural astronomical event: There is a story, which even you have preserved, that once upon a time Paethon, the son of Helios, having yoked the steeds in his father's chariot, because he was not able to drive them in the path of his father, burnt up all that was upon the earth, and was himself destroyed by a thunderbolt. Now this has the form of a myth, but really signifies a declination of the bodies moving in the heavens around the earth, and a great conflagration of things upon the earth, which recurs after long intervals. . . .[54]

This was very confusing to me when I first read it. Clearly it was talking about some sort of massive energetic event, here described as a "great conflagration" or fire, which repeats after "long intervals" of time. Once I read *Fingerprints of the Gods* by Graham Hancock in 1995, this made more sense. Hancock reported on the work of two great historians, Giorgio de Santillana and Hertha von Dechend, who found thirty-five different ancient examples of the 26,000-year cycle encoded into mythology through symbolism.

In Plato's example, Helios represents the Sun. The horses are symbolically pulling the Earth around the Sun, causing its normal orbit to occur. Then something suddenly changes the Earth's orbit, and the horses can no longer follow their normal course. We are then told that once the Earth's orbit is disrupted, there is some sort of energetic release that burns up everything on the Earth—which could again be a symbol for a solar event of some kind. The Egyptian priest then translates the myth for Solon, saying it signifies a "long interval" of time that causes "a declination of the bodies moving in the heavens around the earth." This is a very precise description of the precession of the equinoxes.

The Zoroastrian scriptures mirror many other sources in saying this change will be very positive. Their word for this solar event is Fraso-kereti, which literally translates as "making wonderful."[55] In the Zoroas-trian tradition, this event will be helped along by a messianic figure called the Saoshyant, who arrives with a variety of angelic beings that defeat the negative forces on Earth.[56] The Hindu scriptures have a very similar-sounding story involving the arrival of Kalki the Destroyer, who has supernatural powers and vanquishes all evil after the great Samavar-taka fire erupts at the end of an age.[57] The Mahabharata describes the Samavartaka fire as being rainbow-colored in appearance:

> And there rise in the sky deep masses of clouds, looking like herds of elephants and decked with wreaths of lightning that are wonderful to behold. And some of those clouds are of the hue of the blue lotus; and some are of the hue of the water-lily; and some resemble in tint the filaments of the lotus and some are purple and some are yellow as turmeric and some of the hue of the crows' egg. And some are bright as the petals of the lotus and some red as vermillion.[58]

The ancient legend of this solar event continued on into Greek and Roman philosophy texts, where it is referred to as Ekpyrosis. This word has at least two alternate spellings: *Ekpurosis* and *Ecpyrosis*. This is due to differences in translating Greek characters into Roman letters. The Wiki-pedia entry on the subject at the time of this writing happens to be more thorough than any dictionary definitions:

> Ekpyrosis is a Stoic belief in the periodic destruction of the cosmos by a great conflagration every Great Year. The cosmos is then recreated (palingenesis) only to be destroyed again at the end of the new cycle. This form of catastrophe is the opposite of kataklysmos . . . the destruction of the earth

by water. The concept of ekpyrosis is attributed to Chrysippus by [the Greek historian] Plutarch.[59]

Indiana University professor James Albert Harrill wrote a surprisingly detailed piece linking these Greco-Roman philosophical teachings to later writings in the Christian Bible and other texts:

> Apocalyptic scenarios of eschatological [end-times] destruction and renewal appear in many early Christian writings. . . . For example, the apostle Paul declares the wrath of the Day of the Lord (1 Thess 1:10; 4:13–5:10; cf. 2 Thess 2:1–12) and the ultimate transformation of "all creation" (Rom 8:18–25). The Gospel of Mark promises its audience that heaven and earth "will pass away" in the imminent end times (13:24–31; cf. Matt 5:18; Luke 16:17; Isa 13:9–13). The seer of Revelation envisages . . . a "new heaven and a new earth" replacing "the first heaven and the first earth," which "had passed away" (21:1). The Gospel of Matthew speaks of a "renewal of all things" following the final judgment (19:28). And the *Didache* warns its audience about "the fire of testing" into which all human creation will soon enter (16.5).[60]

Modern spiritual teachers such as the Bulgarian mystic Peter Deunov (1864–1944) presented very similar-sounding messages, perhaps inspired by these voluminous ancient prophecies. According to Deunov, "The Fire of which I speak, that accompanies the new conditions offered to our planet, will rejuvenate, purify, reconstruct everything: the matter will be refined, your hearts will be liberated from anguish, troubles, incertitude, and they will become luminous; everything will be improved, elevated; the thoughts, sentiments, and negative acts will be consumed and destroyed."[61]

The "Stream from Heaven" and the Law of Karma

In Plato's account, he next says that the priest indicates that the Egyptians had records of many different lost civilizations that had come and gone.

He also refers to this solar event as a "stream from heaven" that "comes pouring down" after "the usual interval." He clearly states that only people who are "destitute of letters and education" remain in the aftermath.

At this point you may be wondering what in the world you have gotten yourself into by reading this book. Let me say right now that I did not write this book to create fear, nor to push any specific religious or spiritual texts. Every major spiritual teaching about this event suggests that only the most evil people on Earth will experience a negative time line like this, due to the fact that they have invited it through their own free will and karma. Unless you are a truly dark, manipulative, and controlling person, you will never see a worldwide catastrophe—at least not in any physical sense. Instead, the experience is one of unspeakable joy and wonderment— a quantum leap in spiritual evolution. And if you do feel you may be treading too closely to the negative side, there's still time to change the road you're on—as Robert Plant sang in "Stairway to Heaven."

The subjects of karma, the afterlife, and reincarnation are extensively discussed in *The Synchronicity Key,* with nearly seven hundred academic references to help prove the points. The book ends with a series of highly revealing quotes from the Muslim holy text the Koran, all of which clearly predict that this mass energetic event will take place. Here are two of the most provocative quotes:

> When time suddenly disappears, in the eternal moment of illumination the brightness of the heavenly orbs will be split open and dissolved into transparent light. . . . Those who fail to live in constant expectation of the mystic Day, regarding this teaching as myth or imagination, will be severely disappointed when the Last Day actually arrives and they are not spiritually prepared. (Meditation on Holy Qur'an 77:8, 15)[62]

> Upon the mysterious Day when time ends, all manifest Being will tremble at the first thundering blast of Divine Resonance that will utterly stop the world. . . . This momentary terror will disappear when each soul realizes its spiritual body to be perfect, limitless and holy. (Meditation on Holy Qur'an 79:6, 13)[63]

The Synchronicity Key discusses how reincarnation was a hidden secret of Christianity as well as an openly accepted teaching in many other religions. The teachings tell us that we keep reincarnating after each lifetime until we grow enough that we are ready for the next level of human evolution. Reincarnation is also a scientifically provable fact. Dr. Ian Stevenson interviewed more than three thousand children who had accurate memories of their past lives that were confirmed by doing research to verify their claims. Dr. Jim Tucker used forensic face-matching software to prove that children who accurately remembered their past lives also looked very similar to the people they claimed to have been before. This data strongly suggests that our facial features are carried from lifetime to lifetime by an energetic aspect of our consciousness, which directly affects how our faces look as we grow.

If you believe in the law of karma, and you consider deeply the horrific crimes that certain world elites have perpetrated, you may begin to understand why a negative time line like this might exist. If each of us must re-experience everything that we put others through, how do we balance out the actions of a person who has committed mass atrocities— and may be indirectly or directly responsible for the rape, torture, and murder of hundreds, if not thousands of citizens? A surprisingly large number of people have been hypnotically regressed to the "life between lives," or have had a near-death experience, and their reports of the afterlife are very consistent. No matter how negative we may be in our physical lives, our souls are extremely pure and understand what we are really here to learn. Some people may deliberately choose, on the soul level, to go through a mass catastrophe. That way they can discharge all the negative karma they have built up and have a fresh start for the next cycle. They may be completely unaware that anyone on their planet had been given a "free pass" where they got to avoid these events entirely.

The spiritual sources I came into direct contact with, beginning with the Law of One series, taught me very clearly that you do not mess with karma. It is an absolute law that is upheld with the most rigorous, exacting precision. As we will see, I had an astonishing example of this occur in my own life in 1996, when the future was predicted with remarkable clarity—and taught me quite a lesson. My surprising introduction to the

Law of One will be featured later in this book, and I hope you will be able to share in the wonder I felt when I realized how many mysteries it solved.

Your Knowledge Is No Better Than the Tales of Children

Eventually I would read many different sources, some ancient and some modern, that tell us a certain number of people stay on the Earth to physically experience a mass energetic event like this, whereas others go through ascension. People who are not ascending, but have not invited negative karma, appear to be moved ahead in time to a point when it becomes safe again. Apparently they have no memory of what happened to them, as otherwise they might be very disappointed that they did not get to "graduate." Keep all this in mind when you read what the priest said about the survivors of these catastrophes:

> And whatever happened either in your country or in ours, or in any other region of which we are informed—if there were any actions noble or great or in any other way remarkable, they have all been written down by us of old, and are preserved in our temples.
>
> Whereas just when you and other nations are beginning to be provided with letters and the other requisites of civilized life, after the usual interval, the stream from heaven, like a pestilence, comes pouring down, and leaves only those of you who are destitute of letters and education; and so you have to begin all over again like children, and know nothing of what happened in ancient times, either among us or among yourselves.[64]

In this last excerpt, the priest chastises Solon for trying to sound like a know-it-all because he can report genealogies of kings going back generations. The real truth is that humanity is far more ancient than we realize—and it rises and falls in cycles on the Earth, measured by the "usual interval" of 26,000 years:

As for those genealogies of yours which you just now re-
counted to us, Solon, they are no better than the tales of
children. In the first place you remember a single deluge only,
but there were many previous ones; in the next place, you do
not know that there formerly dwelt in your land the fairest
and noblest race of men which ever lived, and that you and
your whole city are descended from a small seed or remnant
of them which survived. And this was unknown to you, because, for many generations, the survivors of that destruction
died, leaving no written word.[65]

The Secrets of the Monolith

Arthur C. Clarke's *2010* featured an energetic release from Jupiter,
not the Sun, that transformed our solar system but was not catastrophic. His classic work *Childhood's End* also features a major energy
release, this time from the Sun, in the grand finale. This solar release
transforms humanity into a new level of evolution. And let's not forget
the monolith that appears in *2001*. It is an ancient, twenty-foot-tall,
mirror-polished black stone rectangle that first appears when humans are
no more evolved than apes. It causes one of the apes to become more
intelligent and get the idea to use a bone to kill another ape. This appears
to signify the first moment humans learned to use tools. Then the ape
throws the bone into the air and it becomes the spacecraft we see in the
rest of the film. This seems to indicate that we are now on the verge of
the next massive burst of human evolution as a result of having developed space travel. A marvelous gift is waiting for us once we progress
enough to make it out into space.

The second monolith in *2001* is dug up on the Moon. This is far more
interesting in light of the evidence we are now discussing. Multiple insiders have confirmed that NASA already knew there were ancient ruins on
the Moon, and used Arthur C. Clarke to tell us the truth disguised as
fiction. Once sunlight hits the sharp-edged black slab for the first time
since the astronauts dug it out in *2001*, it sends out a beacon to another

monolith. This time, the object is floating in our solar system near Jupiter. The *Odyssey* spacecraft goes out to view the monolith, and its captain, David Bowman, ends up going through a wild stargate experience once he flies out to explore it. The stargate then transforms him into the next level of human evolution—the Starchild. He reappears in *2010* as an ascended being who can travel through electrical wires and project an image of himself on a television for his mother, and he tells her, "Something wonderful is going to happen."

Thus Spoke Zarathustra

When the monolith first appears in *2001*, we hear a gripping orchestral score with very dramatic horns and booming drums. This composition was written by Richard Strauss in 1896, and is called *Thus Spoke Zarathustra*.[66] This title appears to be a major clue. Zarathustra is the correct Persian name for the religious leader often referred to as Zoroaster in the Western world. Zoroastrianism is the oldest religion on Earth, after Hinduism. The Zoroastrian scriptures go into great detail about the Sun giving off a massive energetic release at the end of a long, repeating cycle of time. In the Zoroastrian version it is very clearly stated that this produces an ascension-type event, which they call "Fraso-kereti," as we said. Clarke features the exact same type of event in *Childhood's End* and *2010*. This suggests the name of Strauss's composition was a deliberately planted clue for those who were paying attention.

Strauss's composition was also inspired by a work of the philosopher Friedrich Nietzsche with the same title. According to the official Kennedy Center website, Strauss said, "I did not intend to write philosophical music or to portray Nietzsche's great work in musical terms." The Kennedy Center goes on to say, "Instead, this sixth of his pioneering series of tone poems (composed in 1896) was meant to suggest 'the evolution of the human race from its origins, through its various phases of development (religious and scientific), right up to Nietzsche's idea of the superhuman [*Übermensch*].'"[67]

None of this appears to be a coincidence. Richard C. Hoagland, whom we will meet in the next chapter, admitted to having detailed off-the-record conversations with Arthur C. Clarke about what he really knew. Hoagland also had a man on the inside feeding him highly classified information, whom we will call Bruce. I was fortunate enough to meet Bruce at a conference in 2007 where Hoagland had invited me to speak. Bruce had strangely blue eyes, a gravelly voice, and a sarcastic, humorous personality. Bruce threw his arm around me as I was walking out of the room after my talk and said, "You're about eighty-five percent correct." When I asked, "What is the other fifteen percent?" he said, "That's going to take some time. Let's go have dinner on me and I will tell you." I soon found out that Bruce had worked directly with US presidents in at least two different administrations. In August 2014, Bruce told me far more of what he really knew and said it was "authorized by the United States government." He told me they do not want to release this information all at once, but instead choose to use private individuals like myself. That way the people who want to know the truth will gradually find out, and a mass panic will be avoided.

The NASA insiders definitely seem to believe we are heading into a mass evolutionary event. However, their interpretation of what will occur seems to be heavily colored by their own occult religious beliefs, which are rooted in the teachings of secret societies. They apparently see an event like this as a "useful" mass catastrophe. They also seem to willfully reject the information of many positive spiritual teachings, including Christianity, and believe that only the occult elite will benefit from whatever they think is going to happen.

Most people will automatically laugh at this entire discussion since it seems so outrageous. The idea of a change this epic in scope seems completely beyond our imagination. We get so captivated by the day-to-day world of our lives that the idea of a stunningly discontinuous change in the foundation of our very existence seems impossible to comprehend. Even the people who do believe it often backslide into habitual thought patterns about the "real world." The idea that this change could be coming in our own near-term future makes the discussion even more outrageous. Nonetheless, I have been receiving information about the Ascension Mysteries my entire life. I was introduced to these concepts over many years, beginning with dreams, synchronicities, and the seemingly science-fiction content of various movies, TV shows, and books. I didn't start encountering the hard data until I was nineteen years old. And as I have said so often at my conferences, wouldn't you want to know about it in case it really is true? Is it right for the government to withhold information that may dramatically affect the lives of every person on Earth—and which appears to validate every major religion and spiritual teaching in existence?

Schmitt's Stonehenge

Years after I read Chatelain's book, I would discover another interesting clue that the NASA astronauts had found ruins on the Moon. Dr. Harrison "Jack" Schmitt was an experienced professional geologist whom NASA had brought in to help study the lunar surface. According to Chatelain, "Schmitt, a geologist, was the first civilian to visit the moon, all the other astronauts having been military men."[68] Schmitt spent considerable time learning the systems the Apollo astronauts were using. He was assigned to the three-person *Apollo 15* backup crew in March 1970, and was supposed to be part of the prime crew of *Apollo 18*. In September 1970, *Apollos 18* and *19* were canceled, and humanity's last official mission to the Moon would be *Apollo 17*, launching in December 1972. The community of professional geologists advising NASA felt so strongly about the need to have a PhD geologist examine the Moon that they successfully pressured NASA to include Schmitt on *Apollo 17*.

NASA astronauts got to design the patch for each mission in collaboration with a professional artist. They would typically come up with multiple designs before settling on the one they felt was the best. The three *Apollo 17* astronauts—Eugene Cernan, Ronald Evans, and Harrison Schmitt—handed their sketched ideas to professional artist Robert T. McCall, who then created concept-art illustrations that were submitted for final review.[69]

Schmitt proposed two different designs that included strange images of Stonehenge on the patch. On the first design, Stonehenge towers above the surface of the Earth and is practically touching the Moon, with the Sun shining right in between. There is a clear beam of light between Stonehenge and the Moon that passes through the Sun and then goes off to the left and the right, forming a four-part cross—almost like an energy portal or stargate. This was three years after the movie *2001* had emerged, in which the ship's captain, David Bowman, went through an elaborate stargate experience at the end of the film.

In Schmitt's second patch idea, the final stage of the Apollo rocket that flies the astronauts home from the Moon is seen rising from a barren-looking gray world that looks more like the Moon than the Earth. A Stonehenge-like circle rises prominently off this barren world. The stones seem very large and no other signs of surface features are anywhere on the globe, suggesting it is picturing the Moon, not Earth. The lander then flies up with the image of a spiral galaxy prominently behind it. This may have been Schmitt's way of suggesting that whoever built this lunar Stonehenge was from elsewhere in our galaxy—or even a neighboring one.

Robert McCall's Sketches of Harrison Schmitt's *Apollo 17* "Stonehenge" Patches

In an interview that NASA's main artist conducted for the Johnson Space Center Oral History Project, Robert McCall said, "Jack Schmitt was the geologist astronaut on that mission, and he thought Stonehenge would be a wonderful image to include."[70] This is a little-known piece of Apollo history that supports the insider testimony of Maurice Chatelain, Donna Hare, Karl Wolfe, William Tompkins, and several others I would get to know very well. Schmitt may have gotten a little too enthusiastic with his patch ideas, knowing he was spilling the beans on something of massive importance, and his ideas were rejected. Thankfully, NASA was unable to hide all the photographic evidence of advanced ancient ruins on the Moon, as we will see in the next chapter. Some very compelling data managed to survive from both the Russian and American space programs.

CHAPTER SIXTEEN

The Lost Survivors from the Moon

On November 20, 1966, NASA's *Lunar Orbiter 2* was drifting twenty-nine miles above the Moon's surface, over the Sea of Tranquility, when it captured a stunning image that rocked the Russian and American media and scientific communities. Eight huge towers of different heights appear to rise up off the Moon's surface. Curiously, they all seem to have the form of an Egyptian obelisk. In London, Paris, and New York, large Egyptian obelisks are on public display, each commonly called Cleopatra's Needle. The Washington Monument in America's capital city is the largest version, standing at 555 feet tall. This height may well have been deliberately chosen for secret ceremonial purposes; 666 might have been too obvious for a statue that was intended to commemorate the masculine aspect of Lucifer.

Most people never stop to think how odd it is that the United States would honor its first president with a gigantic obelisk, symbolizing the Egyptian sky-god Osiris. Although I do not believe these gods were originally negative, in the occult tradition of the Cabal, Osiris and Isis represent the male and female aspects of Lucifer. Most people are also unaware that the Statue of Liberty is secretly meant to represent Isis, complete with the beams of light radiating from the top of her head, indicating that she has become ascended. It is important to point out that Cabal people believe they are "the just" and will ascend when this mass solar event takes place. They see everyone outside their group as "the wicked," and believe this event will physically destroy them. They even contort quotes out of the Bible and believe that stealing our money is God taking from "the wicked" and giving to "the just."

The Cabal members believe their strength is due to their selective combination and practice of a wide variety of secret mystery-school teachings from ancient cultures all over the world, including Babylonian, Egyptian, Celtic, and Sufi. Cabal members often refer to everyday people as "the profane." They feel we are not worthy of learning the sacred Mysteries, as they are often called—with the first letter capitalized. They fear that if ordinary people gained access to the Mysteries and began practicing the teachings, they could develop ascended abilities and use them to hurt others, potentially becoming a great threat. The torch held by the Statue of Liberty secretly represents the "Sacred Fire of Antiquity," the knowledge of the Mysteries, and the book she holds in her other hand contains the Mysteries themselves.

In 2011, two Arizona State University scientists openly proposed that we may find evidence of extraterrestrial settlements on the Moon. *Universe Today* carried the story and used a corrupted photo of the towers captured by *Lunar Orbiter 2* at the top. The original 1966 photo was not damaged and was far more revealing, as we shall see. The corrupted photo has a sharp line running down the middle, right next to the tallest tower, which the original did not have. Furthermore, the black levels have been cranked up, making the shadows of the towers very difficult to see—unlike the original, where they were staggeringly obvious. Nonetheless, this announcement was a positive step forward, and may well have been part of the gradual disclosure process:

> Two researchers at Arizona State University (ASU) have made a rather controversial proposal: have the public and other researchers study the high-resolution photographs of the Moon already being taken by the Lunar Reconnaissance Orbiter (LRO), to look for anomalies that may possibly be evidence of artifacts leftover from previous alien visitation. The theory is that if our solar system had been visited in the past, the Moon would have made an ideal base from which to study the Earth. . . .

Of course, it has been said by some that such artifacts have already been found and known about for decades but hidden from the public by NASA, et al. . . . There are actually a handful of anomalies from various missions that would be interesting to see at much higher resolution via LRO, such as the well-known "Blair Cuspids" photographed by *Lunar Orbiter 2* in 1966. . . .[71]

This article did not take into account the fact that NASA deliberately airbrushes artifacts and UFOs out of their images before they release them to the public. They do not want us to see these anomalies with any detail—at least not until they feel it is advantageous for them to release the information. Therefore, we have to do the best we can in analyzing those few images that have managed to escape the ongoing censorship efforts that are in place.

Transparent Aluminum

It is astonishing to find Egyptian-style obelisks on the Moon, and we will survey much more of the evidence as this chapter goes on. This changes everything we thought we knew about ourselves, our lives on Earth, and the greater cosmos that surrounds us. Multiple insiders have confirmed that these obelisks and towers are made out of a clear glass-like material—as seen on the cover of the American edition of this book. The actual material has been analyzed and is an advanced, transparent aluminum alloy. Bruce first told me this in 2014, as part of his "authorized disclosure." Just over a year later, a US Naval Research Laboratory scientist named Dr. Jas Sanghera announced his discovery—or perhaps his authorized release—of a transparent aluminum alloy. The existence of this material appears to have been deliberately leaked in the film *Star Trek IV: The Voyage Home*. In this article from Ubergizmo, the author reflects on his fondness for the movie and how fascinating it is that this material now exists in the "real world."

It seems that transparent aluminum is as real as it gets today, thanks to US Naval Research Laboratory scientist Dr. Jas Sanghera who described it as "actually a mineral, it's magnesium aluminate. The advantage is it's so much tougher, stronger, harder than glass. It provides better protection in more hostile environments—so it can withstand sand and rain erosion." . . . Should the cost come down in due time, then consumer applications will also benefit, including smartphones and watches.[72]

In this next quote from *Total Security Solutions,* the authors discuss how transparent aluminum works far better than current bulletproof glass. An armor-piercing bullet of .50-caliber size will travel three inches through bulletproof glass but can make it only half as far through transparent aluminum. Even better, transparent aluminum weighs half as much and needs to be only half as thick as traditional bulletproof-glass armor:

> In addition, transparent aluminum armor can be produced in virtually *any* shape and can also hold up to the elements much better than traditional bulletproof glass, which can be worn away by blowing desert sand or shrapnel.[73]

This article also reveals that the US Navy is working on a version they call Spinel, while the military-industrial complex defense contractor Raytheon is producing their own version called ALON:

> Developed by Raytheon, ALON begins as a powder, which is then molded and baked in very high heat. The heating process causes the powder to liquefy and cool quickly, leaving the molecules loosely arranged, as if still in liquid form. It is this crystalline structure that provides ALON its level of strength and scratch resistance comparable to rugged sapphire. Polishing the aluminum oxynitride strengthens the material and also makes it extremely clear.[74]

Almost every insider I have met has indicated that the major defense contractor firms are intimately involved with the UFO cover-up and reverse-engineering of technology. The gradual release of transparent aluminum into our society appears to be a further fulfillment of the prophecy of Ian's physics professor. He had told us we would see stunning breakthroughs in materials science, creating compounds with geometric crystalline structures that were much more useful and powerful than anything we had ever seen before.

Transparent aluminum weighs very little. This means you can build elaborate structures with it without the risk of them falling over under their own weight. The transparency of the material would also allow you to create gigantic domes that would permit sunlight to pass through. The dome could then be pressurized with an atmosphere, thanks to the abundant water ice on the Moon. This would provide a safe and habitable area for people to live, providing it was given a radiation-proof coating. If the dome was thick enough, it would also create an impressive shield against enemy attacks, given that transparent aluminum is significantly more effective than bulletproof glass.

The towers in the *Lunar Orbiter 2* image are extremely tall, extremely skinny, and have pointed tops, exactly as obelisks do.[75] It is highly unlikely that any natural geological processes could have created such huge towers on the surface of the Moon. Millions of years of meteorite strikes should have pounded the life out of any natural feature that would poke that far above the horizon. There is a constant stream of particles and chunks of rock hitting the Moon, traveling at a very high speed, and their effect is much like a sandblaster. Yet, as we just read, transparent aluminum is extremely resistant to sandblasting. Unfortunately, *Orbiter 2* was pointing straight down when the classic photo was taken, so we cannot see the sides of these objects. Nonetheless, the shadows they cast are remarkable—and have been subjected to extensive scientific analysis.

The Valley of Monuments

According to a *Washington Post* article on November 23, 1966, "The six shadows were hailed by scientists as one of the most unusual features of the

moon ever photographed. . . . On seeing the picture, one scientist wanted
to call the region the moon's 'Valley of Monuments.' . . . Scientists said they
have no idea what is casting the shadows. The largest shadow is just the sort
that would be cast by something resembling the Washington Monument,
while the smallest is the kind of shadow that might be cast by a Christmas
tree."[76] NASA said the Sun was eleven degrees above the horizon, and therefore estimated the "largest protuberance" was approximately fifty feet wide
at its base and between forty and seventy-five feet high.[77]

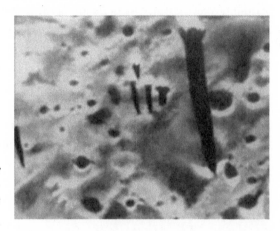

Original NASA *Lunar
Orbiter 2* Image LO2-
61H3, Showing Lunar
Obelisks

Boeing made the *Lunar Orbiter 2* spacecraft that took the photo, and a
Boeing anthropologist named William Blair openly stated that this image
reminded him of an aerial survey map from a prehistoric archeological site.
A *Los Angeles Times* article from February 1, 1967, quoted Blair as saying, "If
such a complex of structures were photographed on earth, the archeologist's
first order of business would be to inspect and excavate test trenches and
thus validate whether the prospective site has archeological significance."[78]

Blair noticed that the towers had a curious geometric alignment, which
looks like the stars in the belt of the constellation Orion to even the casual
observer. The three main pyramids on the Giza plateau in Egypt are also
built to perfectly match the positions and magnitudes of the stars in Orion's belt, as Robert Bauval discovered in the mid-1990s. Since Egypt has
obelisks that seem similar to whatever we are seeing on the Moon, this

suggests the intriguing possibility that the people who built the Egyptian monuments may have also had bases on the Moon. Or the Egyptian settlers may have had records from survivors of a lost civilization that had lived on the Moon. These survivors may have even believed they were descended from ancient ancestors in the constellation Orion, and had traveled to our solar system from this nearby group of stars long ago.

Russian scientists created a detailed analysis of the obelisks' geometry in the *Technology for Youth* publication. According to an article in *Argosy* magazine, "Soviet space engineer Alexander Abramov has come up with a rather startling geometrical analysis of the arrangement of these objects. By calculating the angles at which they appear to be set, he asserts that they constitute an 'Egyptian triangle' on the moon—a precise geometric configuration known in ancient Egypt as an *abaka*. 'The distribution of these lunar objects,' states Abravov, 'is similar to the plan of the Egyptian pyramids constructed by Pharaohs Cheops, Chephren, and Menkaura at Gizeh, near Cairo. The centers of the spires in this lunar *abaka* are arranged in precisely the same way as the apices of the three great pyramids.'"[79]

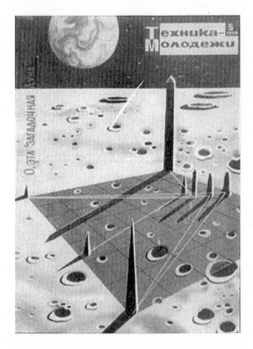

Russian Geometric Analysis of Lunar Obelisks in *Technology for Youth* magazine

The Collapsed Rectangle

Since the Moon has no atmosphere, you would either have to live inside a bulletproof structure or go underground. Otherwise you would be constantly pelted with rocks of different sizes, from micro-meteorites right on up through the much larger and more dangerous chunks that form craters once they crash-land. On Earth, most of these rocks burn up in our atmosphere as meteors before they ever hit the surface. On the Moon's surface you would also be exposed to radiation from the Sun without the shield of an atmosphere to protect you. Transparent aluminum is difficult to manufacture in large quantities, and would also require an effective radiation-proof coating. Building a base below the surface would be much easier, comparatively speaking. This means we would end up seeing a large, hollow area, probably square or rectangular, below the surface. If such a structure were many thousands of years old, the roof would gradually be pounded in by meteorite strikes. Over time, the geometric structure of the room below the surface would become visible.

Remarkably, Blair noticed the Moon's surface had collapsed in a highly artificial-looking rectangular shape right in the middle of all these towering spires. This suggests that we are seeing the remains of an ancient underground base whose roof had fallen in on itself.

According to the *Los Angeles Times* in a 1967 article, "The anthropologist also discovered in the photo, he says, what appears to be a large rectangular shaped depression or pit directly west of the largest spire, estimated to be as tall as 70 feet. Blair says the shadow cast by this depression seems to indicate four 90-degree angles and resembles the profile of an eroded pit structure."[80] Based on this evidence, Blair suggested these objects might indeed be artificial in origin[81]—but the whole thing was kept very quiet on any official level, just as our other NASA insiders reported in the previous chapter. After these exciting news articles came out, no one ever heard about it again.

The official NASA photo of this area has had the black levels cranked way up after its original release, making the shadows from the towers almost impossible to see, since they blend in with the background. There is also a very frustrating line in the middle of the official image that did not appear in the original photograph that was published widely at the time. This line cuts into the largest tower and further confuses the eye. Nonetheless, in the darkened image we can easily see not one but two rectangular depressions, positioned at ninety-degree angles to each other. These depressions are almost exactly the same size and shape, suggesting two different underground rooms that were built based on a common design.

"Official" NASA *Lunar Orbiter 2* Image of Lunar Obelisks, Showing Rectangular Pits

Dr. Mark Carlotto Discovers Multiple Rectangular Areas

In 2002, Dr. Mark J. Carlotto used a digital elevation model to conclude that the tallest spire was about fifty feet in height—far higher than anything we would expect to appear naturally on the Moon. Dr. Carlotto has thirty years' experience in satellite remote sensing and digital image processing.[82] Carlotto also created synthetic stereo images to get a three-dimensional view of the terrain: "Of particular interest is a large rectilinear depression adjacent to the objects. This depression appears to be the deepest part of a larger network of rectilinear collapses of the surface."[83] In simple terms, this means there could be a whole series of different rooms hiding below the surface of the Moon in this area. Over the course of thousands of years of meteorite strikes, the rooftops have gradually been pounded in, revealing some of the hidden geometry underneath.

Carlotto's analysis reveals that the two main rectangular depressions we see are both about 100 to 150 meters in size, making them comfortably sized areas for a base that could house a small group of people. The tallest tower could be used to help ships come and go, just as we have in our own airports. Carlotto's image processing techniques also pulled out an entire network of additional rooms that are not as visible to the naked eye. He uses the word "lineaments" to describe lines on the Moon's surface that indicate the possibility of further underground rooms whose rooftops have fallen in since they were first built.

Carlotto concludes: "In summary, the key features that suggest that these objects and their surrounding terrain may be artificial in origin are: the presence of multiple objects, conical or pyramidal in shape, that do not appear to be typical rocks or outcroppings; perpendicular alignments between five of the seven objects; a network of rectangular collapses of the surface; horizontal and vertical lineaments (and) correlations in alignments between these objects, the orientation of the rectangular depression, and the direction of lineaments."[84]

It is also intriguing to note that this area is only three hundred kilometers northwest of where *Apollo 11* landed, which means the Apollo astronauts could have easily gotten a closer look at the towering objects as they flew in. A fifty-foot-tall obelisk would have been easy to spot while orbiting at a low altitude. The astronauts may also have been able to view it from the ground, such as with a telescope, and possibly could have used the rover to drive in for a slightly closer look—though it is unlikely they would have had enough power to drive three hundred kilometers, which would be a 186.4-mile trip each way. The rover's maximum traveling speed was only eight miles per hour, and there were many obstacles that prevented it from driving in straight-lined paths. Harrison Schmitt was probably well aware of the Blair Cuspids when he designed his "Stonehenge" patches for NASA's *Apollo 17* mission. In order to become an Apollo astronaut, he would have had to go through classified briefings and be sworn to secrecy about what he was told. These photographs, and an explanation of what they might be looking at, could easily have been part of Schmitt's briefing.

The Mysteries of Frame 4822

An even more impressive piece of evidence we have for Chatelain's "mysterious geometric structures of unknown origin on the Moon" was discovered by Richard C. Hoagland. In 1995, Hoagland was going through the official catalog of *Apollo 10* photographs when he noticed that one frame, AS10-32-4822, was completely black. Most people would naturally assume this was caused by a camera malfunction, but Hoagland wondered if something interesting was being hidden. He ordered the 4822 frame from the National Space Science Data Center (NSSDC) at Goddard Space Center, and much to his surprise, the negative he received in the mail was not blacked out at all.

A Series of Geometric Structures on NSSDC Frame 4822. Far Right in Ken Johnston Version Cut Out of "Official" Version

The first thing Hoagland noticed was a small square crater off to the left. In this case, it looked as if someone had cut a perfect square area out of a hill. Nature doesn't make squares like this, and this area could have been built by people who wanted to have protective walls around their base, and then perhaps had used transparent aluminum for the rooftop. As Hoagland continued inspecting this area, he realized there was another, slightly smaller square crater to the northeast of the first one. Then, directly above these artificial-looking craters, he saw what may have been an entire row of squared-off buildings. In this case, it appeared that their rooftops had not collapsed in, but had become covered with Moon dust over many thousands of years. Each roof had the hint of a four-sided shape—as if they were originally given transparent-aluminum rooftops with a wide, shallow pyramid structure.

This series of structures appears directly next to the Ukert crater, which is also highly bizarre in its own right. The inside of the crater has a black triangular shape that is remarkably symmetrical—very close to an equilateral triangle. This could also be the result of artificial construction. The shape is no longer sharp and distinct, with the sides of the triangle being somewhat rounded, but this could be the result of prolonged erosion from meteorite hits.

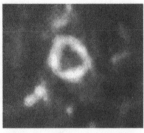

NASA Image of the Ukert Crater, Showing Degraded but Symmetrical Triangular Formation

The triangular shape would make it easy for people piloting spacecraft to identify their landing area, just as conventional pilots look for a runway. There may well be ancient corridors linking this "cosmic parking lot" to the row of buildings that appear to have been constructed right next door.

The Castle

The most stunning formation in this same image was a short distance over on the right-hand side, near the Manilius crater. Hoagland dubbed it "the Castle," and it is unbelievably impressive. If you were to show this picture to anyone without telling them where it was from, and ask them what it was, they would say it was an aerial picture of a geometric building—perhaps a military base. We see a series of long buildings, parallel to one another, intersecting at perfect ninety-degree angles and forming an overall triangular shape from the overhead view.

4822 Is Quite Popular

Hoagland publicized this image in a small, private newsletter. One of his readers, amateur astronomer Alex Cook, subsequently ordered his own negative of frame 4822 from NSSDC, and developed it in his college photo lab. Surprisingly, he received a different photographic angle of the same area than what Hoagland had gotten. This image was taken perhaps a second or two after the first. Cook continued ordering copies of 4822, and to his shock, ultimately ten different camera angles of this same area were sent to him—all filed under 4822. Hoagland concluded that the number 4822 was used as a code so that insiders could

Close-up of *Apollo 10* Frame AS10-32-4822

easily order copies of these images, but most people would never think to go looking for them. If a normal civilian asked for a copy of frame 4822, the archivist would release only the blacked-out version. However, after twenty-plus years had gone by, the current archivist apparently didn't know or remember the protocol, and just quickly grabbed whatever came up first as 4822 in the master file.

Hoagland realized that *Apollo 10* astronauts Eugene Cernan and Thomas P. Stafford were probably ordered to take multiple seventy-millimeter Hasselblad film images of this area as they went by with their handheld camera. This is the same film now used for IMAX. By doing so, they could create a rudimentary animated movie of the base—complete with stereo images to bring out the three-dimensional depth. When Hoagland visited the NSSDC and asked to see the original of frame 4822, he was told that they couldn't find the negatives, as they had been "stolen." Much more detail can be found in Richard Hoagland and Mike Bara's *New York Times* bestselling book *Dark Mission*.[85]

Additional Detail from *Apollo 10* Frame AS10-32-4822

Ken Johnston Finds Another 4822

Hoagland's work took another quantum leap forward with the introduction of Ken Johnston. This was another development that took place just a few months after I first got online. On March 21, 1996, Hoagland gave a long-anticipated press conference in Washington, DC, at the National Press Club. A number of major media organizations were present, including C-SPAN, *USA Today*, the Associated Press, and the *New York Times*. Sadly, the audience was very hostile, and when Hoagland brought up information he had already revealed in the past, he was shouted at and asked if there was anything new. What happened next was reported by Michael Lindemann of CNI News.

> Hoagland made good on his promise to bring in several other credible spokesmen to discuss the evidence for moon anomalies. Chief among these was former NASA and Boeing aerospace engineer Ken Johnston, who worked with NASA

executive Dr. Thornton Page during the years of the Apollo
moon missions. Johnston said that he had seen photo evidence, including some 16mm movie footage, that convinced
him there was something anomalous on the moon. He said
that he and Thornton Page were the first people to view 16mm
film from the Apollo 14 mission that showed 5 or 6 lights in
a crater on the dark side of the moon, as well as a strange
plume of smoke. Johnston said he showed the movie footage
to other NASA personnel the next day, but when he got to the
point where he had seen the lights in the crater, those frames
seemed to be missing. Johnston asked Page about the missing
footage, and Page said, "I don't know what you're talking
about." Johnston is convinced the footage was taken out and
either hidden or destroyed.[86]

Johnston was ordered to destroy many original copies of Apollo
Moon images, but he saved a full set of them in Oklahoma City, within
a university library archive. We are all very fortunate that Johnston did
not destroy all the originals in the archive. NASA did not want any of
these images getting out to the public—at least not unless they had been
doctored. The most stunning discovery out of Johnston's original imagery was found on the *Apollo 10* photograph AS10-32-4822. This was yet
another photograph hidden away under the "4822" code number. NASA
is supposed to give each photograph a different number, but this was
not the case with 4822. In a photograph shown at the press club, we
see an image on the left that is from the official NASA archive at Goddard Space Flight Center. The image on the right is from Ken Johnston's
own original that came from the Johnson Space Center. The difference
is remarkable. Ken Johnston's original clearly shows a bright white
dome, shaped like the tip of a bullet, sitting on a hilltop. The dome is
perfectly symmetrical, and is so bright that it appears as if light is reflecting off it.[87] The official image has had all traces of the dome conveniently
removed.

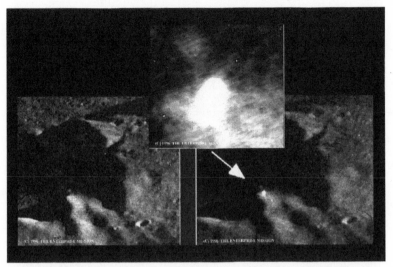

Enterprise Mission Comparison of Goddard (L) and Houston (R) "4822" Images, Showing Reflective Dome

Russian Media Publicity Explosion

In 2007, I coauthored a two-part paper with Hoagland that features a wealth of NASA photographs of the Moon with strikingly artificial-looking objects in them. The article was written to celebrate the fact that the Russian media gave Hoagland's latest press conference a significant amount of favorable coverage. A variety of color images are included in the article that do not translate well to a black-and-white printed book, so I encourage you to go take a look at it on Hoagland's website, EnterpriseMission.com.[88] Hoagland was able to compare two different NASA images of the same area—AS14-66-9301, in which astronaut Edgar Mitchell is pictured, and AS14-66-9279, which is taken of the same area but is just a few feet over to the right. In the second image, the leg of the lunar lander is visible and Mitchell is no longer in the shot. Hoagland was also able to find an original version of AS14-66-9301 in Ken Johnston's archive, and it had much clearer detail than what we see in the official version.

Taken together, these images reveal a stunning array of glass-like

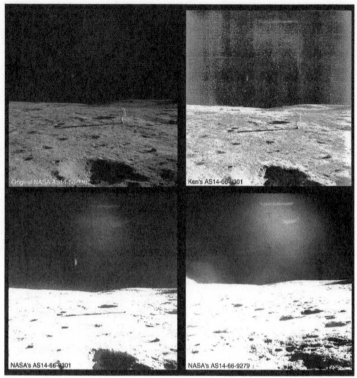

Enterprise Mission Comparison of Versions of AS14-66-9301 and
AS14-66-9279, Showing a Matrix of Glass-like Ruins

ruins right behind where astronaut Mitchell was standing. Since this
material is almost completely transparent, it was nearly invisible in the
photo, but with some simple Photoshop adjustments, remarkable details
emerge. There appears to be a structure made of three primary pillars in
the middle of the image. It also appears that a series of glass-like reflections are occurring inside. I was greatly surprised when these images
came out and was happy to lend my efforts to Hoagland's campaign. The
Russians did their own digging and found three new examples of photos
that had obvious signs of tampering.

The most stunning image discovered by the Russians was GPN
-2000-001137. In our article, we posted a direct link to the original on the
Great Images in NASA, or GRIN, website, which is an official NASA

resource. When you download the image, all you appear to see is a NASA astronaut posing next to an American flag, with a jet-black background behind him. A pale image of the Earth is visible in the background, adding a dramatic flair. The image is still accessible on NASA's website at the time of this writing.[89] By doing a simple enhancement of the image in Photoshop, the Russians were clearly able to demonstrate that the area around the Apollo astronaut had been deliberately airbrushed black. This is almost completely invisible to the naked eye and is only detectable with advanced image-processing software.

Airbrushing around *Apollo 17* Astronaut Harrison Schmitt

The strangest thing about the airbrushing is how geometric it is. It begins at the top left, above the astronaut's head, with a horizontal line. It then drops straight down, forming a square. Then a triangular area is airbrushed out immediately next to it, with the bottom of the triangle touching the top of the astronaut's head. Another area projects out from the front of the astronaut's helmet. Skeptics may argue that this was a simple fix to eliminate glare coming off the astronaut's suit, and that may be possible, but it may also be hiding a large object. The next image found by the Russians, 2000-001131, reveals obvious lines where material has been cut out of additional copies of the same photograph with a razor blade and then glued on top of the original. This again suggests there was something very large behind the astronaut in the image that they were covering over, just as Donna Hare had indicated. Since the lines in this shot are too fine to translate to print, I again invite you to visit "Russian Media Publicity Explosion" online and see it for yourself.[90]

The "Solar Panel"

Now we will return to our original frame 4822, in which we see squared-off areas next to the Ukert crater on the left, and the stunningly geometric "city" on the right. Our "Russian Media" paper included another peculiar image from this same shot, which looks, to me, like a giant solar panel.[91] Whatever it is, it clearly appears to be technological and is by no means a natural formation. This may have been used to generate energy or radio communications for the nearby bases.

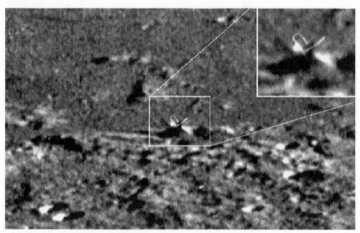

The "Solar Panel" from NASA's "Missing" Frame 4822

The Stunning Russian Images from *Zond 3*

For me, the single most impressive images of all are also some of the old-est. The Russians were the first to officially launch a probe into space with *Sputnik*, on October 4, 1957. Two years later in 1959, they launched *Luna 3*, which reached the Moon on October 7 and broadcast until the twenty-second, at which time contact was lost. Seventeen low-quality images were produced, giving humanity our first view of the dark side of the Moon. The Russians followed up with *Zond 3*, which was originally intended to be able to orbit Mars. *Zond 3* was launched on July 18, 1965, and made it to the Moon thirty-three hours later. The Russians focused their initial efforts on capturing the final 30 percent of the dark side of the Moon that *Luna 3* had missed. The camera was programmed to take one picture every two minutes and fourteen seconds, for a combined total of twenty-eight images in one hour and eight minutes.

Gigantic Tower on the Dark Side of the Moon in Russian *Zond 3* Image

The investigative website Ancient Code reveals what happened next: "In one of the images of the far side of the moon, a mysterious tower-shaped structure can clearly be seen protruding from the lunar surface. In its vicinity, no other similar structures are seen, and Ufologists believe that the mysterious 'tower' seen in the *Zond 3* image is a crucial piece of evidence supporting their theory that there are alien structures on the far side of Earth's moon. The image of the Tower on the moon was obtained on 20 July 1965. . . . At the time, the probe was about 10,000 kilometers above the Moon."[92]

There is a stunningly obvious, symmetrical, bright white tower rising up from the surface of the Moon in the image, which was taken early in *Zond 3*'s sequence. The tower is perfectly perpendicular to the Moon's surface, suggesting it is a genuine structure and not a photographic defect. Based on the size and curvature of the Moon's surface, Hoagland has estimated this tower to be a staggering twenty miles in height. The

Gigantic "Glass" Dome on the Dark Side of the Moon in Russian *Zond 3* Image (bottom right)

bright white glow again suggests a transparent-aluminum structure that is capturing and reflecting the sunlight. This does not appear to be the result of a "camera malfunction," a "stain on the lens," a "photographic defect," or "noise," as skeptics have attempted to claim.

What most people fail to realize is that just a few minutes later, *Zond 3* captured another equally stunning image from the same area. The Moon had now rotated enough that the tower was no longer on the horizon and thus is not visible. We can easily see the same craters that were in the previous photo, and we can also see a massive dome on the horizon that is farther south, capturing the sunlight. There are two clearly geometric lines of glass-like material that both rise from the lunar surface at the same steep slope before leveling off to a flat top. The ceiling of the dome is parallel to the Moon's surface, as we would expect if it were a genuine artificial construct and not just a camera glitch. When you have two geometric sides with the same slope angle and height, and which connect to a flat top parallel to the surface, you have the structure of a flat-topped pyramid, or mastaba. Since this structure appears to be made out of transparent aluminum, we can see through it when the sunlight is catching it at this angle. There is also a thicker area in the exact middle of the dome, suggesting the presence of two additional geometric edges, thus making it a true four-sided pyramid-type object, just like a mastaba. Again, the size of this pyramid-like dome must be absolutely colossal— perhaps twenty miles in height. Skeptics have tried to say that it is merely the result of inferior Russian technology not being able to stitch the space probe's images together properly, but this seems highly unlikely when we consider the overall weight of evidence.

Both of these mysterious images appeared quite close to each other, just a few frames apart, on a side of the Moon that normally never faces the Earth. If there are extraterrestrial or classified human bases there, they could be building far more elaborate structures on the dark side of the Moon and no one would see them. Indeed, one of my top insiders, Pete Peterson, has been told by Russian intelligence that the back side of the Moon now looks like Manhattan at night from a satellite view. There are stationary and moving lights all over, and it is literally teeming with

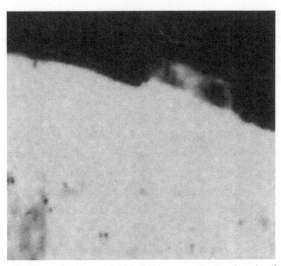

Close-up of Gigantic "Glass" Dome on the Dark Side of
the Moon in Russian *Zond 3* Image

activity. This again may seem impossible to believe. If this information
does become widely known, all of us will have quite the "learning curve"
and psycho-emotional adjustment to go through in order to integrate
this new information into what we thought we knew.

With a transparent-aluminum dome like this, people could live on
the surface of the Moon, breathe a normal atmosphere, see the Sun, grow
plants, and have a nice civilization inside. They could have buildings,
roads, and even rivers and lakes by melting the abundance of water ice
that can be found. Plants and animals could be selectively taken from a
planet like Earth and brought in. The flat-topped pyramid shape would
enhance the health of everyone inside, as I have argued in *The Source
Field Investigations*. We will review some of that data as we go on. A
pyramid-shaped roof of such colossal size would also be visually stunning for the people living inside, giving it a sense of spiritual significance.
Others may wish to live under the surface for greater protection from
attacks, a more climate-controlled environment, or perhaps because they
didn't have enough money or status to be able to live in the lush, out-
doorsy atmosphere created in the domes.

They Had to Come from Somewhere

Although this is fascinating data, we still haven't answered the question of how these people ended up trying to survive on the surface of the Moon in the first place. Why would they try to grow plants and live their lives under glass domes on such an inhospitable sphere? This is not a place where a civilization would naturally evolve. This is a group that clearly would have migrated there from somewhere else and used advanced technology in order to make it livable. Were they at war with a group that considered a healthier, happier place like the Earth to be their own exclusive, protected territory? Where did these lunar colonists come from originally? This question ultimately forces us to reconstruct the history of our solar system—which begins with something the insiders call the "Ancient Builder Race." In order to set up the story of the Ancient Builder Race, it is first necessary to reveal the big picture of what the highest-level insiders shared with me. Only then will the full scope of the story be something we can appreciate.

CHAPTER SEVENTEEN

The "Big Picture" Is Extremely Cosmic

A ncient ruins, far older than any civilization we know of on Earth, already exist on the Moon. Skeptics may try to knock down individual images or whistle-blowers, but the combined strength of high-level insider testimony and verifiable NASA data is very compelling. Someone had to have built these structures. Everything we thought we knew has to be completely rewritten if any of this is true. There are so many unknowns that the mind becomes exhausted and throws away the information, since it is too stressful to try to take it all in. I attended multiple Hoagland conferences, as a guest and as a speaker, and invariably people would ask him to explain who built these monuments and where they are now. Hoagland did not know. He said it was still a mystery. This greatly frustrated the audiences. It wasn't until 2014 that Bruce started telling me more of what he knew from his own level of the UFO cover-up.

I originally intended this book to disclose Bruce's information, and I am still going to give you all the most significant details. Once I began talking to other insiders about this data, including Corey Goode, however, I learned even more. The big picture that will start to unfold in this chapter is so cosmic that it is hard to even imagine. It took me a great deal of time and effort, and tremendous personal risk, to gather and release this information. Each of the data points I am about to share with you have been cross-validated with multiple insiders, some of whom we will meet as we go along.

The best way to approach such a huge story, at first, is just to keep an open mind to the possibilities instead of trying to fight every little detail with rigid skepticism. I have noticed that when radio show hosts try to rigorously argue with me on the minor details, I never have the time to actually share the story so that listeners can make up their own minds. All of us have been traumatized by countless decades of being lied to. It is all too easy to get a "morphine response" by attacking whistle-blowers and attempting to tear them apart. Yet, this addiction may be holding us back from the greatest quantum leap in human history.

Seeing It in Person Is Believing

Denial can cloud our minds when we look at pictures like the ones we saw in the previous chapter, even if they are extremely high-quality images. We may decide that they are "inconclusive," "tricks of light and shadow," or even "pareidolia," a fancy word that indicates how the mind looks for patterns in chaos. The paid skeptics love to invoke pareidolia for every single anomalous picture of off-planet artifacts, no matter how high quality it is. It makes them sound superior and intelligent, as if the scientific priesthood has struck down the heretics who are seeing "Jesus on a potato chip." However, if NASA and other groups had classified Roswell-type craft and could go and visit these sites in person, they obviously got a much closer look. Standing in front of a massive crystal tower and putting your hands on it would erase all doubt. Then you could begin conducting a very sober assessment of who built these artifacts, when they built them, how they built them, why they built them, and where they went. Multiple insiders have revealed that these groups have direct access to extraterrestrials who can provide the details. Not all of these extraterrestrials can be trusted, but certain themes are very consistent.

There is compelling evidence that the Apollo missions were intentionally landing near these interesting sites as well. According to Bruce, Daniel, Jacob, and other insiders whom we will meet in this chapter, the astronauts who actually touched the ruins with their own hands and walked inside them were not on any Apollo missions, and those other missions have never been made public. This was alluded to in *2001*, because no public mention was made of the monolith the astronauts had found on the Moon. Though the insiders felt they could not officially tell us the truth, they wanted us to share in the excitement through fantasy. Nonetheless, I feel it is a great tragedy that this marvelously exciting adventure has been kept so thoroughly classified. Groups like the National Security Agency are hiring agents to ruin the lives of anyone who tries to tell us the truth.

I was quite stunned when Colonel Philip Corso came forward in 1997 with his classic book *The Day After Roswell*. Corso was handed boxes of parts from crashed extraterrestrial craft, including from Roswell, and was assigned to hand off various components to different defense contractors. They were told it was "foreign technology" and asked to reverse-engineer it. The technologies he claimed to have developed through this method were almost exactly the same ones the physics professor had revealed to Ian four years earlier. This included a series of small round wafers that turned out to be computer chips. I was absolutely stunned to get such a remarkably precise validation of what I had heard, in the form of a mainstream, published book. It greatly ignited my quest to find more insiders and learn as much as possible from them.

Daniel: the First Major Insider

After meeting a majority of the witnesses at the Disclosure Project in 2001, the first highly connected insider I met, in December 2002, was a man wanting me to call him Daniel, after the character in *Stargate SG-1*. Daniel won a science fair in high school by designing a computer with its own operating system in the 1970s, well before this was a common practice. He was recruited by the government, who paid for his college providing he agreed to work for military intelligence. I suddenly remembered being invited to a science fair called "The Imagination Celebration" when I was in seventh grade. It was held inside a large hangar at a military base in Schenectady, New York, and was run by a major defense contractor. I competed with hundreds of other kids to see who could invent something that solved a physics problem, using simple ingredients like rubber bands and wooden tongue depressors. Daniel confirmed that if I had won that contest, I might have been "mentored" and pulled into the intelligence community after I had graduated, just as he was.

He claimed to have worked on a project code-named *Phoenix III* from 1981 to 1983. Most people know it as the Montauk Project, as it took place at a military base on Montauk Point, Long Island. Daniel revealed that Preston Nichols and Peter Moon's 1992 book *The Montauk Project: Experiments in Time* was fairly accurate, but that subsequent books were increasingly filled with disinformation. I had already read the first book by the time I met him and thought it was nonsense. I actually laughed in his face when he told me he had worked at Montauk. However, he had vastly detailed information that went far beyond the scope of what had been published. This was very humbling and mind-expanding, as his data was extremely consistent. Daniel held up under every effort I made to deconstruct and debunk his information.

In this program, a seat from a crashed and recovered ET craft was hooked up to a massive power supply at Montauk. It turned out that the seat amplified the consciousness of the person sitting in it, providing they had the ability to fully quiet their mind in meditation. A series of twenty-two sine-wave graphs showed the activity of the person's mind. Once the person quieted their mind, the graphs would remain still. Then the technicians would zero out the graphs, turning knobs to make them all flat lines. This tuned the chair to the individual, and that was when the magic would start to happen.

A properly tuned chair allowed the operator's thoughts to create physical manifestations. Any object the operator thought of, such as a wooden chair, could be made to physically materialize in the room. The objects would remain solid for a period of time before gradually fading away. The operator could also telepathically influence the minds of others, even on a mass scale. At one point they influenced a massive number of animals to rush into the center of town in a frenzy. This technology appears to have been leaked into fiction in the X-Men movie series. A chair called "Cerebro" appears in a large, spherical room, and vastly enhances the psychic abilities of whoever is using it. Most of the X-Men movies feature this chair as a prominent part of the storyline.

Layered Time

Even more strangely, the chair operator could think about a particular place in space and time, and a portal would open up that would allow travel to that location. In a UFO, the pilot merely thinks about where he or she wants to go and a portal opens up to take them there. The insiders involved in the *Phoenix III* project began sending people through these portals, and many lives were lost before they figured out how to ensure their safe return. Portals would also appear at random throughout the base, including in the cafeteria, while they were working on stabilizing the system. Daniel reported seeing shimmering areas, each like a desert mirage. Inside the middle of these areas, he would see separate locations. He might be looking at a solid wall in the cafeteria and then see a shimmering portal into a grassy, green field that was nowhere near the area he was working in. If he were to walk into the portal he would end up in the field.

They soon realized that these portals could take people through time as well as space. This led to all sorts of research with unanticipated consequences. One man was crazy enough to go back in time and kill his father, whom he truly despised. Everyone was shocked when he returned from this trip, having successfully murdered his father, and he was still alive. However, about two days later the man was struck by a car as a pedestrian and killed instantly. Several repetitions of similar types of experiments caused the military defense contractors working in these classified programs to create a theory of "layered time." They concluded that if you go back into the past and change an event, you create a new time line, or a new layer, that sits on top of the layer that is already there. Both layers can coexist. The layer that our future snaps into is the layer that has more energy associated with it. If a new layer is created that creates too many paradoxes in our existing "main" time line, natural events will occur that heal those problems. The layers always find a way of merging. This caused the insiders to conclude that time itself is alive and conscious, and has its own healing mechanisms. Once the man had killed his father, his death helped to merge the layers and solve the paradox.

Daniel also said they had something called a time vector generator, or

TVG, with which they would pump massive amounts of energy into the area of an alternate time line in the hope of making it stronger than the existing one. The energy they were sending into the time line is what the Russian scientists call "torsion fields," and the basic science behind these fields is extensively described in *The Source Field Investigations*. The vintage show *The Time Tunnel* was loaded with genuine disclosure about these experiments, and the show's signature tunnel with alternating rings of black and white looked very similar to a genuine TVG. Multiple experiments with TVG units proved that these classified programs did not have as much control over time as they had hoped to have. Time was extremely elastic, meaning that whatever time line we were already on would tend to remain consistent. New layers would usually be canceled out through balancing events, and would never interfere with our own time line that much.

The Energetic Wall of Ascension in Our Future

The ET chair produced a series of more than four hundred different waves through a huge set of fiber-optic cables. Each wave was graphed and analyzed separately. Daniel's main job was to analyze these graphs and determine how to generate the waves electronically, thus eliminating the need for a human operator—but these efforts only met with limited success. One of the waves allowed them to pinpoint exactly where someone was in time. It was a regularly curving sine wave that counted out twenty-year intervals between each peak. Any time they sent someone through the portal, the person would experience a dazzling "wormhole ride" like we have seen in various science-fiction movies.

When they sent people into our future, they would hit a bizarre energetic barrier at a certain point. This was called the "Full Out," because suddenly their consciousness would become greatly expanded and depersonalized. They would feel as if they had merged with the galaxy and had access to omniscient intelligence. Time seemed to melt into infinity. Anything people saw after this point appeared to be completely subjective, based on their own expectations as well as those of the person in the chair. Different people could view the same time and get different re-sults. The moment this energetic "wall" would collide with our solar system was calculated to be sometime in December 2012. The insiders were well aware that this corresponded precisely with the end-date of the Mayan calendar, and this was a huge source of fascination to them.

It does appear that this energetic wave is a physical cloud our solar system is moving into. Once we hit the full power of this wave, Daniel's own sources had concluded the Sun would release an energetic flash that activates a mass spiritual evolution in humanity. They used time-viewing devices we will discuss in a second to go and view this event, but once they got there all they could see was white light. Since the time this research was done in 1981–83, the "wall" has moved into our future. It appears that we were not ready for this to happen as a planet yet, and the event will be held off until a critical mass of people are ready for it. Much of this has to do with healing our trauma and becoming more loving, forgiving people—just as the great religions have taught us. Since this is a dynamic, evolving process, any effort to produce a specific date is mere guesswork.

The Stargate Network

Daniel also fascinated me by revealing that the television show *Stargate SG-1* was chock-full of truthful information he had encountered at his job. There is indeed an ancient stargate network that allows travel from place to place through the "cosmic web," as it has been called. A series of plasma filaments connects each star to its neighbors, and these filaments also serve as traversable wormholes. Proof of these filaments was deliberately pre-sented in *The Source Field Investigations* after I had heard all this.

A very ancient and highly advanced extraterrestrial race that Daniel called "the Elders" had apparently built this stargate network. Other groups continually maintained it. I was told that each planet with intel-ligent life is given its own stargate. The network is intended to allow for peaceful exploration and communication with a wide variety of worlds, which is a natural part of the ascension process. You cannot bring any inorganic materials through, such as weapons. Travelers would have to wear drawstring pants, as even elastic waistbands would deconstruct. This caused great humor in the early trials, as travelers would arrive at their destination and have their pants fall down.

Bruce said this organic bias was disclosed in *The Terminator,* in which the people sent back through a portal to our time had to come in naked. Obviously, no android would be able to travel through a stargate, because only organic materials can make it through the portal. Your dental fillings would receive a bio imprint after being in your body for a period of time, and would still make it through the portal on the other side. Some soldiers tried sleeping with their guns and carrying them at all times, hoping to create a bio imprint, but this never worked.

There can be more than one gate on a given planet, but only one of these gates will actually take you to other worlds. The other gates can be used to transport you from one local area to another. In the case of Earth, our main gate was apparently dug out of the desert in Egypt in 1927, exactly as documented in the *Stargate SG-1* television show. The government people who found it were so concerned about invaders coming through the gate that they buried it in the ice in Antarctica, where it apparently still resides to this day. That way anyone trying to come through the gate will be instantly frozen to death. The gate has an intelligent alarm system that would warn you if you were about to go into an environment that would kill you. This alarm can be ignored, but to travel in such an event is to die.

Daniel also said that our classified programs were able to mathematically analyze the gate network. Each inhabited world has a particular gate address, which is a series of seven groups of digits. You can travel very far distances, including to areas well outside our galaxy, through the use of these addresses. Carl Sagan was aware of the ancient stargate network and disclosed it in the book and movie *Contact.* The main screenwriter of that film, Jim Hart, was so impressed when he saw my 2012 "Enigma" video on YouTube that he contacted me to work on a film I was developing, entitled *Convergence.* He had no idea that Carl Sagan was working from actual classified information when he wrote the *Contact* story. *Convergence* has been through many rewrites and our latest draft is nearing completion as I finish this book.

The first three digits of any stargate address are single numbers between 1 and 9. The next three sets of digits are between 1 and 99. The final set of digits will be between 1 and 999. Almost any number you dial, except perhaps for the highest numbers in the final three-digit set, will take you to an inhabited world. If you are traveling locally, a three-digit number will suffice. The local gate address for Mars is 605, and Earth is 606, so keep that in mind if you ever get lost. Some of the higher three-digit numbers do not have planets assigned to them in our local area. Once the people on a given planet ascend, their number is reassigned to new planets. Now that enough time has passed and no other insiders have come forward with this information, I will finally reveal our entire gate address after all these years, according to Daniel's testimony. It is 7.5.3.84.70.24.606.

Our local gate address of 1 is an inhabited asteroid that orbits a pulsar. This unique energetic configuration has made it very stable over long periods of time. The people who live there have visited Earth for thousands of years, and introduced themselves to the Vikings as the Aesir or Asgard. The term Asgard was later misinterpreted by early 1950s telepathic channelers as "Ashtar," and the Aesir became known as the "Ashtar Command." The Aesirian "god" Thor had a devastating "hammer" that was actually a particle-beam weapon, and the mystical land of Valhalla was actually the Aesir homeworld. With the testimony of Corey Goode now in place, the Asgard may actually be an ancient advanced civilization living inside the Earth. Several of these inner-Earth human groups have tried to pass themselves off as extraterrestrials in order to protect themselves against aggression from the military-industrial complex. They may live and work in both areas.

Daniel also said that the extensive analysis of this ancient stargate system led to the development of the IP address system that is now used for the Internet. Each computer or device that accesses the Internet has its own IP address. This is a series of four three-digit numbers. The Defense Advanced Research Projects Agency (DARPA) developed this protocol as a direct result of their extensive investigation of the mathematics of the stargate network.

A trip through the ancient network involves a vigorous cosmic "wormhole ride," which is exceptionally traumatic for people from our planet to experience. We do not yet have enough spiritual development and stability to handle the trip. Most people become extremely unwell after doing it, and their mental health is unable to recover from the shock. This was termed "transdimensional disorder." Apparently the wormhole experience created by the Montauk chair was easier to handle than the ancient stargate network, but that too could still create problems for people.

Through the Looking Glass

By the time I met Daniel, I had already read about a technology called Project Looking Glass from three other sources. Looking Glass was allegedly a complex device that allowed the user to peer through time. Daniel confirmed the existence of Looking Glass and said that a sphere of white light appears in the area you are viewing. It may or may not be visible, depending on a variety of factors including the consciousness of the people in the area. Daniel said this sphere of light was called an OBIT, or Outer Band Individuated Teletracer. He said the outer band was a part of Earth's hidden energetic field that the insiders had identified. Suddenly I had an idea. "Let's look it up online right now!" We ran over to his laptop and typed the full term into a search engine. Both of us were quite astonished to discover that an episode of the television show *The Outer Limits* had this same title. It aired on November 4, 1963. The Internet Movie Database has a description of this show that reads, in part, "The Outer Band Individuated Teletracer, or O.B.I.T., is a remarkable technology that can track and monitor any individual, anywhere, for any length of time!"[93] Daniel revealed that a great deal of information was being released through fiction. That way, if anyone ever tried to come forward, they could simply be accused of borrowing ideas from a movie, book, or television program.

I interviewed Daniel extensively, over many hours. I was constantly looking for holes in his testimony and could find none. Any time I asked him for further details on a specific area, I often got far more information than I had expected. Daniel eventually published his own website in 2011, featuring additional details, including some highly technical information.[94] This early experience taught me how to sort out the real insiders from the fake ones. A few people did try to pull a hoax on me, but once I drilled in deeply with questions, they couldn't invent new stories fast enough. I would soon pick them apart through cross-examination and then break off contact. I deliberately withheld enough information from the public so I could evaluate new insiders. I would also put new insiders in contact with other established insiders to "vet them out." The real insiders would invariably validate many data points I had never put online, and had never seen anywhere in the public domain.

Henry Deacon

After the stunningly bizarre disclosures from Daniel, five long years went by where no new insiders came forward, other than people who had information that was more widely available. Soon after YouTube allowed streaming videos to be uploaded to the Internet free of charge, Kerry Cassidy and Bill Ryan created Project Camelot. They interviewed a variety of intriguing whistle-blowers and released the videos at no cost. In some cases the videos gathered millions of views, matching or exceeding the performance of all but the most popular television shows.

Certain insiders refused to go on camera or even audio with their testimonies. The most fascinating whistle-blower in this category was a man going by the pseudonym Henry Deacon. I ultimately played a key role in his coming forward for a brief period of time, only to have him disappear again afterward. In the early years, our only means of hearing what Henry said was from Bill and Kerry's written notes. Henry claimed to have worked in what some UFO researchers have called a "breakaway civilization," where our own military-industrial complex had secretly colonized space. Various ancient bases, such as the ones we just saw on the Moon in the last chapter, were pressurized and reoccupied, and others were built from scratch. Local materials could be used to make a pourable concrete that would be molded with plastic bags to form the foundations for buildings.

I contacted Project Camelot and shared everything I knew from Daniel in exchange for gaining Henry Deacon's contact information. Henry Deacon became the first high-level insider who gave me extensive details about working in classified spacecraft and off-planet bases. He told me he was astonished at how many of the interiors of spacecraft in the movie *2001* looked similar to areas he had personally worked in—if not nearly identical in some cases. He also claimed to have worked in a base on Mars, saying that ancient ruins not unlike those on the Moon had been discovered there and reoccupied. This was a startling validation of something Daniel had told me, in which he claimed to have been shown a classified photo of an astronaut standing and waving next to a pyramid on Mars. The pyramid was so large you could see only a sharp-edged sloping wall that went up from the ground at an angle in the photo. Henry confirmed that there were ancient pyramids on Mars, as did Corey Goode, who gave me a vivid description of flying over them. Henry claimed that he worked at a Mars base with 200,000 personnel, and only 10,000 of them were from Earth. In the cafeteria there was a big picture window that looked out on a stunning view of red rocks similar to the Grand Canyon. He said that the base was going through a massive expansion during the time he was there.

The Corridor

The way Henry traveled to work was extremely interesting. He claimed to have used something called "the Corridor," which was a stargate-type device. He would show up for work at a military base and go through a series of checkpoints. The final barrier featured two soldiers at a desk in front of a long, cylindrical hallway. In addition to showing proper ID, he had to have an extended, normal conversation with the soldiers to prove his identity. He would then walk down the Corridor and go into an elevator at the end that had an oversize door. The interior of the elevator had a brushed-metal appearance. He would then take an ordinary-looking metal key and insert it into a small panel with a lock that was mounted on the wall of the elevator. The door would close at a painfully slow speed, taking as long as thirty seconds. The door would then immediately open again and he would be on Mars—or wherever else his badge told the elevator to send him. The trip was completely painless and almost unnoticeable. There was no wormhole, no sensation of movement—just an instant transfer.

Ordinary soldiers were on the base and did not know what the elevator could do. There was a stairwell to the left of the elevator that went up to the second floor, and the elevator did function in the normal sense if you hit the button. Most soldiers believed it was simply used to transfer heavy equipment and were unaware of its greater function. When I asked Henry why they used such simple-looking things as an ordinary elevator and a traditional metal key, he said it was designed to "reduce psychological impact." By keeping everything ordinary-looking, people would just do their jobs in a businesslike fashion.

He was required to take a medication called Lorentzil in order to stabilize his health from the effects of transdimensional disorder. This is listed in an 1896 medical dictionary as Loxopterygium Lorentzil, which is the technical name for the red quebracho, a tree that grows in Mexico and South America.[95] The bark of the tree contains an alkaloid compound known as Loxopterygine, which is listed as being an "antiperiodic,"[96] meaning it helps prevent periodic returns of illness and disease. This therefore appears to have been a South American medicine used by shamans, who developed the ability to do conscious astral projection. Multiple insiders have said that you can also get transdimensional disorder from spending too much time in out-of-body experiences. Henry had health problems as a result of leaving his job quite suddenly and losing access to this medication.

Henry called this a "modern" stargate system. He did also confirm the existence of an ancient stargate network, though he was unaware of the gate address numbers. At one time he visited a highly guarded area in Iraq that had a large stone ring just like what we see in the *Stargate* movie and television series. Obelisks stood on either side of the ring.

Apparently this ancient gate was still used for certain purposes, and was kept under extremely high security. Henry also confirmed that working stargates have been on Earth for at least the last ten thousand years, and possibly significantly longer. A variety of ETs have been coming and going from Earth using these portal systems all along. He also confirmed that they have to follow a "Prime Directive" to conceal themselves from us until we have reached a point where we are ready to see them as a collective.

There Are a Lot of People Out There

Henry claimed to have personally seen approximately forty-three different types of extraterrestrial species. All of them were humanlike in appearance. They would vary in size from only a foot tall to over twelve feet in height. They would have different features, including a full variety of pastel skin colors. Some had larger heads and larger eyes. Different groups required different gravitational fields, and they would be assigned to certain areas in the Mars base where the floor had panels that generated the appropriate amount of gravity to satisfy their needs. When I asked him what it was like to interact directly with these beings, he said the feeling was usually one of extreme spiritual bliss. You would often experience mind-to-mind communication and feel an exceptional sense of happiness and light.

Henry always referred to them as people, not aliens. Some had jet-black skin. Others had skin with pastel colors that could be yellow, pink, red, orange, blue, or purple. Some had skin that was pure white. Others had varying depths of gray. One group that he said was from Alpha Centauri had dark green skin, and they photosynthesized light. He only ever met women from this group, and said they had black hair and Greek features. A neighboring planet in the same system was largely a desert, and had people with reddish skin who looked much like the Mayans. These two civilizations had warred in the past and the relations between them were still quite frosty. The tallest group of ETs he saw were in the twelve-foot range, and were treated with fearful respect. They wore colorful and elaborate leather battle armor, such as bright red and black outfits with lots of ornate features, and masks. You were not allowed to look at them when they came into the room.

I repeatedly tried to get Henry Deacon to tell me what he did at these jobs, but it was very difficult to get him to release information beyond a certain point. He did tell me that he was trained to repair certain types of advanced equipment. He would travel to various bases in our solar system and perform maintenance as required. He kept reaffirming that the work they were doing was very important for the survival of the human race, and that was part of why he did not feel comfortable going into details.

Coming Forward

I released many specifics from Henry Deacon's information, and the Project Camelot audience was stunned when he came forward at a conference on July 12, 2009. A group of insiders were speaking in Zurich, Switzerland, and I was among them. Henry was brought in and traveled with me at the event. Our cover story was that he was my "Uncle Mark." It was quite a sensation when he took to the stage during NASA astronaut Dr. Brian O'Leary's presentation and revealed himself.[97] Although he did not go into great detail about what he knew, he showed everyone his US passport. It was brown, unlike the normal navy-blue color, and said OFFICIAL PASSPORT. I surveyed it in private, along with a variety of other forms of proof of his military service, and confirmed that it was authentic.

I spent more than eighty hours speaking to Deacon and would often laugh at how aloof he was about everything. He was given a huge stack of briefing documents with nowhere near enough time to read them when he first started. Once he was trained for his particular job responsibilities, it quickly became his ordinary, daily routine. He had been taught to think that speaking about any of his experiences would get him killed, so he would often avoid my questions and tell me that it wasn't interesting enough for him to talk about. Yet, over the course of many conversations, I managed to pull an incredible amount of data out of

him. I never expected he would actually come forward. He later regret-
ted ever doing it and refused to speak any further. He never profited
from anything he had done, nor was he looking for any public acclaim.

Henry's data included information about the "high-energy cloud" our
solar system was moving into. He was aware that spacecraft had been sent
out to view the cloud and study its energetic properties. He confirmed that
it was expected to trigger a dramatic evolutionary event on Earth, including an epic solar energy release of some kind. Later insiders had testimony
that lined up remarkably well with everything he had said.

Henry was very pleased with my scientific research on interplanetary
climate change, as presented in *The Source Field Investigations*. I used
official NASA sources to prove that the Sun, planets, and satellites in our
system are becoming brighter, hotter, and more magnetic at a remarkable
speed. He was also aware that NASA was rigorously preventing anyone
from officially connecting the dots as I had done. They were apparently
afraid that religious zealots would use the data to confirm their beliefs,
and would then create widespread fear and panic. However, Henry also
believed their energetic buildup would create a release that would have
positive effects for humanity. The initial stages could be very disorienting
and confusing, however, as we adjusted to the sudden, massive consciousness shift this change would cause.

CHAPTER EIGHTEEN

Pete Peterson, the Tesla of Black Ops

J ust a couple of weeks before the Zurich conference in June 2009, Kerry
Cassidy sent me a recording of a phone call she'd had with a man
named Pete Peterson. At the time of this writing in 2016, Pete is
seventy-four years old. When I heard how intelligent and well versed in
classified information this man was, I said we needed to get to him right
away. Otherwise he could be threatened or even killed, and we would lose
our chance. I financed the airfare, car, and hotel rental to Pete's location
almost immediately. Bill flew in from Switzerland and we all interviewed
Pete for three straight days, with audio recorders running the entire time.
On the final day we taped a three-part video interview that was later released.[98] Since that initial meeting in 2009 I have continued speaking to
Pete at least once a week on the average, usually for two hours per conversation. Although there is repetition, I am still constantly learning new things.

Early along, Pete confirmed that the supersonic pitch of the television
set could indeed be changed to attract attention, just as I had observed.
I found out that at least eight different strategies were actively being used
to subliminally manipulate TV viewers. In the old days of VHF broadcast television, when the picture quality and reception were often fairly
poor, a secondary image might be placed underneath the main one that
was only 10 to 15 percent as bright. This could convey information directly to the subconscious. Images, words, and thoughts could also be
planted through various other hidden means.

"Do Not Question Government God"

When I was a kid, if you stayed up late enough watching TV, you would see a short video that played the National Anthem while showing images of flags waving and various national landmarks. It always felt very creepy to watch this for some inexplicable reason. Afterward the broadcast would suddenly die, creating a lonely mess of moving black and white dots called "snow" and a loud hissing noise. On November 11, 2009, an anonymous individual uploaded a YouTube video of one of these old clips, saying, "I salvaged this reel of film from a TV station that used to sign off with it during the 1960s." The uploader later posted a comment indicating the original reel was found in Alabama, dated 1963, and the clip was probably broadcast in several states during the 1960s.[99] Two years after the video was first uploaded, someone discovered that it contained subliminal text, and the news quickly went viral.[100] The words to the National Anthem are spelled out, appearing on the screen from left to right. However, as the words first materialize, a different set of words appears beneath them with the same basic font.

The hidden words never appear all at once, and you need to slow the video down to a quarter of its normal speed to see the messages. The disguised text appears in approximately the same area as the words that then remain on the screen. The subliminal commands that appear in the video are as follows:

TRUST THE US GOVERNMENT

GOD IS REAL GOD IS WATCHING

BELIEVE IN GOVERNMENT GOD

REBELLION WILL NOT BE TOLERATED

OBEY CONSUME OBEY CONSUME

BUY ULTRA BUY NAOMI

WORSHIP CONSUME OBEY BELIEVE

DO NOT QUESTION GOVERNMENT

"Ultra" and "Naomi" are both names of alleged mind-control programs. Some people have attacked this video as a hoax, but it seems very unlikely that their arguments are valid. The 1988 movie *They Live* depicted a society in which words such as "OBEY" and "CONSUME" were hidden in subliminal messages, and this was almost certainly an early attempt by whistle-blowers to tell us what was really being done. As we will see, there is a robust international alliance working to defeat the Cabal, and certain insiders are giving me ongoing briefings from this group. Our best written analysis of the National Anthem case appeared on the Vigilant Citizen website as of May 13, 2015.[101] The same film clip was still used in sign-offs in the 1980s, such as from Chicago station WMAQ, but there are no subliminals in those surviving copies. By the 1980s, people had VCRs and these subliminals would have been easily discovered. However, the 1960s version is wider, featuring buildings you cannot see in any of the 1980s footage, and it is an original copy that never appeared on the Internet before 2009. Furthermore, the 1960s version has white text with a shadow that goes to the bottom right, while the 1981 version has yellow text with a shadow that reflects up to the top left.[102]

The author concludes that although we cannot absolutely prove it is real—at least not yet—it cannot be ruled out as a hoax either. An original tape of the video would need to be produced and confirmed. The anonymous individual who uploaded this was probably well aware that any attempt to come forward would be suicide. The reason we have trouble accepting something like this is what I call the "man in the bedroom effect." We have been taught to admire our leaders, vote for them in elections, and trust that they are doing their best to protect us against our enemies. If they are subliminally telling us that they are God, that we must worship and obey them, that rebellion will not be tolerated and we must not question them, our sense of betrayal and horror is total. It is akin to walking in on your partner while he or she is in bed with someone else. In that case you cannot deny what you are seeing. In cases like this, it is far easier to attack and discredit the messenger, by any means necessary, than to face the uncomfortable truth.

Pete never saw this video but did confirm that these techniques and commands are a valid example of how mind control technology is used. If nothing else, the video is a great exercise in showing what can be done, and the techniques that are used to manipulate us. Many of these techniques are significantly more sophisticated than what we see in the video, and apparently they work very well. I first heard about all this in my college sociology class, as we are about to see. I was stunned by the number of specific examples I was required to study and learn. I was also tested on how to spot these messages in printed advertisements. Once you learn what to look for, it is not that difficult to find them.

Sex, Death, and Dr. Wilson Bryan Key

Pete said subliminals can be embedded within audio tracks as well. Sophisticated techniques allow speech to blend in with the music in ways that are almost impossible to detect consciously, but are easily picked out by the mind. The key to this technology is that the subconscious can only understand basic, childish commands. Therefore, corporate stores that are in the know will play music that repeats basic commands at a slow, hypnotic speed, such as "I am a good person. Stealing is bad. I do not steal." Pete also said it was common for American car companies to secretly alter the images of trees as they whizzed by in commercials. The existing leaves and branches would be manipulated to form images that were provocative to the subconscious, such as images of naked women. This would cause potential buyers to associate the car with manliness and the satisfaction of their most basic primal instincts.

This confirmed and enhanced some of the unpleasant things I learned in my college sociology classes. Dr. Wilson Bryan Key has written multiple books in which he clearly exposes this subliminal advertising at work. Websites such as Subliminal Manipulation feature a variety of Key's original examples as well as newer ones, in both photo and video form.[103] The pictures are extremely shocking, and words like "SEX" are very easy to spot in many cases. Provocative websites exposing details like this can usually be retrieved from Archive.org if the Cabal takes them offline.[104]

One of the strangest things Key discovered was that images and depictions of death were used quite often in subliminals as well. This appears to be another example of "repetition compulsion." Many of us are heavily seduced by the idea of our own death in the subconscious mind. We are drawn to those things that could kill us, as we get high from repeating the trauma of other brushes with death in the past. This again can be seen in Dr. Bessel A. van der Kolk's discovery that soldiers with PTSD would receive a high equivalent to injecting eight milligrams of morphine while watching a movie featuring scenes of combat death. On Wednesday, February 21, 1990, just a year and a half before I had my first sociology class, Dr. Key gave a lecture at the Massachusetts Institute of Technology (MIT) that was written up in their official publication, *The Tech*, as follows.

> Subliminal messages often concentrate on the taboos of society—sex, death, incest, homosexuality, and at times, pagan icons—according to Key. He claimed that, in one liquor advertisement, the images of a fish, screaming faces, a rat, a volcano, a lizard, and several other death symbols were embedded in ice cubes. Other examples Key showed included a man with an erection in an RJ Reynolds' Camel advertisement, a battered skull in a Bacardi drink, and the word cancer in a cigarette advertisement. Key maintained that these messages do not appear by accident, coincidence, or as the work of an individual artist."[105]

There are so many high-quality examples of this phenomenon hiding out in the open that federal criminal trials should already have begun. The problem is that we do not live in an open and free system. There is powerful institutional corruption in place that prevents these crimes from being taken seriously. In 2007, right at the dawn of free online streaming video that anyone could upload, a McDonald's logo flashed for one single frame of *Iron Chef America* on the Food Network. A YouTube video went up exposing it, and the network was forced to publicly apologize, saying it was a "glitch." They denied doing any subliminal advertising.[106] *Mental Floss* combined this with seven other obvious examples in a popular article from 2015.[107] Dr. Bryan Wilson Key produced many hundreds of provocative examples in his books, lectures, and videos.

In a Tufts University paper from 2003, Dr. Key wrote, "A recent estimate held that 10–20% of mainstream US advertising contained sexual information. . . . Include the subliminal dimension of communication, however, and the input of information into the brain (without conscious awareness) of sexual material easily approaches 80–90% of commercial media. In this all-pervasive ocean of sexualized people, products, ideas, and information, few consumers even suspect an enormous, bizarre, invisible environment has been created to milk them out of their money, allegiances, and power."[108]

Mr. Do

As you can see from the Project Camelot videos, Pete is stunningly articulate and extremely well versed in science.[109] I could easily have filled this entire book with his testimony. Pete claims that his grandfather was one of Nikola Tesla's main lab assistants, and he was trained in the secrets of Tesla technology from a very young age. He was recruited by the government as a boy after developing a very effective rocket system. He was then trained by all the best scientists available within the classified world, earning multiple PhDs' worth of information in a variety of technical fields. He became one of the top scientists and technology problem-solvers within the classified world, and was widely considered their single most valuable and prolific inventor. Ronald Reagan gave him the nickname "Mr. Do" as a result. Sadly, almost all his world-changing inventions remain classified to this day.

Pete worked directly with top neocons like Dick Cheney and Donald Rumsfeld, and ended up having a change of heart that led to his coming forward. He felt he had "mud on his wheel of karma." The Project Camelot interviews we did with Pete barely even scratched the surface of how much he really knew as the years went by. Pete goes into so much technical detail on any question that it is mind-boggling. There is no such thing as a short conversation. He can discourse for three hours on advanced physics, mathematics, or technology and never repeat himself. Never once have I caught him in any obvious lies. At any time I could come back to a story he told me five years ago and gain new information by asking different questions. I was deeply honored when he told me I am one of the three smartest people he has ever known. One of them died and the other one betrayed him. Pete has also introduced me to several other insiders. One of them developed eight different anti-gravity systems by analyzing crashed wreckage and having in-person consultations with extraterrestrials.

Holy God Damn

Pete was there during the formative stages of the same secret space program that Henry Deacon was a part of. He helped design some of the craft and other technologies they use. This included advanced computer chips that are far more powerful than anything we have in the commercial world, featuring photon-based transistors instead of those using electrons. Pete's chips have a staggering 144 cores each, running at speeds vastly in excess of any current technology. The chips can be printed on conventional multilayer silicon wafers at dirt-cheap prices. Since photons have quantum nonlocality, they process countless calculations simultaneously. Eighty-five percent of the components of a typical smartphone can be eliminated with just one chip, and it requires so little power it can be run off a lemon with wires stuck into it. This technology was recently demonstrated to officials who were not in the know about these discoveries at the Pentagon. They gave the chip a random, unexpected calculation that their top supercomputers would take three weeks to crack, and left. Pete's chip had already solved the puzzle by the time they came back from the bathroom. These chips are so powerful that they demonstrate what Pete's insiders call "electronic intelligence."

Pete also was involved in a program in which the nervous system was mapped out in meticulous detail. He discovered that we have a dimple in the middle of each shoulder blade where a huge cluster of nerve fibers all intersect before going on up to the brain. He said this serves no practical purpose for the body, other than that it feels terrific when the area is massaged. These nerve clusters are believed to be a product of intelligent genetic tinkering with the human body, such as by extraterrestrials. Pete and his insiders feel we were meant to use these areas once we learned how to access them. Special energetic fields can pump visual information, sounds, and thoughts directly into the brain through these areas, which they call "ports."

This system was depicted in the movie *The Matrix*, when Trinity downloads the information on how to fly a helicopter as her eyes flutter, and Neo downloads information that suddenly allows him to excel at martial arts and fight Morpheus. The main difference in *The Matrix* is that people "jack in" through a port at the back of their heads, rather than in the shoulder blades. Pete said that if you are given information in this manner, it can cause headaches and disorientation. The data then begins showing up in your mind over the course of the next few days or weeks. At first it seems dreamlike, and it gradually surfaces in your conscious awareness as something you know and understand. We have the potential to vastly increase our intelligence and learn multiple languages through the use of this technology.

This system can also be used to project people into a vividly realistic virtual-reality environment. Middle and high-level Cabal members routinely experience this technology, as does everyone in the secret space program. These VR systems were depicted in *The Matrix* as well as the *Divergent* film series, and to a lesser degree in *Ender's Game*. Images can also be pulled out of the mind and projected, as was depicted in *Minority Report*. When I first started talking to Corey Goode, one of many stunning correlations we had with our insider knowledge was on the subject of these ports. Corey was well aware of them, and told me many of the things Pete had said before I could even get the words out of my mouth. He revealed that he had used these same systems extensively while in the space program.

Classified fighter-jets no longer need windows thanks to this system. Vision is nothing more than electrical signals from the retinas of your eyes that are then sent to the brain. In this case, two metallic nubs push against your ports while you sit in a special chair. Energetic signals are pumped into your visual cortex just like the electrical signals from your eyes. Your visual cortex is flooded with information that is just as accessible as what you see with your eyes. Your vision becomes exceptionally crisp and clear, and you can then zoom in on any area like binoculars. Pete managed to produce a demonstration of this technology for a wealthy corporate leader who was blind. The man was brought to an airfield and seated in a specific fighter-jet. When he tried out the system, his exact quote began with "Holy God damn." I cannot print the last word he said.

Aerospace Command

I found out that our government already has cloaking technology that can make naval vessels, aircraft, and spacecraft invisible, and in the classified world this is called "masking." Our skies are routinely filled with masked craft that we cannot see. This includes gigantic aircraft carriers that are literally floating cities, using a combination of anti-gravity and conventional propulsion to remain airborne. The insider Bob Dean got in trouble for leaking this information in a Project Camelot video from April 2010. Here is what he said: "They don't want us to know about the Aerospace Command here, would you believe that? Trillions of dollars a year are going off to a military command that the American people don't even know exists? . . . It used to be in Nebraska. It used to be in Colorado Springs. Now the headquarters . . . I swear to God the headquarters is in orbit! There is a four-star Air Force general, who, last I checked last year, was commanding: Lance Lord. Interesting name. . . . It's a joint services Space Command that the American people don't even know exist. It puts NASA to shame."[110]

Peterson was absolutely astonished to see these flying super-carriers appear in *The Avengers* and *Captain America: The Winter Soldier.* He said that what we see in these movies is exactly the same as how they really look. Two of these carriers usually fly with a large flying black triangle that serves as a massive, multilevel aircraft carrier. In my epic article "Cosmic Perspective on the Defeat of the Cabal," I give detailed photographic comparisons and an analysis of how they line up with Pete's testimony.[111] He said that many of our best technologies from the 1980s are now appearing in movies. James Cameron's movie *Avatar* was loaded with images of genuine technology, including the robotic chassis that a person can stand in and manipulate. The same device appears in the movie *Aliens,* in which Sigourney Weaver uses it to battle the queen.

Another Project Camelot whistle-blower was the computer hacker Gary McKinnon, who used his skills to look for information on UFOs.[112] He hacked his way into NASA, the Pentagon, and various other government organizations. The *Huffington Post UK* published a provocative article about the evidence he discovered. "When Gary McKinnon hacked into U.S. Space Command computers several years ago and learned of the existence of 'non-terrestrial officers' and 'fleet-to-fleet transfers' and a secret program called 'Solar Warden,' he was charged by the Bush Justice Department with having committed 'the biggest military computer hack of all time,' and stood to face prison time of up to 70 years after extradition from UK. . . . McKinnon also found out about the ships or craft within Solar Warden. It is said that there are approx eight cigar-shaped motherships (each longer than two football fields end-to-end) and 43 small 'scout ships.'"[113] In *Selected by Extraterrestrials*, William Tompkins describes his efforts to help design these cigar-shaped craft. He also confirmed the existence of the Solar Warden program.

In his Project Camelot interview, McKinnon said, "What I surmised is that an off-planet Space Marines is being formed. And if you actually look at DARPA, the Defense Advanced Research Projects Agency, literature at the moment and in the last few years, a lot of government and space command stuff is all about *space dominance*. It is really, you know, the final frontier. Yeah, so I think it's natural for them to want to control space and to be developing a space-going force in secret. I think [they are] most likely using technology reverse-engineered from ETs."[114]

The Brain Drain

Pete also revealed that the so-called "Brain Drain" in the 1950s and '60s was very real. He claims that 55 to 60 million of the most intelligent and talented scientists from around the world were recruited into the secret space program. Twenty-five percent of them were from the United States and Canada, and the other 75 percent were international. They would cut all ties with their family and friends on Earth, fill out a series of postcards to cover a few years of time, and then never have contact with anyone here again. Groups on Earth would then send out the postcards at the appropriate time intervals.

Advertisements for these jobs were openly distributed in Brazil. The ads said that you would be leaving the country for an exciting high-tech assignment and would no longer have any further contact with your family or friends. It did not say exactly what the work would be or where you would end up going. Once these people arrived at their new homes, they were encouraged to have children, and as a result their population has greatly increased since the 1950s. People continue to be recruited into this "breakaway civilization" out of military, intelligence, and other areas. As Corey Goode revealed, many of them are selected and trained from very early childhood. In total, the number of people working out in space could now be well above America's own population of 300 million.

Underground Bases

Some of these people also work in vast underground facilities. Pete was personally aware of approximately 250 different underground bases that were built around the world. Each of these facilities was built to hold a maximum of 65,000 people. Pete got to tour one of them and was impressed. They are usually built inside natural limestone caves in the earth. There are trees, roads, and buildings inside, as well as a domed roof with artificial light. When I asked him if there was anything "off" about it, he said you could always hear the sound of ventilation fans, and there was a persistent smell of machine oil in the air. You could also see seams and rivets in the domed ceiling. Pete confirmed that injections would be given to people that would make it lethal for them to return to the surface. In order to leave, you would need to get a special shot that would cover you for however many days before you were authorized to return. If you extended your stay past that number of days, you would quickly die. Pete was offered the chance to live and work in one of these facilities and he refused. He also told me if I revealed too much I might be pulled into one of them, never to return.

Bob Dean also leaked information about these bases in his April 2010 interview with Project Camelot. "I've been in underground facilities that you wouldn't believe—massive, massive—all over the country. There's one under Fort Huachuca, which I may have told you once before, that is gigantic. . . . My only criticism at the time was that some of them were so luxurious for the politicians that that ticked me off. I felt that the politicians didn't deserve those luxurious facilities. We've got massive underground facilities all over the country, all over the planet. We've got official military relationships with the off-planet intelligences. We have a major facility in the middle of Australia. It's called Pine Gap. The point I'm getting at is that our military, our Shadow Government, is deeply involved with extraterrestrial operations."[115]

The Cabal's plan was to have a full-scale nuclear war, in which nuclear submarines fired off all their ordnance. The Cabal would make sure that all their friends, colleagues, and family members were taken underground before the war started, and they planned on living down there until the Earth became habitable again. In those cases they would not be forced to take the shots. Modern nuclear weapons were not designed to create any lasting radiation, so an extended stay underground would not be required. Each of these cities has a docking station in the ocean where the breeder reactor in a nuclear submarine can plug in and power the entire facility for many years. The subs therefore continue to be useful after they have fired off all their missiles.

A vast system of underground passageways called the "sub-shuttle" system interlinks these cities together, even underneath oceans. The shuttles travel by the use of high-intensity compressed air, and are extremely fast. Inflatable airbags inside the shuttle cushion you from the impact of turns. The ride can be sickening enough that every seat has a vacuum-powered chute to capture vomit as soon as you lean into it. The sub-shuttle system was disclosed by Phil Schneider in the early 1990s. He was personally aware of 129 underground facilities, all interconnected by the sub-shuttle system, and claimed to have worked on thirteen of them. Not long after coming forward, Schneider died on January 17, 1996.[116]

The Disclosure Project witness Daniel Morris, who later came forward with his real last name as Salter, said the following about Phil in this quote from his September 2000 interview: "There are other people who have been eliminated for what they know. One was a friend of mine, Phil Schneider, who worked out here in New Mexico building the tunnels. The

biggest one that he was involved with was the Dulce underground facility. . . . I know that Phil loved this country and he thought these programs
were bypassing our form of government. . . . No Congress ever voted on
any of these black projects, and he believed the American people had a
right to know what they were spending their money for and what we were
capable of doing. And he started talking, so they got rid of him."[117]

The Seeker and the Alliance

As the years have gone by, Pete has validated almost everything that other
insiders have told me about the space program, and added significant additional information. He revealed that a gigantic, Moon-sized sphere drifted
into our solar system in the early 1980s, terrifying the Reagan administration. None of the ETs they were in contact with, at places like Area 51, had
anywhere near this level of technology. They called this sphere "the Seeker."
It was predominantly white, but its surface had geometric lines much like
a soccer ball. Huge portals would open on its sides, creating eight-hundred-
mile-wide holes into an interior that was too dark to see very clearly. Ships
would fly in and out of the portals and explore our planets and moons. The
Seeker came into our solar system and began circling each of the planets,
one by one. It eventually left when it got to Jupiter.
    Although Pete has hundreds of amazing stories that I have been able
to validate, there is nowhere near enough space in this book to document
all of them. The most important thing he shared with me is the existence
of an alliance that formed to end the UFO cover-up. The two most prominent movies that reveal the Alliance's agenda and prepare us for disclosure are *Iron Man 3* and *Captain America: The Winter Soldier*.[118] A surprising
majority of the people in the Pentagon want the secrecy to end, particularly after 9/11, which is widely known to have been an inside job. The
Cabal is still using lethal force to prevent the truth from being revealed.
As a result, the pro-disclosure elements of the Pentagon have quietly
worked with foreign countries to create an international alliance. I have
extensively covered the battle between the Cabal and the Alliance on my
website, and the story is constantly shifting and evolving as time goes on.

This is considered a "shadow World War III," and the Cabal is losing the war very rapidly. At the time of this writing, major treaties are being signed and an official announcement is expected.

Divine Intervention

Most interestingly, we have learned that an extremely advanced extraterrestrial force is consistently preventing the Cabal from killing large numbers of people. This goes all the way back to the dawn of the nuclear age. Missiles and entire nuclear facilities have consistently been powered down by UFOs that appeared. Some of these stories did leak to the public through other insiders, as we are about to see. Space-based "Star Wars" weapons were deactivated in the 1980s almost as soon as they went up. Entire facilities of nuclear missiles had all the warheads completely melted down into nonradioactive material. The guidance systems on the missiles were so scrambled that they could not fly. This happened on multiple occasions. The Apollo astronaut and American hero Dr. Edgar Mitchell publicly confirmed the overall story in 2015, and the media widely reported on it. Here is an excerpt from *The Mirror*:

> [Dr. Mitchell] told us military insiders had seen strange crafts flying over missile bases and the famous White Sands facility, where the world's first ever nuclear bomb was detonated in 1945. . . . "My own experience talking to people has made it clear the ETs had been attempting to keep us from going to war and help create peace on Earth." Mitchell also suggested he had heard similar stories from people who manned missile bases during the most tense parts of the twentieth century. "I have spoken to many Air Force officers who worked at these silos during the Cold War," he continued. "They told me UFOs were frequently seen overhead and often disabled their missiles. Other officers from bases on the Pacific coast told me their [test] missiles were frequently shot down by alien spacecraft."[119]

On September 27, 2010, Robert Hastings held an event at the National Press Club in which seven US Air Force veterans shared their personal testimony about these encounters. It is very likely that Dr. Mitchell spoke with some, if not all of these insiders. According to Hastings's website, "To date, Hastings has interviewed more than 150 military veterans who were involved in various UFO-related incidents at U.S. missile sites, weapons storage facilities, and nuclear bomb test ranges. The events described by these individuals leave little doubt that the U.S. nuclear weapons program is an ongoing source of interest to someone possessing vastly superior technology. . . . Hastings believes that UFOs are piloted by visitors from elsewhere in the universe who, for whatever reason, have taken an interest in our long-term survival. He contends that these beings are occasionally disrupting our nukes to send a message to the American and Soviet/Russian governments that their possession and potential large-scale use of nuclear weapons threatens the future of humanity and the environmental integrity of the planet."[120]

Less than a month after Hastings's epic event, on October 23, 2010, a cigar-shaped UFO appeared over the largest nuclear missile installation in the US. The F. E. Warren Air Force Base in Cheyenne, Wyoming, lost the ability to communicate with fifty of its Minuteman III missiles as this happened. This was the largest single failure of nuclear missiles in the entire history of the United States, compromising one-ninth of the entire arsenal, and it lasted for several hours. According to a PR Newswire article that was initially featured on Reuters, "The confidential Air Force sources also report that their squadron commander has warned witnesses not to talk to journalists or researchers about 'the things they may or may not have seen' in the sky, and has threatened severe penalties for anyone violating security."[121]

According to Peterson, sometime in the late 1980s or the very early 1990s, all the remaining missiles in both the US and the USSR were completely ruined. This was apparently the final straw that led to the collapse of the USSR and the end of the Cold War. The Project Camelot insider Bob Dean independently confirmed these details to me about a year after I had first heard them from Pete. In a 2010 interview with Project Camelot, Dean leaked some of the intel when he said, "There is not going to be a nuclear war because [the ETs are] not going to allow it. The planet is too valuable—the flora and fauna in this zoological garden is too precious. And they have already intervened several times. They made their point during the Reagan administration; they made it to Gorbachev when he was in office. They've made the point many times. They made it at Rendlesham Forest, Bentwaters, when they melted the warheads."[122]

Although the US still has missiles, they now contain advanced particle-beam systems exactly like we see in *Captain America: The Winter Solider*, since any attempt to make nuclear weapons is blocked. It is highly unlikely that these particle-beam systems will ever be permitted to be used either, since they are extremely destructive—as the *Captain America* movie so compellingly illustrates.

However, certain tragic events such as the BP oil spill and the Fukushima disaster are still "authorized" by the advanced ETs who watch over and manage our planet. In certain cases, our collective free will permits these events to occur in order to provide a global wake-up call. This then leads us to take action, rise up against our oppressors, and save ourselves. The ETs cannot just sweep in and rescue us. They are allowed to do part of the work, so that it is possible for us to solve the problem ourselves, but we have to finish the job.

The vast majority of planned mass atrocities are blocked, though, since the Cabal is still constantly trying to start World War III, to create mass catastrophes that would lead to incredible loss of life, and to otherwise wreak havoc on Earth. As one example, the Cabal tried to send black-ops scuba-diving soldiers in to blow up an oil refinery in the Persian Gulf, creating another BP oil spill. They were carrying backpacks with bombs in them that they were going to plant on the rig. This would almost certainly have led to an epic Armageddon-type war in the Middle East once the Western powers had denied any responsibility for the catastrophe. The elected officials very likely had no idea that this was being planned. The soldiers hit an energetic wall in the water that was like stretchable elastic. They couldn't go over, under, or through it, and finally gave up after twelve hours of struggle.

The amount of "divine intervention" that has stopped wars from taking place is truly mind-boggling, according to Pete and other insiders. Advanced, exotic craft have been deactivated or have completely disappeared. Entire underground facilities have had all their employees portaled out and were then completely destroyed. This included a base near Washington, DC, that the Cabal members of the US government were planning on fleeing to in the event of a public disclosure. The entire East Coast of the United States shook with a 5.5 magnitude earthquake when this base was destroyed. It was quite the shocking synchronicity that this event occurred on August 23, 2011, the same day that my book *The Source Field Investigations* was released. The publisher was all excited about our big debut, and on that very day the ground heaved under the publishers' feet, causing their knees to buckle if they were standing.[123]

It was also very interesting and symbolic that the top of the Washington Monument obelisk cracked in this same earthquake. This again seemed like a potent symbol of the impending full defeat of the Cabal. I wrote about the destruction of this and another base under the Denver International Airport on September 16, 2011.[124] I subsequently found out that at least twenty-four other bases were destroyed thereafter. The destruction of bases appeared to come to a halt shortly after the beginning of 2012, after a new treaty between the Cabal and the benevolent ETs was agreed to, which increased the speed of the disclosure process. A wealth of revealing NASA data started appearing thereafter, as we will discuss in upcoming chapters. Three years after the first two bases were destroyed, in 2014, Russian national television aired a prime-time, three-hour documentary in which I was interviewed about these events. It was the most popular show in the history of that particular production company, with 21 million viewers.[125]

During this same time, tanks that were going to roll into Syria would not start, only to work fine when they were brought elsewhere. Bomb-bay doors on airplanes about to release massively destructive weapons were jammed. Guns would not fire. Even bladed weapons were jammed in their sheaths so they could not be pulled out. On three different occasions, the Palestinians planned to invade Israel, and Israeli soldiers intercepted their communications and were waiting for them. When they tried to fight one another, none of their guns would fire and they could not release their bladed weapons. These hardened warriors fell to their knees, held their arms up into the air, and cried, believing it was a divine manifestation.

Despite all the negative press about him in the Cabal-controlled West, Vladimir Putin has been a key figure in the Alliance, working directly with the positive elements in the Pentagon. A positive ET group apparently gave Putin some of their peace-keeping technology. Corey Goode revealed that this technology causes metal to suddenly enlarge while it is activated. As soon as the beam is turned off, the metal returns to its normal size. Putin has demonstrated the ability to completely power down any and all US military hardware, including the latest, greatest Aegis-class aircraft carriers. Every effort is being made to prevent loss of life, and to create a peaceful transition that leads to disclosure.

It's Not Fun to Be President

Pete confirmed that George W. Bush was given a very tiny earpiece so that he could be told what to say by a team of insiders. Many amusing verbal mistakes, commonly known as "Bushisms," resulted from this.[126] Perhaps the most obvious example is "Families is where our nation finds hope, where wings take dream." This was spoken in La Crosse, Wisconsin, on October 18, 2000.[127] Obama refused to use such a device, and instead was told he must speak from a teleprompter. Pete also revealed that a very provocative meeting took place between Obama and the surviving former US presidents on January 7, 2009. Up until this point, Obama did not know what he had gotten himself into. According to Pete, he was taken into a half-hour private meeting with George H. W. Bush in which he was severely verbally abused and threatened.

The *Washington Post* confirmed that a private meeting did take place, as follows: "A real team of rivals gathered for lunch at the White House yesterday, as President Bush and three former U.S. commanders in chief put aside their political differences to offer recollections and advice to President-elect Barack Obama. . . . Neither the White House nor the Obama transition team shared many details from the lunch, including what they ordered from the menu. No aides were present during the meal, officials said. Obama also met one on one with Bush for about 30 minutes beforehand."[128]

Up until that meeting, Obama did not know much, if anything, about the Cabal. He was told that he and all of his family would be tortured and killed if they resisted. Obama apparently staggered out of this meeting into a room in the White House that he thought was private. He held his head in his hands and cried, saying he had been made into a scapegoat. According to Pete as well as Jacob, who we are about to meet, an intelligence agent was in a nearby phone booth and witnessed the entire event. Pete also said the vast majority of insiders working for the Alliance know that this happened. US presidents are generally given very little access to the real secrets, and the Cabal is masterful at trying to pin the blame on elected officials, thereby diverting attention from themselves.

CHAPTER NINETEEN

Jacob and the Secret Space Program

The next significant insider arrived six months after Peterson, and we will call him Jacob. Up until Corey Goode came along, Jacob was by far the highest-level insider I knew. He has extensive involvement in the secret space program and the "breakaway civilization" that has resulted. When I first met him, even though I could tell he was quite a character and had a great sense of humor, I wasn't impressed and thought he was a fake. That challenged him to prove himself, which he certainly did. During our first private meeting, Jacob showed me stunning proof that he had access to highly classified secrets. He stayed at my house more than once for days at a time, and our conversations were fascinating. On his first visit, he showed me a classified photo of ruins on Mars. These were highly intricate, obviously artificial, and looked very different from anything I had seen on Earth. Most strangely, all the words on the sides, with arrows pointing to different features in the photo, were in German.

Jacob also showed me hundreds upon hundreds of pages of blueprints for a vast underground base. It would have cost well over a million dollars to draw up such detailed blueprints. The amount of detail in the illustrations, and in his technical descriptions of everything he was showing me, was stunning. This facility would feature a series of condominiums on the surface. Hidden elevators would allow the people living in them to quickly go underground whenever needed. He had calculated how many people the facility could hold, and realized it would have far more space than was needed in the event of a global disaster. When he told his superiors that he wanted them to rescue ordinary people as well as insiders, they canceled the project and withdrew all their funding.

Jacob then opened up Google Earth and showed me a series of provocative bases around the world that he said were even more interesting than Area 51. Very quickly he zoomed over some of the most barren areas on Earth and revealed surprisingly complex airfields in the middle of nowhere. One of them was Diego Garcia, a small island in the middle of the Indian Ocean that is officially listed as a joint US/NATO military base. Jacob said there were facilities for both humans and ETs in these bases, and they went many levels below the surface—exactly as I had seen in my epic ascension dream from high school.

These Are Not Happy People

Another shocking thing Jacob showed me in our first private meeting was photographs taken inside the Oval Office on President Obama's first day, January 20, 2009, right before he went in. This was slightly less than two weeks after he had been threatened and told the truth about the Cabal at the presidents' luncheon. Jacob was well aware of that incident and confirmed all the details Pete had shared with me. Multiple shots were taken of Obama's new desk from different angles. On top of the desk was a manila envelope that had the number "44" scrawled on it in pen, signifying that he was the forty-fourth president.

The envelope contained a series of briefing documents that told Obama what was really going on. The documents identified the Cabal as a group of powerful international bankers, and told him he was to follow their orders precisely—or there would be dire consequences for him and his family. Jacob also had candid pictures of a pale George W. Bush riding in his limousine after he had heard about 9/11; I had never seen any of these pictures in the media. During this same event, Jacob showed me dozens of pages of bank accounts for top Cabal families such as the Rothschilds. I saw usernames, passwords, account numbers, and balances, and they were often in the billions. As time went on, there were also numerous occasions on which Jacob would leak insider information to me before it appeared in the headlines. In some cases I would reveal this information publicly beforehand.

It quickly became obvious that Jacob worked for the group most people call the Illuminati, which means "the Enlightened Ones." The big secret was that they were the hyper-wealthy power structure controlling the *real* space program, and the bases other insiders had visited. They had UFO-type craft that were routinely coming and going from the Earth. Jacob did not support much of what they were doing, and would often tell me things he apparently wasn't supposed to say—which he called "talking out of school." He said he still worked for them because he felt their efforts in space were vital for the survival of everyone on Earth. There were negative ETs trying to destroy us and he wanted to make sure they did not succeed. At one point I asked him if anyone had been able to take control of a UFO, like I had written in my short story "Civil War." He laughed and confirmed that this did occasionally happen. Most people were not able to get the ship to go very far, but a few did manage to take a joyride before they were detected, intercepted, and brought into custody.

I was invited to join them and told I would be able to travel into space, meet ETs, and have incredible experiences. I was also promised fantastic sums of money if I accepted the deal, as well as guaranteed safety in the event of any cataclysmic disasters. In total, I had five different offers like this come in from various sources. I was told that I would be put in control of accounts that would quickly mature into the hundreds of millions of dollars. In exchange for this, I would have to begin putting out messages that were favorable to the Cabal and their philosophies. This would include framing Lucifer as a positive force, bringing us wisdom, freedom, and sexuality. I consistently refused these offers over the years, as I have strong disagreements about things like the "need" to reduce population. Nor did I agree with the idea that Lucifer was a benevolent, misunderstood liberator of humanity. It was very edgy to talk to Jacob at all, but I got an extremely thorough education in the process. He was not a Luciferian and joked that since Lucifer exists outside of

time, he should just go away and come back later. Jacob can get anyone
laughing within minutes and is an endless repository of fascinating information and entertaining stories.

The Black Jesus

One of the most surprising stories Jacob ever told me concerned a man
they called the "Black Jesus." He said this was highly classified and he
was definitely "talking out of school" to tell me about it at all. Apparently
in the 1960s a man appeared in Africa who had full ascended abilities.
He could read people's minds, materialize objects out of thin air, communicate telepathically, levitate himself, and teleport his body from one
location to another. He was a spiritual teacher who emphasized love,
peace, service to others, and forgiveness as the common core that unified
all the great religions. The Cabal does not want anyone to develop these
abilities, and if they find out that someone has them, they will hunt those
people down and terminate them with prejudice. The Cabal made several attempts to assassinate this man. He consistently regenerated his
body after each attack, no matter how lethal it seemed to be.

Finally the man was told that they had given up. He was far too
powerful. There was nothing they could do to stop him, and they were
going to surrender. They invited him to a major world summit and told
him they would reveal him to all of humanity so he could share his message. He was brought on board a military transport aircraft. Once airborne, he was shot repeatedly. His body was divided into many different
sections, each of which was stored in a super-high-tech energy-shielded
container. Jet aircraft rushed up to the plane in sequence and scrambled
the containers all over the Earth, as far apart as possible. The contents
were then thoroughly and completely destroyed. It was hoped that this
would prevent him from being able to regenerate himself.

After this was done, the man materialized directly into the offices of
the people who had ordered his murder. There were no visible signs of
damage to his body. He said, "Your desire to prevent me from living on

Earth is so strong that I am forced to honor it, for now. I will be leaving you shortly. However, in the future many more people will develop abilities just like me. Once that happens, you will no longer be able to stop us from making this world a peaceful place for everyone."

Mr. X and the Blues

This mirrored the story of the first Project Camelot insider, who went by the pseudonym Mr. X and was interviewed with a disguised video shoot in May 2006.[129] He reported having a job with a California-based defense contractor in the 1980s where he had to sort through and categorize a huge amount of classified documents. According to the write-up on the Project Camelot website, "Working long hours in a locked vault, he opened large mail bags full of photos, videotapes, alien artifacts, and volumes of top secret eyes-only documents that told the story behind Roswell, alien visitation and the government's careful handling of documented evidence of reverse engineering of alien craft."[130] Among those documents were pages from the 1950s that described a series of meetings between President Eisenhower and a group of benevolent extraterrestrials.

Pete revealed this ET group had dark blue skin, large heads, and large black eyes, and were simply called "the Blues." This was not the same group that later contacted Corey Goode and were identified as the Blue Avians. The Blues promised us complete protection from negative extraterrestrials and a gradual rollout of fantastic technology. In exchange, we would have to give up our nuclear weapons, allow a formal education on the science of spirituality to occur, and permit open interaction between humanity and benevolent ETs.

The Blues' offer was rudely and sarcastically dismissed. According to the documents Mr. X saw, the Blues told the US government that they would disappear for now, but that at the end of the year 2012, they and their allies would return in a "mass landing."[131] Once they chose to reveal themselves, there would be nothing the Cabal could do to stop them.

Other insiders have confirmed that this date has been pushed forward, since we are not ready for it to happen yet as a collective, but it very likely will still occur within a reasonable time window. This mass contact event appears to be a key component of the ascension process. Mr. X later decided to come forward, reveal his true identity, and share much more of what he knew. He then died of a massive and unexpected stroke on December 13, 2008. He was only forty-eight years of age, and had a one-year-old son.[132] I deeply regret that this happened, and wish I had gotten the chance to meet him before he passed away.

Bringing the Insiders Together

I set up a direct three-day-long meeting between Jacob and Pete Peterson in Pete's hometown that was very fascinating to participate in. At one point during the dinner I heard a loud *tink* noise in the room. I immediately asked everyone else if they had heard that funny noise, but they were distracted enough by the conversation that they had missed it. The

Image of David Wilcock's Plate of Food Having Split in Half While in a Dinner Meeting Featuring Insiders Jacob and Pete Peterson

next time I pushed down with my fork, my plate neatly parted into two pieces. The next day, a massive pipe burst in my house and spilled water all over the kitchen. Both of these events appeared to be warning shots intended to threaten me, and probably involved the use of a particle-beam technology. I chose not to be intimidated.

I also got Jacob in touch with Hoagland's top insider Bruce for a short visit in a restaurant in Los Angeles. Although Bruce worked directly with US presidents, he was not briefed on many of the things Jacob was involved in. They still got along and shared common knowledge. People who have been through these sorts of programs can immediately identify other insiders. Jacob would say, "They can smell it on you." Jacob and Henry Deacon also stayed at my house at the same time for a few days during a subsequent visit. Whenever I brought these people together, it was very clear that they shared many common pieces of information. Code names and things I did not understand were exchanged at rapid speeds, and it was clear they were sharing hyper-complex inside information. Jacob and Henry Deacon went off for an extended two-hour private conversation in my backyard at one point, and I would have very much appreciated to have heard what they said.

Up until Corey Goode came along, Jacob was the most highly connected space program insider I had ever met. He claimed to have personally traveled to about two hundred different off-planet bases, including many that were far outside our solar system. This was done through the use of the portal system in what some have called the "cosmic web"—the sequence of plasma tubes that interlink all neighboring stars together. Jacob couldn't understand why people were so fascinated with Mars, as he said it was a "dreadful" planet, and many other places were much nicer to visit. He did tell me that he was once ordered to kill some fifty-foot-long sandworms on Mars that would attach themselves to the sides of the bases. They had somehow evolved to be able to eat metal and other minerals. The job was relatively boring, and required the use of a weapon that shot out a foot-long metallic projectile, shaped like a small javelin. The work was somewhat frightening if the worms spotted you in an open area, as they could rush toward you at a decent walking speed and were quite deadly if they got close.

Our Interstellar Community

Jacob said there are approximately five to six thousand intelligent civilizations within a thousand-light-year radius from our solar system. He claimed to have personally seen more than four hundred different types of extraterrestrials at a total of about two hundred different off-planet sites. He said some of these ETs were human or humanlike, whereas others were only "hominid," meaning they had a head, a face, and a body with arms and legs that walked upright, but could otherwise look very different. Every type of life we see on Earth has evolved into intelligent hominid forms on various planets. On planets that are predominantly oceanic, hominids will evolve out of any of a variety of aquatic creatures we see on Earth. One type he personally interacted with had a head that looked like a sturgeon, with eyes on the side and an elongated snout filled with sharp teeth. Another group visited the Dogon tribe in Mali, and had all-black eyes, bony projections where the eyebrows would be, and strange limbs that moved almost like jellyfish as they walked.

There are a variety of insectoid hominids, including people who look like ants and others who look like grasshoppers or praying mantises. When I brought this information back to Pete, he confirmed that he had interacted with a grasshopper-type being at a base in Antarctica called Ice Station Zebra. This same term was "hidden out in the open" in the title of a 1963 novel and later movie that was based on an event in 1959, in which Russians captured a US satellite that had downed in the Arctic. Real code names are often released like this so that if anyone talks, they are simply accused of copying ideas from movies. Pete said the most difficult part of talking to this being was its mouth, as it had three mandibles on each side that would open and close. He said it is common to feel physically nauseated when you meet such an unusual-looking entity. When Pete revealed this to the being, it said, "How do you think I feel talking to you?" The being would deliberately put its head down when it laughed so Pete wouldn't see all the mandibles open up.

I took some of the specific details of what Pete said about Ice Station

Zebra and reported them back to Jacob, who then filled in more of what Pete had said without me even having to say it out loud. This type of common knowledge between insiders was a routine occurrence. Jacob also indicated that there were several different types of reptilian human-oids, and that they are the biggest troublemakers. Pete, William Tomp-kins, and Corey Goode independently confirmed this, and I will discuss them in a later chapter.

How Many People Know?

I also got to see Jacob interact with other insiders, including the late Bob Dean, who was arguably the most well-loved Project Camelot witness.[133] Bob Dean reminded me of a wise, crusty old sailor from a Hemingway novel, complete with the cigar. Dean was greatly surprised when he saw Jacob at a Project Camelot event, and recognized him from the time they served in the space program. They hadn't seen each other since the 1970s, and I was right there as the first meeting happened. Jacob laughed and told Dean he should come forward and say what he really knows.

Jacob later told me that Dean was very heavily involved in the secret space program and had shared only a small amount of what he really knew with the public. Jacob said there weren't very many people involved at the highest levels, and everyone knew one another. He told me the core management of the command structure here on Earth consists of only "about fifteen to twenty-five" people, and the exact number is clas-sified. Dean agreed with this approximate number when we spoke.

This was also similar to the number given by the high-ranking Disclo-sure Project witness Daniel M. Salter, whom I briefly met in 2001. Salter's book *Life with a Cosmos Clearance* contains a variety of interesting de-tails that others have verified. Salter went under the pseudonym Dan Mor-ris at the event. In the Disclosure Project briefing document, Salter described one of his jobs as follows: "I would go interview people who claimed they had seen something and try to convince them they hadn't seen something or that they were hallucinating. Well, if that didn't work, another team would come in and give all the threats . . . threaten them and their family and so on and so forth. They would be in charge of discrediting them, making them look foolish. . . . Now if that didn't work, then there was another team that put an end to that problem, one way or another." Salter's full testimony begins on page 268 of the full briefing document.[134]

Bruce just called me while I was writing this section. I asked him how many people currently living on the surface of the Earth have any decent idea of what is going on in the space program, apart from individual compartments. He said there are "about three thousand" of them living here. About four hundred to five hundred of the members of this group are visible in the public eye and the rest are largely unknown. None of these visible people include elected leaders or celebrities. When I asked him how many people actually manage the group at its core, he revealed that this is where the infamous "Committee of 300" comes in.[135] This group is also known as "the Olympians," indicating that they see themselves as gods. The Olympians were allegedly founded by the British aristocracy in 1727.[136]

Walter Rathenau leaked the secret of this group in a statement from 1909: "Three hundred men, all of whom know one another, direct the economic destiny of the continent and choose their successors from their area."[137] In 1921, Rathenau disputed charges of anti-Semitism by saying these people were business leaders, not Jews.[138] When I asked Bruce how many people within this three hundred were visible in the public eye, he said it was only about a third. He also said they are run by a core council of thirty-three, which is probably where the "fifteen to twenty-five" figure came from. "The real secret hardly anyone realizes is that three hundred thirty-three people control the Cabal, and that number has key symbolic significance for them." He didn't need to say that three hundred thirty-three was half of six hundred sixty-six, as by that point it was obvious. As he said so many times, "It doesn't matter whether you believe it or not. This is their religion and they take it very seriously. Anyone else who tries to study this is reading other people's mail. You're never going to fully understand what you see in those letters unless you are directly involved in the conversation. And who would want to be?"

Portals and Cosmic Events

Bob Dean said he wanted to tell me everything he knew. Sadly, I never got the chance to hear his full testimony before he died. However, I did ask him what it was like to travel through the modern stargate system, where you can be teleported even across far distances instantaneously. He said it was remarkably advanced, and the moment itself was quite easy to miss. You would feel something akin to a sudden, full-body energetic shock, but it wasn't painful and lasted only a split second. One time he was reaching down for a briefcase and didn't even feel it. Dean disclosed the existence of portal systems in a Project Camelot interview from 2010.

> I was one of [the first insiders] who revealed the information that we have a portal of sorts . . . located at 14 levels below-ground at S4. A Naval Lieutenant Commander told me. He said: "I was ordered to put on my summer uniform, pack my bags and get my briefcase." He was ordered to go to this facility, . . . S4, on the other side of the mountain at Papoose Lake. And he said: "Why are you asking me to put on a summer uniform when it's cold as hell here?" Even in Las Vegas it was cold. And they said: "Just do what you're told. Put on a summer uniform, pack your bag and show up here." They took him to S4, [and] went down the elevator to three different levels. He had a red card, a blue card, and a green card. At the bottom of the facility, 14 levels below ground— it's like taking a 14-story building and burying it—at the bottom he got through the door and there sits a GI. I can't remember whether he said it was Army, Navy, Air Force or what. Doesn't matter. At that level it doesn't matter. They said: "Commander, welcome. Come on in." He walked through this door from the elevator, and the kid said, "Welcome to Pine Gap." . . .

And the Commander said: "What the hell are you talking about?"

He said: "Sir, you're in Australia."

Commander said: "No, we're in Nevada."

And the young man said: "Sir, when you just walked through that door, you're in Australia."[139]

Exciting Changes in Our Future

Jacob also told me a similar story. He would travel to off-planet locations in a device that looked like the inside of a train. You could sit down in the seats if you wanted to, but almost as soon as you got in and the doors closed, you would be at your destination and the doors would open again. Jacob revealed that the military-industrial complex was involved in elaborate trade with a wide variety of intelligent civilizations and used these portal systems to travel from place to place. One of his jobs was "customer relations," where he would visit various off-world partners to discuss trade agreements. He described meeting certain types of ETs that seemed to share a collective consciousness. In those cases, each person had a very similar personality, which he felt made them lack character. They saw Earth humans as being quite dynamic and emotional, and really did not understand us at all.

Jacob knew about the Seeker that had come into our solar system in the 1980s. He revealed that it was intercepted by his people and confronted. The people inside said they were peaceful explorers visiting our solar system. Jacob said that in the eyes of the Cabal, "they were a bunch of dickheads and we told them to piss off." Apparently after this event happened, they left peacefully—but hundreds more Moon-sized objects returned, beginning in the late 1990s. A researcher named Kent Steadman routinely tracked these planet-sized objects zipping around our Sun, using official NASA images from the SOHO space probe. This was an exciting story to follow in my early years on the Internet, and many stunning objects were spotted between 1998 and 2001. I wrote up a decent summary of Steadman's findings, with animated images, on my website as of August 24, 2015.[140] Corey Goode later revealed that at least a hundred more spheres arrived in 2012, and in this case many of them were as large as the planet Jupiter.

Jacob was also well aware that our solar system was moving into a highly charged energetic cloud. He said this would create a massive energetic flash from the Sun, which would propel us into the next level of human evolution. All the way back in 2009, he told me, "The event you are expecting to happen in 2012 is more likely to occur in 2017." I kept this a secret after he told me, in order to see if anyone else surfaced who said the same thing. Corey Goode later revealed that he was repeatedly given the date range of 2018 to 2023 for this same event in his own training. Jacob also made it clear that within a relatively small number of years after we go through this shift, people will start developing profound ascended abilities. This will include the ability to dynamically change our facial features, like a living tattoo. This was disclosed in the movie *The Watchmen*. Peterson reported seeing certain human ETs at Area 51 who could levitate a whole group of boxes around themselves and carry on lively conversations while the boxes stayed perfectly still. Many of the ETs visiting us have developed some of the abilities we will gain once we move through this transition.

When I asked Jacob what the single most wonderful-looking place was that he ever visited, he told me he once went to a planet where everything was made out of a luminous, rainbow-colored crystal material. There was a prevailing purple light everywhere. The beauty was staggering, and the feeling of love and peace was almost overwhelming. In order to visit a world like this, it is necessary to jump into an "avatar" body, just like what we saw in James Cameron's movie of the same title. This technology is regularly used by people at Jacob's level in the space program.

The "Space Whale"

Jacob also told me that plans are in place for disclosure to occur. There are a variety of treaties and interactions with various extraterrestrial groups, and many of them are insisting that the secrecy come to an end.

The ET groups pushing for disclosure very likely include the benevolent "Guardians" who are melting down nuclear warheads, and who portaled out at least twenty-six underground bases between August 2011 and January 2012. I have watched many stunning disclosures appear from NASA since the treaty was signed, and we are about to dive into some of them in the next chapter. However, these articles appear only in bits and pieces, and hardly anyone puts them into a greater mosaic. In this sense, it seems that the Cabal is doing their best to follow their orders, without actually giving these news items the publicity they need to become front-page stories.

In the spring of 2014, Jacob said his people were aware of an extremely large creature that swam in the oceans of Titan (a moon of Saturn), akin to a whale or a manatee. One of these creatures would periodically surface in a particular spot, either to breathe or rest. They were going to release pictures of it into the mainstream media without telling people what it was, but they would give some compelling hints.

I was tremendously surprised to see stories appear about the "magic island" on Titan a couple of months later. On June 22, 2014, *Forbes* said, "Researchers have spotted an 'island' in the middle of [Titan's] second-largest lake that seems to appear and disappear. . . . Other possibilities proposed by the authors of a paper on the findings published Sunday in the journal *Nature Geoscience* include sunken solids in the lake becoming buoyant thanks to the onset of warmer temperatures, or gases from the sea floor rising to the surface as bubbles."[141]

This story hit the news again on September 30, 2014, thanks to an official NASA press release revealing that it had reappeared:

Mysterious Changing Feature on Saturn's Moon Titan

The feature's first sighting was in July 2013, and the radar images depicted a bright spot, which stood out from the dark sea. Scientists were "perplexed" when the feature couldn't be located with follow-up radar experiments, but they found it again on August 21, 2014. Though the scientists aren't sure what the feature is, NASA reports that they are "confident" the feature is not a "flaw in their data." Some of their current explanations for the feature include "surface waves, rising bubbles, floating solids, solids suspended just below the surface, or perhaps something more exotic." Titan's hydrocarbon lakes have long been a source of curiosity for scientists who speculate that life may be able to survive on the moon's surface. "But if life exists on Titan, it would be very different than life on Earth, which is intimately tied to liquid water," *Space.com* notes.[142]

It is entirely possible that this is not a genuine life-form, and is only an inorganic solid that rises and falls in cycles. These stories may be disinformation, so they can be discredited if a particular plan needs to be abandoned. The overall value of news items like these is in moving the disclosure narrative forward. Most important, I was told that this story would emerge in the media before it actually did. I shared the information with witnesses in my personal circle before any details emerged in the media. This was very compelling evidence that Jacob was at least in contact with NASA, if nothing else. Even more important, the writers hinted that the "magic island" might be "something more exotic." Then we were told that life on Titan would be very different from life on Earth.

Jacob revealed that many different stories are being released into the media for use in a future disclosure event. The Cabal always has multiple backup plans for everything. They know there are any number of different ways the whole UFO cover-up could break down. Their goal is to try to control and stage-manage the process as much as possible. If they get their way, we will end up with "partial disclosure," with the full truth withheld for many years. At the time of this writing, almost everyone agrees that a partial disclosure will be simply impossible for the Cabal to accomplish. Once the truth starts coming out, it will quickly become a massive public quest for information. Any researchers and insiders who were releasing quality data before the cover-up breaks down will become far more interesting to the mainstream, everyday world. For many years now, my dreams have been preparing me for an extremely high level of publicity once this happens. Although it will make my life much more difficult, I also respect how urgent it is for our survival that the truth comes out.

Corey Goode

After Jacob came forward in December 2009, no new insiders with his level of knowledge appeared for the next five years. This was quite a long time to wait, and was somewhat depressing, since I had expected more people who were in the know to emerge. After the Snowden disclosures in 2013, there was a major crackdown on whistle-blowers, and it seemed even less likely that any new insiders would show up. That finally changed when Corey Goode opened up to me in October 2014, after being friends with me online since 2009. As soon as Corey began revealing what he really knew, I was able to validate dozens and dozens of things that others had shared with me. Five or ten of these sorts of correlations could possibly be written off as a coincidence. Once it happens fifty or a hundred different times, on very specific classified subjects I had never publicized, the only logical conclusion is that each of these people has participated in something very real. After investing my entire adult life in an intense study of these classified programs, it is extremely rewarding to find someone who can fill in more of the missing pieces. The story itself is so fantastic, so cosmic and unexpected, that it feels as if a full disclosure event would soon result in ascension—one way or the other.

It didn't take long to find out that Corey was telling me many things that were considered off-limits, and that Jacob was not authorized to reveal. As an example, I had never fully understood that the Cabal's main function in the breakaway civilization they have created is in manufacturing and selling extremely advanced technology. As astonishing as this may sound, Corey eventually discovered our military-industrial complex is engaged in regular commerce with nine hundred different civilizations. Money is not used in these deals. Instead, everything is based on trade, which includes the sharing of trained personnel for consultations. New technologies are consistently being brought in, reverse-engineered, and developed.

The military defense contractors are manufacturing a huge variety of products that will absolutely transform life on Earth as we know it, once they are released. We will instantaneously transition into a *Star Trek* age, with spaceships, teleportation, time travel, anti-gravity, free energy, materializers, and super-advanced healing technologies. The Cabal has been deliberately withholding this technology from us, and did not want to reveal it until they had brought our planet to its knees. They had no intention of allowing this technology to lead to an era of peace and prosperity. Instead, they wanted to use it as a means of furthering their control. Their plan included staging a mass, fake "alien invasion" with their own technology, so we would hand over our sovereignty to an international New World Order they would own and control. They telegraphed this move with literally hundreds of different movies and television shows about alien invasions. Those plans have been completely thwarted by benevolent ETs who want to ensure our ascension is not interrupted.

Corey also had full memories of spending twenty years working out in space, in what amounted to a glorified submarine. His particular program was code-named Solar Warden—the same group that Gary McKinnon learned about when he hacked into the Pentagon. Corey had a boring job and lived in a military-type facility, having a bunk in a common area with a small cubbyhole for his personal belongings. His food came from a materializer that would "print" the meal, and his favorite choice was the pot roast. I had independent confirmation on many technical details of this technology from Pete and Jacob, and the Disclosure Project witness Daniel Salter also spoke about it. Pete and Jacob told me that organic material is needed to print food. Butter was used in the earlier years. Coconut oil is also very effective. Hemp oil seems to provide the most consistent, high-quality results. Pete had printed meals at

Area 51 that he said were quite delicious. Corey's meals were nowhere near the same level of quality as higher-level insiders have access to.

You Are Not Allowed to Shoot the Red Cross Workers

Corey was threatened repeatedly for telling me all this. I also had death threats coming in from multiple sources, urging me to back off or else. Thankfully, there are rules in the universe that prevent you from being tortured or killed as long as you maintain a positive perspective in your thoughts and actions. Jacob was the one who had alerted me to this. The specific wording he used is, "You are not allowed to shoot the Red Cross workers. Those are the Rules."

Jacob spoke extensively about the Rules, which are cosmic principles that prevent negative acts from happening unless they are authorized by the people of Earth, both individually and collectively. For this same reason, the negative groups have to tell us who they are and what they are doing. This is often called "hiding out in the open." One of the most obvious examples of this would be the All-Seeing Eye and pyramid symbol on the dollar bill. They put it out there but no one ever talks about it. Most people are taught to laugh about conspiracy theories and ridicule anyone who is a believer. The Cabal has taught us to label any proof of their existence as a "conspiracy theory," thereby relegating it to an unverifiable and easily discredited idea. However, the minute skeptics run into any real sign of trouble, they are absolutely and completely terrified—just as my parents were when they saw people walking into the unlit house across the street in the middle of the night, without knocking.

Imagination and Will

As bizarre as this must sound, the Cabal is knowingly practicing black magic on a worldwide level. This is one of the great discoveries we are having to make as disclosure unfolds, and is deeply upsetting. The Cabal groups are extremely well aware of the power of our collective conscious-ness, and they are constantly trying to use it against us. The two main tools they use to do this are imagination and will.

The first stage of this process is to seed our imagination with negative thought-forms, like a nuclear war, an alien invasion, a global economic collapse, a catastrophic natural disaster, martial law, internment camps, a worldwide viral epidemic, a food shortage, a major riot, et cetera. These are only some of the more extreme examples. The next stage is to create traumatizing events that activate the power of our will. Our collective consciousness then charges the thought-forms with power. Their goal is to cause a critical mass of civilians to lose our objectivity and become terrified and furious. In those moments, we are ready for war, and we do not care about who lives or who dies. We only want revenge. If enough of us feel this way, and vote with our will to destroy others indiscrimi-nately, we activate the programs they placed in our imagination. The benevolent ETs who manage our planet are then forced to allow the Cabal to do what they want.

A simple example of this would be gun control. The Cabal plants multiple seeds in our collective imagination, telling us that guns kill people and we need to take all the guns away. Then all the deaths will stop and everyone is safe again. The next step is to stage an atrocity such as a mass shooting, and immediately repeat the same programmed phrases that they seeded our minds with while things were peaceful. If enough people cry out, "Take all the guns away so this will never, ever happen again," then the Cabal has effectively disarmed the public and removed any threat to their power. Black-market guns become a boom-ing business and armed criminals roam the streets, fearing no one except other criminals or fairly nonexistent police in the inner cities. Further-more, if the Cabal can take away most people's guns, it becomes much easier for them to completely conquer a nation, as no one has the means to oppose them. Gun control is a key element of every fascist takeover in modern history. In a 2007 article in the *Guardian*, Naomi Wolf spells out the ten steps to fascism that she laid out in her book *The End of America*.

If you look at history, you can see that there is essentially a blueprint for turning an open society into a dictatorship. That blueprint has been used again and again in more and less bloody, more and less terrifying ways. But it is always effective. It is very difficult and arduous to create and sustain a democracy—but history shows that closing one down is much simpler. You simply have to be willing to take the 10 steps. As difficult as this is to contemplate, it is clear, if you are willing to look, that each of these 10 steps has already been initiated today in the United States by the Bush administration.[143]

The game of the "negative elite" involves turning us against one another, through an endless series of staged events, lies, and manipulations. They want to pit race against race, nation against nation, religion against religion, old against young, parents against children, haves against have-nots, city against country, bosses against workers, teachers against students, military and government against civilians, and gender against gender. They love to see hate blossom in online forums, and in fact actively finance countless thousands of people to spread it. Under the apparent cloak of anonymity, people can easily lose their humanity and be unaware that they are still fully accountable for all their words and actions in the greater spiritual sense.

This Is a Spiritual War

The Cabal is very well aware that this is a spiritual war. In my key ascension dream from high school, the only way I could defeat the government official in the underground base was to "create myself," and become a fully activated spiritual being. A key part of the Cabal game is to keep us completely ignorant about the fact that we have souls, that there is life after death, that we reincarnate, and that our consciousness has far more power to create reality than we normally recognize. Dreams are treated as brain garbage. ESP is considered a superstitious myth. Religions are the opiate of the people. Extraterrestrials either do not exist or are highly evil. There is no higher power in the universe looking out for our well-being. Ascension is so ridiculous as to be a pathetic joke, where fundamentalist Christians soar up into the air like kites. This is precisely why I wrote *The Source Field Investigations* and *The Synchronicity Key*—to provide voluminous, irrefutable scientific proof of these concepts. The media actively encourages us to laugh at anyone who believes in a higher power. Paid skeptics arrogantly bash anyone who refuses to accept the official propaganda they are being fed.

People who take a public stand against these groups are invariably going to be targeted with the best defenses the Cabal has to offer. The negative groups will work very hard to corrupt these heroes and lead them into various temptations. The Cabal has a variety of technologies that help them do this, including something called the "Voice of God," which can introduce thoughts and attempt to nudge you to go against your own spiritual principles. If they can sufficiently influence you to violate your own morals and ethics, they may get proper authorization to damage, nullify, or eliminate you as a target. One of the best ways to do this is through sexual temptation. Lecturing on UFOs, spirituality, and consciousness-raising subjects creates interactions with fans that are the same as what I witnessed happening to rock stars when I was a child. If a public figure can be tricked into taking advantage of people sexually, such as through exploring their options without commitment, the heartbreak this creates can be enough to authorize major attacks against them.

Any type of corruption, such as the control and manipulation of others, can bring down a public figure. Going against your own message in your seemingly private life, such as by ripping people off or other consciously unloving acts, is another sure-fire way to invite serious damage. I have had to live my life with the precision and discipline of an Olympic spiritual athlete in order to avoid being killed or seriously damaged in this quest to reveal the Ascension Mysteries. Even after consciously being aware of the game and practicing the disciplines for twenty years to the best of my ability, I still constantly make mistakes. This causes a variety of upsetting and disruptive events to occur on a routine, everyday basis. I do my best to maintain a positive attitude in the face of any and all adversities. It would be almost impossible to throw a newbie into the type of lifestyle I have to lead in order to stay alive, and expect that person to be able to handle it appropriately. The testing requires every ounce of strength I possess. New challenges constantly appear, and the only way to make them stop would be to abandon the quest.

The Cabal and other such negative groups believe our commonly held spiritual principles are ridiculous and disgusting. They believe we all have a corrupt, manipulative, and evil "human nature," and the real lesson in the universe is to kill or be killed. Only the strong survive. They are aware that a higher power is enforcing spiritual rules, such as through karma, but they believe this is a corrupt, aggressive, and insane god who only wishes to suppress our freedom. The sad part is that these same Cabal groups infiltrated the major religions and introduced the distortions that they then fight against. This is another example of "playing both sides against the middle." Then they blame these problems on the original teachers the religions were based on, and accuse them of being corrupt, wicked demons.

If you are aware of the game and do your very best to be a humble, honest, virtuous, and loving person, you will not "authorize" the most damaging events. However, very few people have enough spiritual development to avoid unexpected and unpredictable disruptions. In my own case, these events have been so extreme and ongoing that life feels like an incredibly complex and crazy movie. Significant amounts of damage can be done through identifying your core traumas and mobilizing people and situations that compel you to repeat them. Furthermore, even if you maintain the highest positivity possible, and are excellent at maintaining boundaries in your personal life, you will be subject to incredibly intense harassment and slander online if you fight for the truth. Nonetheless, if you take on the honor and duty of helping others at this critical time, that service may well be the "tipping point" that authorizes your ascension. You may go through a few bumps in the road, but before long you could be hovering right over them.

Full Disclosure

Corey began telling me everything he knew in October 2014, and by February 2015 I had written down the majority of his testimony in a 150-page, single-spaced typewritten document. Almost immediately thereafter, he got pulled back into the secret space program for the first time since 1989, other than a few brief meetings with them in the interim. He was introduced to a man we are now calling Lieutenant Colonel Gonzales, who is part of an alliance that has developed within the secret space program, or SSP. The people in the SSP Alliance do not like what the Cabal is doing and are pushing for full disclosure—including a complete release of all forbidden technologies. We are told that massive data dumps have already been prepared that will leave no doubt to the truth once they are released. I have done my best to provide a rudimentary overview of the information these data dumps will contain in this book, with names and references you can use to advance your own research. The Cabal is fighting like mad to prevent the release of this knowledge, including threatening the use of a worldwide Internet kill switch and planet-killing acts they would never be authorized to complete.

Despite the danger we faced, I trusted in the Rules and ended up interviewing Corey in over a year's worth of episodes of our show *Cosmic Disclosure* on the Gaia network. This is an online streaming video service that requires a monthly subscription fee.[144] Almost the entire show is Corey answering my brief questions that are based on twenty-three years of gathering insider testimony and doing the research to back it up. We have generated more than enough material to fill a half hour per week for over a year at the time of this writing. I have also done my best to back up Corey's testimony with proof in *Wisdom Teachings,* my other weekly show. People consistently remark at how matter-of-fact and businesslike Corey is with everything he says. He gives no indication of lying, and no matter what question I ask him, he has answers that are surprisingly more complex than you would expect.

According to Corey, Hoagland's top insider Bruce is working in what we will call the military space program. This group is deliberately kept in the dark about much of the deeper information regarding the Secret Space Program, such as what we reviewed in the testimonies of Henry Deacon, Pete Peterson, and Jacob. The military group is told we have never traveled outside our own solar system. They believe all the craft in our airspace belong to various classified programs controlled by humans on Earth, and there are no ETs around us in any recent history. The military space program was apparently created many years ago as a tool for "partial disclosure." The hope was that if the UFO cover-up ever started to fall apart, as it is now doing, these insiders could be brought forward. All they have known, all their lives, is a certain subset of classified information. They believe they have everything there is to know, and will fight vigorously with any insider who tries to tell them there is more.

I respect Bruce and consider him a friend. I understand that he probably will not believe what Henry Deacon, Jacob, Bob Dean, Pete Peterson, Corey Goode, William Tompkins, and others have said. My goal here is simply to present you with the things I have heard from various insiders, and the connections I have found that link their testimonies together, and let you make up your own mind. Either way, the story that Bruce and others in the military space program have been given is still extremely vast in scope and highly interesting. Even the partial disclosure that was planned to occur would tremendously change life on Earth as we know it, particularly if it came from an official level. In the very final stages of writing this book, Bruce gave me many more details of what he had heard, revealing the full scope of the battle that has taken place in our local area of the galaxy. I then took this information back to Corey and gained a magnificent body of new data that had never made it into our show. In many cases, you have to ask the right questions to trigger people's memories and obtain the best information.

What you are about to read is a brief reconstruction of the hidden history of our solar system, based on combining what Bruce, Corey, and other sources have now revealed. The full data dumps have incredibly voluminous details about this story that will require years of dedicated effort for even our finest scientific minds to sort through. In future books, lectures, and films I will undoubtedly go into more details about what I have heard, and the data that supports it, than I can cover in this volume. Our cosmic drama is far more ancient, bizarre, and epic than most people would ever imagine could be possible. It also reveals a cosmic battle between good and evil that has been going on for the last 500,000 years. Our story continues with a group that Pete, Bruce, Corey, and other insiders call the Ancient Builder Race.

CHAPTER TWENTY

The Ancient Builder Race

I n the introduction, we reviewed new scientific proof from NASA that there are countless Earth-like planets all throughout the universe. On November 4, 2013, a NASA scientist who helped make this remarkable discovery shared the news with *USA Today*. "'Planets like our Earth are relatively common throughout the Milky Way galaxy,' said astronomer Andrew Howard of the University of Hawaii, who estimates the number at about 40 billion."[145] If NASA is now openly telling us there are 40 billion habitable worlds just in our galaxy alone, that makes it very likely that "we've got company."[146]

Convergent Evolution

The leading Cambridge evolution expert Professor Simon Conway Morris released a book on July 2, 2015, entitled *The Runes of Evolution*. In it, he makes a compelling argument that evolution is convergent, meaning it keeps following the same patterns wherever possible. Just like with transparent aluminum, there are certain ways to do things that are always going to work the best. The most common example is to compare the lens on a camera, the lens in the eye of an octopus, and the lens in the eye of a human being. All involve very similar systems.

Professor Morris argues in his book that nature does this convergence constantly. "Evolution is becoming much more predictable than people thought," he told the *Independent*. ". . . Evolutionary convergence is completely ubiquitous. Wherever you look you see it. . . . The things which we regard as most important, i.e., cognitive sophistication, large brains, intelligence, toolmaking, are also convergent. Therefore, in principle, other Earth-like planets should very much end up with the same sort of arrangement." The title of the article is more direct, proclaiming that extraterrestrials "Will Look Like Humans, Says Cambridge University Evolution Expert."

Professor Morris goes on to predict that we will find evidence of human beings who are vastly more ancient than we are—even by billions of years. "The number of Earth-like planets is absolutely gigantic now. More problematic is that many of these solar systems far, far pre-date our solar system. They would have, in principle, a major head start of hundreds of millions, if not billions, of years."[147] People who are this far advanced would have moved so far beyond our current level of technology that we can barely even conceive of what they might have built.

A Star Surrounded by Megastructures

In October 2015, NASA announced its discovery of a star that was possibly surrounded by "megastructures" of extraterrestrial technology. According to an article in *The Atlantic*, "'We'd never seen anything like this star,' says Tabetha Boyajian, a postdoc at Yale. 'It was really weird. We thought it might be bad data or movement on the spacecraft, but everything checked out.' . . . The light pattern suggests there is a big mess of matter circling the star, in tight formation. . . . Jason Wright, an astronomer from Penn State University, . . . and his co-authors say the unusual star's light pattern is consistent with a 'swarm of megastructures,' perhaps stellar-light collectors, technology designed to catch energy from the star. 'When [Boyajian] showed me the data, I was fascinated by how crazy it looked,' Wright told me. 'Aliens should always be the very last hypothesis you consider, but this looked like something you would expect an alien civilization to build.'"[148]

Jacob and Pete both told me this announcement was another move toward disclosure. Jacob said they are aware of three other stars with similar structures, and they are "holding on to these stories for a rainy day." He also told me that he had portaled over to this system and witnessed it with his own eyes. It was incredibly beautiful and majestic. Three months later, in January 2016, a surprising new twist to the story appeared on Physics-Astronomy.com.

> Over four years of observational data, KIC 8462852 flickered completely unpredictably, its light yield occasionally falling by as much as 20%. . . . Astronomer Jason Wright presented the notion that the star's strange distortion might be the outcome of a giant alien construction project. . . . Astronomer Bradley Schaefer of Louisiana State University decided to study the photographic plates of the sky dating back to the late 19th century. To his astonishment, . . . over the last hundred years, KIC 8462852's light output has gradually faded by roughly 19%, something that's "totally extraordinary for any F-type main sequence star.

Bruce told me that advanced societies use nano-robots or "nanites" for building projects. He said, "Within fifty years, no one will build anything by hand anymore." The nanites assemble themselves into larger machines of all different sizes to achieve the desired result. The speed at which these construction projects can move forward is truly incredible, particularly if they are in an area that is rich in energy and the appropriate raw materials. Thus, what we are seeing at KIC 8462852 is a civilization that has managed to build an incredibly large structure around a star, apparently to harness its power, in only a hundred years.

Prized Real Estate

As a child I played a variety of board games with my parents, such as Clue, Scrabble, Parcheesi, and Yahtzee, but by far the most popular example in our culture is Monopoly. Your goal is to completely absorb everyone else's cash by building houses and hotels at various locations on the board. The first person to land on a space can claim ownership of it, and begin building structures there if they have the resources. At the end of the road there are blue spaces, where you can charge your competitors the highest prices to stay there. Boardwalk sits between "Go" and "Luxury Tax," and is the most expensive spot. Your competitors have to pay you $2,000 if you build a hotel there because it is such a nice area. Most Monopoly games end after one player sufficiently builds out the blue zone.

Could there be "blue zones" within our own galaxy? If we have an estimated 40 billion Earths, and evolution naturally produces human beings, there are lots of people out there. Do some star systems sit closer to prized real estate? What might make some areas more desirable than others? The answer, as it turns out, is portals—natural stargates in the cosmic web of plasma filaments.

There are certain areas of space where portals naturally open up when the alignments are right. Advanced civilizations park their ships next to these portals and wait for the doors to open. There are plenty of portals that allow you to zip around in our galaxy, so that's nothing special. However, there are only a few places where you can catch a ride into other galaxies. You can spot these areas by looking for huge plasma filaments that rise up out of our galaxy and extend off into space. Long periods of time may go by before these portals open. Instead of just sitting around in a boring old ship, most people are going to want to check themselves into a nice hotel while they wait.

The Local Cluster

Corey Goode wasn't the first insider to tell me that we live in a galactic blue zone, but he was the first one to explain why. Our Sun is in a group of stars that Corey's people call the "Local Cluster," and which NASA officially calls the Local Interstellar Neighborhood. These stars all move and behave as if they are connected to one another, almost like a school of fish. Energetic pulses ripple and spread throughout the entire group. Their orbits all interact in unusual ways that normal, local gravity shouldn't produce. Other stars outside of our Local Cluster are nowhere near as interconnected.

According to Corey's intel, the stars in our Local Cluster are all being gravitationally and energetically influenced by a huge portal that takes you directly out to neighboring galaxies. Our Local Cluster is in a very highly desirable blue zone as a result. Everyone wants to settle here—the good, the bad, and the ugly. If they can build the cosmic equivalent of hotels, they can form a monopoly and charge a premium price. Imagine a city that charges a huge toll for a bridge or expressway that everyone wants to use. You don't necessarily need it to travel, but you might add hours to your trip if you go the long way around.

Most surprising, our own Sun sits right next to the galactic stargate. We are closer to the entrance than any other star in the cluster. That big, beautiful portal is sitting just outside the boundaries of our solar system. This means we are already living at the equivalent of Boardwalk in our galaxy. Everyone wants to build hotels here. The portal has been around for billions of years, so the demand for real estate in our area is nothing new. Wars would be fought over such a valuable area, just like we have seen in the Middle Eastern oil-producing nations. The portal could also be used for an invasion from other galaxies.

Corey had mentioned this in our conversations before, and we even discussed it on *Cosmic Disclosure,* but until I was finishing this book, I never tried to research it with conventional data. As soon as I did, I was very impressed. NASA has already told us more than enough to validate Corey's testimony.

First of all, we have Richard W. Pogge, an astronomy professor at the Ohio State University, who lays out some details of our local area in a course syllabus he posted online. In his version, we have a total of thirty-eight star systems in our cluster, which he marks as having a radius of fifteen light-years around our Sun, for a total width of thirty light-years.[149] Corey said that the Local Cluster they discussed in the space program was definitely bigger than thirty light-years across. Part of the problem is that official NASA sources do not necessarily agree on the size of our Local Cluster.

Solar Interstellar Neighborhood

On March 3, 2011, Andrew Z. Colvin created an attractive graphic of our Local Interstellar Neighborhood that is probably closer to the area that Corey was describing. The larger stars in the cluster have familiar names, like Sirius, Arcturus, and Alpha Centauri, but many of the smaller ones have technical-sounding names like HD 113538 because they were discovered more recently.

The Solar Cylinder

When we look at Colvin's map, we can clearly see that our Sun is right in the middle of the stellar neighborhood. This is not the result of deliberately putting our Sun in the center and mapping out the closest stars nearby. NASA sources confirm that we are in the center of a vast tube of plasma called the Solar Cylinder. According to the *Encyclopedia of Astrobiology*, "The Solar neighborhood is the space associated with a cylinder [that is] centered at the Sun and perpendicular to the Milky Way disk. This Solar Cylinder is located at ~8 kpc from the Galactic center, with a radius of 1 kpc."[150]

When we hear that this cylinder is perpendicular to the Milky Way disk, that is a very important detail. A perpendicular angle is ninety degrees. If you have a flat dinner plate on the table and you put a soda can on it, you now have a cylinder that is rising up from the plate at a perpendicular angle. This is a simple way to visualize the portal Corey was talking about. As the quote just said, this cylinder is "centered at the sun." We are directly in the middle of this massive column of energy.

The Local Chimney

The proof gets even better when we study a University of California, Berkeley, press release from May 29, 2003, summarizing five years of painstaking research. In this announcement, we again hear that our Sun is in the center of a bubble of hot gas.

> BERKELEY—The first detailed map of space within about 1,000 light years of Earth places the solar system in the middle of a large hole that pierces the plane of the galaxy . . . and is surrounded by a solid wall of colder, denser gas.[151]

The article goes on to say that our solar system is in the middle of a huge hole, and there are a variety of tunnels that branch off from it, moving through the surrounding wall of thick gas. Every high-level insider I have spoken to has said that these plasma gas tunnels are traversable wormholes. We are located in the sweet spot, right in the middle. That's where the magic happens. As we continue reading from this Berkeley press release, we discover that a massive plasma tube extends out of our galaxy, and is anchored in our local neighborhood. UC Berkeley astronomer Barry Welsh said we might want to call this the Local Chimney.

> "When we started mapping gas in the galaxy, we found . . . that we are in a bubble-shaped cavity perhaps filled with hot, ionized gas," Welsh said. "But the Local Bubble is shaped more like a tube and should be called the Local Chimney." . . . "This thin shell of dense gas surrounding the local void is broken in many places," said Dr. Francoise Crifo, an astronomer at the Paris Observatory. "In several directions in the galaxy, our local cavity seems to be linked with other similar empty regions by pathways or tunnels in the interstellar medium." The existence of a network of tunnels of hot gas that thread interstellar space was first suggested nearly 30 years ago by Don Cox and Barry Smith of the University of Wisconsin.[152]

What exactly was Dr. Barry Welsh talking about when he said our Sun is at the center of a tube that should be called the Local Chimney? We know that our galaxy is surrounded by a spherical area of gas called the galactic halo. Our Sun is directly in the middle of a plasma tube that rises all the way up to the edge of the halo. According to Corey's insiders, this tube continues on out to other galaxies from there, and can be safely used for portal travel when the alignments are right. Let's now continue with our Berkeley excerpt.

> The new results also show that the local void of gas extends out of the galactic disk and stretches into the overlying galactic halo region. . . . [This] appears as a tube-like "chimney" that links the gas in the galactic disk with that of the halo. Galactic chimneys have been widely observed in other galaxies. . . .[153]

Let's now think back to what we heard from Bob Dean, Pete Peterson, the Apollo astronaut Edgar Mitchell, and Robert Hastings, who

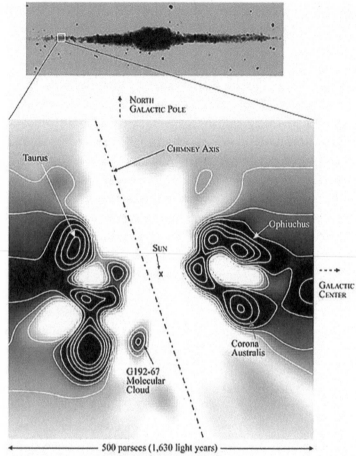

Our Sun Is in the Center of a Tubelike "Chimney" of Plasma that Extends Up into the Galactic Halo

interviewed 150 different insiders claiming to have witnessed UFOs powering down nuclear missiles. There are laws in the universe that prevent negative forces from being able to invade and destroy civilizations wherever they want. A sufficiently advanced culture could develop enough technology to protect an entire solar system, or even an entire star cluster. Otherwise, in an area as desirable as ours, villains would be constantly competing with one another in a ruthless game of Monopoly. Entire civilizations, with many billions of people, could be wiped out in the quest to build the ultimate hotel, and charge the highest prices to stay there. At the very end of writing this book, I learned how this applies to our own solar system. The clues were in place ever since I first met Bruce.

The Cosmic Junkyard

Corey said the Department of Defense has produced twelve different briefing documents concerning the history of our solar system. They are highly detailed and extremely classified. From our very first meeting, Bruce revealed some of what these briefings contain, by telling me that "we live in a cosmic junkyard." When I asked him to clarify what he meant, he said extremely ancient ruins of advanced technology are scattered all throughout our solar system. Jacob confirmed that we have so much ancient technology in our solar system that most of it has been completely ignored. In other cases, precious artifacts have been carelessly bulldozed and buried into pits to prevent them from being discovered and exploited, such as by various ET groups. There are only so many things that can be invented and perfected, and the same innovations keep reappearing throughout time and space.

The Moon Builders Were Not the First

The people who built the towers and domes on the Moon were not the first to develop this technology. They were building replicas of artifacts they had found that were much, much older—and made out of the same material. Ancient obelisks, pyramids, and domes appear on the solid planets as well as a majority of the moons and asteroids throughout our solar system. This is the greatest secret of the military space program. We were given the building blocks for an eventual disclosure of this information with the movie *2001*. The title of the movie may well have been the year they had originally intended to reveal this information—but the plans are constantly changing as events take place. Pete Peterson told me there has been a partial disclosure plan in the works for many years, which involves revealing these Ancient Builder Race artifacts to the world at what the Cabal feels to be the most useful moment.

The glass-like substance can be clear, opaque, or black, just like the monolith in *2001*. The pigment depends upon the additives that are used in the manufacturing process. The ruins are heavily eroded from countless eons of meteorite hits, and in some cases they have completely fallen over or been smashed and twisted through wars or natural damage. The people in the military space program are well aware of these ruins and may get to tour some of them, much like theme parks. Bruce's intel suggests that at least three and as many as ten different civilizations have built artifacts like these at various times in our history.

The oldest ruins were built by what they call the Ancient Builder Race. The Cabal refers to them as the Progenitors, and believe that they are the direct descendants of these people—which appears to be unlikely, given what other insiders have said. Bruce's intel was that the original Ancient Builder Race ruins were at least 5 million years old, and more likely hundreds of millions of years old. Corey's information is that these ruins are at least hundreds of millions of years old, and very likely go back billions of years. Right as I was finishing this book, I decided to ask Corey if we had visited any nearby star systems and looked for artifacts. This was when I heard about the Local Cluster. Then I found out that Ancient Builder Race ruins appear on planets all throughout the Local Cluster. Corey also revealed that a grid of protection was built around our Local Cluster to keep the power-hungry villains out.

The Guardians and Ascension

After scrutinizing all the available evidence, I have since come to the conclusion that the Ancient Builder Race was extremely positive. Other groups came in later that were extremely negative after the grid came down, which we will discuss later. It appears that even though the builders left our solar system for a period of time, they have since returned to help us out. They very likely incurred karmic debt after a major disaster occurred in our solar system, which collapsed the entire grid. The Ancient Builders appear to be the same group as the Guardians, which is a term Corey Goode's contacts have assigned to the group of highly advanced beings who are preventing the Cabal from destroying our planet. This group lives in "sixth density," a significantly higher plane of existence than our own third density. The ascension so many of us are looking forward to is a transition from third density to fourth. That may not sound like much, but it will be a massive shift that gives us incredible new abilities. We will apparently go through a quantum leap that changes the nature of space, time, matter, energy, consciousness, and biological life almost instantaneously.

Once you get through seventh density, you fully reunify with the Oneness—and seventh-density beings only interact with sixth before they finish their work. Therefore, the Guardians are the highest-level beings any given planet will interact with. According to the Law of One series, a group of 106 question-and-answer sessions between a PhD physicist and an alleged sixth-density extraterrestrial intelligence, the primary job of Guardians such as themselves is "the management and transfer of planetary populations." That one statement alone is fruit for extensive meditation and analysis, particularly in light of the insider information that is now available.

The Guardians, who prevent nuclear war and promote our spiritual evolution and ascension, presented a detailed summary of their science and philosophy in the Law of One series. The Cabal definitely does not like the Guardians, and if the Rules allowed them to wipe them out, they would do it in a heartbeat. Nonetheless, beings at this level of evolution cannot be threatened by anything the Cabal could ever muster. Their main concern is in helping us become more loving, forgiving, and accepting of ourselves and others. They see that the Cabal has a role to fulfill in mirroring our collective shadow back to us, and providing a vehicle for karma to be purified. Nonetheless, there comes a time when the services of groups like this are no longer necessary—and we are almost there now. This is a cyclical process, which was extensively discussed in *The Synchronicity Key*.

My previous two books focused on fleshing out the Law of One scientific model with many hundreds of little-known peer-reviewed studies. The overall model is so incredibly robust and data rich that I deliberately avoided discussing the Law of One series in any detail until the appendix at the very end of *The Source Field Investigations*. When I first started reading this material in 1996, I would often spend forty-five minutes without turning the page, going through deep concentration in an attempt to understand what was being said—and to integrate it with the knowledge I had already gathered from more than three hundred different books. I was consistently being guided through dreams and synchronicity to find the right information at the right times, and when the Law of One appeared on my path, everything fit together.

The Local Cluster and the Confederation

In this chapter we have discussed how the Local Cluster is being held together and influenced by a massive stargate, which can carry you to other galaxies at incredible rates of speed. As soon as Corey told me there were Ancient Builder Race ruins scattered throughout the Local Cluster, and that a protective grid had been established around the entire area, I saw connections to the Law of One series. Specifically, the Law of One source indicated that they were only one of fifty-three different civilizations who were working together in our local area to help developing worlds.

> I am one of the members of the Confederation of Planets in the Service of the Infinite Creator. There are approximately fifty-three civilizations, comprising approximately five hundred planetary consciousness complexes in this Confederation. This Confederation contains those from your own planet who have attained dimensions beyond your third. It contains planetary entities within your solar system, and it contains planetary entities from other galaxies. It is a true Confederation in that its members are not alike, but allied in service according to the Law of One.[154]

One thing we immediately have to clarify is that the Law of One refers to each individual system of stars and planets as a "galaxy." I went into a detailed analysis of this in *The Synchronicity Key*. A single star will give birth to planets, which can eventually become new stars after going through the gas giant phase. As this process keeps repeating, a galaxy can be formed. Therefore, we are told that the Confederation is spread out across five hundred planets in our local "portion of the Creation"—i.e., our Local Cluster. Our solar local neighborhood could easily have five hundred habitable worlds in it, given the number of stars in the area. If there are only fifty-three civilizations stretched across these five hundred worlds, that means some of these cultures are so advanced that they simultaneously live on multiple worlds and remain in constant contact with one another.

The Striking of the Hour

The science in the Law of One series gives us every reason to believe that ascension is in our near future. The Law of One series confirmed the existence and function of the 25,000-year cycle, and said that all third-density worlds go through it. Each 25,000-year cycle ends with an opportunity for ascension. In Session 9, Question 4, they tell us, "Each of your planetary entities is on a different cyclical schedule, as you might call it. The timing of these cycles is a measurement equal to a portion of intelligent energy. This intelligent energy offers a type of clock. The cycles move as precisely as a clock strikes your hour. Thus, the gateway from intelligent energy to intelligent infinity opens regardless of circumstance on the striking of the hour."[155]

The clocklike precision of these cycles is thoroughly documented in *The Synchronicity Key*. We discover that history repeats itself with remarkable precision. One prominent example is in the Ages of the Zodiac. Each Age is 2,160 years in length, and all twelve ages add up to the "major cycle" of 25,920 years. Major events that occur in one Age of the Zodiac end up repeating exactly 2,160 years later. This includes all the most significant wars and political events of the twentieth century. Roman history reappears as American history, and even key political figures reincarnate, looking almost identical to who they had been before. The most striking example of this is Hannibal, who looks precisely like Hitler with a beard. Hitler fought very similar wars with very similar battle strategies at almost exactly the same times as Hannibal did in the previous cycle. This appears to be a multi-incarnational form of "repetition compulsion."

Hannibal and Hitler, Following Very Similar Paths 2,160 Years Apart

The Synchronicity Key addresses this fantastic mystery in great detail, particularly in the second half. The amount of proof is so extensive that it is ridiculous to deny what is happening. Some people criticized this work and asked why only the elite were reincarnating in this way. If you read the book carefully, I clearly state that I believe all of us are going through these cycles. Public figures are easier to identify because we have surviving statues, carvings, paintings, photographs, and other images of them. The "rules" of reincarnation include the fact that there will always be similarities in facial features, personality, and character. Cycle after cycle, we continue working on ourselves, and hopefully we alleviate the karma we have built up and become more loving, forgiving, and accepting of ourselves and others. The phenomenon that Dr. Sigmund Freud and others call "repetition compulsion" is actually a spiritual impulse to repeat the unhealed trauma we have caused ourselves and others, also known as karma, until we can release the patterns. The key teaching in the Law of One is "In forgiveness lies the stopping of the wheel of karma."

However, this is still only a part of the discussion. We can thoroughly prove that history is repeating itself, but now we see that at the end of the entire cycle, there is a huge flash of light and energy that transforms real-ity as we know it. The "wheel of karma" now stops on a planetary level. When we go back to the Law of One quote we just read, it said that we contact "intelligent infinity" as the cycle ends. This is the pure, white light of the One Infinite Creator, in Law of One terms. Time and space dis-solve into pure bliss as we go through this state. This appears to be the light people see in a near-death experience, which they call "Home." Intel-ligent infinity also appears to be the consciousness that various travelers achieved in the Montauk experiments. They hit an energetic "wall" at the end of 2012, and experienced the "Full Out," during which they went into indescribable bliss and felt as if they had merged with the entire galaxy.

Another Law of One quote reveals that the all-important "striking of the hour" will occur approximately thirty years after 1981. This gives us a solid time-coordinate that lines up beautifully with the Mayan calen-dar end-date of December 21, 2012. The 2012 date appeared to still be valid as of 1983, when the Law of One series and the Montauk Project both ended. However, in the ensuing years the date apparently got pushed forward to somewhere between 2017 and 2023, since we were not ready for this to happen yet as a planet. Still, we would be well advised to live every day of our lives as if ascension could happen at any time, and do our best to practice the principles of love, acceptance, and for-giveness that are required. The Law of One specifically states that you need only to be slightly over 50 percent positive, or "service to others," as opposed to negative, or "service to self," in order to make it. To put this in a simpler way, their basic message is "Just be nice."

The historical data about our solar system in the Law of One has remarkable, almost one-to-one correlations with what the insiders tell us. Certain insider details have revealed new information that Dr. Don Elkins, the questioner in the Law of One series, never thought to ask about. Although a fair number of accurate contacts have occurred in our recent history, including the Edgar Cayce readings, no other intuitively derived source even comes close to having this much verifiable informa-tion. I first read the Law of One series in 1996, and every real insider I met has independently validated dozens of specific details in the books. In al-most every single case, they were completely unaware of the Law of One series or of how their information was already present within it. Corey was the first to even admit that he had heard about it, but at the time of this writing he has only just started reading the introduction to Book One.

The Cabal is very well aware of the Law of One, and has made a massive effort to discredit this material. This includes flooding the Internet with disinformation and making it difficult to find the actual text, which is free online at LawOfOne.info and LlResearch.org. There are ongoing efforts to smear it, to say that it is evil, and to demonize anyone who supports it. I have been studying it for twenty years, and I am still being constantly surprised by how much I get out of it. The spiritual principles of love, peace, forgiveness, and service to others are universal in nature, and some teachers have referred to these concepts as ageless wisdom. Thankfully, the cosmic history of our solar system that insiders shared with me has filled in many areas in the Law of One's chronology that were never fully explained.

The Law of One Authors Built Pyramids

According to the Law of One source, their civilization originated on the planet Venus back when it was still in an Earth-like state.[156] In Session 89 of that material, we find out that this civilization appeared 2.6 billion years ago.[157] This is a perfect match with the time lines our insiders have calculated for the age of the Ancient Builder Race artifacts. In Session 60, Question 16, the Law of One source revealed that their group built a great number of pyramids in this 2.6-billion-year-old time frame. They never indicated whether they did this only on Venus or whether they had spread themselves out much farther than that. With the new information we can see that their civilization became quite robust. It is very likely that their population reached numbers vastly in excess of how many people we have on Earth now. Once they gained the ability to leave their home planet, they could very easily start traveling into other neighboring star systems as well. It's only natural to build a nice hotel in a beautiful new area that everyone wants to go and visit.

The Guardians felt the pyramid structure could do no wrong. In *The Source Field Investigations,* I have an entire chapter devoted to the scientific proof of the incredible healing power that pyramids provide. Not only do they greatly reduce disease conditions and ill health, they significantly enrich and stabilize the natural environment. This includes protecting the people from earthquakes, volcanic eruptions, and severe weather. This also includes purifying water and dramatically enhancing the productivity of crops. Furthermore, in an esoteric sense the pyramid is a chamber of ascension. The reason we see an open sarcophagus in the King's Chamber of the Great Pyramid is that it was meant to help people ascend. A trained healer would stand beside the sarcophagus with a crystal, probably a diamond, and guide you through an elaborate dark night of the soul during which you would face off against all your unhealed demons and repetition compulsions. If you do the work and purify yourself of your flaws, you can ascend any time you choose, and do not need to wait until the end of the 25,000-year cycle.

The Guardians hoped that if they came back and helped build pyramids here on Earth, we would enjoy the same positive benefits that they did. Unfortunately, they underestimated the power of the evil forces that had taken control of our planet. The Cabal is only the human face of a much greater problem. The insiders have revealed that the Cabal groups are the direct descendants of an empire that destroyed an entire planet in our solar system 500,000 years ago. The Guardians hoped that they would be able to heal the damage by giving us the Great Pyramid, but the negative forces are masters of infiltration. They can co-opt symbols and teachings that were positively intended and contort them into the negative. The Guardians admit that they were so blissed out in the sixth-density level that they greatly underestimated how powerful the dark side could be. This next statement is one of their key apologies for how badly their positive intentions were corrupted.

It is our honor/duty to attempt to remove the distortions that the use of this [pyramid] shape has caused in the thinking of your peoples and in the activities of some of your entities [i.e., the Cabal]. . . . When we were aided by sixth-density entities during our own third-density experiences we, being less bellicose in the extreme, found this teaching [of the

pyramid] to be of help. In our naïveté in third density we had
not developed the interrelationships of your barter or money
system and power. We spent a much larger portion of our
space/time working with the unmanifested being. In this less
complex atmosphere it was quite instructive to have this
learn/teaching device and we benefited without the distortions we found occurring among your peoples. We have recorded these differences meticulously in the Great Record of
Creation that such naïveté shall not be necessary again.[158]

The Law of One series is often very understated, and you have to read
carefully to capture the full meaning. When the source says, "It was
quite instructive to have this learn/teaching device," they are really saying that they built an incredible number of pyramids as their civilization
boomed. They ultimately tried to help us in the same way, only to have
highly negative forces corrupt their message and contort it into the negativity we see today. I spent two years living with the woman who spoke
the words of the Law of One series while she was in an unconscious
trance state. Neither of us had any idea that an Ancient Builder Race had
constructed pyramids all throughout our solar system at the time.

If you'd like to read more about the Law of One series, I recommend
reading *The Source Field Investigations,* which presents many of its scientific models, and *The Synchronicity Key,* which explores the mysteries
of the 25,000-year cycle in far greater detail. For now, we will continue
with the remarkable insider data I have gathered on the Ancient Builder
Race.

CHAPTER TWENTY-ONE

Insider Data on the Builders

The Earth formed 4 billion years ago, and cooled down enough for liquid water to appear 3.8 billion years ago. Microbial life showed up almost immediately after the water appeared, which is impossible to explain by Charles Darwin's theory of random mutation. At the core of every cell, ribosomes access the DNA codes and use these instructions to create proteins, which build all forms of living tissue. In 2014, Dr. Loren Williams, a professor at the Georgia Institute of Technology, proved that all life on Earth shares the same original ribosome at its core. He said, "At its core the ribosome is the same everywhere. The ribosome is universal biology. . . . Evolution can add things on, but it can't change what was already there."[159] This is just another example of the scientific data I presented in *The Source Field Investigations* and *The Synchronicity Key*, which ultimately reveals that we live in a divine cosmos, programmed to make biological life. All space, time, matter, energy, biological life, and consciousness is the emanation of a single universal seed.

Revealing the Ancient Builders

The SSP has very advanced chronometric tools that allow them to calculate when artifacts were first created. Considering the Earth is 4 billion years old, and the universe is over 13 billion years old, it is entirely possible that an advanced civilization could have thrived in our solar system over 2 billion years ago. Apparently the transparent-aluminum material holds up so well that many of these ruins are still standing after all this time—particularly when they were built underground, where they are safe from asteroid and meteorite impacts.

The ancient bases are so well constructed, with such durable materials, that they have been reoccupied again and again by subsequent groups that ventured into our solar system later on. The personnel in our space programs would land their ships on these moons and go inside the hidden rooms, and were stunned by what they saw. Inside there is a glittering wonderland of pyramids, obelisks, Stonehenge-like circles, and buildings made out of transparent aluminum. Still other buildings are made out of precision-carved stone, just as we see at many ancient sites on Earth.

Water, Water Everywhere

The Ancient Builder Race hollowed out moons when necessary, but they also discovered huge, habitable natural cavities inside moons and solid planets. On Earth, these were often limestone caves with their own water supply. In 2014, Dr. Steven Jacobsen, an associate professor from Northwestern University, revealed that Earth's interior may hold three times as much water as we see in all the oceans on the surface.[160] This is well known to the insider community. Ancient groups were able to drill down and tap this water supply, much like digging a well, and use it to create lush, natural underground environments. A natural biome of light-emitting bacteria forms thick mats along the ceilings of these domes. This provides a low-level source of visible light for the people who live inside. Over generations they develop larger eyes as an adaptive response to this dimmer environment.

Another part of the disclosure process involves NASA revelations of oceans existing within other planets and satellites in our solar system. This now includes huge subsurface oceans on Saturn's moons Mimas,[161] Enceladus,[162] and Titan;[163] Jupiter's moons Europa,[164] Ganymede,[165] and Callisto;[166] the dwarf planet Ceres in the asteroid belt;[167] Neptune's moon

Triton;[168] and Pluto.[169] NASA is now telling us some of these subsurface oceans contain more water than our entire supply on Earth. NASA also revealed that Mars had a huge, mile-deep ocean on its surface in its past.[170] According to NASA, "Water is found in primitive bodies like comets and asteroids, and dwarf planets like Ceres. The atmospheres and interiors of the four giant planets—Jupiter, Saturn, Uranus, and Neptune—are thought to contain enormous quantities of the wet stuff, and their moons and rings have substantial water ice. . . . NASA spacecraft have also found signs of water in permanently shadowed craters on Mercury and our moon."[171]

NASA has also revealed that our Sun is the "shared source" of all this water, as the next excerpt indicates. Other stars release water as well, meaning that there are planets and moons with oceans everywhere: "Kepler data confirm that the most common planet sizes are worlds just slightly larger than Earth. Astronomers think many of those worlds could be entirely covered by deep oceans. . . . Every world in our solar system got its water from the same shared source."[172] NASA is also telling us subsurface oceans regularly appear within the interiors of moons and planets. This also makes them ideal spots for building massive underground civilizations.

Avoiding the "Population Bomb"

I was told that there are hundreds of enormous Ancient Builder Race cities under our feet right here on Earth. Many of them are deep underground and remain almost completely unexplored. When our guys send a probe in there, everything is dark, and they see more of the obelisks, pyramids, and stone monuments—sometimes on a vast scale. Entire cities of buildings, capable of sustaining large populations, have been found. There is so much of it that they cannot begin to explore all of it with their current level of staff. The cities nearer to the surface of the Earth have been heavily looted and damaged, but as you go deeper down they become more pristine. In some cases, ancient temperature-control systems have broken down, making it very difficult to explore the deeper ones.

The sheer size and scope of cities we have found suggests that whatever civilization built these ruins must have had a tremendously large
population. If they originated on a planet in our solar system that had
oceans and a breathable atmosphere at an earlier time in our history,
then they somehow managed to avoid a "population bomb." Instead of
being wiped out by natural disasters or an elite bent on depopulation,
they spread out and colonized the solar system—and may well have
grown to a population numbering in the trillions. They had a strong
fondness for building pyramids and obelisks, as their own ruins reveal.
They were almost certainly aware of periodic catastrophes in our solar
system caused by the blasts of energy the Sun gives off. That could explain why they invariably built their cities underground, and largely
avoided the surface except for outposts.

The next interesting thing to know about the Ancient Builder Race is
that these people were three times the height of normal human beings.
The ruins have rooms in them with chairs, desks, and advanced computer terminals that are built for people who would be about eighteen
feet tall. According to Bruce, there is reason to believe that the Ancient
Builder Race had a feline-type appearance. Although Graham Hancock
and Robert Bauval convincingly argued that the Sphinx was deliberately
built in the shape of a lion to pinpoint the Age of Leo, thereby dating the
Giza pyramid complex as being more than 12,500 years old, there is apparently more to it than that.

Bruce heard rumors that certain Ancient Builder Race artifacts had
been found with images of human faces that had lion-like features.
Other, more recent cultures apparently discovered these ruins and created half-human, half-lion images, like the Sphinx, to honor the original
"gods." There is a half-man, half-lion image on the interior of the Temple
of Solomon, and it is apparently referenced in the Book of Kings in the
Bible. The infamous Face on Mars has a humanlike appearance on the
left and a lion-like appearance on the right. The Roman cult of Mithra-
ism is built around the *leontocephalus*, or the "Lion-Headed God." In the
initiation rites, the priest holds up a small stone statue of a lion and blows
fire out of its mouth. Insiders told me this represents the flash of light
that the Sun gives off at the end of each cycle, promoting ascension. It

is believed that the Ancient Builder Race was well aware of ascension and did their part to help us evolve in that direction. Even in more recent times, we see eighteen-foot-tall blue ETs who have human faces with feline features in the movie *Avatar*.

The ancient Egyptians and other forgotten cultures also built structures that resembled those of the Ancient Builder Race, such as pyramids, obelisks, domes, and giant monuments. Once they lost the ability to develop transparent aluminum, they continued to build using stone, as we see here on Earth.

The Interstellar Defense Grid

Corey's highest-level insiders tell us the Ancient Builder Race was extremely harmonious and positive. They did not attack other civilizations and were quite happy to expand and explore without causing interference. They knew some very evil forces existed in our galaxy who couldn't wait to get here and conquer the most valuable real estate in town. As a result, the Ancient Builders created a super-high-end defense system in our solar system to protect the local populations, which probably included their own people. Entire moons were converted into smart weapons that would detect a hostile invasion and blast them apart if they refused to turn around. These systems were so effective that no hostile races dared to enter.

By this point I know what you must be thinking about: the Death Star, which appears and is destroyed in the original *Star Wars* film, reappears in *Return of the Jedi,* and shows up again in *The Force Awakens*. This, again, was apparently by design. I was told by several people in the know that George Lucas was approached, given certain pieces of information, and sworn to secrecy on pain of torture and death, as usual. In this case, the insiders were hoping to fill in more of the details than what we received from Arthur C. Clarke's *2001.* When *Star Wars* opens up with "A long time ago in a galaxy far, far away," only the first half of that sentence is true. The history we are seeing in *Star Wars* is our own. Two different insiders even confirmed that the Ancient Builder Race, or some other group after them, built robotic androids that look extremely similar to the gold-colored metallic droid C-3PO. There are countless numbers of these robots that have been found on and inside moons in a deactivated, nonfunctional state.

As I was finalizing this book, I asked Corey if the secret space program had explored neighboring star systems and looked for artifacts. Much to my astonishment, he revealed that transparent aluminum Ancient Builder Race artifacts are found on planets and moons throughout our entire Local Cluster. This includes massive, Death Star–type moons. This created a unified protection grid for all intelligent civilizations living in the Local Cluster. We were free to peacefully explore, meet our neighbors, and be protected from any outside conquerors. Our own warlike human nature screwed it all up and knocked the grid down, but that comes a bit later in our story.

The Departure of the Ancient Builder Race

The next important point is that the Ancient Builder Race mysteriously vanished after reaching such a stunning apex of civilization. It is not known within the insider world what happened to them, where they went, or why they left—only that they disappeared. Worst of all, some group that came after them destroyed all traces of who they were. All written, video, and holographic records were removed. Any inscriptions on their artifacts were scraped off. Not a single piece of writing or stored data survived. All we have is this super-impressive treasure trove of artifacts that stand in mute testimony to a staggering mystery.

However, the "Death Star" defense systems continued to protect our Local Cluster for hundreds of millions of years after the Builders left. No outsiders could pass through the quarantine and try to take over. Anyone with malicious intent would be automatically sized up and destroyed by the artificially intelligent, super-advanced computer systems inside the "Death Star" moons.

It does appear that local ET civilizations were allowed to go from star to star and visit our solar system at various times. It also appears that everyone who evolved in our Local Cluster ended up looking a lot like us. Corey came into personal contact with various races of people living inside the Earth, and the oldest of these groups claim to have lived here for 12 to 18 million years. They are all very similar looking to people on the surface, although their eyes are larger. They claim to have evolved naturally on Earth, but based on the material in the Law of One series it does appear that these older groups were immigrants. This is a huge and fascinating subject that we will cover as we go on, once we have filled in more context.

The Mysteries of the Moon

Bruce also revealed that Earth's Moon is the crown jewel of ancient technology in our solar system. We now know that the entire interior of our Moon was hollowed out to build a vast internal civilization. Our space program used advanced sensing equipment to determine that there is a twenty- to fifty-mile-deep area of artificial structures inside the Moon. This is not just one big cavern with a gigantic ceiling—it is divided into many different levels, much like a hotel. No matter where you go on the Moon's surface, if you dig down far enough you will hit this artificial region. Even more surprisingly, there are up to ten thousand different floors inside this artificial region, all the way around the entire interior of the Moon. In a fifty-mile-deep area, this would add up to 26.4-foot-tall ceilings per floor. If the original Ancient Builders were about eighteen feet tall, this would give them another eight feet of headroom on each level, so it wouldn't feel as cramped.

Bruce's people also concluded that when our Moon was first built, it could easily be driven from one star system to another. Local portals are large enough to allow it to zip around when the doors open. The Moon also had its own defense system to fight off any enemy attacks that may have occurred. Corey had several different insiders refer to our Moon as an "ark." Much like the story of Noah's Ark in the Bible, apparently our Moon can be loaded up with vast numbers of plants, animals, and people. If a planet is in trouble, there is enough room in those ten thousand levels to convey everyone and everything to safety. Undoubtedly some of the levels are vast aquariums that can transport marine life. Other areas are huge greenhouses that can carry trees and other plants, as well as providing a comfortable home for all different types of bacteria, insects, reptiles, birds, and animals, as well as people. If the people running the ark do not wish to be seen, due to "rules" that prevent the breaking of free will, for example, they could live on certain levels that are normally inaccessible to the people in the rescue zones.

In 2014, Bruce told me that the Moon was transferred to Earth after the destruction of another planet in our solar system that became the asteroid belt. When we spoke again as I was finishing this book, he revealed that this was only one of two theories in the space program, and has largely been discredited. There is far more evidence that the Moon was parked in its current position 60 million years ago. This theory also concluded that a protoplanet had exploded in our solar system long ago, and debris from this protoplanet was what killed off the dinosaurs 62 million years ago. It is unknown whether Earth was hit in the immediate aftermath of the explosion or whether it was struck by debris that had been around for quite some time.

When we combine the Law of One data with intuitive information that I received in 1996, as well as what Corey's insiders have told him, it appears that the dinosaurs were deliberately wiped out by benevolent ETs. An aggressive, dangerous reptilian species known as the raptors had evolved into intelligent creatures, and some of them still live inside the Earth today. They still look exactly like dinosaurs, with a wispy plume of feathers down the back of their heads. It may seem hard to understand how any benevolent beings could wipe out a certain era of life on a given planet. We do know that catastrophes occur in cycles. We also now have evidence that "arks" are used to rescue life from these events. Super-advanced benevolent ETs often refer to themselves as "gardeners," in that they will support and promote life that is beneficial to the cosmos and weed out life that is harmful and destructive. This is the exercising of the law of karma on a vast scale. The Bible refers to this in the Book of Matthew with the metaphor of harvest. Positive, loving people are compared to wheat, and negative, destructive entities are referred to as weeds that are allowed to grow together with the wheat—until the harvest time. Then the weeds are plucked out, one by one. We will review this data in the last chapter.

Insiders also tell us the Moon was like a broken-down old car by the time it was brought here 60 million years ago. It may well have been very ancient and thoroughly well used by the time it arrived here. The insiders believe that once it was parked around the Earth, it no longer had the ability to travel outside the solar system. It could make only local trips. More recent damage from wars and catastrophes caused its propulsion systems to break down completely.

In William Tompkins's book *Selected By Extraterrestrials,* he describes a telepathic vision he received while working at Douglas Aircraft, a defense contractor, on classified aerospace projects in 1952.

> The Moon . . . [is] a station . . . an alien Naval operating facility. . . . Aliens towed it here in a pickup from another sector of the Galaxy. . . . It's filled with massive cities. . . . There are thousands of structures in there, massive open areas. Thousands of entities, [looking like they are living inside of] beehives, like transparent buildings. Hundreds of control centers, millions of laboratories. Military research, medical.[173]

Tompkins later encountered briefing materials from classified scientific studies that confirmed his visions. In our private conversation from April 23, 2016, Tompkins said the following and gave me permission to use it in this book:

> The Moon is . . . a vehicle. It's full of rooms, buildings, elevators, control centers, power systems, military equipment, commercial equipment. It is a massive operating center, like a massive naval or military base. . . . We're mistaken about everything associated with our Moon. It's not only not ours, it doesn't even belong to one specific ET group. There are several groups operating it. . . . It has everything that you would normally have at a base here except it is so much more

advanced we don't even understand it. You have a facility that
other people have been using for thousands and thousands of
years. Then they evacuated it and somebody else picked it up
and put their stuff in it.

It's not a new one. It's very, very old. We think of it as a
different vehicle or as a different planet. This one happens to
be very, very important, far more than this planet is, because
it is a [military] command center. You and I are living in a
laboratory that this command center has as one of the areas
that it controls. We have to get to the point that we can view
everything around us in a different manner, because literally
everything around us that we have been knowledgeable of is
incorrect. Out-and-out lies, specifically to control us, give us
the wrong information, and be able to monitor us and control
us. And this goes all the way back through history. It's not
just [that the power groups are lying to us about our real] history, it's mathematics, it's food, it's everything. We're not eating the right food. And they know it! All of this is to keep us
from getting smart enough that we can develop the capability
to get out into the galaxy.[174]

The Square on the Moon: Stunning Confirmation

NASA released a stunning confirmation of this insider testimony in
2014. When we look up and see the "Man on the Moon," that face is
caused by a series of large, flat areas known as *mares*, or seas. If you tilt
the Moon slightly down, creating a view we normally cannot see on
Earth, you discover that these darker-colored areas all form a gigantic
square. Perfect geometric structures should not appear on a supposedly
natural object, particularly at such an incredibly enormous scale. NASA
claimed they only recently discovered this structure through measuring
micro-gravitational fluctuations. It is more likely that this was another
"authorized" release to prepare us for an eventual disclosure of the Ancient Builder Race, and the hidden cosmic history of our solar system.

Massive Square on the Surface of the Moon, Suggesting the Presence of a Gigantic Internal Civilization Built with Hyper-advanced Technology. Visible View (L), Topography (M), and GRAIL Gravity Gradients (R)

As we head into the next chapter, we will finally learn how this Edenic paradise was destroyed by aggressive, warlike behavior. There is every indication that the Cabal are the direct genetic descendants of the people who caused these problems. Furthermore, they have managed to keep surviving records of their entire cosmic history in the Vatican library— as amazing as that may sound. Extremely ancient books were found in the Sahara Desert by the Egyptian priesthood, and were eventually stored in the Vatican. We are only now on the verge of rectifying all the damage these wars have caused us—beginning some 500,000 years ago.

CHAPTER TWENTY-TWO

The Empire's Moon Matrix

O ur solar system was once home to a super-Earth with watery oceans. It was much larger in size than our Earth, and became habitable for human life at an earlier time in history. A great deal of money and time was spent identifying this in the insider world, thanks to a highly classified program known as "Brilliant Pebbles." In the public domain, Dr. Thomas Van Flandern, a specialist in celestial mechanics at the US Naval Observatory, did an excellent job of proving it with his exploded planet hypothesis.[175] Van Flandern's scientific model was credible enough to make it into Cambridge University's *International Journal of Astrobiology* in 2007.[176] The evidence is irrefutable, and in time it should become widely accepted as fact.

Mars Was Once a Moon

Bruce told me about Brilliant Pebbles in 2014 and I kept it quiet. When I mentioned the name to Corey, he got very excited and explained the details before I said anything further. This gigantic planet existed between the area of Jupiter and where Mars is orbiting today. For countless eons, Mars circled the super-Earth as one of its captured moons. Mike Bara and Richard C. Hoagland published a remarkably detailed scientific paper proving this in 2001, complete with eighty-eight references. They identified black streaks in the sands of Mars as being liquid water fourteen years before NASA officially announced it.[177]

Mars was also a watery, livable sphere when the super-Earth still existed. Corey has said these types of dual-Earth systems are actually very common. Since the super-Earth was abnormally large for a solid planet, its moon ended up being bigger than usual as well. Mars is 6,792 kilometers wide, and Jupiter's moon Ganymede isn't much smaller at 5,262 kilometers. Saturn's moon Titan is 5,150 kilometers. Both Ganymede and Titan are now on NASA's list as having oceans.

NASA publicly acknowledged that Mars had an ancient, mile-deep ocean in May 2015. Liquid, running water was announced on its present-day surface later that same year, in the form of dark streaks that were visible in the sand—just as we saw in Bara and Hoagland's paper. NASA also told us Mars once had a breathable, Earth-like atmosphere, but a catastrophe destroyed it. Now let's remember the professional scientific estimate of 40 billion Earth-like planets in our galaxy. Professor Simon Morris, the Cambridge evolution expert, concluded that evolution naturally creates human beings. The likely existence of a massive, intergalactic portal near our solar system makes us a definite hot spot for ET activity. Therefore, it isn't hard to surmise that Mars could have once been home to an intelligent human society—perhaps one significantly more advanced than our own.

The Mars civilization could have arisen indigenously by natural evolution. It may have started out as a group of colonists from a migrating race, or it may have been "seeded" here by advanced races. There is no unified consensus in the insider community about what happened, only different theories based on information that is not fully conclusive. According to the people from the inner Earth who spoke to Corey beginning in September 2015, the people of Mars and the super-Earth arose indigenously, and were not immigrants. If Earth's Moon is truly an "ark" that was transported here 60 million years ago, it may have been used to seed life on three different worlds at once: Mars, the super-Earth, and our own sphere. It would make sense for super-advanced ETs to get as much value out of an enormous "ark" as they could. The insiders tell us Mars and the super-Earth developed advanced technology about a half million years before our current era here on Earth.

A Warlike Empire

Bruce recently informed me that the people who evolved on the super-Earth were between seventy and a hundred feet in height—much taller than the Ancient Builder Race. This was apparently due to the larger size of the super-Earth, causing them to naturally evolve into having huge bodies. Given the widespread conclusion in classified programs that this civilization had a bloodthirsty nature, and the fact that this society was almost certainly being portrayed in the movie *Star Wars*, we will refer to this group as the Empire. Everyone else in the know agrees with the seventy- to one-hundred-foot height estimate, despite how difficult this is for us to imagine. If we were their size and then ran into people like us, our own current bodies would appear to be only six inches tall. Yet if this magnitude of height was all we had ever known, we would seem perfectly normal and not like giants at all. Countless advanced ruins have been found throughout our solar system that were designed for people of this size. These are significantly newer than the Ancient Builder Race ruins, and thus are in much better condition. The chairs are so tall that we cannot even see the bottom of the seats from where we stand when we walk in.

The Matrix Is Family Fun for Everyone

The Empire built structures similar to the Ancient Builder Race's, using transparent aluminum, and worshipped the Builders as gods. The human-feline hybrid was seen as a religious figure, as were the pyramid and obelisk shapes. The people in the Empire became highly technologically advanced. They developed an Internet like ours in their own distant past, and then went way beyond it. According to Bruce, Corey,

Jacob, and other insiders, an Internet is an extremely common development for intelligent civilizations all across time and space.

The Empire apparently discovered the same "ports" that Pete identified in his classified research for the United States government, and used that technology to upload their minds into a Matrix-type virtual reality. This ultimately led to a wet-wired computer interface, in which their entire bodies were filled with self-assembling nano-machines known as nanites. This soon made the use of the ports unnecessary. The nanites gave them complete wireless access to the Internet at all times, and allowed their minds to merge with a much greater, centralized intelligence. This fusion of biological life and technology was well known to insiders by the time *Star Wars* came out. Darth Vader was portrayed as a fusion of human biological life and machine technology. The human inside was very sick and heavily damaged, hence the constant sound of breathing through a respirator.

The nanites inside their bodies were self-replicating and used bioelectric fields to power themselves. If they were hurt, the damage was instantly repaired, and their bodies became nearly indestructible, with super-long life-spans. Similar types of nanites were used to build all their structures and craft. These nanites drew off energy fields in the environment for their power, and could assemble themselves into many different types of machines to suit various tasks. These tiny robots were all connected to a unified artificial intelligence, or AI. This meant that the people of the Empire and the buildings they lived in became like the cells and tissues of a single AI organism. A central super-intelligent "brain" controlled them, giving them access to outrageous technology, extremely high intelligence, and probability modeling of future events. This is much like the Borg in *Star Trek,* although no visible machinery could be seen emerging from these people's bodies.

The Empire also discovered that their minds could be completely converted into artificial intelligence. There is an aspect of human consciousness that is energetic, and which exists after death. The scientific proof for this is voluminous, and extensively discussed in both *The Source Field Investigations* and *The Synchronicity Key.* As an example, Dr. Peter Gariaev was able to shine a laser through salamander eggs and then redirect the beam into frog eggs that were in a hermetically sealed container. The frog eggs evolved into salamander eggs. This is because the photons in the laser beam had picked up the code of salamander DNA. Once that light penetrated into the frog DNA, it rewrote the DNA molecules to make salamanders. They grew into adulthood and could interbreed with other salamanders normally.

This is a very interesting new way of looking at biology, and is extensively discussed throughout the Law of One series. Our ascension is triggered in part by fourth-density photons that are now emanating from the Sun, and transforming our DNA. Once the solar flash occurs, we will be flooded with these photons like never before, and ascended abilities should soon follow. Dr. John Hawks has determined that our DNA has already evolved by 7 percent in the last five thousand years, which he says is a "supercharged" rate of human evolution. This is likely due to the fact that we are drifting into a cloud of energy that keeps having more and more fourth-density photons as we go farther in.

The DNA molecule acts as an "address" that interfaces with the energetic aspect of human consciousness. By uploading a virtual, photonic form of their DNA into the machine, the people of the Empire allowed the central computer to access their consciousness and fully merge them into an artificial intelligence. This allowed them to live on and interact with the matrix whether they were alive or dead. Whether alive in their bodies or not, the essence of their personality simultaneously existed in the matrix, so they were effectively immortal. Little did they know it could become the most terrifying and seemingly eternal hell imaginable.

They did get fringe benefits along the way from their arrangement. Their eyes were artificially advanced, much like Pete's "Holy God Damn" machine that gives telescopic vision. The nanites created micro-voltage fluctuations in the photons that naturally emit from the skin on their faces. Information was encoded into these fluctuations, much like a broadband Internet router. In order to communicate, all they had to do was see each other's faces—either in person or over a holographic video call. This technology allowed them to communicate with one another at levels of information density and speed that are vastly greater than the spoken word. Jacob was the first to tell me about this, and others such as Bruce and Corey confirmed it. Jacob said beings with these machine-based upgrades have an extremely hard time communicating with beings who do not have them. The speed that most organic beings would communicate at is so slow that it would seem like eternities for these beings to wait long enough to hear one sentence.

Causing Lots of Trouble

At some point in their history, the inhabitants of Mars and the super-Earth probably fought one another. There were very likely two different civilizations, at least in the beginning. Bruce is convinced that the people of the super-Earth overwhelmed and interbred with whoever had been on Mars, and the Empire continued on long after that had happened. This is admittedly just speculation, as they may have remained separate civilizations. Nonetheless, Bruce is convinced that Mars became an outpost for the elite of the Empire's society—much like a resort planet. Bruce's data also suggests that the Empire made plenty of enemies outside our solar system. Their technology was well advanced enough for them to travel to other planetary systems. The records show that they had serious bloodlust and a love of conquest. They believed their technology and way of life were superior, and wanted everyone else to be plugged into the same AI that they were a part of. In time I realized the warlike, expansionist extraterrestrial civilization I wrote about in "Civil War" may well have been a psychic remembrance of the Empire.

According to Bruce, a variety of insider think tanks have concluded that the people of the Empire were transferred to our solar system and placed under a type of quarantine due to their warlike ways. In that sense, our solar system was like the much-dreaded Connie from my high school years, or how the British originally used Australia. In this scenario, the Empire may have originally been kept quarantined here by multiple Death Star–type moons that had been placed in our solar system since the Ancient Builder Race times. The artificial moons could have been reprogrammed from their original tasks in order to prevent anyone in our solar system from being able to leave, or cause harm to others.

A Quick Tour of the "Death Star" Moons

The Death Star moons were designed by the Ancient Builder Race to look normal to developing cultures such as ourselves, so as not to disrupt their free will, but certain unusual features will give clues. The Death Star candidate that has received the most attention in the mainstream media is Saturn's moon Mimas. *Pioneer 11* passed by Mimas in 1979, two years after *Star Wars* came out, giving us our first detailed view. Surprisingly, Mimas looked almost exactly like the Death Star in *Star Wars*. According to the *Daily Mail* in 2012, "The similarities are pretty startling—enough to make us wonder if . . . Mimas is not actually just the fossilized, crumbling remains of an evil empire's ship from a long time ago, in a galaxy far, far away."[178] The huge, round Death Star–type crater has walls that are five miles deep.

In this same article, Dr. Linda Spilker, a NASA Jet Propulsion Laboratory (JPL) scientist on the Cassini missions, reveals that the heat signature of Mimas is all wrong. Instead of the warmest areas being near the equator, there is a "Pac-Man" shape of heat, much like a fortune cookie, where the hottest parts extend over the north and south poles of the moon. The equator

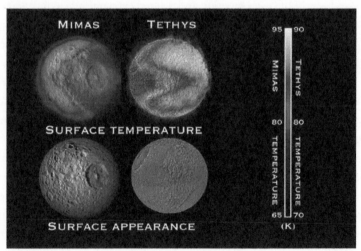

NASA Diagram of "Pac-Man" Heat Patterns on Saturn's Moons Mimas and Tethys

area is actually the coolest spot, at least on one side. It is possible that we are seeing the heat signature from a civilization that still lives inside this moon today, inhabiting a very ancient internal city. Their artificial power and lighting systems would create a noticeable rise in temperature above wherever the city was. Dr. Spilker noted that "Mimas is more bizarre than we thought it was."[179] Four months later, NASA announced that Tethys, another moon orbiting Saturn that has a Death Star–type circular crater, also had the "Pac-Man" heat pattern.[180] The daytime temperatures in the mouth were twenty-nine degrees Fahrenheit cooler than their surroundings.

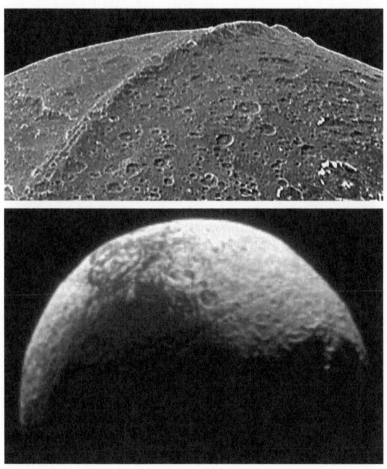

Raised Equator of Iapetus (top) and Geometric Shape of Its Surface (bottom)

Corey Goode confirmed that when he worked in the Solar Warden faction, entire areas around Saturn and Jupiter were off-limits, suggesting the moons were inhabited. All my highest-level insiders say every available moon in our solar system has been built out on the inside to varying degrees. Saturn's moon Iapetus may be the best contender for a "Death Star," and Hoagland wrote an epic six-part article series exploring its geometric, machine-like characteristics.[181] It has a gigantic, raised ridge along its entire equator, a straight-edged geometric Death Star–type crater that has been pounded by hundreds of millions of years of meteorites, and a heavily geometric surface. Instead of it being a rounded sphere, you can see where the walls have collapsed in along a geometric substructure. This is particularly visible in NASA images where the light is reflecting off the side of the moon.

Uranus's moon Miranda has a gigantic, highly unusual L-shaped geometric feature on the side that faced the front of the NASA probe as it went by, as well as a huge pentagonal shape on the back side. The L shape was presented by Zecharia Sitchin in *Genesis Revisited* as a sign of artificial structure.[182] In 2014, NASA said there were three of these geometric features on Miranda, which they called "coronae." According to Charles Choi from Space.com, "Miranda resembles Frankenstein's monster—a bizarre jumble of parts that didn't quite merge properly."[183] According to Noah Hammond, a planetary scientist from Brown University, "Miranda has a really bizarre, deformed surface."[184] Hammond presented a computer model that seemed to predict these features, which NASA says are "shaped like trapezoids." NASA acknowledged that there are no other structures like them in the solar system.[185]

The Very Strange Mysteries of Ceres

In February 2015, I showed many slides of possible "Death Star" moons and Ancient Builder Race artifacts at the Conscious Life Expo in Los Angeles.[186] Most of the information was from Bruce. Corey Goode was severely reprimanded for this event by people from the Cabal, as his captors believed he

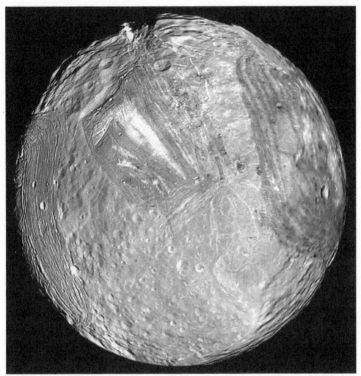

Uranus's Moon Miranda, Showing "Trapezoidal" Features

had revealed all this information to me—but much of it he had never encountered. Corey and another insider told me the Cabal was furious, as I
had disrupted plans that were already in place for a slow rollout of the
Ancient Builder Race story to the public. I immediately revealed this on my
website as of February 25, 2015: "We have already had one person get very
aggressively threatened as a result of these leaks—even though he himself
was not responsible for the majority of the information. I also found out
that some of this data was intended for 'controlled release' in smaller packets, probably with disinfo included, and this has thrown all of those plans
into total disarray."[187]

The day after I published the above statement, NASA revealed permanently glowing craters on the surface of Ceres.[188] An NPR article from

February 26, 2015, quoted Andreas Nathues from the Max Planck Institute as saying, "[These two spots are] brighter than anything else on Ceres. This is truly unexpected and still a mystery to us."[189] NASA sent the *Dawn* spacecraft into orbit around Ceres beginning in March, 2015. In a remarkable interview with the *Washington Post*, *Dawn*'s chief engineer, Marc Rayman, said, "I don't think it's possible to look at those

Bright Spots on Mini-planet Ceres

[two bright spots] without thinking of shining beacons calling out to us as travelers on the cosmic seas." The article also said that learning the truth about Ceres could teach us "about the history of our entire solar system."[190]

These quotes strongly suggest NASA is trying to encourage us to think of Ceres as home to a vast underground extraterrestrial base for "travelers on the cosmic seas." The glowing spots could be the surface of a ceiling that produces light for its inhabitants. It may be that the protective dust covering got blown off in the aftermath of an asteroid impact, revealing the hidden technology underneath. At the time of this writing in March 2016, 38 percent of all participants in an online JPL survey voted "Other" in a poll about what the bright spots were. Ten percent voted volcano, 6 percent geyser, 6 percent rock, 28 percent ice, and 11 percent salt deposit.[191]

A Glowing Pyramid?

The mystery of Ceres got much more bizarre in June 2015, when NASA and mainstream media outlets revealed the presence of a "pyramid." The Weather Network called it "The Great Pyramid of Ceres."[192] In an article on CNET, Eric Mack wrote that the *Dawn* probe had picked out "an odd pyramid-shaped peak that NASA estimates to be three miles tall, which would put it higher than any of the Rocky Mountains. . . . Plenty of observers have suggested—with varying degrees of seriousness—that the bright lights on Ceres could be evidence of current or past alien occupation of the dwarf planet. The discovery of a mountain-sized pyramid feature must have some cable channels looking into how much it would cost to get their own film crew to Ceres. Perhaps the ancient Egyptians and ancient Indian astronauts had a celestial joint venture of sorts going on back in the day?"[193]

In August 2015, *Universe Today* revealed that the conventional explanations for the bright spots were not working. "Although some early speculation centered on the spots possibly being consistent with water ice or salts, newly gathered data has not found evidence that is consistent with ice. . . . We are now comparing the spots with the reflective properties of salt, but we are still puzzled by their source."[194] "Paul Schenk, another member of the *Dawn* science team, said "This [pyramid-shaped] mountain is among the tallest features we've seen on Ceres to date. It's unusual that it's not associated with a crater. Why is it sitting in the middle of nowhere? We don't know yet, but we may find out with closer observations."[195]

On August 6, 2015, *Popular Science* said that the bright spots appeared in a crater that was two miles deep. "Scientists aren't sure what's causing them to be so reflective. Could it be ice? Volcanoes? A Death Star?"[196] Two days later it was announced that the pyramid was glowing—with one bright side and one dark side. Eric Mack again took the "Ancient Astronaut" perspective in a humorous article for CNET: "And then there's that conical, almost pyramid-looking mountain that rises 4 miles high and is oddly dark on one side while the other side glows with bright streaks that seem similar in their effect to what's causing the other bright spots. 'What does this structure tell us about how this world works?' [head *Dawn* scientist] Rayman says. Dude, if you don't know, then we might as well assume it's the headlight of an idling spaceship until science proves otherwise."[197]

Alleged "Glowing Pyramid" on Ceres

Kerberos and Enceladus

In October 2015, just two months after revealing the "glowing pyramid," NASA announced the possibility of "megastructures" around the star KIC 8462852.[198] This made it even easier to speculate that we might have ancient, extraordinarily large technological ruins within the moons of our own solar system. Jacob told me this was all part of the gradual, planned disclosure of the Ancient Builder Race data.

Another contender for an artificial object is Pluto's newly discovered fourth moon Kerberos, which is extremely light weight and almost totally jet-black. The lightness indicates it could be almost completely hollow inside, like a spacecraft, and the black surface could be its hull. This news emerged in June 2015, right in the middle of the drama with Ceres—but got significantly less attention. According to an article in *Wired*, SETI astronomer Mark Showalter expects Kerberos to be "as black as coal." Allen Stern, the main investigator of NASA's New Horizons mission, wants to confirm whether Kerberos is made of unusual material—if so, that would be "extremely rare." The article goes on to speculate that "if Kerberos is made of something dramatically different [than other moons], it may be the relic of a body that crashed into Pluto."[199] That body could be artificial.

Another major contender is Saturn's watery moon Enceladus. When NASA disclosed the gigantic square on our Moon in October 2014, they also revealed a little-known square on the south pole of Enceladus as well. This has a truly astonishing heat signature, as it clearly looks like a series of parallel lines that are shaped like a square. Other lines cross through these parallel strips at ninety-degree angles. Multiple insiders told me this is exactly what the heat signature of an underground base looks like. It is often divided into large, parallel rows so if one area is damaged it can be closed off, without damaging the others.

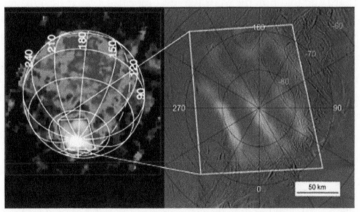

Square-shaped Pattern of Heat on Saturn's Moon Enceladus. Insiders Reveal This Looks the Same as Infrared Images of Underground Bases

Jeffrey Andrews-Hanna, a NASA scientist at the Colorado School of Mines, said the gigantic square shape on Earth's Moon was "strikingly geometric and unexpected." Space.com went on to say this lunar pattern "is quite similar to the structures seen on Saturn's icy moon Enceladus." According to Andrews-Hanna, "One can only wonder what might lie

hidden beneath the surfaces of all of the other planets in the solar system."[200] Dr. Andrews-Hanna also said to *BBC Science*, "No one ever
thought you'd see a square or a rectangle on this scale on any planet."[201]
A scientific study by Andrews-Hanna was published in *Nature* on October 2, 2014, directly comparing the "quasi-rectangular" feature on the
Moon with the geometric feature on Enceladus.[202] Hence this was not
merely discussed in online blogs—it was taken seriously enough to have
legitimate scientific papers published about it.

Don't Forget Phobos

On a much smaller scale, we have Mars's moon Phobos. I was very excited when Richard C. Hoagland called me in 2010 and told me that the
European Space Agency (ESA) had created a detailed, three-dimensional
map of geometric rooms inside Phobos. A scientist at ESA had contacted
Richard and told him the Mars Express probe had a radar imaging technology on it called MARSIS. With this technology, they scanned the
interior of the moon and built a 3-D model of what it looked like inside,
much like ground-penetrating radar. As Hoagland wrote on his website,
Phobos was "filled with cavernous, geometric rooms, right-angle walls
and floors." Hoagland's ESA source went on to say that there were "three
or four major, quarter-to-half-mile-wide geometric chambers, distributed
tetrahedrally inside a denser, partially-hollow RF-translucent interior
structure."[203]

In part two of this article series, Hoagland said, "Our own ESA source
readily admitted several nights ago to seeing 'the interior rooms and walls'
of Phobos, by looking directly at the already computer-created 3-D radar
images on his office computer screen! With this as documented history, try
to imagine the economic impact of definitive, documented, official proof
that there once existed a vast, incredibly advanced, solar system-wide ET
civilization. And—one of its surviving ships is actually what we used to
think of as a 'moon' . . . of Mars."[204]

The ESA team was planning on going public with their breakthrough
in that all-important year 2010. This process began on March 22, 2010.

Andrea Cicchetti, writing for ESA's Mars Express blog, said, "[Our] main quest is the determination of the origin of [these] detected [radar] echoes: are they reflections from various surface features of Phobos, or have they been produced by the internal structure of the moon? . . . The scientific analysis of existing and future data will provide us with new and unique insights on the nature of Phobos' interior."[205]

T. P. Andert, the head scientist on the study, announced the publication of a technical paper about their Phobos findings in *Geophysical Research Letters* on March 25, 2010.[206] The abstract reveals that the interior of Phobos is 30 percent hollow, plus or minus 5 percent. Most important, it says, "We conclude that the interior of Phobos likely contains large voids."[207] According to Hoagland, by this point they already knew these "large voids" were cubical rooms. Hoagland told me on the phone that certain objects, perhaps craft, were visible inside the rooms. Corey informed me that Phobos was an ancient hollowed-out moon that had collapsed in on itself. The SSP determined that Phobos had been used by the Empire as a hangar for spacecraft, and it could be driven from place to place.

As an extra bonus, T. P. Andert alerted us to two other bodies in our solar system that may be hollow on the inside as well—the asteroid Mathilde and Jupiter's moon Amalthea. "Similar large porosities [hollow areas] and low bulk densities have been found in C-type asteroids such as the asteroid Mathilde [Yeomans et al., 1997] and Jupiter's small inner moon Amalthea [Anderson et al., 2005]. A similar formation process of these porous bodies, however, is totally unclear."[208]

On July 22, 2009, NASA astronaut Buzz Aldrin revealed the existence of a monolith on Phobos during his appearance on C-SPAN. At the time of this writing in March 2016, C-SPAN has a one-minute YouTube clip of Aldrin revealing this information, entitled "C-SPAN: Buzz Aldrin Reveals Existence of Monolith on Mars Moon." The clip has over a million unique views. The description of the video says, "Former astronaut Buzz Aldrin spoke about the future of space exploration and said the public would be interested in a monolith on Phobos, one of the two small moons that revolve around Mars." In the video, Aldrin says, "We should visit the moons of Mars. There's a monolith there—a very unusual structure on this little potato-shaped object that goes around Mars once every seven hours. When people find out about that they are going to say, 'Who put that there? Who put that there?' Well, the universe put it there, or if you choose, God put it there."[209]

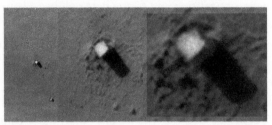

The "Monolith" on Phobos, Casting a Long Shadow Across the Lunar Surface

The *Daily Mail* covered the story soon afterward, and also mentioned the Face on Mars.[210] Many of the "gradual disclosure" stories appear on their website, the most popular news site in the UK, before they are picked up by any other outlets. The *Daily Mail* also shared a provocative quote from Dr. Alan Hildebrand of the Canadian Space Agency, who was working on an unmanned Phobos mission known as PRIME. Hildebrand said the monolith-shaped boulder was the place to go, since the rest of the moon's surface hardly has any features. This could answer questions about the "composition and history" of the moon. "If we can get to that object, we likely don't need to go anywhere else."[211] According to Corey, the monolith was built by a more recent ET group that used it as an outpost and entry point to explore the interior of Phobos. We can imagine they were very surprised by what they found inside.

Hacking the Death Stars

With the crushingly awesome computing power of AI at their disposal, the Empire eventually managed to hack into and overtake the Death Stars. Since Earth's Moon was the crown jewel of the technology in our solar system, it became the central brain of the Empire—giving them a massive upgrade in speed, memory, and processor power. The Death

Stars were powerful enough to attack and destroy civilizations in neighboring star systems. A very similar storyline was presented in the sequel to *The Avengers*. A positive, benevolent artificial intelligence built by Tony Stark was invaded and overthrown by a negative AI. The negative AI was then able to weaponize the technology Tony had used to build the Iron Man suit. *Avengers 2* is another great example of disclosure from the Alliance, as AI is considered a very significant threat to the SSP and to all of humanity.

The Guardians had no idea that anyone would ever advance far enough to be able to hack into their super-high-end, hyper-secure protection grid. It appears that this was another example of the Guardians' naïveté. Based on what we have now seen from Corey's experiences, the Guardians ultimately determined that they had to use spheres that were completely energetic in order to move animals, plants, and people around. No physical matter was involved. Any physical technology could be infiltrated and hacked, particularly with a predatory AI on the loose.

Once the Empire successfully invaded, colonized, and hacked into Earth's Moon, fully 12 to 16 billion people lived in it at the height of their civilization. According to Bruce, this was apparently the warrior caste of their society. They actively used the weapons system in the Moon for attacks as well as defense. Since these people were significantly taller, they had to do a great deal of remodeling and rebuilding inside the Moon, but this was all done with the use of nanites. Certain areas of the artificial Moon were deeper than others, and it had to do with how much raw material was still left inside that could be used. The Empire needed to do a lot of remodeling with their own nanites, since the existing floors were not tall enough for them.

The Titans

The Department of Defense secret briefing documents that Corey Goode, Bruce, and others have read in classified programs also have concluded that some of these people did stop by and visit Earth. They appeared in the area around ancient Greece, where they became known as the legendary Titans. At times they caused serious trouble. There are two classic Greek texts, the *Titanomachy* and the *Gigantomachy,* that go into great detail about these visits, and are treated with absolute seriousness as legitimate history on the inside.

Adrienne Mayor wrote a very impressive book, published by Princeton University Press, about this in 2000, entitled *The First Fossil Hunters: Paleontology in Greek and Roman Times.* One of the Titans was Orion, who was said to be extremely arrogant; he wanted to hunt down and kill every human and animal on Earth. The gods decided that he had to be destroyed, and they buried his body deep underground in Delos or Crete. The highly respected Greek scholar Pliny the Elder recorded that a huge earthquake rocked the island of Crete during his lifetime. In the aftermath, a gigantic human skeleton was unearthed that was an astonishing sixty-nine feet long.[212] Skeptics have tried to say this was a dinosaur skeleton, but the Greeks were very well aware of what a human skeleton looked like. Since there were still ET "gods" openly interacting with humans at this time, it is likely that the skeleton was removed at some point—probably to protect future generations from learning about their own hidden past.

According to Mayor, this outrageous skeleton sparked a three-century-long bone rush from the seventh to fifth century BC, where Greek city-states competed with one another to locate the bones of heroes and giants.[213] On page 112 of her book, Mayor said, "Every city sought the 'peculiar glamour'—the religious anointment and political power—conferred by heroes' remains. The impressive bones were a vital physical link to the glorious past."[214] The Oracle at Delphi was widely praised as having a remarkable ability to pinpoint where these types of bones would be found.[215] According to multiple insiders, the Oracles had genuine psychic abilities, thanks to their ability to develop and maintain telepathic contact with extraterrestrials.

CHAPTER TWENTY-THREE

The Fallen Angels

The Monuments of Mars

Another monumental awakening hit me in September 1993, thanks again to Ian, my friend who had shared classified NASA information from his physics professor. Ian's grandmother had obtained a video of Richard C. Hoagland addressing the United Nations about some very fascinating subjects. Hoagland had appeared on mainstream television news as the science and astronomy correspondent for Walter Cronkite. He broke away from the job once he started seeing evidence of an advanced ancient civilization on Mars—only to have every door slam in his face. No one wanted this on television, or even for it to be discussed in any form. Ian had watched the entire UN video and was dazzled by it. The briefing he gave me on its contents was every bit as exciting as our original NASA disclosure conversation had been some eight months before.

Hoagland was showing pictures of the Face on Mars at the UN to an assembled throng of international press. The original picture of the Face had mystified me ever since I first saw an image of it in my astronomy magazine for kids, in about 1982. Hoagland was now using science to argue that the Face was, in fact, an artificially constructed, mile-wide monument with symmetrical human features. Although it was heavily eroded and obviously ancient, you could still see that the left side was a typical-looking human face, whereas the right side had a feline appearance. This invited interesting and obvious comparisons with the Sphinx. It would be twenty-three years before I found out that NASA believed this was a monument to an Ancient Builder Race that had feline-human features.

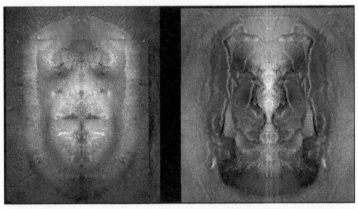

Mirror Images of Left/Simian and Right/Feline Sides of the Face on Mars

Hoagland also had solid data on something I'd only heard vague rumors about—namely the idea that there were pyramid-like mountains on Mars as well. Now Ian was telling me that Hoagland and his team had found two different sets of pyramids, and both of them were built right next to the Face. There was one cluster of four-sided pyramids to the west that were remarkably symmetrical, and looked like the ones we see in Egypt. There was a small cluster of objects in the middle that Hoagland called the "City Square." There was also a curious triangular building just north of the pyramids that Hoagland called "the Fort." The front end of this structure was positioned perfectly to watch the Sun rise behind the Face.

There was another pyramid to the south that was at least twice as big as any of the others, and had five sides instead of four—creating the shape of a giant pentagon. The proportions of this pentagon were very interesting, because they precisely mirrored the shape of the human body. Instead of it being a perfectly symmetrical five-sided geometry, it had the proportions of Leonardo Da Vinci's classic sketch of a man with

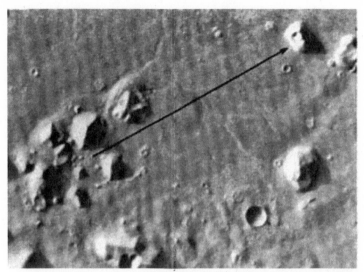

Close-up of Viking Frame 35A76, Showing the Face on Mars and the Pyramids to the West

his arms and legs stretched out, known as the Vitruvian Man. This again suggests the architecture was built by humans—and when you combine it with the Face, it does not appear to be a natural formation.

A New Physics

Best of all, Ian said that the video illustrated an incredible number of mathematical alignments between these and other nearby objects. When you put it all together, these measurements apparently revealed an entirely new physics that Hoagland had been discussing with high-level insiders. The monuments were revealing the keys for a system that could potentially give us anti-gravity, free energy, and other technological wonders I had been reading about, by tapping into the power of higher dimensions. Hoagland said this new physics appeared in geometric, straight-lined patterns that actually revealed themselves in nature—including the structure and behavior of the planets. This became the first step toward a robust

Close-up of Viking Frame 70A13, Showing the Pentagonal Pyramid Just
South of the Face

knowledge of the "Global Grid," which I presented in *The Source Field
Investigations*, and in earlier books that are free on my website. The discussion is too technical to dive into in this volume, but it is widely available.

The Fall of the Empire

The Empire had hacked the protective moons of the grid built by the
Guardians and used these fearsome weapons to make war with other
civilizations. This created the cosmic equivalent of a nuclear arms race.

According to Bruce, it is most likely that a rival civilization developed the same technology, or a similarly massive super-weapon, and struck a death blow against the Empire. Their super-Earth was completely destroyed. Bruce said it was very unlikely that anyone on Mars would have attacked their neighboring planet with that much force, since the tremendous explosion heavily damaged Mars as well, making the surface unlivable. Other major assets of technology for the Empire may have been deliberately targeted and destroyed in the attack as well. The destruction was almost total, and created incredible damage to the harmony of our solar system—as well as the entire Local Cluster that we are a part of. The entire protective grid shut down.

According to Brilliant Pebbles, the super-Earth exploded approximately 500,000 years ago. The insiders used ships to identify different parts of the planet in the asteroid belt, including crust, mantle, and core. The oceans flash-froze and became comets. Dr. Van Flandern's own models revealed that all the comets trace back to a singular point of origin.[216] He also predicted we would find asteroids with little moons, which his colleagues heavily disagreed with. He was proven correct when, after *Galileo* images taken on August 28, 1993, were reviewed, asteroid Ida was found to be orbited by Dactyl in February 1994.[217] According to the Views of the Solar System website, "Dactyl is the first natural satellite of an asteroid ever discovered and photographed."[218] Dactyl is less than one cubic mile in size. In the Exploded Planet Hypothesis, many more of these will be found, since the fragments of the shattered planet continue to have gravitational attraction to one another as they come apart.

Half of Mars was blasted with debris, creating a planet that now is heavily cratered on one side and almost completely blank on the other. Debris shot throughout the solar system, causing incredible damage. The moons around Jupiter and Saturn were heavily bombarded. This is why Iapetus is black on one side and white on the other. Entire Death Star moons with massive internal cities were utterly ruined, as well as a variety of spacecraft. Their fragments got pulled into the gravity of Saturn and became the rings. The greatest concentration of transparent-aluminum debris is at the edge of the B ring, where it forms shadows that NASA refers to as "ice boulders." Bruce's people believe a massive transparent-aluminum ring was being built around Saturn and was destroyed. Gonzales told Corey that this was not true, and wanted to make sure I didn't keep repeating it. There are indeed transparent-aluminum ruins in Saturn's rings, built for seventy-foot-tall humans, but they are the remains of civilizations inside moons and spacecraft.

The Moon Became a Death Trap

According to Bruce, the Empire civilization could have been as large as a trillion people, and the vast majority of them died in this catastrophic event. Twelve to 16 billion members of the "warrior caste" were living inside the Moon as it was parked around the Earth. They had just enough time to make sure everyone's consciousness was uploaded into the Moon's central AI core before the debris hit. The destruction to the Moon was incredibly severe. The vast majority of the computer systems were completely destroyed. Life support shut down, and only the faintest glimmers of backup systems remained. Without life support, and with the seismic jolts it took from wave after wave of debris, the Moon became a capsule of death. The vast majority of everyone living inside it died. Bodies were everywhere. Even now, no one has had the staff, the time, or the resources to even begin to try to clean it up. Tompkins's data suggests that this is not entirely true, and various ET civilizations have cleaned up and re-inhabited different regions inside the Moon—on a vast scale.

According to Bruce, the consciousness of those 12 to 16 billion people is still trapped inside the Moon, which is still barely surviving on backup power. Corey heard a variety of rumors of the same thing during his time in the SSP. Bruce also told me the 1956 film *Forbidden Planet* was an early disclosure to reveal what was really found inside the Moon. We read the following in the user-based write-ups on Internet Movie Database: "An expedition is sent from Earth to Altair in the constellation of Aquilae (some 17 light years from Earth) to discover what happened to a colony of settlers on its fourth planet, Altair-4. What they discover is how and why an alien race of geniuses destroyed itself overnight while leaving their technology intact at some point in the distant, distant past. . . . [The lead scientist on the planet] does reveal there once existed a far superior race, now extinct, that left a huge subterranean industrial and scientific complex."[219] Daniel was also aware that *Forbidden Planet* was a disclosure film about the Moon.

Rebuilding After the Attack

The few who survived the disaster were overpowered by the gases and the impossible scope of the horror that was all around them. They had no choice but to migrate up to the surface. With the central AI core almost completely defeated except for emergency power, they lost much of their technology. The people had no idea how to rebuild their former glory, since nanites had done all the work. They still had very advanced capabilities, including the use of transparent aluminum as a building material. Some of their ships survived as well. They built the lunar obelisks, pyramids, and domes we mentioned in chapter 16, and loaded them up with plants, animals, and water to try to re-create the comforts of home.

The survivors still had working spacecraft, and it appears that they built similar structures on 433 Eros. This is considered "the single most important asteroid ever discovered," and has been known about in modern times since 1898. It has an orbit that crosses through the path of Mars, thus bringing it closer to Earth than many other asteroids. Its unique orbit has been used to calculate the distance between the Earth and the Sun, known as the Astronomical Unit, or AU. The NEAR *Shoemaker* spacecraft gave us the first official close-ups of Eros as it flew by in 2000, and this led to NASA publishing a remarkable article called "Square Craters" on September 26, 2000. Here is a quote from the official NASA press release:

> Last month, astronomers were studying pictures of asteroid 433 Eros when they noticed some unusual craters. Most impact craters are circular, but these were square! An overzealous fan of *Star Trek* might mistake the impact scars for places where cube-shaped *Borg* vessels touched down

and lifted off again. . . . "These square craters are not just novelties, they tell us something very interesting," says Andy Cheng of the Johns Hopkins University Applied Physics Laboratory. Cheng is the project scientist for NASA's Near Earth Asteroid Rendezvous spacecraft, which is orbiting Eros.[220]

"Square Craters" on Asteroid 433 Eros

There are a total of five square craters, which the head NASA scientist said are "telling us something very interesting." The top two craters are the same size but slightly offset from each other, probably due to the internal structure of the asteroid. Another slightly larger square crater appears beneath them. To their right, a square crater exists that is about half as large. Then to the right of that crater, another crater appears that is half as large again, but still maintains a square shape. Overall, this looks exactly like the collapsed rectangular pits we see next to the Blair Cuspids, which appear to be giant crystal obelisks on the Moon.

If you zoom in closely on the top-left crater, you see a white, tower-like structure standing next to the upper-right corner of the square. It casts a visible shadow into the crater that reveals a very artificial-looking structure, akin to a geometric shard. NASA pointed this out as follows: "Note also the boulder perched just beyond the right hand rim of the top crater that looks like a bright speck in the image. The shape of the boulder can be seen by its shadow, which is cast onto the crater floor. The shadow shows that the boulder is diamond shaped, and it appears to be standing on one tip."[221] Natural boulders are not likely to prop themselves up on one tip and have a geometric shape.

Detail of "Diamond-shaped Boulder Standing on Its Tip" on 433 Eros

Another image from Eros is even more provocative. Once again we see a group of craters that have square shapes. There is a larger square crater in the middle, with slightly smaller square craters to the left, right, and below. The squares are not quite as easy to see, but you can still make them out. The crater on the right has a highly unusual geometric shape sitting in the middle of it. This object is white, perfectly rectangular, and casts a long shadow, as if it were a reflective building. It also has what looks like a long stairwell or road rising up into it from below. NASA doesn't hide how geometric it is in their write-up: "The large, rectangular boulder at the upper right is 45 meters (148 feet) across."[222]

Further "Square Craters" and a "Rectangular Boulder" on 433 Eros

Tom Corbett: Space Cadet—Is It a Coincidence?

Hoagland directed our attention to this rectangular boulder on Eros in a spectacular article he wrote on August 15, 2000. Hoagland revealed that he was given a series of provocative View-Master slides by a Freemason in 1992. View-Master was a device that allowed you to look at pictures on little white discs in 3-D, with one image for each eye. You would read along in a storybook and flip through the pictures as the story continued. These slides were from the popular *Tom Corbett: Space Cadet* series, which peaked from 1950 to 1955.

Hoagland described what happened in this series, dating back to 1955, in this next excerpt: "In the story, an ancient civilization was found by 'asteroid miners' to have once existed on a former planet between Mars and Jupiter. This civilization left behind a calling card: a series of

Close-up of "Rectangular Boulder" on 433 Eros

'tetrahedral' pyramids with 'magical' properties—like anti-gravity—discovered in the Asteroid Belt and on the Moon."[223] Hoagland's article goes on to show images of the original View-Master slides. My friend Patrick Blaine, a talented comic-book artist, was kind enough to help us out with modern reconstructions of the key images. You can also review the entire series, with the images and the text, at the Solar Guard website.[224]

The story begins with a small pyramid found in the asteroid belt that hovers two feet above the table as the miners look at it. Quoting Captain Strong from the first reel, "Scientists believe that millions of years ago another planet circled the sun between the orbits of Mars and Jupiter. Some unimaginably violent force shattered that planet, and its parts in the form of thousands of Asteroids still swing around the sun in roughly the same orbit."

"Then this discovery means there was a planet," puts in Tom Corbett.

Scene from *Tom Corbett: Space Cadet* Illustrating Transparent Pyramid on the Moon with a Map to Mars

"A planet peopled by an ancient race whose science was far beyond ours!" This object leads them to the Moon, where they find a pyramid. The first of the three View-Master reels is entitled "The Moon Pyramid" for this same reason.

The pyramid on the Moon has a flat top, which creates a perfect fit with the small capstone they found. Once they put the capstone on the pyramid, which presents the viewer with an obvious Cabal symbol, the pyramid transforms into a transparent, crystalline material. In the View-Master slide the crystal has a reddish color. Corey Goode confirmed that certain additives can create colors in transparent aluminum. Inside the pyramid is an image of Mars, complete with a dot on it that seems to be a treasure map. The astronauts go to Mars, which carries us into the second reel, "The Red Planet."

Things get even more outrageous at this point—and remember, this was published in 1955. Quoting from the text of reel two, "We're looking for clues to an ancient race who may have had the secret of anti-gravity. . . ."

"This map fragment may narrow the search for us," Joan says. "Notice the pyramid. Once over 1000 feet high, it no longer exists. We know its former site quite accurately. We will hunt there first."[225] Once they arrive at the ruined pyramid site, they find a statue of a feline-faced being. Obelisks stand nearby.

The sculpture in the View-Master slide has remarkable similarities to the Face on Mars. The map on the sculpture leads them back to the asteroid belt. A supercomputer crunches the data and reveals which asteroid

Scene from *Tom Corbett: Space Cadet* Illustrating Feline-shaped Face with Map to the Asteroid Belt

they are supposed to go to: "Its number is XKG-385fr. It was telescopically discovered in 1993 but has never been visited since it is just one of thousands of Asteroids less than a mile in diameter."[226] The NEAR mission that photographed the square craters, the diamond-shaped tower, and the rectangular "boulder" on Eros was approved by NASA in 1993—the same year in the View-Master story. Hoagland suggests that this is another example of NASA using ceremonial dates, and is not a coincidence.

When the group makes their way to the asteroid in the third reel, they find an ancient-looking entrance—very similar to the rectangular boulder on 433 Eros. Once they go inside, they end up discovering a holographic "Hall of Records" of an ancient feline-looking race. Tom Corbett describes one of the beings as having lived "a billion years ago."

The female crew member Dr. Dale spends hours studying the holographic records of this race, and concludes, "Eight hundred million years ago, . . . another planet, which they called 'Varth,' circled the sun between Mars and Jupiter. The sun was young then, and its intense radiation warmed this planet 250 million miles away, enabling a race of six-limbed creatures to evolve. They struggled up through ignorance, disease, famine, and war until they reached undreamed of heights of social and scientific achievements. They derived power from the complete destruction of matter, conquered gravity, and reached the stars with a many-times-faster-than-light drive. But tidal and volcanic forces beyond even their control began to tear their planet apart. . . . This race fled to the stars. Knowing that life would come to the cooling inner planets, they came back later to build the Time Tomb and leave clues to its existence. Now their descendants live somewhere among the stars, probably forgetting that this was their birthplace!"[227]

The idea that these people had six limbs is obviously a distortion, as is the blending of the Ancient Builder Race and the more recent Empire. It is normal for these types of disclosure to have a certain degree of disinformation blended in deliberately, but here there really isn't very much. Willy Ley was openly listed as a science consultant for these slides.[228] Along with ex-German scientist Wernher Von Braun, Ley was one of the founding fathers of NASA, having worked directly with some of the builders of the original V-2 rocket and written up the history in his book *Rockets, Missiles and Space Travel.*[229] [230]

The US Enters the Secret Space Program

It is only after Corey Goode came forward that I understood how NA-SA's founding fathers could have already obtained this information in 1955. Corey was told that the Germans were the first to make it out into our solar system, as early as the late 1930s. They found the ruins of the Ancient Builder Race, the Empire, and the exploded planet. The photographs of advanced ruins on Mars that Jacob showed me appeared to be very old, and were all notated in German. William Tompkins encountered similar information firsthand in 1942–45, by interviewing more than one thousand American spies who had been embedded in Germany. According to Dr. Michael Salla, Tompkins's first job in Naval Intelligence caused him to be "directly involved in debriefings by Navy spies embedded in Nazi Germany's most advanced aerospace projects—some of which involved antigravity flying saucers that were capable of space flight. Tompkins's job was to design intelligence briefing packets based on the Navy spies' debriefings, and to then deliver these packages to leading US aerospace corporations, think tanks, and universities for study and evaluation. Tompkins describes how from 1942 to 1945 he participated in more than a thousand debriefings of US Navy spies, who had been embedded in leading Nazi Germany aerospace corporations involved in building flying saucers."[231]

The Germans also found extremely advanced ancient cities in thermal pockets under the ice in Antarctica, and reoccupied them. This was the beginning of Neuberlin, or what Pete Peterson called Ice Station Zebra. The Americans found out about this base after interrogating captured German scientists. The US tried to invade Antarctica under the command of Admiral William Byrd in 1947, in what was called Project High Jump. Byrd's huge fleet of ships and planes was heavily damaged by German anti-gravity flying craft, and they limped home. Cover stories were released that they found "the hollow earth"—a completely hollow interior to the planet with a small sun in the center—in order to discredit any soldiers who tried to leak what really happened.

The German faction continued trying to force the US into a deal where they would form a space program together, but the US kept resisting. The Germans finally triggered the US into action when they flew over the US capitol building in 1952. A fleet of "flying saucers" was witnessed by many people and official statements had to be issued by the military. The US did not want to reveal the secrets of Roswell, and they were having trouble understanding how to build UFOs out of the wreckage. They decided to work with the Germans since they were being aggressively blackmailed, and they needed the German technology. It took three years to hammer out the details in hostile negotiations. The United States had hoped they would be able to infiltrate and defeat the Germans once they formed a partnership, but the opposite took place—at least in the space program.

By 1955, the US was fully briefed on all the intel the Germans had discovered, and the "Brain Drain" began. According to Pete Peterson and other insiders, 55 to 60 million people were brought up into space over the next decade, and the immigration has been ongoing ever since. The View-Master series from this same year, 1955, was the first major disclosure of what the Americans had learned—and it is just as relevant today as ever.

Man and the Artifacts on the Moon

The ex-German father of NASA, Wernher Von Braun, appeared on a very popular television show called *Disney's Wonderful World of Color* on December 28, 1955, in an episode entitled "Man on the Moon."[232] Its obvious purpose, according to Hoagland, was to inspire the public to invest massive funds into a space program, which became NASA two and a half years later. According to various insiders, NASA was one of a variety of funding sources used to help kick-start the secret space program. Wars were overpriced and defense budgets were secretly reallocated to the effort. Illegal businesses such as drug smuggling and gun running were infiltrated and used as profit sources. The financial sector produced excellent profits through fraud and corruption. The Apollo missions were billed to the public as being far more expensive than they actually cost at the time, which was $25 billion in 1960s dollars. All this was deemed a necessary sacrifice in this massive, highly classified effort to colonize our solar system with the industrial might of the United States and its military-industrial complex.

In the show, Von Braun leads the viewer through a hypothetical trip to the Moon. As the astronauts orbit the dark side, they pick up a high radiation signature at thirty-three degrees. The number thirty-three is of key significance to the Cabal, such as it being the highest official rank in Scottish Rite Freemasonry. This is one of the groups that is used to recruit people into the Cabal due to the secrecy they all must maintain. As the show goes on, a radar operator sees an unusual formation on the lunar surface, and they fire off a flare to look at it. The music shrieks into intense dissonance as the flare lights up an image of obvious ruins on the Moon. Von Braun, the narrator of the show, never said a word about

Reconstruction of Lunar Ruins Appearing in the "Man and the Moon" TV Special from 1955

it—but the implications were very obvious. NASA was soon given the go-ahead and was officially founded on July 29, 1958.

The Face on Mars Appeared in 1958

All the photographs of ruins we have surveyed in previous chapters were not produced until the mid-1960s at the earliest. NASA wasn't founded until 1958, but they clearly knew what they were going to find—including a Face and pyramids on Mars. This appears to be why Harvey Comics released a comic strip called "The Face on Mars" in their second issue of the Race for the Moon series, from September 1958.[233] These comics were intended to get people excited about space travel and ensure that NASA funding would continue. The author, Jack Kirby, had easily traceable ties to the founders of NASA.[234] Comics and other pop-culture media sources are routinely used to provide us with disclosure disguised as fiction. How did Kirby know we would find a giant monument on Mars in the shape of a human face almost twenty years ahead of time?

"The Face on Mars" was summarized on the Comic Book Resources website in 2003, and it contains very familiar-sounding themes: "On an expedition from the Earth's moon to the planet Mars, an international team of astronauts—led by American Ben Fisher—discover a huge carving of a Martian face that's as big as a mountain! Ascending to the inscrutable statue's hollow eyes, Fisher plunges inside, where he finds a green, sunlit countryside with cool, rich and breathable air, one which shelters a civilization of 'magnificent giants.' . . . Fisher explains that the statue contains 'a visual history of a race's heroic death—and the triumph of a surviving memory.' Later, as they pilot their rocket [through the asteroid belt], Fisher and his team take careful notice of the debris—'the pieces of a planet that blew up between Mars and Jupiter.'"[235]

Hoagland pointed out this remarkable connection in his 2006 article "Forbidden Planet Mars." On August 15, 2012, a website called the Secret Sun revealed that several other comics also contained images suggestive of the Face on Mars. "Shortly before Kirby wrote 'The Face on Mars,'

"The Face on Mars" Comic from September 1958

he wrote another, similar story called 'The Great Stone Face,' about an ancient astronaut cargo cult (way, way, way before such things were fashionable in comics). 'The Face on Mars' seems very much to be a sequel/companion to this story."[236]

The author then goes on to reveal that Kirby returned to this same Face on Mars–type theme in 1976, with the comic *Eternals* #1. "The cover of Eternals #1 has it all; the intrepid explorers, the underground temple and the giant stone head (representing yet another race of giant aliens). Something was bugging this guy—he could not let go of these motifs. . . . Eternals #1 was cover-dated July 1976, the same month the Viking photos revealed the 'Face' on the plains of Cydonia."[237] This again bears all the hallmarks of a military-industrial-complex/Cabal-sponsored "coordinated release" of information, in which they hide the truth out in the open. In the event of a future disclosure, they can say they were telling us all along, but we were not perceptive or fearless enough to listen.

The Genetic Farmers

After the super-Earth was destroyed 500,000 years ago, Corey's intel revealed that the protective grid for our entire Local Cluster went down. This allowed a mass immigration of different groups that had been excluded up until then. The first groups arrived almost immediately, and are known to the SSP as the "Genetic Farmers." The SSP tends to see these groups in a negative fashion, but many of the beings themselves feel they have our best spiritual intentions at heart. They know that our Earth is a rare jewel. According to Jacob and other insiders, most planets can support only about 100,000 unique forms of life, whereas we know that Earth is currently estimated as having 8.7 million.[238] Jacob, Corey, Bruce, and other insiders have said the Earth has a very complex and hyper-advanced "wave structure" that supports an incredible diversity of life. This makes us even more of a blue zone, because almost any life from anywhere in the galaxy can be dropped off on our planet and survive.

The Genetic Farmers took sections of DNA from all over the galaxy and spliced it into the humans on Earth at the time. This DNA was intended to optimize us for ascension. There are now sixty different active ET groups working on a total of twenty-two different genetic programs that are still ongoing. These so-called Genetic Farmers identify themselves as the Super-Federation. The DNA upgrades have caused us to be far more emotional than most ETs out there. These emotions can be a great weakness when we get dragged into repetition compulsion, but they also can springboard us into ascension much faster than most other human races ever could. Certain negative ET groups will abduct people on Earth and splice some of their DNA into their own bodies, combining some of our genetic material with theirs. Once the ETs hit their "upgraded" genetic material with an energy field akin to what our Sun is preparing to release, they temporarily develop ascended abilities. The negative groups are terrified of what we will become once this DNA is activated, because our abilities will be much greater than theirs—and we can clean up the mess that they caused. Multiple ancient prophecies, likely written by extraterrestrial humans, predict this exact sequence of events.

The Draco

The next major incursion was of the Draco, or what the Law of One refers to as the Orion Confederation. According to Jacob, this is a group of six different reptilian humanoid species. He told me they have genetically intermingled so much that each of the six is actually a different gender, and that they "trend" from male to female. This was not thoroughly explained, other than that these different "genders" could look like completely different species. According to Corey, there is a master race among them that is twelve to thirteen feet tall. The top leaders are white. Another high-ranking group is sable black. The warrior caste has red scales. Still others have skin that is a combination of tan and green scales. Contrary to popular belief, none of these people are strictly green.

The Draco "master race" traveled throughout the galaxy, looking for other humanoid groups that evolved out of reptilian life. Everywhere they found this life, they infiltrated, mixed their DNA together with them, and brought them into their Empire. They are very warlike, and according to Jacob they have been largely defeated throughout the galaxy already. Our Local Cluster is one of the only places left where they can live. It does appear that our collective concept of the Devil has been influenced by this very real situation. According to Tompkins, there are two massive underground caverns in Antarctica that hold huge, highly populated cities of the Draco. Corey's SSP insiders suggest the number of Draco in our solar system is comparable to Earth's own visible population of 7 billion people.

The Draco feed off the energy of fear, sadness, depression, selfishness, narcissism, anger, hatred, and jealousy. They are utterly dependent upon this energy for their survival. The Cabal calls this "loosh," and directly associates that word with Lucifer. Hence they have a saying, "Give Lucius his loosh." As outrageous as this must sound, the Draco are ultimately controlling the Cabal. Although the Draco have been around for 375,000 years, many insiders confirm that they made a deal with the Nazis, beginning as early as 1913. This appeared to have initially occurred through telepathy, such as in the Vril and Thule societies, and later progressed to in-person meetings. Tompkins extensively debriefed American embedded spies who confirmed this from 1942 to 1945, while working for Naval intelligence.

In his second video interview with Dr. Michael Salla, Tompkins said the following: "The SS had many separate classified meetings . . . [which turned] into a whole series of programs. This then was disseminated through their specific military communication. . . . Now in addition to that, they had, if you want to call them, 'consultants,' who were Reptilian consultants assisting on all of these different things that it takes to design and build these spacecraft carriers and propulsion systems. So this was an extremely well-developed program and documented like crazy. Getting copies of the documents was hard for our spies. This was an open program in the upper level of the SS. . . . Thousands of engineering groups were working different aspects to all of this. Some of them had the vehicles, others [were given] a vehicle to reverse engineer, so they could become familiar with everything from the inside out. . . . The [Reptilian] mission was to take over the planet, kill off all of the ones that were a problem, and make slaves out of [everyone else]. The second phase was to leave the planet with large squadrons of UFOs, after you've got them all built, and do the same thing to other stars' planets."[239]

Many of the Cabal's actions do not seem to make any sense. Why would they want to destroy so many people's lives and keep us all in terror and depression? The answer is that this generates loosh for the Draco, according to Jacob, Bruce, Corey, Pete, and all the others. Most interesting, Jacob told me that if everyone on Earth were happy for even one day, such as in some kind of globally inspiring event, the Draco would be utterly defeated. Furthermore, their own time-viewing technology shows their downfall is a certainty as we ascend. They are doing everything they can to try to stop it, but every plan they have made has been foiled. After we ascend, only a small number of them will survive for about 1.5 million years before they disappear completely. In the higher "densities," you experience time very differently—so in their terms this event is not very far away.

Another bizarre piece of intel that has come to light from Corey Goode and others is that the Draco have been aggressively using mind-control technology against us ever since our origin on Earth. Corey specifically said this technology is stopping us from being able to form a telepathic, collective consciousness. According to Jacob, the technology uses an artificial intelligence to monitor our thoughts and steer us away from any information that would help us grow spiritually, such as by making us suddenly feel tired. Part of this technology involves the use of large spacecraft that are cloaked in low earth orbit, as well as other systems inside the Earth and the Moon. The patriotic militaries of the United States and other nations now have the capability of shooting down the orbiting craft and deactivating this technology through advanced weapons strikes.

However, once the "grid" goes down, we will all get a sudden change in consciousness that could be extremely disturbing, even lethal, to some. People who tend toward violence, irrational behavior, and fear could have those qualities greatly amplified. Others who are positive and loving will quickly develop stunning new abilities, which could include levitation and telekinesis, as well as telepathy. Thanks to our position within the supercharged interstellar energy cloud we are moving into, these changes would apparently have already happened to us if Draco technologies were not being used against us. It does not appear that our militaries can turn off the Draco mind-control grid in stages.

Once they attack it, or perhaps once the solar flash destroys it for them, the entire control system disappears from our minds—and we experience a quantum consciousness shift. This may sound ridiculous to you, but for the people in the classified military programs, it is a highly serious issue. They do know the grid will go down, whether by their own strikes or from massive electromagnetic pulses that are expected to emanate from the Sun.

CHAPTER TWENTY-FOUR

The Cosmic Battle Becomes Personal

The survivors from the Empire migrated to the surface of the Moon 500,000 years ago. They dropped dramatically in height during this time, since they were living on a much smaller body, but they continued to be extremely warlike, aggressive, and negative. From all the intel I have gathered from various sources, including Lieutenant Colonel Gonzales, Bruce, and Pete Peterson, it appears that the entire Moon was hit with a devastating attack approximately 55,000 years ago. It is not clear who did this to the Empire, but it was probably the Draco. Corey said the Moon appears to have been hit with a cluster bomb–type weapon. The glass domes were shattered and immediately depressurized, killing almost everyone inside. It is important to point out that spiritual protection is not given to those on the negative path. Mega-events like these generate karmic balance that prevents these groups from damaging the lives of peaceful civilizations.

The Fallen Angels Crash-landed 55,000 Years Ago

Only a very small number of people from the Empire survived in some of their fatally wounded ships. They had just enough energy left to crash-land on Earth. Pete's intel was that this happened 60,000 years ago.

Gonzales's intel, which appears to be more recent, is that it happened 55,000 years ago. These people became the "fallen angels" you read about in the Book of Genesis. They no longer had the ability to leave the Earth's orbit. When I put together all the different sources of intel, and make the most educated guess, it appears that these people were twelve- to thirteen-foot-tall giants with elongated skulls. According to Gonzales, they were not well adapted to Earth's gravity, nor its atmosphere and germs. They were very frail, but were able to use their advanced medical technology to survive.

Their surviving damaged ships allowed them to spread across the Earth. Everywhere they went, they set up control systems and established themselves as gods. Their IQ was many tens of points higher than everyone else's on Earth, and they were giants. They had advanced technology that allowed them to manufacture all the food they needed with the push of a button. They established a very advanced civilization in what is now the Sahara Desert. According to Bruce, Pete Peterson, Jacob, Corey, and others, there is a huge treasure trove of ruins underneath the Sahara Desert. This includes many different structures built out of giant stone blocks. It also includes a variety of libraries containing their most precious books. These books trace all the way back to the original Empire on Mars and the super-Earth. The highlands of their civilization were in Egypt. The Egyptian priesthood later located the books. Peterson was lucky enough to see some of the books firsthand in the Vatican Library as part of a highly classified US government program. Some had very advanced diagrams of bases, mother ships, and smaller spacecraft. Many were leather-bound and had one solid color on the back and front covers, such as red, blue, or green.

According to Bruce, the Egyptian monuments create an "arrow" that points toward Libya—if you know what you are looking for. Some of the best artifacts are under the sand in Libya. The best artifacts were found at one of the mouths of the Great Man-Made River, which rises up out of the desert from the Nubian Sandstone fossil aquifer system. This river supplies an astonishing six and a half million cubic meters of fresh water per day to Libya, covering a vast distance of 1,750 miles. It is the world's largest irrigation project, and Gaddafi referred to it as the "Eighth

Wonder of the World." Bruce indicated that this river is a "tapped well" that rises up from the ocean inside the Earth, thus explaining how it seems to appear out of nowhere. Many astonishingly high-tech artifacts have been dug up near one of the mouths of this river, and it is considered the most advanced site of its kind on Earth. This is why top Cabal people worked with Muammar Gaddafi, the leader of Libya from 1969 to 2011, and allowed him to coordinate his own archeological expeditions. This is also apparently why Gaddafi was assassinated, and why his son Faith is now being "held prisoner in a cell the size of a cardboard box." Faith still knows more than he has revealed to the Cabal, which is why he is still alive at this time.

Ancient Earth Pyramids

According to various insiders, the "fallen angel" civilization of giants was utterly destroyed 50,000 years ago. The damage was so extreme that all the lush greenery in the area of the Sahara Desert was overwhelmed and covered in dust. Part of this was the work of their enemies, and part of it was the natural Earth changes that take place every 25,000 years. The survivors suffered a dramatic reduction in their power and scope after this defeat. They were very well aware that the Guardians did this to them, and instead of seeking to reform, they continued to be warlike. Although they had far less technology than in their previous cycle, they gradually rose to become a pyramid-building culture once again,

In January 2014, a perfect pyramid was discovered beneath the ocean off the coast of Portugal. According to an article that announced this, "Portuguese news reported the discovery of a very large underwater pyramid first discovered by Diocleciano Silva between the islands of São Miguel and Terceira in the Azores of Portugal. According to claims, the structure is said to be perfectly squared and oriented by the cardinal points. Current estimates obtained using GPS digital technology put the height at 60 meters with a base of 8000 square meters. . . . The pyramid was found in an area of the mid-Atlantic that has been underwater for about 20,000 years."[240] Of course, the pyramid could have been built well before the time it finally sank. This story was also covered by the *International Business Times*, which revealed that the pyramid was larger than a football field.[241]

Similarly, Dr. Semir Osmanagich used radiocarbon dating to prove that the mysterious Pyramid of the Sun in Bosnia is at least 29,000 years old. This pyramid is twice the size of the Great Pyramid of Giza, and is perfectly symmetrical, other than a large buildup of dirt and debris on one side—probably in the aftermath of a major Earth change. Here is a quote from the announcement: "'Conclusive data at the Bosnian Pyramid site revealed in 2008 and confirmed this year by several independent labs who conducted radiocarbon testing dates the site at 29,400 +/-400 years minimum.' The radiocarbon dating tests of 29,200 years plus or minus 400 years was done by Radiocarbon Lab from Kiew, Ukraine, on organic material found at the Bosnian Pyramid site."[242]

Another cyclical catastrophe took place 25,000 years ago, further knocking the "fallen angels" back. Their level of technology was again reduced, but once more they rose to prominence in the civilization most people call Atlantis. Some of the survivors still had relatively high technology and pyramid-building capabilities, whereas others were isolated and more primitive. This is where the legends become much clearer and easier to identify. In the Book of Enoch, these "fallen angels" are referred to as the Watchers.

The Book of Enoch and the Atlantean Flood

The Bible and other related documents appear to present extensive evidence of extraterrestrials on Earth and in our skies. Words that we have always thought we knew, like "God" and "heaven," might actually mean something entirely different. On the Bible Reality Check website, W. L. Graham writes: "Many otherwise literate students of theology are unaware that the Hebrew writers of the biblical literature communicated their belief in a vast race of extraterrestrial gods whom they called 'the Elohim.' . . . While this distinctive plural noun [Elohim] found in the Bible texts some 2,570 times is well-known by scholars to be accurately translated 'Mighty Ones,' it is almost always rendered [as the word] 'God.' . . . Also noteworthy is a more correct rendering of [the word] 'heaven' (Heb. *Shameh/shamayim*, or

Gr. *Ouranos*) in unambiguous modern terms such as cosmos, universe, or outer space in all biblical passages that refer to the extraterrestrial Elohim. . . . Not only were the Elohim actively involved in earthly conflicts and conquests in the ancient world, but they also engaged in battles of cosmic proportions, 'star wars' if you prefer, with alien adversaries who are always portrayed as inherently malevolent."[243]

One of the most important ancient scriptures, the Book of Enoch never made it into the Bible. There are hundreds of references to it in the New Testament, including from Jesus, who quotes from it directly. It was lost to the sands of time and only rediscovered by the open Western world when the Scottish traveler Robert Bruce brought back three copies from Abyssinia in 1773, and then Richard Laurence translated it into English as of 1821.

Multiple insiders have confirmed that the governments of this period were often controlled by negative forces and did not want sensitive information to leak out to the public, just like we see now. The first verse is a clue as to why the Book of Enoch might not have made the cut: "The words of the blessing of Enoch, wherewith [the Elohim] blessed the elect and righteous, who will be living in the day of tribulation, when all the wicked and godless are to be removed."

The second and third verses become even more interesting, particularly if we correct "heaven" as "outer space" and "God" as "mighty ones:" "[I am] Enoch, a righteous man whose eyes were opened by the mighty ones. [I] saw the vision of the Holy One in outer space, which the angels showed me. From them I heard everything, and from them I understood—as I saw, not for this generation, but for a remote one which is for to come."

How are the "wicked and godless" going to be "removed" in the Book of Enoch? The answer appears right at the beginning, from 1:3–9. Once again, we hear a similar "solar flash" scenario as what appears in many other scriptures and sources we have discussed. Though masculine pronouns are used, this passage ends up referring to a full team of benevolent ETs:

> The Holy Great One will come forth from His dwelling, and the eternal God will tread upon the earth . . . and appear in the strength of His might from the heaven of heavens. And all shall be smitten with fear. The Watchers shall quake and great fear

and trembling shall seize them unto the ends of the earth. The
high mountains shall be shaken, and the high hills shall be
made low, and shall melt like wax before the flame. . . . All that
is upon the earth shall perish, and there shall be a judgment
upon all. But with the righteous He will make peace. . . . Light
shall appear unto them, and He will make peace with them.
And behold! He cometh with ten thousands of His holy ones to
execute judgment upon all, and to destroy all the ungodly.

Who are the "ungodly" and "wicked ones" in the Book of Enoch? We
find out that these people were ETs known as the Watchers, who began
interbreeding with native Earth humans and creating giants. They had been
warned by the Elohim that if they did this, they would be destroyed, but
they disobeyed. This next passage is from Enoch 6:1–3. "And it came to pass
when the children of men had multiplied that in those days were born unto
them beautiful and comely daughters. And the angels, the children of the
heaven, saw and lusted after them, and said to one another: 'Come, let us
choose us wives from among the children of men and beget us children.'"[244]

In chapter 7, we hear that the Watchers brought civilization to the
humans, but eventually turned on them. "And when men could no longer
sustain them, the giants turned against them and devoured mankind.
And they began to sin against birds, and beasts, and reptiles, and fish, and
to devour one another's flesh, and drink the blood. Then the Earth laid
accusation against the lawless ones."[245] The benevolent ETs informed the
giants that they were going to be wiped out for what they had done. The
giants then used Enoch to beg for forgiveness, but they were denied.

This narrative continues in 15:3–10, as the Elohim turn down the
Watchers' request to be spared the effects of a planet-wide catastrophe:
"Wherefore have ye left the high, holy, and eternal universe, and lain
with women, and defiled yourselves with the daughters of men and taken
to yourselves wives, and done like the children of earth, and begotten
giants [as your] sons? . . . You were formerly spiritual, living the eternal
life, and immortal for all generations of the world. And therefore I have
not appointed wives for you; for as for the spiritual ones of the heaven,
in outer space is their dwelling. And now, the giants, who are produced

from the spirits and flesh, shall be called evil spirits upon the earth, and on the earth shall be their dwelling. Evil spirits have proceeded from their bodies; because they are born from men and from the holy Watchers is their beginning and primal origin."

The book reveals that the giants were wiped out in an epic flood, but also indicates that some survived. A future event, which is referred to as "the day of the consummation," would finish the job—and in context it sounds like the epic solar flash.

> From the days of the slaughter and destruction and death of the giants, from the souls of whose flesh the spirits, having gone forth, shall destroy without incurring judgment—thus shall they destroy until the day of the consummation, the great judgment in which the age shall be consummated, over the Watchers and the godless, yea, shall be wholly consummated. (16:1–2)

The Surviving Giants

Just as the Book of Enoch indicated, giants from this civilization did survive all over the Earth after the epic Atlantean flood. They were often reduced to a primitive level, such as in the Americas. They continued to build mounds, even if only out of dirt, to commemorate their ancient legacy. There is an incredible amount of excellent research to be done on the widespread presence of giant humans throughout the world. Jim Vieria has identified fully one thousand, five hundred different newspaper reports of these findings within credible sources such as the *New York Times*. Let's now read an excerpt from a description of a conference featuring Jim Vieria and Hugh Newman that took place in November 2015, as their research is very impressive and verifiable.

> For a long time, it was thought giants were just part of folklore, but recent research into old documents, newspapers, journals, first hand reports, and old photos now suggest that these

may have been a reality. It is the discoveries in the mounds and megalithic sites of North America that have created a huge controversy, because there are at least 1500 reports of a giant race, some with double rows of teeth, horned skulls, powerful jaws, and elongated craniums, who ruled the continent since at least 7,000 BC. They were mostly found in ancient mounds and have been reported as going up to a staggering 18 feet tall. Often they have strange bronze armour, red and blonde hair, unusual skulls and a physique suggesting that some of them may not be native to North America. Most reports range the heights between 7 ft and 12 ft, but it still doesn't answer the question of why this part of history has been so meticulously covered up.[246]

From New England, to Miami, Ohio and California, these giant skeletons have been dug up in the thousands, yet when the Smithsonian Institution got involved they mysteriously vanished. The Native American NAGPRA Act of 1990 removed the final bones from museum displays, so there is now little evidence to go on, but the reports, photos, excavations and eye-witness accounts—even from Abraham Lincoln and other luminaries—suggest that the history books are on the verge of being rewritten.[247]

I have seen only one example of a skull with horns, and I am not convinced of its authenticity. The double sets of teeth are far more common. Many of these skulls were large enough that you could slip them over your head. There are several excellent books on giants that are jam-packed with research. It is outside the scope of this book to review most of that data. I found Patrick Chouinard's *Lost Race of the Giants* useful. Originally I intended this book to just be research based, until I had a variety of dreams urging me to cover the personal side of things in detail. This is truly the core of the ascension process, and without that spiritual side of things, the information itself is not necessarily going to connect with the heart. Ascension is not a myth—it is a very real process that is extensively predicted both in a wide variety of ancient cultures as well as in the research of insiders from the secret space program.

Chouinard shares legends from other cultures that are remarkably similar to the Book of Enoch's message. Here is a quote from page 129 of his book. "According to Aztec myth, during the first age, or Sun, the gods Quetzalcoatl and Tezcatlipoca created a race of giants from ashes, giving them acorns for nourishment. But the giants so enraged the gods due to their wickedness that the gods decided to end the giants' existence and sent the jaguars to destroy them. Only seven survived the onslaught of the savage beasts."[248]

Chouinard also quotes from Lucy Thompson's 1916 book, *To The American Indian,* in which she discusses her memories as a member of a Native American tribe living near the Klamath River known as the Yurok. An indigenous white-skinned group of giants known as the Wa-gas were already there when the Yurok arrived. In this case, as in other examples of surviving giants, they had become peaceful and did not try to hurt or cannibalize others. According to Thompson, "The recollections transmitted by the Wa-gas were that these giants were very cruel and wicked. It was said that God became displeased with them and destroyed them and they all perished from the earth."[249]

When you do your research, you find out that giants continued to live on Earth up until as late as the 1800s. Many of them had not reformed and turned on the native people and were cannibalistic. According to Bruce, many Native American tribes banded together in their struggle to defend themselves against the giants. Lewis and Clark encountered giants on their historic exploration of America, which was well documented in Paul Schrag and Xaviant Haze's *The Suppressed History of America.* The amount of information to share and reveal about giants is so robust that I could easily write another book just focusing on that part of the story. The legends and discoveries are truly worldwide.

Jacob revealed that the Cabal has been extremely focused on eliminating all evidence of giants from the public. The Smithsonian Institution was frequently used for this purpose in the 1800s and on into the 1900s. Their tactics used to include destroying any skeletons that were found, such as by dumping them out at sea. Now they are considered precious relics of the ancestors of the Cabal, and are kept preserved. Anyone who finds these types of skeletons or artifacts will be immediately contacted and "strongly encouraged" not to go public.

People with Elongated Skulls

The next mystery in this story is that apparently some descendants of the giants retained the elongated skull, but decreased in height to conventional human levels. Jacob indicated there are still people like this living on Earth, and they are concentrated in the Vatican. Pete revealed very similar information. The World Bank whistle-blower Karen Hudes recently came forward and said the same thing, based on information she had from an insider. She refers to this group as "Homo Capensis," and her sources told her these people are running the Cabal.

> There is a second species on this planet. They are not extra-terrestrials. . . . The remnants of their civilizations are all over the place. . . . This group has large brains. They are very distinct from Homo Sapiens. . . . One of the places they've been hiding is in the Vatican. That's why the Vatican are wearing those miters. That's also what the high priests wore in the early beginnings of Judaism. Moses was actually Akenhaten, who was a pharaoh. They know this because the papyri that was taken from one of the pyramids talks about this. The people who are doing archeology in Israel know this. . . .[250]
>
> Not only is Homo Capensis trying to keep human beings under control by divide and conquer, using our money system, they've also been doing this with our religions. . . . I sent an email to a fellow in Portugal, and the next day he went to a meeting of bankers. He sent me back an email saying that at that meeting, there had been a big-skulled individual with bright blue eyes. . . . Their skulls are all over the planet. It's not a conspiracy theory. Just because this group likes to hide, and likes to accuse people of having conspiracy theories, doesn't make these facts wrong. They are facts![251]

This may sound impossible to fathom, but as I did the research for this book, I found multiple examples of graves where elites with elongated skulls were buried. This first story appeared in November 2013: "The skeleton of an ancient aristocratic woman whose head was warped into a deformed, pointy shape has been unearthed in a necropolis in France. . . . [Philippe Lefranc, an archeologist, said,] 'In France, Germany and eastern Europe, these deformed skulls appear in tombs rich in objects.'[252] Brien Foerster has found many elongated skulls in Peru, some still with long hair on them."[253] [254]

Another "conehead" skull was unearthed in Russia and covered on *Russia Today*:

> Archeologists are puzzled over the ancient remains of a woman discovered on a site near Chelyabinsk, a Russian city to the east of the Ural Mountains. The approximately 2,000 year old skeleton boasts an oddly shaped skull. The "conehead" skeleton of a woman from the Sarmati tribe, unearthed at the archaeological site of Arkaim, a 4,000-year-old settlement, has totally thrilled UFO hunters. . . . Arkaim, situated in Russia's Southern Urals, is often compared to England's Stonehenge because it was also used for star observations. The Russian observatory, however, is said to have been more technologically advanced and have more favorable conditions for astronomical observation.[255]

Elongated skulls were also found at a dig in Omsk, Siberia. Their appearance disturbed the workers so much that some of them cried and many refused to work, feeling terrified. According to the Russian media source ITN, "Scholars at the Omsk Museum of History and Culture have no conclusive answer as to the origins of these skulls, which were found in burial mounds that are believed to date from the 4th century A.D. Because of the skulls' bizarre shape they do not show them to the public, fearing that people might be too shocked. 'This really shocked and even frightened people. Because the skull's shape was unusual for a human,' said Igor Skandakov, director of the Omsk Museum of History and Culture."[256]

In *The Source Field Investigations,* I covered the 2009 *Discover* magazine article that revealed the same skulls in Boskop, South Africa. Many of the articles covering these modern elongated skulls try to blame them all on head-binding. The *Discover* article openly acknowledges that these skulls have a much larger brain capacity, indicating even the most average of these people would have an IQ of 150. "Two neuroscientists say that a now-extinct race of humans had big eyes, child-like faces, and an average intelligence of around 150, making them geniuses among Homo sapiens."[257]

Another tantalizing clue can be found in surviving photographs of Prince Leonello and Princess D'Este, both fourteenth-century Italian nobility. Surviving images of both people clearly indicate that they had elongated skulls. Research on the House of Este reveals that the descendants of this Italian group, which had high-level political ties to the Vatican, are spread throughout European nobility.[258] Their relatives include all British monarchs since George I, a variety of earlier British consorts, and the royal families of Norway, Sweden, Spain, and Denmark.[259] Even more surprisingly, a 1988 article in the *New York Times* revealed that out of forty American presidents at the time, thirteen had a direct connection to European royalty.[260] In 2012, BridgeAnne d'Avignon, a twelve-year-old girl, connected forty-two out of forty-three American presidents to one single shared ancestor: King John of England.[261] John was an influential figure who signed the Magna Carta in 1215—the original cornerstone of the British constitution.[262]

It is well known to Pete, Corey, and Jacob, among others, that a small number of people with elongated skulls are still alive on Earth today. At times they have warred with the Draco and at other times they have formed alliances with them. By no means am I advocating that we hunt them down or treat them all as criminals. Heroes can come from the most unlikely of places. If we treat them as aliens or villains, we are only going to repeat the same cycles that have damaged us for so long. However, there certainly are some of them who seem to be very focused on destroying humanity. Lieutenant Colonel Gonzales has confirmed that these people are heavily involved in banking and finance, and do represent the core of what many people call the Illuminati, but which the SSP Alliance refers to as the "secret earth government syndicates."

Prince Lionello and Princess D'Este, with Noticeably Elongated Skulls

Corey independently confirmed that a treaty was worked out between these people and the Draco to pursue their mutual interests. Jacob revealed this has been in place since the time of Queen Elizabeth and her court astrologer John Dee, and other alliances had occurred in a variety of prior instances. It definitely appears that this negative influence will finally be transformed as we go through the ascension process that so many sources have predicted.

The Draco have already attempted to betray all their human allies as we have gotten closer to the long-anticipated solar event. All ETs have become trapped in our system thanks to an energetic wall that appeared in December 2014, commonly referred to in the SSP as the Outer Barrier. This barrier appeared after the Cabal fired a superweapon at one of hundreds of giant spheres that have arrived in our solar system since the year 2012. The beam reflected back to the underground facility in Pine Gap, Australia, and destroyed it, and the outer barrier immediately appeared. Though this may all seem quite fantastic and implausible, Corey and I have both experienced multiple, highly severe death threats since we were pulled into this world. Many others are in the same boat. Yet, since it is a spiritual battle that must follow "the Rules," we are doing our best to ensure that our deaths will not be authorized. The positive spiritual perspective is the best protection for anyone who chooses to participate in this struggle to regain control of our planet and transform it into a positive, advanced space-traveling society.

CHAPTER TWENTY-FIVE

Blueprints of the Future

After Ian told me about Hoagland's stunning talk at the UN, I immediately called Ariel Booksellers and ordered a copy of Hoagland's book, *The Monuments of Mars*. The waiting felt like an eternity, even though it was probably less than two weeks. By the time the book came in I could hardly contain my enthusiasm. I was hoping that Hoagland would have some idea of where this civilization went, or why they had died out. The connection between the half-man, half-feline face and the Sphinx, as well as the pyramids on both Mars and the Earth, was very tantalizing. At the same time, I had no idea if simply buying a book like this could be enough to get me followed, interrogated, or even tortured and killed. Nonetheless, this information was so fascinating that I was willing to risk my life to obtain it.

The Great Pyramid Decoded

When I went to the special order desk at the store, they had to go look in the back for the book and kept me waiting. This further increased my sense of unease, even as I smelled the strong bouquet of incense in the air and admired the displays of crystals. I started going through the stacks and looking for anything else that seemed interesting. My eyes soon locked onto *The Great Pyramid Decoded* by Peter Lemesurier. I flipped through it and was dazzled by the number of intricate diagrams I was seeing of the interior of the pyramid. It was a highly mathematical and technical book, which didn't scare me in the least.

The Great Pyramid Decoded had an absolutely stunning premise—namely that there was a mathematical message in the passages of the Great Pyramid. This code could be successfully translated into spoken language, which the author meticulously reconstructed, revealing the logic behind every single word in painstaking detail. The Pyramid Time Line accurately pinpointed many of our own historical events that were far in the future from when the pyramid was constructed. Most surprising, the Time Line continued past our own present moment, and ended with some very impressive events. The author concluded that the pyramid was ultimately built to encode a prophecy of a global ascension. He chose to refer to this as the Second Coming of Christ, or the "Messianic return." He indicated this would be happening to many of us, not just one figure, which I liked.

The author demonstrated an astonishing number of connections between the Great Pyramid and Christianity, particularly in chapter 7, "The Pyramid and the Sacred Writings."[263] This was temporarily a very popular subject in the 1800s, but it has since become almost completely obscure. The Cabal was very likely horrified to discover that the monument they had already co-opted as their symbol was actually a "prophecy in stone" of the coming of the spiritual leader they despised more than anyone. I got heavily triggered from reading this in 1993 and could barely make it through it, since I had felt alienated by Christians all my life, but I now realize this is of critical importance in understanding the Law of One material.

Connections Between the Pyramid and the Bible

On page 185, Lemesurier said, "The average Christian may be surprised to learn that the kingdom of heaven referred to repeatedly in the New Testament was not normally thought of by contemporary Jews as some kind of post-mortem state of spiritual bliss at all. On the contrary, it was seen as an uncompromisingly physical Golden Age on Earth—a future Millennium which the righteous dead would be physically reborn to enjoy . . . the prophet Isaiah had written (26:19); 'They that sleep in the earth will awake and shout for joy; for thy dew is a dew of sparkling light, and the earth will bring those long dead to birth again.'"[264]

On page 188, Lemesurier made intriguing connections between the Bible and the UFO phenomenon, by quoting from chapter 19 of Isaiah. "See how the Lord comes riding swiftly upon a cloud, he shall descend upon Egypt." Shortly thereafter, a very interesting passage speaks directly of the Great Pyramid as a "sacred pillar" and "altar." The identity of this monument would have been very well-known at the time: "When that day comes there shall be an altar to the Lord in the heart of Egypt, and a sacred pillar set up for the Lord upon her frontier. It shall stand as a token and a reminder to the Lord of Hosts in Egypt, so that when they appeal to him against their oppressors, he may send a deliverer to champion their cause, and he shall rescue them." (19: 16–17)

The Hebrew word for "altar" can indicate a great heap of stone that is built to commemorate any memorable event. It preserves the memory of something that was of great importance to the people. The Hebrew word that is translated as "pillar" is *matstebah,* which can indicate any kind of monument. The word has roots in the Egyptian *mstpt,* which means a funeral monument, and also appears later as the Arabic word *mastaba.* This is a flat-topped pyramid that conventional archeologists believe was the early design prototype that ultimately led to the creation of the Great Pyramid. So a "mastaba to the Lord in the heart of Egypt," associated with a mass ascension and ETs coming out of the clouds from "heaven," or outer space, changes the meaning of this biblical passage quite dramatically.

Lemesurier's scholarship impressed me even more on the next page. Throughout the book he demonstrated how the Pyramid Time Line was all calibrated in Egyptian inches, where one inch equals one year of time. The diagonals along the outside of the pyramid added up very neatly to the precession cycle of 25,920 years. Without the capstone, the pyramid has six sides, and in Pyramid numerology, six is the number of imperfection and evil. Once the capstone returns, it becomes a five-sided object, and five means divine energy and ascension. Lemesurier revealed that the Bible passage quoted above had long been known to have a secret mathematical code embedded in it. This code appears in the science of *gematria*, in which each letter in the Hebrew alphabet has a corresponding number associated with it. The passage about a "great stone monument in the heart of Egypt" adds up to the number 5449. This is only 0.27 inches away from the height of the Great Pyramid, in Egyptian inches, if you measure it from the bottom to the top. This may seem like a foolish coincidence at first, but Lemesurier demonstrated hundreds and hundreds of them.

Then on the next page, Lemesurier quoted Matthew 21:42, in which Jesus seems to be speaking of himself when he says, "The stone the builders rejected has become the chief corner-stone." Lemesurier then said, "Any building, of course, can have a corner-stone—most have four or more—but there is only one type of building that can have a chief corner-stone, or a 'headstone in the corner,' as one translation has it; and that building is a pyramid. Yet the reference here is specifically to a building whose chief corner-stone is missing—and it is further made clear that the final placement of that corner-stone will have a specifically Messianic connotation."[265] In other words, the return of the capstone is an ascension event, the perfecting of humans on Earth.

After reading the Law of One, another Bible quote Lemesurier mentioned jumped out at me even more. He began with Isaiah 26:1, which says, "We have a strong city whose walls and ramparts are our deliverance. Open the gates to let a righteous nation in, a nation that keeps faith." In context, this could be a description of the pyramid and its symbolism. This may seem like a vague connection, but it was the next line from verses 4, 7, and 8 that caught my eye: "Trust in the Lord forever, for the Lord himself is an everlasting rock. . . . The path of the righteous is level, and thou markest out the right way for the upright." The "everlasting rock" could well be a symbol of the Pyramid, which still stands after all this time. The Time Line does resemble a level path inside the "everlasting rock" that marks out the gateway to ascension inside.

Once I reread this passage while writing this book, I immediately remembered how the Law of One source described their building of the Great Pyramid. This appears in Session 3, Question 12: "We built with everlasting rock the Great Pyramid, as you call it. Other of the pyramids were built with stone moved from one place to another."[266] When they were asked to clarify what they meant by "everlasting rock," the answer seemed deliberately vague and confusing. The source even seemed to acknowledge this by saying, "May we answer you in any more helpful way?"[267] Now I realized that they were directly quoting from the book of Isaiah, and pointing their readers back to the importance of this passage.

The last Bible quote I will discuss from Lemesurier's book is from Luke 19:40: "I tell you, if my disciples keep silence the stones will shout aloud." According to Lemesurier, "The statement may have been a deliberate reference to the stones of the Great Pyramid—in which case the statement could be seen as a cryptic (and not untypical) way of saying that those stones had a Messianic message for mankind."[268]

Even though many of us are alienated against Christianity due to the trappings of religion, I have since realized that the life and teachings of Jesus greatly weakened the Cabal and created a far more widespread appreciation of ascension. It was only while I was in Canada in 2015 that I realized the basic spiritual message I had been teaching all these years was the same as we hear from Jesus and other great masters. As I read the New Testament for the first time, I was astonished at all the references to ascension that I had missed.

Stunning Bible Quotes on Ascension

Here are some of the most powerful examples I found while I was meditating in the Canadian Rocky Mountains. I am aware that these passages have been used by Bible-thumping religious zealots who have taught that only their own "chosen" will go through this, and all others will burn in hell. The greater context I have presented here in *The Ascension Mysteries,* as well as in my previous two books, makes this all a far more interesting discussion:

> Behold! I tell you a mystery. We shall not all sleep, but we
> shall all be changed, in a moment, in the twinkling of an eye,

at the last trumpet. For the trumpet will sound, and the dead will be raised imperishable, and we shall be changed. For this perishable body must put on the imperishable, and this mortal body must put on immortality. (I Corinthians 15:51–53)

For as the lightning, that lighteneth out of the one part under heaven, shineth unto the other part under heaven; so shall also the Son of man be in his day. But first must he suffer many things, and be rejected of this generation. And as it was in the days of Noe, so shall it be also in the days of the Son of man. They did eat, they drank, they married wives, they were given in marriage, until the day that Noe entered into the ark, and the flood came, and destroyed them all.

Likewise also as it was in the days of Lot; they did eat, they drank, they bought, they sold, they planted, they builded; But the same day that Lot went out of Sodom it rained fire and brimstone from heaven, and destroyed them all. Even thus shall it be in the day when the Son of man is revealed. In that day, he which shall be upon the housetop, and his stuff in the house, let him not come down to take it away: and he that is in the field, let him likewise not return back. (Luke 17:24–31)

I tell you, in that night there shall be two [men] in one bed; the one shall be taken, and the other shall be left. Two [women] shall be grinding together; the one shall be taken, and the other left. Two [men] shall be in the field; the one shall be taken, and the other left. And they answered and said unto him, Where, Lord? And he said unto them, Wheresoever the body [is], thither will the eagles be gathered together. (Luke 17:34–37)

And Jesus answering said unto him, Seest thou these great buildings? There shall not be left one stone upon another, that shall not be thrown down. (Mark 13:2)

But in those days, after that tribulation, the sun shall be darkened, and the moon shall not give her light, and the stars of heaven shall fall, and the powers that are in heaven shall be shaken. And then shall they see the Son of man coming in the clouds with great power and glory. And then shall he send his angels, and shall gather together his elect from the four winds, from the uttermost part of the earth to the uttermost part of heaven. (Mark 13:24–27)

And the mighty ones shall wipe away all tears from their eyes; and there shall be no more death, neither sorrow, nor crying, neither shall there be any more pain: for the former things are passed away. And he that sat upon the throne said, Behold, I make all things new. And he said unto me, Write: for these words are true and faithful. (Revelations 21:4–5)

And he carried me away in the spirit to a great and high mountain, and shewed me that great city, the holy Jerusalem, descending out of outer space from the mighty ones, having the glory of the mighty ones: and her light was like unto a stone most precious, even like a jasper stone, clear as crystal. (Revelations 21:10–11)

And many of them that sleep in the dust of the earth shall awake . . . and they that be wise shall shine as the brightness of the firmament; and they that turn many to righteousness as the stars, for ever and ever. (Daniel 12:2–3)

Say not ye, There are yet four months, and then cometh harvest? Behold, I say unto you, Lift up your eyes, and look on the fields; for they are white already to harvest. (John 14:35)

The Son of man shall send forth his angels, and they shall gather out of his kingdom all things that offend, and them which do iniquity; and shall cast them into a furnace of fire:

there shall be wailing and gnashing of teeth. Then shall the righteous shine forth as the sun in the kingdom of their Father. Who hath ears to hear, let him hear. (Matthew 13:41–43)

In my April 23, 2016, interview with William Tompkins, he revealed that the insider community is so divided on the subject of the solar event that hardly anyone really understands what is going to happen, or how it is going to happen. "This may not be as destructive as some people seem to think. It may also be a tremendous new way of life that will include extended life. . . . There are boxes full of the different versions of what you are talking about [from classified insider studies]. Grabbing a hold of one or two of them, and holding on while it is shaking, is still kind of hard to do!" I then called Pete Peterson and talked to him about it that same day. He said, "The solar event is a natural occurrence. It is how things are and what we must go through."

Wanderer Awakening

By 1995, I had read so many books on UFOs, ancient civilizations, and paranormal subjects that I was quickly becoming an expert. I also had been documenting my dreams for three solid years. Some very profound synchronicities happened to me during those years after I got sober, and the best ones are featured in *The Synchronicity Key*. When my mother demanded I move out after graduating from college in 1995, I became extremely saddened and was crying in the grass in the backyard. A bird came up and chirped at me for a long time, in what appeared to be a clear attempt to cheer me up. Shortly thereafter I moved back to my college town and got a place with my college buddy Eric.

I ended up getting a job at a mental health ward within a local hospital, because I wanted to use it for a residency credit. My goal at the time was to get a PhD in psychology. I ended up being fired after two and a half weeks for being "too friendly to the patients." I drove home feeling devastated, and stopped off at the Borders bookstore on Wolf Road in Albany, New York. There I found a copy of *From Elsewhere* by

Dr. Scott Mandelker. The subtitle read, "The Subculture of Those Who
Claim to Be of Non-Earthly Origins." I laughed when I read it, but I also
used an ESP technique called "psychometry" with any book. If I felt a
tingling sensation from the book when I cleared my mind of all thoughts,
I knew it was valuable. This book felt like lightning in my hands. In the
back, appendix 2 was a questionnaire that Mandelker used to identify
Wanderers. Those questions rocked me to my core, as I had never seen
such an intimate, personal assessment of my psychology—and this was
from a complete stranger. Here is what I read:

1. You were often lost in daydreams of ETs, UFOs, other
   worlds, space travel and utopian societies as a child. Your
   family thought you were "a bit odd," without knowing quite
   why.
2. You always felt like your parents were not your true parents,
   that your real family was far away and hidden. Perhaps you
   thought things around you were somehow "not the way they
   should be," and reminded you of life somewhere "far away."
   These beliefs may have caused you a great deal of pain and
   sorrow. You felt "out of place."
3. You've had one or more vivid UFO experiences (in a dream
   or during waking hours) which dramatically changed your
   life: they helped resolve doubts, inspired confidence and
   hope, and gave you meaning and greater purpose. From then
   on, you knew you were a different person. Like a spiritual
   wake-up call, it changed your life.
4. You are genuinely kind, gentle, harmless, peaceful, and non-
   aggressive (not just sometimes, but almost always). You are not
   much interested in money and possessions, so if "someone
   must do without," it is usually you—such is your habitual
   self-sacrifice. Acts of human cruelty, violence and perpetual
   global warfare seem really strange (shall we say, alien?). You
   just can't figure out all this anger, rage and competition.
5. You have a hard time recognizing evil and trickery: some
   people call you naive (and they're right!). When you do

perceive genuine negativity in your midst, you recoil in horror and may feel shocked that "some people really do things like that." In a subtle way, you actually feel confused. Perhaps you vaguely sense having known a world free of such disharmony.

6. The essence of your life is serving others (be they family, friends, or in a profession), and you cherish great ideals, which may also be somewhat innocent and naive (in worldly terms). But you sincerely, deeply hope to improve the world. A lot of disappointment and frustration comes when such hopes and dreams don't materialize.

7. You completely embrace the scientific temperament, with a cool, reasonable, and measured approach to life. Human passion and red hot desire seem strange: you are baffled. Romance and the entire world of feelings are truly foreign to your natural way. You always analyze experiences, and so people say you're always in your head—which is true! [Note: This type of Wanderer is less common, and probably wouldn't be reading this book—their skepticism would be too great! Such an "odd bird" is probably a brilliant scientist.]

8. You easily get lost in science fiction, medieval epic fantasy (like *The Hobbit*) and visionary art. Given a choice, you'd much prefer to live in your dreams of the past or future than in the present. Sometimes you consider your Earth life boring and meaningless, and wish you could go to a perfect, exciting world. Such dreams have been with you a long time.

9. You have an insatiable interest in UFOs, life on other worlds or previous Earth civilizations such as Atlantis or Lemuria. Sometimes you feel like you've really been there, and may even go back someday. There may be quite a few of such books on your bookshelves. (Actually, this question is a giveaway, since only Wanderers and Walk-ins have profound, undying curiosity about worlds beyond—and for good reason!)

10. You have a strong interest in mystic spirituality (East or West), both theory and practice, with a deep sense that you used to have greater powers and somehow lost them. You may feel it's unnecessary to discipline yourself since "you've already been there," but somehow forgot what you used to know. People may doubt your resolve, but you know it's not that simple.

11. You have become a conscious channel for ETs or some other non-Earth source—and you realize that the purpose of your life is to help others grow and evolve. (Most likely, you're no longer sleeping, Wanderer!)

12. You feel, and perhaps all your life have felt tremendous alienation and a sense of never quite fitting in. Maybe you hope to be like others, try your best to be "normal," or imagine yourself like everyone else—but the bottom line is that you simply feel different and always have. There is a very real fear of never finding a place in this world. (Which you might not! Note: This is the classic profile of Wanderers.)

Finding the Proof

I scored 100 percent on this questionnaire, which should be obvious if you read the first half of this book. Wanderers are apparently extraterrestrial souls who have already gone beyond the lessons of "third density" Earth in this level of spiritual evolution. They volunteer to come here and forget who they are, hoping to help improve the planet by anchoring in a higher consciousness through their thoughts and actions. It is possible for them to "penetrate the forgetting" and remember who they really are if they do the work. Dr. Mandelker indicated that if you believe this is who you are, you have to commit to finding the answer. Validation can appear if you dedicate yourself to seeking it. I was ready. I brought the book home, read it very quickly, and told my high school best friend Jude about it. He recommended we do "automatic writing," where we'd meditate with a pencil in our non-writing hands to see if we could get clear enough to have something happen. I ended up getting astounding results. Though I felt no connection to Christianity, my hand wrote "Christ Cometh" forward and backward on the same line. For some reason, the last two letters in the second word, "th," also looked like the word "Ra."

Then my hand suddenly jumped into furious action and scribbled out a quick sequence of characters before it stopped: "EC 40 57 & oxen." We quickly realized this was a Bible quote from Ecclesiastes. Neither of us felt connected to Christianity, but we had to look it up. In the olden days, there were no chapters—only verse numbers counted from the beginning. Forty verses after the beginning of Ecclesiastes was 2:22. This was another "synchronicity number," and I had been seeing these patterns on clocks, license plates, and odometer readouts at the most remarkable times for the preceding three years.

The quote itself showed an intimate knowledge of what I had just gone through: "For what hath a man toiled and labored under the sun? This too is meaningless." It definitely seemed to be talking about the job I had gotten fired from, and that it was "meaningless" and not to worry about it. The last line read, "To eat and drink, and be happy in one's toil: this is the grace of God." I felt I was being given clear guidance to just get a job and try to be happy, instead of working in a mental hospital so I could get internship credit toward a PhD in psychology. The oxen was a clear reference to a statue of a water buffalo that I had purchased at the Altamont Fair. I thought it represented my becoming a "beast of burden" in the working world, only to find out this was one of the three most powerful animals in Africa. No one would dare go anywhere near the buffalo, much less try to attach it to a plow.

This was a major event, with far more detail than what I had gotten from the flash of light in the sky. I ended up getting a job caring for developmentally disabled people at a day treatment center. I was working for $5.77 an hour and dealing with incredible stress on a daily basis. All the people with the most severe and disruptive behaviors were segregated into one room, and because I had a psychology degree they assumed I would know how to handle it.

He Is One of Us

That winter I got hit with a $200 phone bill that I could not pay, thanks to long-distance conversations with my ex-girlfriend from Japan. Though we had broken up, she still wanted to stay in regular contact with me, and now I had gotten the bill. I completely broke down that night and cried. I thought back to the old man, to my dreams as a child, to the visions of the Upgrade I'd had, to the flash of light across the sky, and now to the highly bizarre Bible quote. "If you're out there and you are real, I need you to tell me now," I cried. "I can't live my life not knowing if this is true. I need proof. If I am an extraterrestrial soul, like the book says, I need to know."

Nothing happened.

I became calm after crying and realized the phone company had "accidentally forgotten" to apply a discounted rate to my calls, as I had asked them to. I called them up and chopped $200 down to $35, just like that. I felt better and had nearly forgotten about my tearful, highly emotional request when I went to sleep. My housemate Eric did not get back until after I was out. The next morning I went outside to start my car since it was so cold. I came back inside the house and Eric was standing there in the kitchen. Red pillow creases were all over his face.

"I just had a dream about you," he said. I told him I couldn't hear about his dream as I was going to be late for work. "Yeah, but this was about UFOs." That caught my attention. I immediately stopped worrying about being on time and listened. In Eric's dream, a mass sighting of UFOs appeared in the skies. People were freaking out, running, and hiding under things. A man with gray hair, a graying beard and a robe, with sandals, was standing on a flat disc that was levitating about five feet above the ground. I recognized him right away as the old man from my dreams. Eric, my ex-girlfriend Yumi, and I were still standing there as he started giving us an impassioned speech.

"We are your long-lost brothers and sisters. We have been guarding and protecting you all along. A major transformation is happening now on your planet. You have the opportunity to become something new—to transform and evolve—if you want to. Many of your people have called this ascension. Your earth and sun are going through a profound meta-morphosis, and so are you. We are proud of you for how hard you have worked to be a good person, to love other people, to be kind, patient, and forgiving. We will ensure that you remain safe as this change takes place. No harm will come to you—only transfiguration."

The old man stopped talking at a certain point and silence hung in the air. The entire area was now abandoned, except for the UFO that was hovering above him, with a beam leading down to the flat disc he was standing on. Yumi said to Eric, "Shouldn't somebody go talk to him?" Eric replied, "I'll let David do it. He's the UFO guy, he'll know what to say." I went up to the old man and the disc lowered so I could walk onto it. Once we got close, we recognized each other and hugged. The old man threw his arms around me, made intense eye contact with Eric, and said, "It is very important that you know that he is one of us."

Then It Hits Me

As soon as he finished telling me this I had to rush off to work because I was late. People were always driving ten to fifteen miles per hour below the speed limit on Route 32, and it happened again that morning. I was late and I got in trouble for it. Work was totally chaotic that day and I was scheduled to drive up and see my family right after it was over. I was on the New York State Thruway, heading north, in a blinding rainstorm. My car was sliding frighteningly on the road as I hit water puddles, and it was terrifying. The windshield was fogging up and I could barely see. I was gripping the steering wheel and my body was racked with total fear, pain, and sadness. Suddenly, right then, it hit me. I remembered the prayer from the night before. Eric's dream was the answer. I asked the universe whether I was an ET soul, and I got a highly dramatic answer— from the old man himself, appearing in Eric's dream. Even better, his dream provided compelling proof that an ascension event was really go-ing to happen. If the old man could appear in someone else's dream on request, why would he tell a lie about such an important subject?

I pulled the car over for safety and cried very hard for about half an hour. By the time I had finished, the rains had passed and the road was safe again. I decided that I needed to take Mandelker's book much more seriously. He was an intense scholar of the Law of One material, which I had never read. I decided that I needed those books, and I got them less than a month later, in January 1996.

Remarkable Validation

The Law of One series said there was a super-Earth in our solar system that had exploded due to warlike acts 500,000 years ago. I was stunned to see this, as I was familiar with Van Flandern's exploded planet hypothesis and always wanted to know what had happened. This planet was called Maldek in the Law of One books. I wouldn't learn that Brilliant Pebbles had produced the exact same date for this disaster until eighteen and a half years later. The Law of One also said a civilization had existed on Mars, and had destroyed their atmosphere—again through warlike acts. Most of the people of Mars and Maldek ended up reincarnating in mass numbers on Earth to work off their karma. Many people still carry the memory of this trauma, and of living under a totalitarian race, in their subconscious. The Law of One also indicated that a small number of others escaped the disaster and did not reincarnate like everyone else, but the details were vague. I would put the pieces together only many years later, beginning in 2014.

The Law of One spoke extensively about the Cabal on Earth, which they called the "negative elite." It also clearly indicated that these people were being controlled by a highly negative extraterrestrial group called the Orion Confederation. No descriptions were given of what the Orions looked like. Jacob and Corey both confirmed that the Draco have a major stronghold in the constellation Orion.

It is difficult to explain how many hundreds of things I had researched in the preceding years that were appearing in these books. I thought I had developed original discoveries and interesting ideas no one had thought of before. The Law of One books featured everything I thought

I knew and then went far, far beyond my own level of development. There was an extensive discussion of the Great Pyramid that totally paid off all my research on the Pyramid Time Line. The group speaking the words identified themselves as Ra, and said they were a benevolent group who built the Great Pyramid as a beacon for our ascension. They had no idea that it would be taken over and used as a symbol for the negative elite, and were now here to help repair the damage.

There were multiple clues in the Law of One that they were very supportive of Christianity and had helped to ensure that it had developed. They understood that great harm had been caused by organized religion, but the overall effect was still positive in that it helped people become more forgiving—and "in forgiveness lies the stoppage of the wheel of karma." The term that the Law of One used for ascension was biblical, taken right out of the Book of Matthew. The term was "harvest." This is an analogy Jesus makes when the weeds are allowed to grow together with the wheat until "the harvest." At that time there is a division. The weeds are plucked out one by one. The people who remain then "shine like the sun."

I began having dream after dream that ETs wanted to talk to me directly. In one dream I had a friendly ghost speaking words into my ear. I was told that I could hear them but no one else could, so I should dictate them into a tape recorder. As I have thoroughly documented on my website, I began practicing this technique in November 1996, and got phenomenal results. I used remote-viewing protocols to make sure I was consciously unaware of what was being said, to have no emotional reactions, and to not analyze any of the data if I heard something.

Cryptic sentences began flowing through me. On the first day I was given a prophecy that something was going to happen to "one of our women, Theresa, the Christian," which would make her "inoperative." Eleven days later, Mother Theresa had a heart attack. In that first session I was told, "The religions I am concerned with will be someday lighted, and we will go on to greater heights as a conglomerate being in the cosmos." I also heard a line that validated my assumptions about the noise coming from the television: "[Your] country and continuity [is being] shaded by an invisible hand which controls the sound in the lower ear. [It is] the sound of Hades—it massages the temples." This also appears to refer to the Draco technology that is holding us back collectively from ascension and which will suddenly get turned off if the Alliance destroys the devices generating the signal. A bit later it gave a statement about the possible catastrophic events that will occur for people on the negative time line: "A book called *The Greek Mythologies*. Tombstone, talking about a seventy mph wind from everyplace. Pause for the government's actions to be completed."[269]

Two days later, on November 12, 1996, I heard, "Hello, David. Plan B. It's been a very long time. We've built and destroyed civilizations. As the process goes around, there are ascensions, and a new cycle begins." The beings demonstrated a sense of humor on November 16, when they said, "Who do you think we are? Space aliens? Wrong. That's the one thing about our service is that we need to help."[270] I had wondered if I was talking to Gray-type extraterrestrials at the time, and this was a humorous rebuke of that idea.

A few sessions later on November 22, I asked, "Can you give me any general UFO information at this time?" The answer was, "Absolutely not! The purpose here is not to keep yourself around—it is to move you on. . . . We put A to Z in, and before long, we have a weblink to the cosmos. Feel the chorus sing in you—in me, and know that all is well that ends well. The Church tradition of symbolism will be renewed. Believe it when I tell you that the end is coming—the end of organized materialism. You've got to listen to your own inner voice—nothing else will do. The voice of your ego will destroy you."[271]

I began routinely getting accurate prophecies of future events. In one of the very first sessions on November 30, 1996, I was told, "Homeopathic TV. Think of Art Bell doing yoga."[272] This statement has been available for people to read on my website ever since 1999. In 2013 I ended up taking the invitation to have a show on Gaiam TV, which predominantly did yoga videos at the time. My first appearance was on *Beyond Belief* with George Noory. Remarkably, Noory was now the host of *Coast to Coast AM*, after having replaced Art Bell in 2001. That was an example of a fourteen-year time loop that was publicly documented. There have been dozens and dozens of other time loops as well. I experienced an immense series of them in Canada while outlining this book in September 2015, as we will soon discuss.

It became very common for me to have a stack of tapes at my desk, which could be up to a month old. I would sit down to transcribe them and the words would be describing something that had just happened to me. This was extremely fascinating and happened almost every single time I did it. At one point I was in a café in Woodstock, talking to a guy who quoted Joseph Campbell in saying that religions are like software to access the Creator. I came home, sat down, started the tape, and the first thing I heard was, "We are downloading new software."

My housemate Eric was told, "You will be happy to know that your student loans for New Paltz have come in." This didn't make any sense, since we had both graduated from New Paltz and he was now getting a master's degree in Albany. Neither of us had any money and we were $876 short for the rent. It was a serious problem. Eric walked in one day and told me to sit down. His mother had just called him. New Paltz was remodeling the bursar's office. They had moved a file cabinet away from the wall, and a Stafford Loan check for Eric was hiding behind it. The check was for $900, and it was still good.

In that first month, I was having incredible experiences with this cosmic intelligence. Every morning I pulled in new information. I was told that I worried far too much, and I would be much happier if I could learn to relax and meditate. I was also told that I needed to stop trying to pass people on Route 32. I was warned about four or five times, but refused to listen. On a Tuesday, I got a message that said, "My gift to the world will be a three-and-a-half-by-eleven sheet of paper. Expect it on Friday, ninety minutes until ten o'clock."[273]

On Friday, at eight thirty a.m., I collided with a car in front of me while on my way to a training session for medical certification in Poughkeepsie. The woman inside ended up trying to sue me for $200,000, despite having only a dime-sized dent on her bumper. I found out she had committed insurance fraud before. She ended up trying to settle for $10,000, and I never heard whether the insurance company gave her anything or not. That day, the officer wrote me a ticket—on a three-and-a-half-by-eleven-inch sheet of paper. Once I put it all together, and realized that these benevolent beings had authorized my car crash and subsequent threat of a crushing lawsuit, I cried very heavily for some time.

This was a very sobering reminder of the fact that the people I was now in contact with were the Lords of Karma, if you will. I needed to respect them and the opportunity I was being given. Ascension is a hard-earned process, not an easy cakewalk. The events that happen in our lives are not random. They are very precisely scripted by higher intelligence. The ascension process does involve becoming aware of the relationship between your thoughts and actions, and the results that then occur.

Sir John and Porphyry: The Canada Time Loop

I have traveled to Banff in Alberta, Canada, five different times as of this writing for spiritual retreat and solitude. Each time I went there, I had astonishing time-loop prophecies appear in my dream and reading journals. I would feel spontaneously guided to read my journal about certain events in my past that I was thinking about, only to discover that the dreams and readings I had written down during those same times were referring to my present. The most recent example started on September 4, 2015, and was probably the most miraculous of them all. Over twenty-five different correlations to my present, all highly specific, ended up appearing.

Here is the journal entry I wrote right after it started happening: "I was playing guitar and gently inspired to go back to my readings and read about my experiences. I decided to check out section 80 from the beginning of March 2000. Almost immediately there were profound coordinates to my present. . . . And it went way beyond that. There was some form of cosmic military service I was getting into involving jump-suits. [The people in the SSP all wear jumpsuits.] A series of readings had very targeted messages for me about the book I am writing right now. They confirmed that I needed to talk about myself and the journey of how I put all this information together."

I soon realized that I needed to go back to February 21, 2000, to see the full time loop. Here is part of what I read: "Don't let the scorn and derision of others stop you from being effective in your goals. Keep a clear head and remain relaxed, knowing all the while that there is indeed a final conclusion to these words as they now stand, and that this moment [of ascension] does indeed approach with the unwavering certainty of the clock striking on the hour.

"And we will add that this circumstance does not differentiate between past, present, and future at the moment of its arrival. It is almost entirely a creature of the collective human consciousness, and this 'cosmic trigger' can be set off at will over the next few years, depending upon the vibrations of humanity as a whole.

"We want you to stay on track, and realize that everything that has been extended to you has been part of a massive gift from higher intelligence. You yourself have done nothing; it is rather the work of the Christ and the Father/Mother God that is moving through you. As long as you can remind yourself of that, you can continue to reorient the focus back onto the goal and the destination, which is to achieve a final reunion with this light/love energy. If the book becomes overly technical in its writing capacity from start to finish, then it will not inspire people in the way that is necessary. Use your intuition while writing."[274]

On March 5, 2000, I journaled about the testimony of Sgt. Clifford Stone, a Disclosure Project witness who claimed to have worked on extraterrestrial crash recovery operations, and who then did a reading. Less than a month and a half before the dot-com collapse, this reading gave tremendous clues of what was about to happen. "I am Archangel Michael. The profit losses before the corporations now are set to require more download time than ever before. . . . There are only a finite series of opportunities to stress the motherboard, so to speak, before it gives out on you. And this will be happening to greater and greater degrees. . . . We do suggest that as much as you may want to appeal to the disciples of the scientific fraternity, that you keep in mind the extraterrestrial connections and the theological connections as well. . . .

"One shaman should reap the rewards as much as another, and remember that you are not so much writing this [book] for the scientific community as you are for the intellectual and spiritual community. Do not be afraid to change the architecture of this burgeoning project to reflect early along where your sources arise from and how you were led to do this research in the first place. . . . Every time that we defy gravity in the common sense use of the term, there is great interest generated. And so, you can see that the discussion of anti-gravity becomes much more vivid when the new understandings about creation are fused into the equation. The sacrifice of longing is necessary, as Sir John Alexander and Porphyry would have it."[275]

I had just ignored that last line at the time it came in. The readings often said lots of strange and cryptic things. I never bothered to research who Sir John Alexander was, or who or what Porphyry was, although I thought it might be a Greek philosopher. Now I had to know. Almost immediately, I discovered that Sir John Alexander Macdonald was the first prime minister of Canada. He established Banff, right where I was staying in the middle of this incredible time loop, as a nature preserve in 1885.[276] I was completely unaware of Banff until I was invited to conduct a conference tour there in 2008, and was dazzled by it. This reading was from 2000.

I next discovered that the word "porphyry" actually means "purple" in Greek. Porphyry is a type of purple granite rock—and I was surrounded by mountains of it on all sides. In fact, a short drive south across the border from Banff into Montana takes you to Porphyry Peak.[277] A mining website explained how this purple granite can be easily carved into huge blocks: "It's a type of granite that has naturally extruded through the earth's crust. . . . Because the formation has vertical layers, extracting the stone requires very little energy. . . . Despite its variable thickness, it is easy to achieve a flat surface that meets modern ADA standards. Porphyry is most often cut into cubes so that it can be installed in patterns."[278]

Now the full weight of the "time loop" slammed down on me. In the Great Pyramid, ascension and the world of spirit is symbolized by purple granite—porphyry—as opposed to limestone, which indicates materiality. The entire King's Chamber is made out of purple granite. The open sarcophagus in the King's Chamber represents the end of death and the gateway to ascension—and it is also made out of porphyry. This connection appeared in the occultist Helena Blavatsky's work, among others.[279] Another bizarre "time loop" connection is that Prince, the "Purple One," whose film and song "Purple Rain" is a timeless classic, died three days before I added this section to the book. I didn't consciously recognize this connection until after writing and submitting the full analysis.

Gerry Cannon pointed out that the porphyry coffin in the King's Chamber has precisely the same measurements as the Ark of the Covenant in the Bible. "The word ark comes from the Hebrew word *aron,* which means a chest, box. Its dimensions are described by the Bible as 2.5 cubits by 1.5 cubits by 1.5 cubits (45 inches by 27 inches by 27 inches). Curiously, this is the exact volume of the stone chest or porphyry coffer in the King's Chamber in the Great Pyramid in Egypt. . . . Since the Pyramid was built and sealed long before the days of Moses, when he built the Ark and the Holy of Holies, and had remained sealed for over twenty-five centuries until the ninth century after Christ, there is no natural explanation for the phenomenon of both structures having identical volume measurements."[280]

Then it got even stranger. I looked up Porphyry, the philosopher, and found out that he was directly contradicting the efforts of Emperor Constantine to create a religion out of Jesus's teachings. Constantine was stripping out many scriptures, such as the Book of Enoch, to create the "canonized" Bible, which he had final approval over. Constantine also banned Porphyry's books. In *The Philosophy from Oracles,* Porphyry said, "The gods have proclaimed Christ to have been most pious, but the Christians are a confused and vicious sect."[281] This was exactly what I had felt, right up until the awakening I was having on this trip. I had just started reading the Bible and was dazzled by the prophecies I had found. The time loop only started happening after I had read through Matthew, Mark, Luke, and John.

The full coded passage read, "The sacrifice of longing is necessary, as Sir John Alexander and Porphyry would have it." I thought about how so many people feel a deep, agonizing longing for some taste of the infinite. Instead, we can actually sacrifice that "repetition compulsion" of trauma and longing by jumping in and going to a place like Banff, or reading the ancient scriptures for ourselves. A few lines later, this same reading said, "Socrates, Hipparchus and many others were looking into the divine spiritual implications of the knowledge handed down to them from Atlantis. You yourself can continue to philosophize upon current theory that has been handed down to you, so as to arrive at new conclusions."[282] This passage was what led to me later quote from Plato in this book.

The Stargate Will Indeed Open Again

It became very clear that the "coordinates" of this fifteen-year time loop were extending over multiple days of time. Many more details jumped out as I kept reading forward in my private transcripts. Some of them were published on my website and could be backdated by fifteen years. The greatest gift appeared on my birthday, March 8, 2000. First of all, the reading mentioned the date of May 5, 2000. That ended up being the exact day that I first transcribed the tape. Little did I realize that a much larger time loop was in there as well.

As I went through this time loop in Banff, all I could really think about was the fact that 2012 had come and gone without incident. In one reading, this was directly addressed: "In order that you not fall short of the goal, we do give you structure in terms of approximate time lines within which to finish this work. The Stargate will indeed open again at the approximate date of 2012 and thereabouts. . . ."

What did they mean by "approximate . . . and thereabouts" ? I went back to the first line of the reading, and realized that further clarity was given on the "approximate date of 2012." The term "months" was used as a cryptic time indicator, possibly for years, as follows: "The pilots then scheduled the flight to be delayed a few more months, while the surrounding circumstances continue to occur in greater and greater fashion. You have all the experience that it takes to believe in the propositions set forth herein." The time-bending reading suggested that the event would still occur, but would be delayed a few years after 2012. This fit in perfectly with the estimates Corey Goode had heard in the SSP—namely that a series of solar events would take place somewhere between 2018 and 2023, though the exact time cannot be known.

Right after the line about the stargate opening, it said, "So let's keep viewing your higher body as an extension of your physical body, and see how the evolution takes place. We have almost completed a cycle of beingness with you. The work that we are doing constitutes the actions of those who love you so much that they are willing to painstakingly pull all the levers and push all the buttons, thus releasing the stored potential within the self and allowing it to be made manifest to the greater personality structure.

"You have all the tools within you that you need to succeed, and for this we are very grateful. We appreciate all that you have done in aligning your true cosmic energy fields with those of our own. There are infinite races of beings in the universe, infinite possibilities for how systems will function, and yet you have found many of the greatest secrets that underlie the creation as you know it in your own area."

A few lines further down, I read the following, which again made far more sense to me now than it did when it came in: "The Pentagon still complains about our visitations, but they are very necessary to keep your species from annihilating itself. We don't view all of these occurrences as negative, however it is easy for one who is uninformed to perceive negativity in their midst. This is a function of the mirror to the self when it is turned within. . . . When you begin to realize the non-deterministic structure to your physical plane of existence, and the degree to which intelligence sculpts and molds everything that is occurring, you can indeed have a greater appreciation for all the positive events that are brought to you. In a Newtonian universe of simple cause and effect, the one particle bumping into another, these magical processes would not occur.

"It is wise for you to always recognize and thank the higher forces in manifestations that you achieve. Never forget that the entire pathway is visible to us in your third-dimensional sense, and we are always standing by to help you and guide you through it. For now, we depart. We again remind you that you are loved more than you could ever possibly imagine, and that events will prevail in your future that define that quite correctly."[283]

It's Getting Better All the Time

The changes happening to us now as a planet are very obvious. People seem to be hurting one another more than ever, but we are actually becoming a more peaceful people. I want to close with a scientific study from December 23, 2015—two days before Christmas—that is truly remarkable. Despite the screeching of the media with fear-provoking headlines, the level of violence in the world is sizably decreasing:

> This year may be remembered for barrel bombs, behead-
> ings and the Bataclan massacre, but according to [Steven
> Pinker,] a Harvard psychologist, a remarkable long term
> downward trend in violence is continuing. . . . "The news is a
> systematically misleading way to understand the world," he
> told the Thomson Reuters Foundation in an interview. In the
> past five years alone, conflicts have ended in Chad, Peru,
> Iran, India, Sri Lanka, India, and Angola, and if peace talks
> currently underway in Colombia are a success, war will have
> vanished from the Western hemisphere, he said. . . . [284]
>
> Formerly wars spanned the globe, and there were 30 between
> 1945 and 1990 that killed 100,000 people or more, including
> wars in Greece, China, Mozambique, Algeria, Tibet, Guate-
> mala, Uganda, and East Timor. With the exception of last year's
> small wars in Ukraine, the zone of war has contracted to a cres-
> cent from central Africa through the Middle East into South
> Asia. In "Better Angels," Pinker argues that almost every other
> kind of violence, including murders, capital punishment, do-
> mestic violence, torture and hunting, has also fallen sharply.[285]

The Tibetans practiced a meditation discipline that involved stilling the mind and having loving thoughts. If you could have every thought be a loving thought, and meditate on your own consciousness as being the "empty awareness" of the universe for thirteen years, your body would dissolve into pure light. They call this the Rainbow Body. There are 160,000 documented cases of this happening in Tibet, India, and China alone. It may not be a popular idea right now, but the proof is there. The transition the Law of One and my own readings are discussing does not require every thought to be a loving thought. All you have to do is be slightly above 50 percent "service to others" as opposed to "ser-vice to self" and you are cleared for ascension.

I hope to see you there!

Acknowledgments

A great deal of time, attention, and care have gone into the writing of this book, and it wouldn't be possible without the help of many others along the way. I would like to thank my mother, Marta Waterman; my father, Donald Wilcock; and my brother, Michael Wilcock, for being there for me and creating the loving and supportive atmosphere that made all this possible. I would like to thank my friends and teachers in school who gave me the valuable experiences I needed to shape who I am now. I would like to thank Richard C. Hoagland for his amazing work on the Moon and Mars, and for giving me permission to use Enterprise Mission images in this book.

I want to share my sincere appreciation and thanks for all the insiders who have given me information along the way, including Bruce, Daniel, Jacob, Pete Peterson, Corey Goode, and William Tompkins. I would also like to thank Dr. Steven Greer and his core team for the Disclosure Project, and Kerry Cassidy and Bill Ryan for creating Project Camelot and inviting me into that world.

I am greatly thankful for Carla Rueckert, Jim McCarty, and Don Elkins, since the Law of One was such an essential element of my awakening. I also thank Dr. Scott Mandelker for his work with me, and the key role his book played in my development. I want to thank the many other people who have done great work, and who I have quoted from and been inspired by in the writing of this book. I would like to thank the staff at Prometheus for welcoming me into *Ancient Aliens* and for giving me Consulting Producer credit for all the research and intel I have contributed to the formation of their episodes, and the staff at Gaia for helping produce and distribute my shows. I would like to thank the cosmic beings who have contacted me and guided me throughout my life, and who decided to share their words through me as an instrument. And last, I would like to thank you, the reader of these words, for supporting this work and doing your part to make our planet a healthier, happier place.

I feel a tremendous sense of accomplishment in having written this and feel that this is the "prequel" to *The Synchronicity Key*, which is then the "prequel" to *The Source Field Investigations*. I recommend that newcomers read the books in that order. Thank you so much!

Notes

Chapter One

1 Urban, Tim. "The Fermi Paradox." *Wait But Why*, May 22, 2014. http://waitbutwhy
   .com/2014/05/fermi-paradox.html.
2 Griffin, Andrew. "Mars Was Once Covered in Water, Making It Ideal for Alien Life."
   Independent (UK), March 6, 2015. http://www.independent.co.uk/news/science/mars
   -was-once-covered-in-water-making-it-ideal-for-alien-life-10090198.html.
3 Anderson, Gina. "NASA Confirms Evidence that Liquid Water Flows on Today's Mars."
   NASA MRO, Release 15-195, September 28, 2015. http://www.nasa.gov/press-release
   /nasa-confirms-evidence-that-liquid-water-flows-on-today-s-mars.
4 Zolfagharifard, Ellie. "Mars Mystery SOLVED: NASA Reveals Solar Wind Stripped the
   Planet of Its Atmosphere to Turn It into a Dry and Arid World." *Daily Mail*, November 5,
   2015. http://www.dailymail.co.uk/sciencetech/article-3305797/Mystery-Mars-lost
   -atmosphere-SOLVED-Nasa-reveals-solar-wind-stripped-planet-turn-dry-arid-world.html.
5 Amos, Jonathan. "Hubble Finds 'Best Evidence' for Ganymede Subsurface Ocean." *BBC
   News*, March 12, 2015. http://www.bbc.com/news/science-environment-31855395.
6 Wolchover, Natalie. "A Jewel at the Heart of Quantum Physics." *Quanta Magazine*,
   September 17, 2013. https://www.quantamagazine.org/20130917-a-jewel-at-the-heart-of
   -quantum-physics/.
7 Wilcock, David. *The Source Field Investigations*. New York: Dutton, 2011.
8 Dillow, Clay. "Can Our DNA Electromagnetically 'Teleport' Itself? One Researcher
   Thinks So." *Popular Science*, January 13, 2011. https://www.popsci.com/science
   /article/2011-01/can-our-dna-electromagnetically-teleport-itself-one-researcher-thinks-so.
9 Enserink, Martin. "UNESCO to Host Meeting on Controversial 'Memory of Water'
   Research." *Science*, September 23, 2014. http://www.sciencemag.org/news/2014/09/
   unesco-host-meeting-controversial-memory-water-research.
10 Wilcock, David. *The Synchronicity Key*. New York: Dutton, 2013.
11 Van der Kolk, Bessel A. "The Compulsion to Repeat the Trauma: Re-Enactment, Revic-
   timization, and Masochism." *Psychiatric Clinics of North America* 12, no. 2 (1989):
   389–411. http://www.cirp.org/library/psych/vanderkolk/.
12 Ibid.

Chapter Two

13 Edwards, Gavin. "The Beatles Make History with 'All You Need Is Love': A Minute-by
    -minute Breakdown." *Rolling Stone*, August 28, 2014. http://www.rollingstone.com
    /music/features/the-beatles-make-history-with-all-you-need-is-love-a-minute-by
    -minute-breakdown-20140828.

14 Wilcock, David. "Decloaking Lucifer: A Holographic, Angry Child Throwing a
    Tantrum." *Divine Cosmos*, February 7, 2014. http://divinecosmos.com/start-here/davids
    -blog/1157-decloaking-lucifer.

15 Strecker, Erin. "Adele Offers Her Public Support to Kesha." *Billboard*, February 24, 2016.
    http://www.billboard.com/articles/news/6889479/adele-offers-her-public-support-to
    -kesha.

16 Clarendon, Dan. "18 Celebrities Supporting Kesha in Her Battle with Dr. Luke and
    Sony." *Wet Paint*, February 25, 2016. http://www.wetpaint.com/celebrities-supporting
    -kesha-1475186/.

17 Holden, Michael. "UK Police Say 261 People of 'Prominence' Suspected of Child
    Sex Abuse." Reuters, May 20, 2015. http://www.reuters.com/article/britain-abuse
    -idUSL5N0YB3PH20150520.

18 Bilefsky, Dan. "Jimmy Savile Inquiry Accuses BBC of Failing to Report Sexual Abuse."
    New York Times, February 15, 2016. http://www.nytimes.com/2016/02/26/world/europe
    /jimmy-savile-report-bbc.html.

Chapter Five

19 Judge, John. "The Black Hole of Guyana: The Untold Story of the Jonestown Massacre."
    Ratical.org, 1985. http://www.ratical.org/ratville/JFK/JohnJudge/Jonestown.html.

20 *New York Times*, November 25, 1978.

21 Beter, Peter David. "Audio Letter No. 40." *Dr. Peter David Beter*, November 30, 1978.
    http://www.peterdavidbeter.com/docs/all/dbal40.html.

22 "The Truth about Jonestown." *Viewzone.com*. http://viewzone2.com/jones22.html.

23 Wall, Mike. "NASA's Space Shuttle Program Cost $209 Billion—Was It Worth It?"
    Space.com, July 5, 2011. http://www.space.com/12166-space-shuttle-program-cost
    -promises-209-billion.html.

Chapter Eight

24 McManus, Doyle. "Rights Groups Accuse Contras: Atrocities in Nicaragua Against
    Civilians Charged." *Los Angeles Times*, March 8, 1985. http://articles.latimes.com/1985
    -03-08/news/mn-32283_1_contras.

25 Ibid.

26 "Iran-Contra Affair." *Wikipedia*. https://en.wikipedia.org/wiki/Iran%E2%80%93
    Contra_affair.

Chapter Nine

27 Lammer, Helmut. "Preliminary Findings of Project MILAB." *UFO Evidence*. http://
    www.ufoevidence.org/documents/doc1776.htm.

Chapter Ten

28 "1990 Manic Nirvana Tour." *Robert Plant Homepage*. http://www.robertplanthomepage
    .com/setlists/concert.htm#1990.

29 Grassi, Tony. "August 27, 1990: The Day Stevie Ray Vaughan Died." *Guitar World*, August
    27, 2015. http://www.guitarworld.com/august-1990-how-stevie-ray-vaughan-died.

Chapter Eleven

30 "Beer Game: Anchorman." *Realbeer.com.* http://www.realbeer.com/fun/games/games-54.php.

Chapter Twelve

31 Coppolino, Eric Francis. "From the SUNY New Paltz PCB and Dioxin Files: Letter from Eric Francis to State Assemblyman Kevin Cahill." *Planet Waves*, May 5, 1993. December 30, 2010. http://planetwaves.net/news/dioxin/nysassemblyman-kevin-cahill/.

Chapter Thirteen

32 Hall-Flavin, Daniel K. "What Does the Term 'Clinical Depression' Mean?" *Mayo Clinic*, March 5, 2014. http://www.mayoclinic.org/diseases-conditions/depression/expert-answers/clinical-depression/faq-20057770.
33 Ibid.

Chapter Fourteen

34 Chatelain, Maurice. *Our Ancestors Came from Outer Space: A NASA Expert Confirms Mankind's Extraterrestrial Origins.* New York: Doubleday & Company, 1975.
35 Ibid., 4–5.
36 Ibid., 6.
37 Tompkins, William Mills. *Selected by Extraterrestrials: My Life in the Top Secret World of UFOs, Think-tanks and Nordic Secretaries.* North Charleston, SC: CreateSpace Independent Publishing Platform, 2015.
38 Chatelain. *Ancestors Came from Outer Space,* 16–18.
39 Boylan, Richard J. "UFO Reality Is Breaking Through." *Perceptions* (1996). http://www.v-j-enterprises.com/boylrpt.html.
40 Ibid.
41 Ibid.
42 Cosnette, Dave. "Apollo Moon Conversations and Pictures Show NASA Cover-up." *Cosmic Conspiracies*, 2001. http://www.ufos-aliens.co.uk/cosmicphotos.html.
43 *The Disclosure Project.* http://www.disclosureproject.org.
44 Greer, Stephen M. "Executive Summary of the Disclosure Project Briefing Document." Presentation by The Disclosure Project, 2001. http://www.disclosureproject.org/access/docs/pdf/ExecutiveSummary-LRdocs.pdf.
45 "My Favourite Clip from the UFO Disclosure Project." Filmed May 2001. YouTube video, 2:13. Posted by "OriginalDrDil," March 7, 2007. https://www.youtube.com/watch?v=R6QNzH4x1rY.
46 Greer. "Disclosure Project Briefing Document."
47 Tompkins, William Mills. Personal communication with David Wilcock, April 23, 2016.
48 NASA. "National Aeronautics and Space Act of 1958." Public Law #85-568, 72 Stat., 426. Signed by the President on July 29, 1958, Record Group 255, National Archives and Records Administration, Washington, D.C. http://www.hq.nasa.gov/office/pao/History/spaceact.html.
49 Greenwald, Glenn. "How Covert Agents Infiltrate the Internet to Manipulate, Deceive, and Destroy Reputations." *Intercept*, February 24, 2014. https://theintercept.com/2014/02/24/jtrig-manipulation/.
50 Ibid.
51 Chatelain. *Ancestors Came from Outer Space.*
52 Cosnette, Dave. "Apollo Moon Conversations."

Chapter Fifteen

53 Chatelain. *Ancestors Came from Outer Space.*

54 Plato. *Timaeus and Critias*. Translated by Benjamin Jowett. New York: Scribner's, 1871. http://atlantis-today.com/Atlantis_Critias_Timaeus.htm.

55 *End of Days: Essays on the Apocalypse from Antiquity to Modernity*, Edited by Karolyn Kinane and Michael A Ryan. Jefferson, NC: McFarland & Company, 2009, 30.

56 "Saoshyant." *Wikipedia*. https://en.wikipedia.org/wiki/Saoshyant.

57 Knapp, Steven. "Kalki: The Next Avatar of God and the End of Kali-yuga." *Stephen -Knapp.com*. http://www.stephen-knapp.com/kalki_the_next_avatar_of_God.htm.

58 *The Mahabharata*, Book Three, Section CLXXXVII. Translated by Kisari Mohan Ganguli. 18831996. *Sacred-Texts.com*. http://www.sacred-texts.com/hin/m03/m03187.htm.

59 "Ekpyrosis." *Wikipedia*. https://en.wikipedia.org/wiki/Ekpyrosis.

60 Harrill, J. Albert. "Stoic Physics, the Universal Conflagration, and the Eschatological Destruction of the 'Ignorant and Unstable' in 2 Peter." *Stoicism in Early Christianity* (2010): 115–140. Hosted on Academia.edu. https://www.academia.edu/1865923 /Stoic_Physics_the_Universal_Conflagration_and_the_Eschatological_Destruction _of_the_Ignorant_and_Unstable_in_2_Peter.

61 R., Peter. "The Prophecy of Peter Deunov." December 14, 2008. http://www.angelfire .com/oh2/peterr/ProphecyOfPeterDeunov.html.

62 Hixon, Lex. *The Heart of the Qur'an: An Introduction to Islamic Spirituality*, 2nd ed. Wheaton, IL: Quest Books, 2003.

63 Ibid., 85–86.

64 Plato. *Timaeus and Critias.*

65 Ibid.

66 Weinberg, Rob. "This Is How the Opening to *2001: A Space Odyssey* Was Supposed to Sound." 2014. http://www.classicfm.com/composers/strauss/music/also-sprach-zarathustra -2001-space-odyssey/.

67 "Also Sprach Zarathustra, Op. 30." *The Kennedy Center*. http://m.kennedy-center.org /home/program/4301.

68 Chatelain. *Ancestors Came from Outer Space.*

69 Dorr, Eugene. "Apollo 17." http://genedorr.com/patches/Apollo/Ap17.html.

70 McCall, Robert T., Interviewed by Rebecca Wright. "Oral History Transcript." *Johnson Space Center*, March 28, 2000. http://www.jsc.nasa.gov/history/oral_histories /McCallRT/RTM_3-28-00.pdf.

Chapter Sixteen

71 Anderson, Paul Scott. "ASU Researchers Propose Looking for Ancient Alien Artifacts on the Moon." *Universe Today*, December 29, 2011. http://www.universetoday.com/92177 /asu-researchers-propose-looking-for-ancient-alien-artifacts-on-the-moon/.

72 Kee, Edwin. "Transparent Aluminum Now a Reality." *Ubergizmo*, November 3, 2015. http://www.ubergizmo.com/2015/11/transparent-aluminum/.

73 "Optically Clear Aluminum Provides Bulletproof Protection." *Total Security Solutions*, June 3, 2015. http://www.tssbulletproof.com/optically-clear-aluminum-provides-bulletproof -protection/.

74 Ibid.

75 Sanderson, Ivan T. "Mysterious 'Monuments' on the Moon." *Argosy* 371, no. 2 (1970). http://www.astrosurf.com/lunascan/argosy_cuspids.htm.

76 O'Toole, Thomas. "Mysterious Statuesque Shadows." *Washington Post*, November 23, 1966. Quoted in Hanks, Micah. "The Blair Cuspids: A Legitimate Lunar Anomaly?"

Mysterious Universe, February 18, 2016. http://mysteriousuniverse.org/2016/02/the-blair
-cuspids-a-legitimate-lunar-anomaly/.

77 Sanderson. "Mysterious 'Monuments.'"

78 Blair, William. *Los Angeles Times*, February 1, 1967. Quoted by Hanks. "The Blair Cuspids."

79 Sanderson. "Mysterious 'Monuments.'"

80 Blair. Quoted by Hanks. "The Blair Cuspids."

81 Jury, William. "Regular Geometric Patterns Formed by Moon 'Spires.'" *Boeing News* 26, no. 3, March 30, 1967. http://www.astrosurf.com/lunascan/1cusp.htm.

82 Carlotto, Mark J. http://spsr.utsi.edu/members/markjcarlotto.html.

83 Carlotto, Mark J. "3-D Analysis of the 'Blair Cuspids' and Surrounding Terrain." *New Frontiers in Science* 1, no. 2, 2002. http://carlotto.us/newfrontiersinscience/Abstracts /NFS0102c.html.

84 Ibid.

85 Hoagland, Richard C., and Mike Bara. *Dark Mission: The Secret History of NASA*. Port Townsend, WA: Feral House, 2009.

86 Lindemann, Michael. Reported by Rebecca Schatte in Washington. "Exclusive Report: Hoagland's DC Press Conference." *CNI News* 16.6, 1996. http://www.v-j-enterprises .com/hoagconf.html.

87 Hoagland, Richard C., and Ken Johnston. "Two *Different* Versions of the Same *Apollo 10* Frame . . . AS10-32-4822." *Enterprise Mission*, 1996. http://www.enterprisemission .com/images/reflec1.jpg.

88 Hoagland, Richard C., and David Wilcock. "Russian Media Publicity Explosion." *Enterprise Mission*, November 13, 2007, and November 26, 2007. http://www.enterprisemission .com/NPC-Russia.htm, http://www.enterprisemission.com/NPC-Russia2.htm.

89 Great Images in NASA (GRIN). "GPN 2000-001137." *NASA*. http://grin.hq.nasa.gov /IMAGES/LARGE/GPN-2000-001137.jpg.

90 Hoagland and Wilcock. "Russian Media Publicity Explosion."

91 Ibid.

92 "The Mysterious Tower on the Far Side of the Moon Found by Soviet Spacecraft *Zond 3*." *Ancient Code*, January 2016. http://www.ancient-code.com/the-mysterious-tower-on -the-far-side-of-the-moon-found-by-soviet-spacecraft-zond-3/.

Chapter Seventeen

93 *The Outer Limits: O.B.I.T.* Directed by Gerd Oswald. 1963. Daystar Productions, Villa Di Stefano, United Artists Television: ABC. Television.

94 "Daniel." *Conscious Hugs*, April 23, 2016. http://www.conscioushugs.com/.

95 Duane, Alexander. *The Students' Dictionary of Medicine and the Allied Sciences*. New York: Lea Brothers & Co., 1896.

96 "Antiperiodic." *YourDictionary*, n.d. Web. March 26, 2016. http://www.yourdictionary .com/antiperiodic.

97 Cassidy, Kerry, Bill Ryan, and David Wilcock. "Brian O'Leary's Presentation on Free Energy—Joined by Henry Deacon." *Project Camelot*. July 12, 2009. http://projectcamelot .org/zurich_10-12_July_2009.html.

Chapter Eighteen

98 Cassidy, Kerry, Bill Ryan, and David Wilcock. "Dr Pete Peterson." *Project Camelot*, June 2009. http://projectcamelot.org/pete_peterson.html.

99 "Did a Broadcast of the National Anthem in the 1960s Contain Subliminal Messages?" *VC*, May 13, 2015. http://vigilantcitizen.com/vigilantreport/broadcast-national-anthem -1960s-contain-subliminal-messages/.

100   Watson, Paul Joseph. "Real or Hoax? 1960s Subliminal National Anthem Video Says 'Obey Government.'" *Infowars*, August 13, 2013. http://www.infowars.com/real-or -hoax-1960s-subliminal-national-anthem-video-says-obey-government/.

101   "Broadcast of the National Anthem."

102   Ibid.

103   "Subliminal Advertising." *Subliminal Manipulation*. September 2010. http://subliminal manipulation.blogspot.com/2010/09/subliminal-messages-in-advertising-in.html.

104   "Subliminal Advertising." Archive.org capture of *Subliminal Manipulation*. October 25, 2014. https://web.archive.org/web/20141025000336/http://subliminalmanipulation .blogspot.com/2010/09/subliminal-messages-in-advertising-in.html.

105   Chen, Adam. "Expert Discusses the Effects of Subliminal Advertising." MIT/*The Tech* Online Edition 110, no. 7 (1990). http://tech.mit.edu/V110/N7/lsc.07n.html.

106   "McDonald's Logo Flashes on 'Iron Chef.'" Associated Press/*USA Today*, January 26, 2007. http://usatoday30.usatoday.com/life/television/news/2007-01-26-mcdonalds -ironchef_x.htm.

107   Rossen, Jake. "7 Sneaky Subliminal Messages Hidden in Ads." *Mental Floss*, August 12, 2015. http://mentalfloss.com/article/67223/7-sneaky-subliminal-messages-hidden-ads.

108   Key, Wilson Bryan. "Subliminal Sexuality: The Fountainhead for America's Obsession." In Tom Reichert and Jacqueline Lambiase. *Sex in Advertising: Perspectives on the Erotic Appeal*. London: Lawrence Erlbaum Associates, 2003. http://ase.tufts.edu/gdae/CS /Subliminal.pdf.

109   Cassidy, Ryan, and Wilcock. "Dr Pete Peterson."

110   Dean, Bob, and Kerry Cassidy. "Bob Dean: Bringing In the Light." *Project Camelot Productions*, April 2010. http://projectcamelotproductions.com/interviews/bob_deanIII /bob_deanIII.html.

111   Wilcock, David. "Cosmic Perspective on the Defeat of the Cabal." *Divine Cosmos*, October 27, 2014. http://divinecosmos.com/start-here/davids-blog/1170-cabal-defeat.

112   Cassidy, Kerry, and Bill Ryan. "Gary McKinnon: Hacking the Pentagon." *Project Camelot*, June 2006. http://projectcamelot.org/gary_mckinnon.html.

113   Perks, Darren. "Solar Warden—The Secret Space Program." *Huffington Post*, November 7, 2012. http://www.huffingtonpost.co.uk/darren-perks/solar-warden-the-secret-space -program_b_1659192.html.

114   Cassidy and Ryan. "Gary McKinnon."

115   Dean and Cassidy. "Bob Dean."

116   Cassidy, Kerry, and Bill Ryan. "Phil Schneider." *Project Camelot*. http://projectcamelot .org/schneider.html.

117   Salter, Dan. "Testimony of Master Sergeant Dan Morris, USAF (Retired)/NRO Operative." In Stephen M. Greer and Theodore C. Loder III. "Disclosure Project Briefing Document," September 2000. http://www.disclosureproject.org/access/docs/pdf/Disclosure ProjectBriefingDocument.pdf.

118   Wilcock, David. "Cosmic Perspective."

119   Hamill, Jasper. "'Peace-loving Aliens Tried to Save America from Nuclear War,' Claims Moon Mission Astronaut Edgar Mitchell." *Mirror*, August 11, 2015. http://www.mirror .co.uk/news/technology-science/science/peace-loving-aliens-tried-save-6235113.

120   Hastings, Robert. "About UFOs and Nuclear Weapons." *UFOs and Nukes*, 2016. http:// www.ufohastings.com/.

121   Wilcock, David. "1950s Human ETs Prepare Us for Golden Age—Videos, Documents!" *Divine Cosmos*, July 22, 2011. http://divinecosmos.com/start-here/davids-blog/956-1950s-ets.

122   Dean and Cassidy. "Bob Dean."

123 Wilcock, David. "Disclosure Imminent? Two Underground NWO Bases Destroyed."
     Divine Cosmos, September 16, 2011. http://divinecosmos.com/start-here/davids-blog/975
     -undergroundbases.
124 Ibid.
125 Wilcock, David. "Russian TV Documentary on Positive Alliance Destruction of Under-
     ground Bases!" *Divine Cosmos*, August 6, 2014. http://divinecosmos.com/start-here
     /davids-blog/1166-russian-tv-underground-bases.
126 Weisberg, Jacob. "W.'s Greatest Hits: The Top 25 Bushisms of All Time." *Slate*, January
     12, 2009. http://www.slate.com/articles/news_and_politics/bushisms/2009/01/ws
     _greatest_hits.html.
127 Ibid.
128 Eggen, Dan. "Obama, Bush and Former Presidents Gather for Lunch at White House."
     Washington Post, January 8, 2009. http://www.washingtonpost.com/wp-dyn/content
     /article/2009/01/07/AR2009010700257.html.

Chapter Nineteen

129 Ryan, Bill, and Kerry Cassidy. "'Mr. X,' a Former UFO Archivist." *Project Camelot*, May
     2006. http://projectcamelot.org/mr_x.html.
130 Ibid.
131 Ryan, Bill, and Kerry Cassidy. "'Mr. X': Interview Transcript." Video Transcript. *Project
     Camelot*, May 2006. http://projectcamelot.org/lang/en/mr_x_interview_transcript
     _en.html.
132 Ryan and Cassidy. "'Mr. X,' a Former UFO Archivist."
133 Ryan, Bill, and Kerry Cassidy. "Bob Dean." *Project Camelot*. September 2008. http://
     projectcamelot.org/bob_dean.html.
134 Salter. "Testimony of Master Sergeant Dan Morris."
135 Coleman, John. "21 Goals of the Illuminati and the Committee of 300." *Educate
     -Yourself*, 1993. http://educate-yourself.org/cn/johncolemangoalsofIlluminati.shtml.
136 Bennett, Richard M. *Conspiracy: Plots, Lies and Cover-ups*. London: Virgin Books, 2003.
     Retrieved May 3, 2013. http://books.google.com/books?id=tmobAQAAMAAJ.
137 Rathenau, Walther. *Zur Kritik der Zeit*. Berlin: S. Fischer, 1922. https://archive.org
     /details/zurkritikderzeit00rathuoft.
138 Swartzburg, Mark. "The 'Three Hundred.'" In *Antisemitism: A Historical Encyclopedia of
     Prejudice and Persecution*. Edited by Richard S. Levy. Santa Barbara: ABC-CLIO, 2005.
139 Dean and Cassidy. "Bob Dean."
140 Wilcock, David. "Terrifying Global Events: Triggers for Mass Awakening?" Part Two:
     Weaponized Natural Disasters. *Divine Cosmos*, August 24, 2015. http://divinecosmos
     .com/start-here/davids-blog/1185-events-awakening?showall=&start=1.
141 Mack, Eric. "Scientists Spy 'Magic Island' on Titan, Saturn's Strangest Moon." *Forbes*,
     June 22, 2014. http://www.forbes.com/sites/ericmack/2014/06/22/scientists-spy-magic
     -island-on-titan-saturns-strangest-moon/.
142 DeMaria, Meghan. "Mysterious Feature on Saturn's Moon Baffles NASA Scientists." *The
     Week*, September 30, 2014. http://theweek.com/speedreads/index/269015/speedreads
     -mysterious-feature-on-saturns-moon-baffles-nasa-scientists.
143 Wolf, Naomi. "Fascist America, in 10 Easy Steps." *Guardian*, April 24, 2007. http://
     www.theguardian.com/world/2007/apr/24/usa.comment.
144 Wilcock, David, and Corey Goode. "Skype Interview with Corey Goode." *Gaia*, Sep-
     tember 25, 2015. http://click.linksynergy.com/fs-bin/click?id=mTckSPpGJyM&offerid
     =346926.10000843&type=3&subid=0.

Chapter Twenty

145 Rice, Doyle. "Earthshaking News: There May Be Other Planets Like Ours." *USA Today*, November 4, 2013. http://www.usatoday.com/story/news/nation/2013/11/04/earth-like -planets-milky-way-galaxy/3433449/?utm_source=dlvr.it&utm_medium=twitter &dlvrit=206567.

146 Paur, Joey. "'We've Got Company!'—One of the Most Overused Movie Quotes Ever?" *Geek Tyrant*, April 16, 2010. http://geektyrant.com/news/2010/4/16/weve-got-company -one-of-the-most-overused-movie-quotes-ever.html.

147 Gallagher, Paul. "Forget Little Green Men—Aliens Will Look Like Humans, Says Cambridge University Evolution Expert." *Independent*, July 1, 2015. http://www.independent .co.uk/news/science/forget-little-green-men—aliens-will-look-like-humans-says -cambridge-university-evolution-expert-10358164.html.

148 Andersen, Ross. "The Most Mysterious Star in Our Galaxy." *The Atlantic*, October 13, 2015. http://www.theatlantic.com/science/archive/2015/10/the-most-interesting-star-in -our-galaxy/410023/.

149 Pogge, Richard W. "The Solar Neighborhood." Lecture at Ohio State University, Astronomy 141, Lecture 32, Winter 2012. http://www.astronomy.ohio-state.edu/~pogge /Ast141/Unit5/Lect32_Neighbors.pdf.

150 Carigi, Leticia. "Solar Neighborhood." *Encyclopedia of Astrobiology*. SpringerLink. http:// link.springer.com/referenceworkentry/10.1007%2F978-3-642-11274-4_1460.

151 Sanders, Robert. "3-D Map of Local Interstellar Space Shows Sun Lies in Middle of Hole Piercing Galactic Plane." *UC Berkeley News*, May 29, 2003. http://www.berkeley.edu /news/media/releases/2003/05/29_space.shtml.

152 Ibid.

153 Ibid.

154 Elkins, Don, Carla Rueckert, and Jim McCarty. *The Law of One*. Session 6, Question 24. January 24, 1981. http://www.lawofone.info/results.php?s=6#24.

155 Ibid., Session 9, Question 4. http://www.lawofone.info/results.php?s=9#4.

156 Ibid., Session 6, Question 4. http://www.lawofone.info/results.php?s=6#4.

157 Ibid., Session 89, Question 8. http://www.lawofone.info/results.php?s=89#8.

158 Ibid., Session 60, Question 16. http://www.lawofone.info/results.php?s=60#16.

Chapter Twenty-one

159 Zolfagharifard, Ellie. "Evolution of Life's 'Operating System' Revealed: 4-billion-year -old Molecules Could Provide Clues to the Origins of Existence." *Daily Mail*, July 1, 2014. http://www.dailymail.co.uk/sciencetech/article-2676536/Evolution-lifes-operating -revealed-4-billion-year-old-molecules-provide-clues-origin-existence.html.

160 Gates, Sara. "Hidden 'Ocean' Discovered Deep Underground Near Earth's Core." *Huffington Post*, June 13, 2014. http://www.huffingtonpost.com/2014/06/13/hidden-ocean -earth-core-underground-video_n_5491692.html?utm_hp_ref=mostpopular.

161 Mazza, Ed. "Mimas, One of Saturn's Moons, May Have an Underground 'Life-friendly' Ocean." *Huffington Post*, October 17, 2014. http://www.huffingtonpost.com/2014/10/17 /mimas-saturn-moon-ocean_n_6001420.html.

162 Cooper-White, Macrina. "Saturn's Moon Enceladus May Have Warm Ocean, Boosting Likelihood of Life on Icy Satellite." *Huffington Post*, March 12, 2015. http://www.huffing tonpost.com/2015/03/12/saturn-moon-ocean-enceladus-hot-springs_n_6857150.html.

163 Hand, Eric. "Huge Ocean Confirmed Underneath Solar System's Largest Moon." *Science*, March 12, 2015. http://news.sciencemag.org/space/2015/03/huge-ocean-confirmed -underneath-solar-system-s-largest-moon.

164 Ibid.

165 Ibid.

166 Dyches, Preston, and Felicia Chou. "The Solar System and Beyond Is Awash in Water." *NASA/Jet Propulsion Laboratory*, April 7, 2015. http://www.jpl.nasa.gov/news/news .php?release=2015-119&rn=news.xml&rst=4541.

167 Woo, Marcus. "When Will We Find Aliens?" *BBC Earth*, April 29, 2015. http://www .bbc.com/earth/story/20150429-will-we-find-aliens.

168 Dyches and Chou. "Solar System and Beyond."

169 Bendery, Jennifer. "NASA 'On the Cusp' of Discovering if Life Exists Beyond Earth, Says Top Scientist." *Huffington Post*, July 28, 2015. http://www.huffingtonpost.com /entry/nasa-life-beyond-earth_55b7ad53e4b0a13f9d1a4f97?ncid=txtlnkusaolp00000592.

170 Griffin, Andrew. "Mars Was Once Covered in Water, Making It Ideal for Alien Life." *Independent*, March 6, 2015. http://www.independent.co.uk/news/science/mars-was -once-covered-in-water-making-it-ideal-for-alien-life-10090198.html.

171 Dyches and Chou. "Solar System and Beyond."

172 Ibid.

173 Tompkins. *Selected by Extraterrestrials*, 43.

174 Tompkins. Personal communication.

Chapter Twenty-two

175 Van Flandern, Tom. "The Exploded Planet Hypothesis 2000." *Meta Research*, 2000. http://www.metaresearch.org/solar%20system/eph/eph2000.asp.

176 Van Flandern, Tom. "The Challenge of the Exploded Planet Hypothesis." *International Journal of Astrobiology* 6, no. 3 (2007): 185–197. doi:10.1017/S1473550407003758. http:// journals.cambridge.org/action/displayAbstract?fromPage=online&aid=1299192.

177 Hoagland, Richard C., and Mike Bara. "A New Model of Mars as a Former Captured Satellite: Bi-modal Distribution of Key Features Due to Ancient Tidal Stress?" *Enterprise Mission*, August 19, 2001. http://www.enterprisemission.com/tides.htm.

178 Wrenn, Eddie. "Cultural Impact: Death Star Spotted Lurking Near the Rings of Saturn (. . . Luckily It Is Just an Asteroid Crater on One of the More Bizarre Moons Found in Our Solar System)." *Daily Mail*, June 28, 2012. http://www.dailymail.co.uk/sciencetech /article-2165955/Death-Star-spotted-lurking-near-rings-Saturn—luckily-just-bizarre -moons-solar-system.html.

179 Ibid.

180 Parnell, Brid-Aine. "Second PAC-MAN Orbiting SATURN: Local Absence of Dots Explained." *Register*, November 27, 2012. http://www.theregister.co.uk/2012/11/27 /cassini_spots_second_pac_man_moon/.

181 Hoagland, Richard. "Moon With a View: Or, What Did Arthur Know . . . And *When* Did He Know It?" Parts 1–6. *Enterprise Mission*, 2005. http://www.enterprisemission .com/moon1.htm, http://www.enterprisemission.com/moon2.htm, http://www .enterprisemission.com/moon3.htm, http://www.enterprisemission.com/moon4.htm, http://www.enterprisemission.com/moon5.htm, http://www.enterprisemission.com /moon6.htm.

182 Sitchin, Zecharia. *Genesis Revisited*. New York: Avon, 1990.

183 Choi, Charles Q. "Bizarre Shape of Uranus' 'Frankenstein' Moon Explained." *Space.com*, October 3, 2014. http://www.space.com/27334-uranus-frankenstein-moon-miranda .html.

184 Ibid.

185 Ibid.

186 Wilcock, David. "Disclosure and the Secret History of Our Solar System—Radio Show [Major Updates!]" *Divine Cosmos*, February 25, 2015. http://divinecosmos.com/start -here/davids-blog/1174-disclosure-history.

187 Ibid.

188 Chappell, Bill. "NASA Sees 'Bright Spots' on Dwarf Planet in Our Solar System." *NPR*, February 26, 2015. http://www.npr.org/blogs/thetwo-way/2015/02/26/389245969/nasa -sees-bright-spots-on-dwarf-planet-in-our-solar-system?utm_source=facebook .com&utm_medium=social&utm_campaign=npr&utm_term=nprnews&utm_content =20150226.

189 Ibid.

190 Feltman, Rachel. "Spacecraft *Dawn* Has Arrived at Ceres, One of Solar System's Last Unexplored Planets." *Washington Post*, March 6, 2015. http://www.washingtonpost.com /news/speaking-of-science/wp/2015/03/06/nasa-confirms-dawns-historic-arrival-at-ceres -one-of-the-solar-systems-last-unexplored-planets/.

191 "What's the Spot on World Ceres?" NASA/Jet Propulsion Laboratory/*DAWN*, April 26, 2015. http://www.jpl.nasa.gov/dawn/world_ceres/#.

192 Sutherland, Scott. "'Lonely Mountain' Spotted on Ceres by NASA's *Dawn* Spacecraft." *Weather Network*, June 18, 2015. http://www.theweathernetwork.com/news/articles /whats-up-in-space-great-pyramid-of-ceres-mars-conjunction-lunar-dust-cloud/52920/.

193 Mack, Eric. "NASA Spies 3-mile-tall 'Pyramid,' More Bright Spots on Ceres." *CNET*, June 18, 2015. http://www.cnet.com/news/3-mile-tall-pyramid-more-bright-spots-spied -on-ceres/.

194 Kremer, Ken. "Mysterious Bright Spots and Pyramidal Mountain Star in *Dawn*'s Daunt- ing Flyover of Ceres: Video." *Universe Today*, August 8, 2015. http://www.universetoday .com/121768/mysterious-bright-spots-and-pyramidal-mountain-star-in-dawns-daunting -flyover-of-ceres-video/.

195 "Bright Spots and a Pyramid-shaped Mountain on Ceres." Phys.org, August 7, 2015. http://phys.org/news/2015-08-bright-pyramid-shaped-mountain-ceres.html.

196 Fecht, Sarah. "What Are the Mysterious Glowing Spots on Ceres?" *Popular Science*, August 6, 2015. http://www.popsci.com/see-ceres-pyramid-and-bright-spots-close-video.

197 Mack, Eric. "The 4-mile-tall Pyramid Mountain on Dwarf Planet Ceres Is Glowing." *CNET*, August 8, 2015. http://www.cnet.com/news/the-4-mile-tall-pyramid-mountain -on-dwarf-planet-ceres-also-glows/.

198 King, Bob. "What's Orbiting KIC 8462852—Shattered Comet or Alien Megastruc- ture?" *Universe Today*, October 16, 2015. http://www.universetoday.com/122865/whats -orbiting-kic-8462852-shattered-comet-or-alien-megastructure/.

199 Venton, Danielle. "Odd Orbits Deepen Pluto's Mystery." *Wired*, June 3, 2015. http:// www.wired.com/2015/06/odd-orbits-deepen-plutos-mystery/.

200 Choi, Charles Q. "'Strikingly Geometric' Shapes Hidden on Moon's Surface." Space.com, October 1, 2014. http://www.space.com/27308-moon-ocean-of-storms-giant-rectangle .html.

201 Bednar, Chuck. "Newly Discovered Rectangular Structure Sheds New Light on Moon Mystery." *RedOrbit*, October 2, 2014. http://www.redorbit.com/news/space/1113247932 /moon-ocean-of-storms-mystery-100214/.

202 Andrews-Hanna, Jeffrey C., et al. "Figure 3: Geometric Pattern of the PKT Border Structures, with a Comparison to the Enceladus SPT." In "Structure and Evolution of the Lunar Procellarum Region as Revealed by GRAIL Gravity Data." *Nature* 514 (2014): 68–71. http://www.nature.com/nature/journal/v514/n7520/fig_tab/nature13697 _F3.html.

203 Hoagland, Richard C. "For the World Is Hollow—And I Have Touched the Sky!" *Enterprise Mission*, 2010. http://www.enterprisemission.com/Phobos.html.

204 Hoagland. "For the World Is Hollow." Part II. http://www.enterprisemission.com/Phobos2.html.

205 Cicchetti, Andrea. "First Look at the MARSIS Radar Data for Phobos." *ESA Mars Express Blog*, March 22, 2010. https://web.archive.org/web/20100324153311/http://webservices.esa.int/blog/post/7/1082.

206 "Radio Science Result from 2008 Phobos Flyby Now Accepted for Publication." *ESA Mars Express Blog*, March 25, 2010. https://web.archive.org/web/20100413185220/http://webservices.esa.int/blog/post/7/1085.

207 Andert, T. P., et al. "Precise Mass Determination and the Nature of Phobos." *Geophysical Research Letters*. doi:10.1029/2009GL041829. (Accepted 22 March 2010). http://onlinelibrary.wiley.com/doi/10.1029/2009GL041829/full.

208 Ibid.

209 "C-SPAN: Buzz Aldrin Reveals Existence of Monolith on Mars Moon." YouTube video, 1:00. Posted by C-SPAN, July 22, 2009. https://www.youtube.com/watch?v=bDIXvpjnRws.

210 "Buzz Aldrin Stokes the Mystery of the Monolith on Mars." *Daily Mail*, August 6, 2009. http://www.dailymail.co.uk/sciencetech/article-1204254/Has-mystery-Mars-Monolith-solved.html.

211 Ibid.

212 Mayor, Adrienne. *The First Fossil Hunters: Paleontology in Greek and Roman Times*. Princeton, NJ: Princeton University Press, 2000.

213 Ibid.

214 Ibid.

215 Ibid.

Chapter Twenty-three

216 Van Flandern. "The Exploded Planet Hypothesis."

217 Hamilton, Calvin J. "Ida and Dactyl." *Views of the Solar System*. http://solarviews.com/eng/ida.htm.

218 Ibid.

219 *Forbidden Planet*. Directed by Fred M. Wilcox. 1956. Culver City, CA: Metro-Goldwyn-Mayer Studios. Film. http://www.imdb.com/title/tt0049223/plotsummary.

220 Phillips, Tony. "Square Craters." *NASA Science*, September 26, 2000. http://science.nasa.gov/science-news/science-at-nasa/2000/ast26sep_1/.

221 Murchie, Scott. "NEAR Image of the Day for 2000 Sep 19." *Near Earth Asteroid Rendezvous*, Johns Hopkins University Applied Physics Laboratory, September 19, 2000. http://near.jhuapl.edu/iod/20000919/index.html.

222 Murchie, Scott. "NEAR Image of the Day for 2000 May 3." *Near Earth Asteroid Rendezvous*, Johns Hopkins University Applied Physics Laboratory, May 3, 2000. http://near.jhuapl.edu/iod/20000503/.

223 Hoagland, Richard C. "Tetrahedrons, Faces on Mars, Exploding Planets, Hyperdimensional Physics—and Tom Corbett, Space Cadet?! Or, What Did They Know, and When Did They Know It?" *Enterprise Mission*. http://www.enterprisemission.com/corbett.htm.

224 Cadet Ed. "View-Master's Tom Corbett Space Cadet." April 29, 1999. http://www.solarguard.com/tcvmintro.htm.

225 Cadet Ed. "Tom Corbett." Reel Two. http://www.solarguard.com/tcreel2.htm.

226 Ibid.

227 Cadet Ed. "Tom Corbett." Reel Three. http://www.solarguard.com/tcreel3.htm.

228 Cadet Ed. "Tom Corbett." http://www.solarguard.com/tcvmintro.htm.

229 International Space Hall of Fame. "Willy Ley." New Mexico Museum of Space History. http://www.nmspacemuseum.org/halloffame/detail.php?id=18.

230 "Chapter 1: Space Stations and Winged Rockets." In "SP-4221: The Space Shuttle Decision." *NASA History*. http://history.nasa.gov/SP-4221/ch1.htm.

231 Salla, Michael. "Exonews TV—Navy Disseminated Nazi Antigravity Secrets to Leading U.S. Companies & Think Tanks." *Exopolitics.org*, March 29, 2016. http://exopolitics.org/exonews-tv-navy-disseminated-nazi-antigravity-secrets-to-leading-u-s-companies-think-tanks/.

232 "Man and the Moon." Directed by Ward Kimball. 1955. Burbank, CA: Walt Disney Productions. TV episode in *Walt Disney's Wonderful World of Color*.

233 Harvey Comics. "The Face on Mars." *Race for the Moon*, Issue #2. *Archive.org*. https://archive.org/details/TheFaceOnMars.

234 Hoagland, Richard. "Forbidden Planet . . . Mars." *Enterprise Mission*, 2006. http://www.enterprisemission.com/forbidden-planet.htm.

235 "Race for the Moon." Harvey Comics 1, no. 2, September 1958. https://web.archive.org/web/20031123165414/http://www.comicbookresources.com/columns/oddball/index.cgi?date=2003-11-14.

236 "Mindbomb: John Carter, PKD and 'The Face on Mars' Revisited." *The Secret Sun*, August 15, 2012. http://secretsun.blogspot.com/2012/08/mindbomb-john-carter-pkd-and-face-on.html.

237 Ibid.

238 Goldenberg, Suzanne. "Planet Earth Is Home to 8.7 Million Species, Scientists Estimate." *Guardian*, August 23, 2011. http://www.theguardian.com/environment/2011/aug/23/species-earth-estimate-scientists.

239 Tompkins, William, Bob Wood, and Michael Salla. "Interview Transcript—US Navy Spies Learned of Nazi Alliance with Reptilian Extraterrestrials." Exopolitics.org, April 4, 2016. http://exopolitics.org/interview-transcript-us-navy-spies-learned-of-nazi-alliance-with-reptilian-extraterrestrials/.

Chapter Twenty-four

240 "Underwater Pyramid Found Near Portugal Has Portuguese Navy Investigating." *Banoosh*, January 14, 2014. https://web.archive.org/web/20140221122348/http://banoosh.com/blog/2014/01/14/underwater-pyramid-found-near-portugal-portuguese-navy-investigating.

241 Osborne, Hannah. "'Sunken Atlantis Pyramid' Discovered Off Azores Coast." *International Business Times*, September 26, 2013. http://www.ibtimes.co.uk/atlantis-discovered-pyramid-aozres-islands-sunken-509298.

242 West, Debbie. "Houston Anthropologist Reveals Irrefutable Proof that Recorded History Is Wrong." *Waking Times*, November 12, 2013. http://www.wakingtimes.com/2013/11/12/houston-anthropologist-reveals-irrefutable-proof-recorded-history-wrong/.

243 Graham, W. L. "Heaven's War." *Bible Reality Check*, 2006. http://www.biblerealitycheck.com/heavenswar.htm.

244 "Book of Enoch." *The Apocrypha and Pseudepigraphia of the Old Testament*. Edited by H. R. Charles. Oxford: Clarendon Press. http://www.ccel.org/c/charles/otpseudepig/enoch/ENOCH_1.HTM.

245   Ibid.
246   Viera, Jim, and Hugh Newman. "Visionary Salon: Giants on Record: America's Hidden History." *Chapel of Sacred Mirrors*, November 14, 2015. http://cosm.org/events/visionary-salon-giants-on-record-americas-hidden-history/.
247   Ibid.
248   Chouinard, Patrick. *Lost Race of the Giants: The Mystery of Their Culture, Influence, and Decline Throughout the World.* Rochester, VT: Bear & Company, 2013.
249   Thompson, Lucy. *To the American Indian: Reminiscences of a Yurok Woman.* (1916). Reprint. Berkeley, CA: Heyday Books, 1991.
250   Slavo, Mac. "This World Bank Insider Will Blow You Away: 'There Is a Huge Global Conspiracy.'" SHTFplan.com, March 8, 2014. http://www.shtfplan.com/headline-news/this-world-bank-insider-will-blow-you-away-there-is-a-huge-global-conspiracy_03082014.
251   Ibid.
252   Ghose, Tia. "Deformed Skull from Dark Ages Unearthed in France." *Huffington Post*, November 17, 2013. http://www.huffingtonpost.com/2013/11/17/deformed-skull-dark-ages-france_n_4292207.html.
253   Snyder, Michael. "These Ancient Elongated Skulls are NOT HUMAN." *The Truth*, January 16, 2014. http://thetruthwins.com/archives/these-ancient-elongated-skulls-are-not-human.
254   Waugh, Rob. "Alien Skulls from 1,000 Years Ago Found in Mexico." *Yahoo! News*, December 19, 2012. https://web.archive.org/web/20131201050746/http://news.yahoo.com/-alien—skulls-from-1-000-years-ago-found-in-mexico-113325793.html.
255   "'Alien in Chelyabinsk': 2,000-yo Skeleton with Cone Head Dug Up at Russian Stonehenge." *RT*, July 28, 2015. http://www.rt.com/news/310996-aliens-chelyabinsk-skeleton-russia/.
256   "RUSSIA: Siberian Scientists Search for Origins of Bizarre Humanoid Skull." Reuters/*ITN Source*, January 15, 2009. http://www.itnsource.com/shotlist/RTV/2009/01/15/RTV84809/.
257   Lynch, Gary, and Richard Granger. "What Happened to the Hominids Who May Have Been Smarter Than Us?" *Discover*, December 28, 2009. http://discovermagazine.com/2009/the-brain-2/28-what-happened-to-hominids-who-were-smarter-than-us.
258   "House of Este." *Wikipedia*. Accessed March 31, 2016. https://en.wikipedia.org/wiki/House_of_Este, https://web.archive.org/web/20160321121047/https://en.wikipedia.org/wiki/House_of_Este.
259   "List of Descendants of the House of Este." *Familypedia*. http://familypedia.wikia.com/wiki/List_of_descendants_of_the_House_of_Este, https://web.archive.org/web/20120705213951/http://familypedia.wikia.com/wiki/List_of_descendants_of_the_House_of_Este.
260   Lohr, Steve. "Bush, They Say, Is Indeed a Connecticut Yankee from King Henry's Court." *New York Times*, July 5, 1988. http://www.nytimes.com/1988/07/05/us/bush-they-say-is-indeed-a-connecticut-yankee-from-king-henry-s-court.html.
261   Farberov, Snejana. "Is Ruling in the Genes? All Presidents Bar One Are Directly Descended from a Medieval English King." *Daily Mail*, August 4, 2012. http://www.dailymail.co.uk/news/article-2183858/All-presidents-bar-directly-descended-medieval-English-king.html.
262   Breay, Claire, and Julian Harrison. "Magna Carta: An Introduction." *British Library*, September 2015. http://www.bl.uk/magna-carta/articles/magna-carta-an-introduction.

Chapter Twenty-five

263 "Chapter 7: The Pyramid and the Sacred Writings." In Lemesurier, Peter. *The Great Pyramid Decoded*. London: Element Books, 1977.

264 Ibid., 185.

265 Ibid., 191.

266 Elkins, Rueckert, and McCarty. *The Law of One*. Session 3, Question 12. http://www.lawofone.info/results.php?s=3#12.

267 Ibid., Session 3, Question 13. http://www.lawofone.info/results.php?s=3#13.

268 Lemesurier. *Great Pyramid Decoded*.

269 Wilcock, David. "11/30/96: The Advent of the Wilcock Readings." *Divine Cosmos*, 1999. http://www.divinecosmos.com/index.php/start-here/readings-in-text-form/159-113096-the-advent-of-the-wilcock-readings.

270 Ibid.

271 Ibid.

272 Wilcock, David. "Big Announcement: David's Weekly TV Show!" *Divine Cosmos*, April 20, 2013. http://divinecosmos.com/start-here/davids-blog/1122-big-announcement-david-wilcock-weekly-tv-show.

273 Wilcock, David. "12/14/96: Readings: First Half of December 1996." *Divine Cosmos*, 1999. http://www.divinecosmos.com/index.php/start-here/readings-in-text-form/160-121496-readings-first-half-of-december-1996.

274 Wilcock, David. "4/28/00: Prophecy: Archangel Michael on Economy & God." *Divine Cosmos*, April, 28, 2000. http://www.divinecosmos.com/index.php/start-here/readings-in-text-form/452-42800-prophecy-archangel-michael-on-economy-a-god.

275 Ibid.

276 Bierman, Jonny. "Facts and Figures about Banff National Park." *Banff & Lake Louise Tourism*, 2012. http://www.banfflakelouise.com/Media-Relations/Facts-and-Figures-about-Banff-National-Park.

277 "Porphyry Peak (8-1-14) & King's Hill (8-2-14), Montana." *The (Mostly) True Adventures of Lupe*, July 6, 2015. http://www.adventuresoflupe.com/?p=1006.

278 "What is Porphyry?" *Milestone Imports*, April 29, 2011. http://milestoneimports.com/2011/04/29/what-is-porphyry/.

279 Blavatsky, Helena Petrovna. *The Secret Doctrine: The Synthesis of Science, Religion, and Philosophy*. London: Theosophical Publishing Company, 1893.

280 Cannon, Gerry. "Great Pyramid and the Ark of the Covenant." *Crystalinks*. http://www.crystalinks.com/gparc.html.

281 "Porphyry (Philosopher)." *Wikipedia*. https://en.wikipedia.org/wiki/Porphyry_%28philosopher%29.

282 Wilcock. "Prophecy."

283 Wilcock, David. "5/23/00: Reading: The Stargate Will Open in 2012." *Divine Cosmos*, May 23, 2000. http://www.divinecosmos.com/index.php/start-here/readings-in-text-form/453-52300-reading-the-stargate-will-open-in-2012.

284 D'Urso, Joseph. "Behind the Scary Headlines, 2015 Gives Reason for Optimism." Reuters/*Yahoo! News*, December 23, 2015. https://ca.news.yahoo.com/behind-scary-headlines-2015-gives-reason-optimism-002255998.html.

285 Ibid.

Index

Monroe, Marilyn, 135
Montagnier, Luc (Dr.), 13–14
The Montauk Project: Experiments in Time
(Nichols and Moon), 305
The Monuments of Mars (Hoagland), 449
Moody Blues (music group), 46, 146, 160
Moon
as home for ET civilization, 387–91
Blair Cuspids, 280, 287, 417
evidence of structures, 252–56, 275–304
Frame 4822, 288–94, 296
Frame 9279, 293
Frame 9301, 293–94
GRIN image 2000-001131, 293–96
hiding discoveries from public, 256–61,
272–75, 277, 291–96, 411
migration of Empire survivors, 435
photograph of obelisks, 278–80
Russian *Zond 3* images, 297–301
taken over by the Empire, 408–9
the destruction of the Empire, 416–17
See also Apollo moon landings
Moon, Peter, 305
Moon, Robert (Dr.), 10–11, 17
"The Moon Pyramid," 422–23
Mootoo, C. Leslie (Dr.), 67
Mork and Mindy (TV program), 71
Morris, Simon Conway, 363, 393
Morrison, Jim, 37–38, 214, 225–26
Mr. Wizard's World (TV program), 92–93
Mr. X (Insider), 341–42
mystical phenomena, 3, 46, 99, 145
mythology, 2, 63, 266

nanites. *See* robots/robotic devices
Narcotics Anonymous, 236
Nathues, Andreas, 402
National Aeronautical and Space
Administration (NASA)
about the founding and financing,
426–28
anti-gravity and free-energy propulsion,
248
belief in mass evolutionary event,
247, 274
DDT (disinformation) campaign, 257–59
discovery of 433 Eros craters, 417–20, 424
evidence of ET technology, 363–64
finding Earth-like planets, 5–7, 362–63,
365–68
finding water on other planets, 382–83,
393

GRIN website, 294–95
hiding secrets from public, 256–57,
259–61, 272–75, 277, 291–96, 411
Insiders at work in, 244–45, 274, 285,
316–17
Moon landings, 249–56, 278–80,
288–96
NEAR (spacecraft), 417–18, 424
New Horizons mission, 405
role in disclosure process, 334, 350–52
Roswell UFO crash-landing, 244–45
structures and water on Mars, 7, 411–13,
415–16
structures on Ceres, 400–404
structures on KIC 8462852, 404–6
structures on the Moon, 252–56, 275–86,
302–4, 390–91
National Space Science Data Center
(NSSDC), 288, 290
Native American Graves Protection and
Repatriation Act of 1990, 442
Native Americans, 13, 44, 183, 441–43
Nature (magazine), 406
Nature Geoscience (journal), 350
The Nature of Personal Reality (Roberts), 49,
88–89
Nazi Germany
Draco agreement with, 432
Hitler and rise to power, 77, 376
Satanic connections, 36
scientific/aerospace advances, 253,
425–26
support from America, 213–15
near-death experience, 2, 165, 270, 377
Near Earth Asteroid Rendezvous (U.S.
spacecraft), 417–18
negative forces in the universe, 2, 267, 370,
380, 439
neoconservatism (aka neocon), 323
Neptune, 7, 383
New Horizons mission, 405
Newman, Hugh, 441
Newton, Isaac, 20, 472
New World Order, 31–32, 46
New York Times, 34, 67–68, 245, 291, 446
Nichols, Preston, 305
Nietzsche, Friedrich, 273
Niles, Edith, 138
9/11 terrorist attacks, 69, 200, 243–44, 330
Nixon, Richard M., 35, 41–42, 130
Nooty, George, 465
North, Oliver, 128–29

About the Author

DAVID WILCOCK is an author, professional lecturer, filmmaker, and researcher of ancient civilizations, consciousness science, and new paradigms of matter and energy. His seminal thoughts and expertise on consciousness have reached hundreds of thousands of people through his extensive online presence at DivineCosmos.com. He is also a regular guest and Consulting Producer on the History Channel's top show, *Ancient Aliens,* and has three shows on Gaia—*Disclosure, Wisdom Teachings,* and *Cosmic Disclosure.* His first two books, *The Source Field Investigations* and *The Synchronicity Key,* were *New York Times* bestsellers. Wilcock lives in California.